Praise for *Plunder*

"As shorthand for the crazy unfairness of financialized modern capitalism, more accurate than *Wall Street* or *hedge fund* is *private equity*—the state-of-the-art corporate-takeover mode that has brought predatory greed and ruthlessness to new levels, wrecking companies and workers' lives as a matter of course. Plunder is the right word, as Brendan Ballou lucidly explains in his infuriating, illuminating, essential book. And his practical plan for reining in this monstrous new centerpiece of our system makes total sense."
—Kurt Anderson, author of *Evil Geniuses:*
The Unmaking of America

"As private equity has risen to seize everything from nursing homes to clothing retailers to private prisons to our retirement savings, Ballou has written a cogent and indispensable book on this strange financial world. Ballou shows how these modern-day robber barons not only target the poor and serve themselves, but also bore into the foundations of our economy and society, weakening it for everyone. He ends with a stirring road map for reform."
—Jesse Eisinger, ProPublica, author of
The Chickenshit Club: Why the Justice Department
Fails to Prosecute Executives

"Private equity might be the biggest economic story of the century, and yet so few people understand what it is or how it's crippling our economy and our democracy. In *Plunder*, Ballou tells a complicated story clearly and explains how private equity shapes your life and, importantly, how it can be stopped. For anyone who wants to understand why our economy has become so broken and so unjust—and for anyone who wants to fix it—*Plunder* is required reading."
—Zephyr Teachout, professor of law,
Fordham Law School, and author of
Break 'em Up: Recovering our Freedom from Big Ag,
Big Tech, and Big Money

"*Plunder* offers a clear and critical analysis of the private-equity industry. Ballou shows how some private equity firms have ruined retail businesses, made housing more expensive, reduced the quality of health care and nursing homes, and wreaked havoc on families. If you're interested in understanding the hidden sources of our economic problems—and in fixing them—read this book."
—Ganesh Sitaraman, professor of law,
Vanderbilt University, and author of
The Crisis of the Middle-Class Constitution

"Private equity firms don't just transform our economy: they co-opt and compromise our government and our democracy. As few other people can, Ballou has shown how private equity has been so phenomenally successful in advancing its agenda at every level of government, and how government has been so tremendously solicitous of private equity. For anyone who wants to understand what's happening in our economy and our democracy, *Plunder* is required reading."
—Russ Feingold, former senator, president of the
American Constitution Society,
and author of *The Constitution in Jeopardy:
An Unprecedented Effort to Rewrite Our
Fundamental Law and What We Can Do About It*

"Despite owning companies with tens of millions of workers and impacting the lives of tens of millions more by buying up hospitals, nursing homes, housing, and other services we depend on, giant private-equity firms still largely operate in the shadows—and prefer it that way. Ballou's *Plunder* shines an important light on these finance giants that have reshaped the global economy to their advantage, connecting private equity firms' actions directly to the lives of people who are impacted, from workers, to patients, to students, and many more. Ballou reminds us that in nearly all these cases, private equity firms have not acted alone—instead they have been aided and abetted by, and profit massively from, the willing assistance of government. Perhaps most importantly,

Plunder points us toward solutions—the concrete actions we can take to halt the doom loop of private-equity-driven inequality and press for a more just economy."

—Jim Baker, executive director,
Private Equity Stakeholder Project

"The mysterious private-equity industry is one of the most destructive forces in American society—and one that too few people truly understand. Ballou's *Plunder* promises to change that. At a time when private equity has never been more powerful, his book shines a floodlight on the corporate raiders ravaging our economy and lays out a comprehensive road map for policymakers willing to take them on. For people who want to understand why America suffers from enormous disparities in wealth and power—and what we can do to change it—*Plunder* is essential reading."

—Sarah Miller, executive director,
American Economic Liberties Project

PLUNDER

PLUNDER

Private Equity's Plan
to Pillage America

BRENDAN BALLOU

PUBLICAFFAIRS

NEW YORK

PublicAffairs
Hachette Book Group
1290 Avenue of the Americas, New York, NY 10104
www.publicaffairsbooks.com
@Public_Affairs

Printed in the United States of America

First Edition: May 2023

Published by PublicAffairs, an imprint of Perseus Books, LLC, a subsidiary of Hachette Book Group, Inc. The PublicAffairs name and logo is a trademark of the Hachette Book Group.

The Hachette Speakers Bureau provides a wide range of authors for speaking events. To find out more, go to hachettespeakersbureau.com or email HachetteSpeakers@hbgusa.com.

PublicAffairs books may be purchased in bulk for business, educational, or promotional use. For information, please contact your local bookseller or Hachette Book Group Special Markets Department at special.markets@hbgusa.com.

The publisher is not responsible for websites (or their content) that are not owned by the publisher.

Print book interior design by Jeff Williams

Library of Congress Cataloging-in-Publication Data has been applied for.

ISBNs: 9781541702103 (hardcover), 9781541702127 (ebook)

LSC-H

Printing 3, 2024

To Mom

CONTENTS

PART II: HOW THEY GET THEIR WAY

PART III: HOW TO STOP THEM

WE MUST BREAK THE MONEY TRUST OR THE
MONEY TRUST WILL BREAK US.

—LOUIS BRANDEIS, *Other People's Money
and How the Bankers Use It*

INTRODUCTION

A New Gilded Age

Private equity surrounds you. When you visit a doctor or pay a student loan, buy life insurance or rent an apartment, pump gas or fill a prescription, you may—wittingly or not—be supporting a private equity firm. These firms, with obscure names like Blackstone, Carlyle, and KKR, are actually some of the largest employers in America and hold assets that rival those of small countries. Yet few people understand what these firms are or how they work. This is unfortunate because private equity firms, which buy and sell so many businesses you know, explain innumerable modern economic mysteries. They explain, in part, why your doctor's bill is so expensive and why your veterinary clinic seems to be in decline. They explain why so many stores are understaffed or closing altogether. They explain why there are ever fewer companies in America and why those that remain are selling ever lower-quality products. In fact, despite their relative anonymity, private equity firms are poised to reshape America in this decade the way in which Big Tech did in the last decade and in which subprime lenders did in the decade before that. And as we will explore, they're doing it all with the government's help.

Consider the pillaging of HCR ManorCare, which was once the second-largest nursing home chain in America.[1] In 2007, a private equity firm, the Carlyle Group, bought ManorCare for a little over $6 billion, most of which was borrowed money that ManorCare, not Carlyle, would have to pay back. As the nursing home chain's new owner, Carlyle sold nearly all of ManorCare's real estate and quickly recovered the money that it put into the purchase. But the move forced ManorCare to pay nearly half a billion dollars a year in rent to occupy buildings it once owned. Moreover, Carlyle extracted over $80 million in transaction and advisory fees that ManorCare paid for the privilege of being bought and owned by Carlyle. These sorts of payments made Carlyle's founders billionaires many times over.[2] But they drained ManorCare of the money it needed to operate and care for its residents.[3]

As a result of these financial machinations, ManorCare was forced to lay off hundreds of workers and institute various cost-cutting programs.[4] Health code violations spiked. And an unknowable number of residents suffered. The daughter of one resident told the *Washington Post* that "my mom would call us every day crying when she was in there. It was dirty—like a run-down motel. Roaches and ants all over the place."[5] Such cost cutting eviscerated the business, and in 2018, the company filed for bankruptcy with over $7 billion in debt.[6] Yet despite the bankruptcy, the deal was almost certainly profitable for Carlyle. It recovered the money it invested through the sale of the real estate and made millions more in various fees.[7] That the business itself collapsed was, in a sense, immaterial to Carlyle. (In statements to the *Post*, ManorCare denied that the quality of its care had declined, while Carlyle claimed that changes in how Medicare paid nursing homes, not its own actions, caused the chain's bankruptcy.)

Moreover, Carlyle managed to avoid legal liability for the consequences of its actions. For instance, the family of one resident, Annie Salley, sued Carlyle after she died in an understaffed facility.[8] Though she struggled to go to the restroom by herself, Salley was nevertheless forced to do so and fell and hit her head on a bathroom fixture. Afterward, nursing home staff reportedly failed to order a head scan and failed to report her to a doctor, even though in the days that followed, Salley showed confusion, vomited, and thrashed around. Salley eventually died of subdural hematoma—bleeding around the brain—and doctors found that blood had pushed her brain fully to one side of her head. Yet when Salley's family sued for wrongful death, Carlyle managed to get the case against it dismissed. As a private equity firm, Carlyle explained, it did not technically own ManorCare. Rather, Carlyle merely advised a series of investment funds—funds with names like Carlyle Partners V MC, L.P.—that did.[9] In essence, Carlyle performed a legal disappearing act, and the court dismissed the Salley family's case against the firm.[10] Carlyle would not be held responsible for Salley's death, or for the sordid sorry outcomes that resulted from its plunder of ManorCare.

※

THE STORY OF ManorCare and Carlyle is both common and confounding. The leaders of this industry, including Carlyle, but also Blackstone, KKR, Apollo, Warburg Pincus, Bain, and many other smaller firms are, at best, only vaguely known to most Americans. But their companies fill and shape our lives. If you rented an apartment, you may have done so through a company owned by Blackstone. If you visited a doctor or rode in an ambulance, you may have been billed by a company owned by KKR. If you bought insurance, you may have done so through Apollo, or if you paid your student loans, you might have done so through a Platinum Equity company. If you bought contacts, pet food, slacks, or a new dress, you may ultimately have paid KKR, BC Partners, Leonard Green & Partners, or Sycamore Partners.[11] In some municipalities, the very water you drink has been provided by private equity. The industry is quite literally right in front of you. The font used in this book is owned and licensed by a private equity portfolio company.[12]

Today, the industry owns more businesses than all those listed on US stock exchanges combined.[13] KKR's portfolio companies employ over 800,000 people;[14] Carlyle's 650,000;[15] and Blackstone's 550,000.[16] Considered together, they would be the third-, fourth-, and fifth-largest employers in America, behind only Walmart and Amazon.[17]

Yet, few of us have heard of these firms, let alone understand how they work. In a sense, their business is simple. Private equity firms invest a little of their own money, a lot of investors' money, and a whole lot of borrowed money to buy up companies (typically making them the sole, or private owner, hence the name). They then use various tactics to extract money from those companies, with an eye toward reselling them for a profit a few years later. Some of the companies that private equity firms buy go on to great success. But many others collapse or limp along, gutted of the assets that made them worth buying in the first place.

The basic business model of private equity firms often leads to disasters like that at ManorCare for three fundamental reasons. *First*, private equity firms typically buy businesses only for the short term. *Second*, they often load up the companies they buy with debt and extract onerous fees. And *third*, they insulate themselves from the consequences, both legal and financial, of their actions.[18] This leads to a practice of extraction, rather than investment, of destruction, rather than creation. While not every company owned by private equity firms goes bankrupt, the chance of disaster meaningfully increases under their ownership.[19]

Consider the following: J.Crew. Neiman Marcus. Toys "R" Us. Sears. 24 Hour Fitness. Aeropostale. American Apparel. Brookstone. Charlotte Russe. Claire's. David's Bridal. Deadspin. Fairway. Gymboree. Hertz. KB Toys. Linens 'n Things. Mervyn's. Mattress Firm. Musicland. Nine West. Payless ShoeSource. RadioShack. Shopko. Sports Authority. Rockport. True Religion. Wickes Furniture. The list goes on. All these companies went bankrupt after private equity firms bought them.[20] Some were restructured, often by firing workers or abandoning retirees' pension obligations. Many simply no longer exist. These bankruptcies, as we will see, are the consequence of private equity's business model. As we will see, though these liquidations and restructurings are usually bad for consumers and workers, counterintuitively, companies' bankruptcies may be desirable, even profitable, for their private equity owners.

The collapse of so many well-known companies is distressing by itself. But more than the failure of specific businesses, private equity helps to explain how whole industries and ways of life are being transformed. With its reliance on debt and fees and its focus on short-term profits, private equity is part of the reason why the quality of care at your dentist's office is going down and why your doctor seems perennially overbooked. It's part of the reason why so many people die in prisons and in nursing homes, why it's so hard to buy a house, and why so many companies are suing their own customers. These aren't unhappy accidents: they are fundamental to the industry's business model.

Moreover, private equity helps to explain our ever-widening economic inequality. These firms take money from productive companies, their employees, and their customers and redistribute it to themselves. Typically, they load up the businesses they buy with debt and often impose fees on their companies for the privilege of being owned by them. The result of this wealth transfer is that the leaders of the largest private equity firms are some of the richest people in America: the cofounders of KKR, Apollo, and Blackstone are worth $7 billion, $9 billion, and $29 billion, respectively.[21] Their wealth is more than the gross domestic product of some countries[22] and an order of magnitude greater than that of the merely absurdly rich. While the CEO of the investment bank JP Morgan made a little over $80 million in 2021, the CEO of the private equity firm Blackstone made over ten times that: $1 billion.[23]

As the chapters in this book explain, private equity firms also hasten the "financialization" of the American economy through the increased power of banks and other financial institutions over companies that make and sell useful products and tangible goods. Today, the finance industry gets a quarter of all corporate profits, up from a tenth in the "greed is good" 1980s.[24] At the same time, it employs just 5 percent of the country's workforce and largely fails to deliver a useful product for many Americans: a quarter of households, for instance, don't have access to a bank account.[25] By controlling the operation of companies in the rest of the economy, private equity hastens this trend toward financial control.

The predatory practices of private equity exacerbate inequality and eviscerate our economy by taking money from productive businesses and giving it to largely unproductive ones. But private equity firms have done more, by taking on much of the work in lending to big businesses that was once the domain of investment banks before the financial crisis of 2007. In other words, private equity firms you may not have heard of—Blackstone, Apollo, and so forth—are replacing the investment banks you probably know: Goldman Sachs, JP Morgan, and others. These private equity firms are taking on much of the work of the very institutions that precipitated the Great Recession and are now doing so with vastly less oversight—if such a thing were possible—than the investment banks faced before that crisis.

❋

THAT SOME BUSINESSES may be rapacious or even dangerous is concerning yet unsurprising. The new and important point— and the subject of this book—is that the stunning success of private equity is all happening with the support of the government, whose various arms—from courts and Congress to the executive branch, states, and localities—have not only allowed private equity to grow and dominate but have actively encouraged it. This is unsurprising, in part, because the industry has given hundreds of millions of dollars to politicians[26] and has welcomed untold senior government officials into its employment after their careers in public service came to an end. These have included

- Timothy Geithner, former treasury secretary under President Obama, now president of Warburg Pincus[27]

- Jacob Lew, another former Obama treasury secretary, now a managing partner at Lindsay Goldberg[28]

- Newt Gingrich, former Speaker of the House, now a strategic partner at JAM Capital[29]

- Paul Ryan, another former Speaker of the House, now a partner at Solamere Capital[30]

- David Petraeus, former general and CIA director, now chairman of the KKR Global Institute[31]

- Leon Panetta, former secretary of defense, now an adviser at Cerberus Capital Management[32]

- Kelly Ayotte and Evan Bayh, former senators and now director of Blackstone and senior adviser to Apollo, respectively[33]

Other luminaries in the private equity–government complex include former vice president Dan Quayle;[34] generals Barry R. McCaffrey and Anthony Zinni;[35] former cabinet members James Baker, John F. Kelly, Dan Coats, and John Snow; former FCC chairmen William Kennard, Julius Genachowski, and Ajit Pai; and former SEC chairmen Arthur Levitt and Jay Clayton, among so many others.[36]

As a cause and effect of this cross-pollination, the government has been extraordinarily solicitous of private equity firms. Whole private equity–owned businesses have been built based on getting government money. Where regulations stood in the way of these companies, they have been removed. As described in future chapters, Fannie Mae helped private equity firms buy up foreclosed homes and flip them into rentals. Local police departments helped private equity–owned companies buy prison phone, food, and health care operations and gut their quality of care. Courts helped private equity firms slough off pension obligations, and federal regulators helped them access 401(k) funds. Cities sold their own water systems to private equity–owned firms, and Congress gave them billions of dollars.

What is perhaps most ironic is that those who have the most to lose from private equity are enabling it. Pension funds—the investments of unions and middle-class workers—are some of private equity's largest investors. Private equity firms then use the money of these funds to buy companies in which they often cut wages and abandon pension obligations. Extraordinarily, we appear to be creating the tools of our own destruction.

✳

WE CAN STOP the industry's worst abuses. But we have to act now. Policies by the Federal Reserve before and during the pandemic to lower interest rates made it vastly easier for private equity firms to buy up companies. While many businesses struggled during the pandemic, private equity spent $1.2 trillion in 2021—over $500 billion more than it spent the year before—to buy them up.[37] Meanwhile, deregulation by the Trump administration allowed private equity to access potentially trillions more dollars in people's 401(k) accounts, including, possibly, yours. This will give the industry vastly more money with which to buy up companies.

Yet, despite its size, we can stop the ever-outward movement of the industry. We can do so because we've done it before. Today's private equity industry bears a striking resemblance to the great "money trusts" that Louis Brandeis denounced a century ago in his book *Other People's Money and How the Bankers Use It*. Then, as now, financiers captured productive companies with the savings of others.[38] Then, as now, they gutted their portfolio companies, extracted fees, and forced partnerships among their various businesses.[39] And then, as now, the financiers—often ignorant of the actual operations of the companies they bought—arrested the development of their businesses. As private equity firms buy companies across the disparate industries of health care, construction, retail, and leisure, so it is today.

But then—and perhaps now—people organized to break the great trusts of their time, including the money trusts. The government banned anticompetitive acquisitions and "interlocking directorates" between competing companies. It created the Federal Trade Commission and investigated, and eventually destroyed, monopolies in steel, sugar, tobacco, and elsewhere. We can do so again, and this book endeavors to show us how.

The chapters that follow proceed in three parts.

Part I explains how private equity firms make their money: both their tactics of extraction and their businesses of focus, from mobile homes and nursing facilities to retailers and prisons. A recurring theme of these chapters is that, surprisingly, private equity firms buy businesses that target the very poor, rather than the very rich, because, in a sense, these customers have no recourse when quality falls and prices rise.

Part II explains how the industry has advanced its agenda across virtually every arm of government, from Congress and courts to regulators and localities. As these chapters describe, sometimes private equity firms have lobbied directly to change laws and regulations: for instance, to fight rent control laws or to preserve tax advantages. At other times, the industry has benefited from larger trends over several decades: the reshaping of antitrust law, for instance, or the rise of forced arbitration.

Part III explains how we can stop the industry's worst excesses. These chapters offer a specific agenda for what we must accomplish and a path for how we might effect change—through litigation, regulation, and state and local legislation—at a time of extraordinary political dysfunction.

To the arguments thus far, and those to come, a world-weary reader may offer three skeptical replies.

First, the skeptic may say, "for better or worse, private equity is just an extreme form of free-market capitalism." The debt that private equity forces onto companies, and the short deadlines it demands for profits, force sluggish companies to reform and demand the survival of the fittest. Or so the argument goes. As the chapters that follow show, private equity firms do not offer simply an extreme version of capitalism but, rather, something much darker: a twining of big business and big government that finds profits by creating and exploiting legal gaps and obscure government programs. When forced to actually run businesses, private equity firms often show surprising ineptitude. Their executives' talents often come not from operating the levers of business but from the levers of power: securing financing, identifying regulatory holes, and creating them when they don't exist. Capitalists and social-ists, and everyone in between, should all be united in their concern over this business philosophy.

Second, the skeptic may ask, "Yes, private equity is bad, but is it meaningfully different from other parts of the finance indus-try?" Yes, it is. Hedge funds might short businesses. Investment banks may create ruinous bubbles. But private equity firms can do both and more. Because their business model—which requires short-term thinking, leverage and extractive fees, and escape from liability—produces uniquely bad outcomes, they are uniquely worthy of your attention.

Third, the skeptic may say, "Yes, private equity is uniquely bad, but it is inevitable, or at least irremediable." And this is the most important point of the book, namely, that we can stop this from happening. We do indeed live in a second Gilded Age, a time of gaping inequality and aching political dysfunction. But a cen-tury ago, we rejected immiserating poverty and politics in favor of populist and progressive reforms: unions, suffrage, antitrust, worker and environmental protections, and graduated taxation. We can do so again. We just need the collective will to act.

And that is the final message of this book, a message of hope. Private equity is part of the larger financialization of our economy, and perhaps its worst exemplar. It was created with the active support of our government, and as the pages that follow show, it has trans-formed whole industries and upended lives. But if we created private equity, we can also contain it. I am here to tell you that we can write our own future. A better world *is* possible. The following chapters show us how.

PART I

HOW THEY MAKE THEIR MONEY

CHAPTER ONE

OTHER PEOPLE'S MONEY, AND HOW THEY USE IT

The Tactics of Private Equity

In 2005, Sun Capital bought Shopko for a little over a billion dollars. A regional retailer like Fred Meyer, Gabe's, or Bi-Mart, Shopko's operations were focused primarily in the Midwest.[1] Its first store opened in Green Bay, Wisconsin, in 1962 and began what a commemorative plaque at the site later called "a new era in retailing."[2] The company's innovation: putting pharmacies and, later, groceries in their larger stores.[3] Over time, the business expanded to other states, like Minnesota, Michigan, and Iowa.[4] Eventually, it became a regional institution. "Shopko was at the heart of our community," said Sarah Godlewski, Wisconsin's state treasurer.[5] "As a kid my mom would ask me if I needed anything for school. I would mention different supplies, and she would say, 'OK, go put it on your Shopko list.' It was never a shopping list, it was always a Shopko list."[6]

Despite its regional importance, in 2019, Shopko filed for bankruptcy and, shortly thereafter, ceased operations entirely.[7] How did this happen? How did a respected institution flail and eventually fail? The short answer was that a private equity firm bought it.[8] Over nearly fifteen years of ownership, Sun Capital bankrupted Shopko while making hundreds of millions of dollars for itself. It did so through a variety of tactics that drained Shopko of assets, locked the chain into unfavorable deals, denied employees pay, and transferred money that the retailer needed to modernize and grow. These tactics were surprising—perhaps even shocking—but they were not unusual, for as the pages below explain, they are often the means by which private equity firms succeed, even if the very companies they buy fail.

First, Sun Capital made Shopko sell most of its property. It's important for a retailer to own its own stores, if it can: it saves the company from having to pay rent in good times and gives the company something to borrow against in bad times. By forcing the chain to give up most of its stores, Sun Capital made Shopko a quick $815 million.[9] But it also saddled Shopko with paying rent on the very stores it once owned, an expensive and unending obligation. To compound the problem, Sun Capital locked Shopko into fifteen- and twenty-year leases,[10] which made it hard for Shopko's management to move stores.

Then Sun Capital began extracting fees. It forced Shopko to borrow nearly $180 million to pay Sun Capital "dividends": financial rewards to owners usually given only in good times.[11] It also required Shopko to pay a quarterly $1 million "consulting" fee, and a 1 percent fee on certain large transactions. The latter fee applied to Shopko's dividend payments, so that Shopko actually had to pay Sun Capital a fee just for paying Sun Capital.[12] And while Sun Capital was extracting this money, under its watch, Shopko skirted its tax obligations: in 2019, the Wisconsin Department of Revenue alleged that the company failed to pay over $13 million in sales taxes and penalties.[13] (The Department ultimately withdrew its claim after reaching an undisclosed settlement with the holding corporation for Shopko's bankrupted assets.)[14]

Then Sun Capital began layoffs. In December 2018, Shopko announced that it would close thirty-nine stores.[15] In January the next year, Sun Capital pushed Shopko into bankruptcy and closed an additional thirty-eight. And in March, unable to find a new buyer, Shopko announced that it was liquidating entirely and closing its remaining 360 or so locations. At the time, Shopko had fourteen thousand employees:[16] most all of them would lose their jobs.

As Shopko's employees were fired and the company's assets liquidated—even the plaque commemorating the company's first location was sold—Sun Capital asked some employees to stay on through the bankruptcy process. But after they did so, Sun Capital reneged on its promise to pay them severance. "We risked losing potential job opportunities by sticking around," one former employee told the Green Bay Press-Gazette.[17] "Then the day we officially found out about not getting the severance was the last day we were open. It felt like a false promise."[18] Ultimately, a bankruptcy judge approved $3 million in pay for nearly four thousand workers, but only after labor organizers filed a class action lawsuit. And even then, the agreement excluded thousands of employees who were among the last to work at the company.

The effects of Shopko's collapse lived on in the company's former workers. At a memorial event a year after the bankruptcy, Trina McInerney, tearing up, explained to the Washington Examiner that "Sun Capital left me jobless, with nothing. . . . The devastation was real, the heartbreak was real, having no income, losing your work family, losing your work dignity—all real."[19] Linda Parker, who managed several Payless ShoeSource stores housed within Shopkos, said that she had to take on three part-time jobs that together didn't make as much as her old one.[20] "Holding Wall Street and private equity and hedge fund billionaires accountable is crucial," she said. "It's just going to get worse. They feel no empathy for us, they feel no guilt over what they're doing. . . . It's time to take action and do something to stop these horrible business practices."[21]

But who are these private equity billionaires? Sun Capital is run by two Wharton classmates, Rodger Krouse and Marc Leder. Both men are worth hundreds of millions of dollars, though Leder is the public face of the company and by far the brasher of the two. The New York Post described him as the "Hugh Hefner of the Hamptons"[22] and alleged that he threw parties in which "guests cavorted nude in the pool and performed sex acts, scantily dressed Russians danced on platforms and men twirled lit torches to a booming techno beat."[23] Said one acquaintance, "So many girls think they're dating him. There are [at] least three that I know of."[24]

Despite his lavish lifestyle, Leder supports the politics of austerity. Recall when Mitt Romney declared that "47 percent of the people" would vote for President Obama "no matter what" because they "believe the government has a responsibility to care for them, who believe that they are entitled to health care, to food, to housing, to you-name-it."[25] Romney made that statement at a private fundraiser that Leder hosted in his Boca Raton home.[26] Leder has also given money to David Perdue,[27] Marco Rubio,[28] Jason Chaffetz,[29] Clay Shaw,[30] and Mitch McConnell,[31] who have all attempted to cut various cables of the social safety net on which so many of Leder's former employees now rely.[32]

It is important to understand that Shopko is not some fluke, a rare failure in Sun Capital's otherwise brilliant investments. In 2005, the firm bought Garden Fresh Restaurant Corporation, but pushed it into bankruptcy in 2016.[33] In 2006, it bought Marsh Supermarkets, which filed for bankruptcy in 2017. In 2007, Sun Capital bought a majority stake in Limited Stores, which filed for bankruptcy a decade later. And in 2008, it bought Gordmans, which went bankrupt in 2017, but not before Sun Capital forced the company to borrow $45 million to pay in dividends. And yet despite these failures, Sun Capital continued to prosper, making over $1.4 billion in the most recent year for which it published data.[34]

The point is that Sun Capital's—and private equity's—success does not always depend on the success of the companies they own. Through a range of tactics described below, they can extract money from the businesses they buy, whether or not those businesses thrive or die. In this way, the whole industry of private equity is unnervingly similar to the "money trusts" of the early twentieth century, when financiers like George F. Baker and J. P.

Morgan oversaw disparate empires of railroads, banks, steel mills, shipping, and insurance companies.[35] In 1914, Louis Brandeis observed that the men of the money trust "start usually with ignorance of the particular business which they are supposed to direct."[36] When the Steel Trust was signed into existence, one of the lawyers present declared that, "[t]hat signature is the last one necessary to put the Steel industry, on a large scale, into the hands of men who do not know anything about it."[37] So it is today, as a firm like Sun Capital invests in businesses as diverse as an industrial manufacturer,[38] a dermatology network,[39] a chain of barbecue restaurants,[40] and a high-end women's clothing retailer.[41] Like the money trusts of the Gilded Age, Sun Capital, as with private equity firms, lacks the institutional skills necessary to manage the operations of such a diverse set of companies. But it isn't just that private equity firms lack the knowledge to improve their companies' operations; often, they lack the interest. As shortly explained, their skill frequently comes not in making companies better but in extracting more money from them.

Today's private equity firms bear another similarity to the money trusts of a century ago, namely, that their power is obtained not, as Brandeis wrote, through "the possession of extraordinary ability" but through "the savings and quick capital of others."[42] Which is to say that private equity titans are rarely themselves masters of running companies but rather geniuses at getting and spending other people's money. The difference now is simply a matter of scale. When the Gilded Age financier George F. Baker, reportedly twice as rich as J. P. Morgan, died in 1931, he was worth an estimated $1.4 billion in today's money.[43] Now, Stephen Schwarzman of Blackstone is worth nearly twenty times that.[44]

What accounts for this increase in these men's wealth is not the quality of people running private equity firms but the availability of money, which is largely the decision of the government. In 1979, Congress reduced the capital gains rate—the tax on money made from investments—and in 1981 did so again.[45] Along the way, the Labor Department permitted pension funds to make riskier investments, clarifying that while such funds must exercise the caution of a "prudent man" as a whole, individual speculative purchases "may be entirely proper" under the standard.[46] These two changes allowed a flood of investment in venture capital and the emerging business of leveraged buyouts. One of the first was Gibson Greetings. In 1981, a consortium of investors led by former Nixon treasury secretary William E. Simon bought the company—a manufacturer of greeting cards—for $80 million.[47] Simon and his investors put up just $1 million of their own money (Simon himself contributed about a third of that) and borrowed the remaining $79 million. Sixteen months later, they turned the company public at a valuation of $290 million. In a little over a year, Simon had made himself $66 million on a $330,000 investment. His astounding success inspired others. "I didn't know what a leveraged buyout was," said David Rubenstein, the founder of the behemoth Carlyle Group, "but it sounded more attractive than practicing law."[48]

Between 1979 and 1989, there were some two thousand leveraged buyouts worth $250 million or more,[49] capped at the end of the decade by Kohlberg Kravis Roberts & Co.'s (later called KKR) $24 billion takeover of RJR Nabisco.[50] During this time, the story of leveraged buyouts was told in tandem with that of junk bonds: speculative investments that promised high yields but also high risks of failure. These bonds financed leveraged buyouts and made the whole industry possible. But by the end of the 1980s, the market collapsed: as foreshadowed by its very name, a number of junk bond–financed buyouts prominently failed. Drexel Burnham Lambert, the investment firm that powered much of the junk bond industry, imploded, and several of its most prominent bankers were criminally prosecuted.[51] Meanwhile, hundreds of savings and loan associations (S&Ls), which had been primary purchasers of junk bonds, were closed, with the subsequent bailout costing taxpayers over $100 billion.[52]

But leveraged buyouts didn't die after this first frenzy; they were simply rebranded as "private equity." After a fallow period in the early 1990s, firms in this renamed business bought big companies like Snapple,[53] Burger King,[54] Houghton Mifflin,[55] Harrah's

Entertainment,[56] MGM,[57] and Toys "R" Us.[58] The industry found new sources of money: in 2006, KKR was the first firm to take itself public, followed by Blackstone, Apollo, and Carlyle. Countries like Russia and Saudi Arabia created "sovereign wealth funds" to invest their oil fortunes in private equity. And a secondary market developed, so that institutions that invested with private equity companies could in turn sell those investments to others. Shorn of its rougher public associations with junk bonds, S&Ls, and Drexel Burnham Lambert, this "superior form of capitalism,"[59] as the former leader of Yale's endowment once described it, entered a new golden age.

The Great Recession briefly depressed private equity, and the 2012 presidential campaign scoured some of the gilding off the industry, such that its leading firms no longer even describe themselves primarily in terms of private equity. Blackstone generically calls itself "a leading global investment business,"[60] while Apollo claims simply to be an "alternative asset management business."[61] But whatever its reputation, after each crisis, private equity emerged more powerful than before. In fact, while the COVID-19 pandemic was a disaster for most Americans, it was a boon to private equity. Private equity firms need borrowed money to buy companies, the interest rates for which are determined in large part by the Federal Reserve. At the outset of the pandemic, the Fed's chairman, Jerome Powell (himself a private equity alum), helped drive interest rates to nearly zero. As a result, and coupled with the pandemic struggles of many ordinary businesses, private equity spent an astounding $1.2 trillion on acquisitions in 2021,[62] or about one-twentieth of gross domestic product of the entire country.[63] KKR's "assets under management"—the money it controls to invest—grew 87 percent that year, to $471 billion.[64] Blackstone's rose to nearly twice that: $881 billion.[65] These are stores of wealth bigger than the economies of many countries. And they are big enough to change the world.

✳

THE CHAPTERS THAT follow describe how private equity spends its money, how it transforms industries, and how the arms of the government helped at every step. But before examining the details, it is important to understand the larger matter of just how private equity works, for while the term *private equity* is frequently used, its meaning is rarely understood.

Private equity firms are different from investment banks, which originally centered on helping other businesses buy one another or issue stock. They are also different from hedge funds, which tend to buy and sell public securities, such as stocks and bonds. Rather than buying individual securities, private equity firms buy whole companies. And rather than doing so on behalf of other businesses, they do so for themselves. The line between different kinds of financial institutions is porous: firms that call themselves hedge funds sometimes engage in private equity, and as a future chapter explains, private equity firms are increasingly taking on the business of investment banks. Nevertheless, the general division is that while banks and hedge funds tend to invest in companies, private equity firms tend to buy them.

Private equity firms' basic business model is simple. In a typical case, a private equity firm—or, more accurately, a legally separate fund that the firm controls—buys a company.[66] The separate fund helps to insulate the firm from liability, as we saw with ManorCare, and is generally the sole, or private, owner of the company, hence the "private" in private equity. Through a series of operational and financial changes, the private equity firm works to make the company more valuable and, after a few years, tries to sell it or take it public at a profit.

To make its business model work, the private equity firm needs money, which it gets from three sources. The firm itself contributes a small percentage of the funds needed to buy the company, while the firm's investors—pension funds, sovereign wealth funds, wealthy individuals, and the like—provide some of the rest necessary for the acquisition. The firm then leverages all those assets (hence the "leveraged" in leveraged buyout) to borrow most of the money it needs from banks and other lenders. Crucially, the responsibility for paying back the money the firm borrows sits not with the firm itself but with the company it buys. Thus, if the company fails, the private equity firm loses only its small initial investment. But why would the company agree to take on this debt? And why would banks and other investors lend this money in the first place? Executives at the acquired company may agree to borrow money because they stand to make a great deal from the sale to a private equity firm. With the prospect of a windfall, they may authorize borrowing that, ordinarily, they might not. As for the banks and lenders, when interest rates are low, they are often willing to make riskier loans in an effort to make more than inflation. Furthermore, lenders are often able to "syndicate" their loans to others, meaning that those who make loans often are not responsible for getting that money back.

But while private equity firms stand to lose only a little if their investments fail, they stand to make enormous sums if they succeed. As mentioned above, firms make their purchases through legally separate funds, each of which has money, provided by investors, with which to buy companies. Private equity firms are typically entitled to 2 percent of that money every year, no matter how well or poorly their funds do. This means, for instance, that a firm with a billion-dollar fund is guaranteed to make $20 million—2 percent—every year, even if its investments fail.[67] On top of this, a firm usually takes 20 percent of the fund's profits once it clears a certain hurdle, often an 8 percent rate of return.

As private equity experts Eileen Appelbaum and Rosemary Batt have explained, there are three fundamental problems with the business model just described.[68] *First*, because private equity firms own the companies they buy for just a few years, they must extract money from them exceedingly fast; there's simply not much reason for them to consider the long-term health of the companies they buy. *Second*, because private equity firms invest little of their own money but receive an outsized share of potential profits, they are encouraged to take huge risks. In practice, this means loading companies up with debt and extracting onerous fees. And *third*, partly because legally separate funds technically own the companies, private equity firms are rarely held responsible for the debts and actions of the companies they run. These facts of short-term, high-risk, and low-consequence ownership explain why private equity firms' efforts to make companies profitable so often prove disastrous for everyone except the private equity firms themselves.

But how exactly does a private equity firm make money? In theory, it should make a company's operations more efficient by bringing in new management and modern business practices. This may be so for the small and midsized companies that private equity firms acquire, which are often run by families or first-time entrepreneurs. But it is rarely so for big companies, whose professional managers are schooled in best practices and experienced in running large organizations; in other words, there is only so much need for outside assistance. Instead of offering better management, firms often use a range of tactics described below—leasebacks, dividend recaps, strategic bankruptcies, rollups, forced partnerships, tax avoidance, and layoffs—to extract money from businesses. These tactics are endemic to the industry and fundamental to the way it operates.

LEASEBACKS

After Sun Capital bought Shopko in 2005, it forced the company to sell most of its stores and lease in perpetuity the property that it once owned. This leaseback tactic is a great source of revenue for private equity because it allows the firm to post a quick profit and often take a transaction fee along the way. But it is often devastating for the underlying company, which is permanently shorn of assets. And it is particularly hard for businesses in cyclical industries. As mentioned, owning property saves companies from having to pay rent and gives them something to borrow against in bad times.[69] Without assets, and burdened with an ongoing expense, companies that merely survive when demand waxes may die when it wanes.

There is a darker purpose to leasebacks too. A few decades ago, private equity firms began buying nursing homes, and today they own between 5 and 11 percent of all facilities in America.[70] To save money, these firms often gut homes' quality of care. Studies have found that after private equity firms buy nursing homes, average nursing and staff hours fall while violations of industry protocols increase.[71] Hospital readmission rates—the pace at which residents are sent back to hospitals within thirty days of discharge—also rise, a sign of declining care.[72] As a result, more than twenty thousand people are estimated to have died due to private equity firms' ownership of such homes.[73]

And this is where leasebacks come in. After buying nursing homes, private equity firms often sell their underlying assets and separately incorporate each facility in a nursing home chain.[74] This means that if there is negligence in one facility—if a resident dies needlessly—that resident's family often can only recover assets from that facility. And because that facility no longer owns its own property, there often aren't many assets to recover. The result is that nursing home residents are needlessly dying and families are failing to get damages, and because of sale-leasebacks, there is little legal incentive for private equity firms to ever change their ways.

DIVIDEND RECAPS

Private equity firms use dividend recapitalizations, or recaps, to take companies' borrowed money and give it to themselves. Ordinarily, a company's shareholders will take an occasional cut of its profits, called a dividend, as a reward for the risks of ownership. They usually do so when times are good and the company can afford to shed the money. Private equity firms are different. They often force the companies they own to borrow money, in good times or in bad, to pay themselves. It's like using someone else's credit card to pay yourself. And like using someone else's credit card, the practice often damages the company's credit rating.[75]

Consider the case of Hertz. When the rental car company filed for bankruptcy in 2020, *Axios* described it as "a Frankenstein of financial engineering."[76] Fifteen years earlier, the private equity firm Clayton, Dubilier & Rice (CD&R) had led a consortium of investors to buy the company from Ford for $14.8 billion, nearly half of which was debt. Clayton quickly forced Hertz to borrow an additional $1 billion to pay it a dividend. By loading Hertz up with debt, Clayton and its coinvestors managed to make much of their initial money back while substantially retaining control of the company.[77] But in the opinion of observers, after Hertz disastrously overpaid for its acquisition of rivals Thrifty and Dollar under CD&R's watch, the private equity firm sold its remaining stake in the company in 2013.[78] Hertz limped along for a number of years, but burdened in part by the debt that CD&R had forced upon it, the company filed for bankruptcy. When it did, Hertz owed over $24 billion, with barely $1 billion in cash on hand.[79]

Stories like Hertz's are not uncommon. But if private equity firms own the companies they force to borrow money, don't they ultimately have to pay the loans back, one way or another? Not necessarily. Recall that private equity firms buy companies with heaps of other people's money. In other words, these firms control companies while making only modest investments themselves. Dividend recaps are a way for private equity firms to make back their investments—eliminating all risk—while still controlling the companies they buy. That's what Sycamore Partners did when it forced Staples to give it a $1 billion dividend recap.[80] The office supply store then had to pay $130 million a year on interest payments alone.[81] That fact was almost immaterial to Sycamore, however, given that it made back through the recap most of what it paid to buy the company.

Dividend recaps can be devastating. The retailer Payless Shoe-Source, lab testing company Trident USA, and urinalysis firm Millennium Health, for instance, all went bankrupt after being forced to make recaps.[82] After the hospital chain Prospect Medical Holdings was forced to pay its private equity owner $457 million in 2018, it closed five facilities and fired over one thousand employees. And after the Environmental Protection Agency alleged that the medical device sterilization company Sterigenics was potentially emitting toxic carcinogens around its suburban Illinois production facility, a flood of lawsuits followed.[83] According to plaintiffs, however, Sterigenics had shoveled over $1 billion in dividend recapitalizations to its private equity owners in the years before so that the company would have less money to pay to its victims.[84] Hundreds of cases against the company remain ongoing.

Unfortunately, the federal government's actions to stave off the worst economic effects of the pandemic may have made recaps easier. By driving interest rates down at the outset of the COVID-19 pandemic, the Federal Reserve made it cheaper for private equity–owned companies to borrow money. The effect was that in the second half of 2020, in the midst of a global recession, private equity firms forced the companies they owned to borrow an astonishing $27 billion to pay for dividend recaps or debt restructurings.[85] Reflecting later on this trend, Davide Scigliuzzo of Bloomberg wrote that "[i]t looks likely billionaires and private equity firms will keep loading up companies with debt to turn them into dividend-paying ATMs."[86] Jim Baker of the Private Equity Stakeholder Project, which researches and publicizes abuses in the industry, added that these recaps "do nothing to help private equity–owned companies and only put those companies at greater risk."[87]

STRATEGIC BANKRUPTCIES

Private equity firms sometimes push the companies they own into bankruptcy to avoid paying debts to their employees, retirees, and creditors. Such seemed to be the case with Sun Capital and Marsh Supermarkets, which Sun Capital bought in 2006. Marsh, a regional institution in Indiana, was the kind of place where generations of employees could spend decades working. It was also something of an innovator: in the 1970s, it was the first grocery store in the world to use a barcode scanner (the first purchase was a pack of gum).[88]

As reported by Peter Whoriskey of the *Washington Post*, when Sun Capital bought Marsh, it did not bring any particular expertise in the grocery industry to the purchase. Amy Gerken, a former assistant manager at a Marsh Supermarket, told the *Post* that Sun Capital "didn't really know how grocery stores work. We'd joke about them being on a yacht without even knowing what a UPC code is."[89] But Sun Capital did execute some of its now-familiar tactics. For instance, it forced Marsh to sell many of its stores for $260 million and then had the grocer lease back the stores it once owned. It also collected transaction fees from Marsh for selling various assets, on top of a $1 million annual management fee for the privilege of being owned by the firm.

At the same time, Sun Capital was unable or unwilling to make the investments necessary for Marsh to succeed. Perhaps this is because Marsh's property was reportedly worth more than the cash Sun Capital paid for the company,[90] making the survival of the business a pleasant but ultimately unnecessary proposition. Instead, Sun Capital pushed the company into bankruptcy. When Marsh filed for bankruptcy, it owed $62 million in pension fund obligations to its warehouse workers, plus millions more to its store employees.[91] (A separate pension for Marsh's most senior executives remained fully funded.) Through bankruptcy, Sun Capital was able to heave Marsh's unfunded pension obligations onto a government agency, the Pension Benefit Guaranty Corporation, or PBGC, which pays a portion of promised benefits for retirees when pension funds become insolvent. In Marsh's case, the PBGC was able to pay nearly the entirety of the store employees' pension obligations but not the warehouse workers', whose benefits were cut by a quarter.[92] "They did everyone dirty," Kilby Baker, a retired warehouse worker, told the *Post*. "We all gave up wage increases so we could have a better pension. Then they just took it away from us."[93] Said another worker who had been with the company since 1967: "If I lose my pension, what am I going to do? Who's going to hire a 75-year-old man?"[94]

Marsh was not an isolated incident. In 2005, Sun Capital bought Indalex, an aluminum parts manufacturer. After taking a multimillion-dollar dividend for itself, the firm forced Indalex into bankruptcy and pushed the pensions of thousands of employees onto the PBGC and taxpayers.[95] Similarly, in 2006, Sun Capital bought Powermate, a manufacturer of electric generators. Two years later, it pushed Powermate into bankruptcy too, and the PBGC was forced to pay the underfunded pensions of some six hundred employees. Sun Capital did the same with Fluid Routing Systems and the restaurant chain Friendly's, and both times it improbably managed to keep running the companies after bankruptcy. The whole thing is "pension laundering," Joshua Gotbaum, the former director of the PBGC, claimed to the *Post*. "What we've seen is that financial firms essentially take the money and run, leaving their employees and the PBGC holding the bag."[96] All of which is to say that Sun Capital and others used the bankruptcy system to slough off the obligations to employees that they did not want to pay, while continuing to extract money for themselves.[97]

FORCED PARTNERSHIPS

Private equity firms can also extract money by forcing the companies they buy into arranged marriages with other businesses in their portfolio. For instance, in 2012, Sycamore Partners bought the midmarket women's clothier Talbots.[98] At the time of its acquisition, Talbots had sold smart, preppy women's clothes for over sixty years, having developed its initial specialty selling to women moving to the suburbs after World War II.[99] For women "looking for classic styles at affordable prices,"[100] as the *New York Times* put it, Talbots was an institution. After Sycamore bought the company, however, it executed some now-familiar tactics. It cut the company's staff and narrowed its product selection.[101] It gutted Talbot's assets by selling the company's credit card receivables: that is, its promise of future payments. It made over half a billion dollars for itself.[102] (Sycamore's managing director declined to comment to the *Wall Street Journal* on his firm's tactics.)

As relevant here, Sycamore also forced Talbots to work with MGF Sourcing Holdings, a supply agent it owned.[103] In the clothing industry, supply agents broker transactions between factories and retailers. By forcing Talbots to use MGF Sourcing, Sycamore ensured that it would make money on the clothes that Talbots bought, whether or not it was ultimately able to sell them. The arrangement created a perverse incentive for Sycamore to push

Talbots to buy clothes it didn't need, and by 2021, the company had a junk rating of CCC–, indicating a high risk of default.[104]

Sycamore was accused of using this tactic to push another retailer into bankruptcy. In 2013, it took a minority stake in the teen retailer Aeropostale and offered the company a substantial loan in exchange for, among other things, using MGF as its supply agent.[105] But after negotiating the deal, Sycamore imposed harsh new payment terms through MGF. As subsequently alleged by Aeropostale, Sycamore's true purpose was to push the company into bankruptcy, which Sycamore could then purchase at a discount. And Sycamore's tactics—for instance, demanding full payment on the delivery of goods, an unusual practice in the clothing industry—successfully disrupted the company's supply chain and cost Aeropostale an alleged $25 million per year.

Sycamore denied the allegation, and ultimately, a judge rejected Aeropostale's argument that Sycamore purposefully pushed the company into bankruptcy to buy it at a discount.[106] But whether Sycamore intentionally tried to sabotage the company or not, the effect was the same: Aeropostale filed for bankruptcy in March 2016, about a month after MGF began making its demands,[107] and ultimately, the company was forced to close over one hundred stores.[108]

TAX AVOIDANCE

Private equity firms, their investors, and their executives also use a number of tactics to avoid paying taxes. Many of these tactics are legal, but some are not. Most famously, there is the carried interest loophole.

Most private equity firms are paid on the 2-and-20 model: a 2 percent annual fixed fee on all the money it invests and 20 percent of all profits above a certain threshold. The United States taxes money made from investments—so-called capital gains—at a lower level than money made through ordinary labor, whether at a factory or in an office. The distinction is ambiguous and unfair, but even more so, private equity firms have convinced the IRS that their 20 percent income should be taxed at the lower capital gains rate than at the higher ordinary income rate.[109] This means that many private equity executives often pay a lower effective tax rate than the retail employees, secretaries, and factory workers they employ. But the industry as a whole has fought hard, and successfully, to defend this imbalance.

Private equity firms use so-called management fee waivers to give more of their income this preferential treatment. Here, private equity firms waive some or all of their 2 percent management fee (which is taxed at a higher rate) in exchange for a priority claim on the profits earned (which is taxed at a lower rate). Through a variety of tactics, however, the firms virtually guarantee that they will make this money back.[110] Some of the biggest firms—KKR, Apollo, and TPG Capital—used these fee-waiver provisions.[111] Many of these schemes might violate the spirit, if not the letter, of the law. The IRS investigated fee waivers during the Obama administration but very little came of it. An audit of Thoma Bravo for use of the tactic, for instance, took four years and resulted in no actual adjustments to the company's tax returns. In 2015, the Obama administration proposed regulations to bar the most aggressive forms of fee waivers. But nothing came of that either: the regulations were never finalized. Ultimately, both of President Obama's treasury secretaries—Tim Geithner and Jack Lew—left the government to work for private equity firms.

More daringly, private equity firms use offshoring tactics to reduce the tax obligations on themselves and their investors. For instance, most public corporations must, in theory, pay the federal corporate tax rate on their income. There is an exception, however, for companies that make most of their money through dividends, interest, or capital gains. Private equity firms are active businesses, but they try to get this preferential treatment by establishing blocker corporations in offshore tax havens.[112] The income due to the private equity firm instead goes to the blocker corporation, which pays the low local corporate tax rate. The blocker corporation then pays the money to the private equity firm as dividends or interest, on which the private equity firm pays a lower rate in the United States than it otherwise would. While this tax arbitrage lowers the effective rate paid by the private equity firm, it does nothing to improve the operational efficiency of the companies it owns and gives tax revenues to haven nations that would ordinarily go to the United States.

Finally, at least some private equity executives engage in ordinary tax evasion. For instance, Robert Smith, the cofounder of Vista Equity Partners, is worth an estimated $8 billion[113] and was number 125 on the *Forbes* 2020 list of wealthiest Americans.[114] That same year, however, Smith admitted to evading more than $200 million in income taxes over fifteen years.[115] As part of his agreement with the government, Smith disclosed that he funneled money into hidden or undeclared bank accounts in Belize, Nevis, Switzerland, and the British Virgin Islands.[116] He also revealed that he paid a Houston lawyer $800,000 to maintain a false paper trail for these accounts (the lawyer died by suicide the day before his own trial was to begin).[117] Smith negotiated a plea deal to avoid prison time—an astonishing feat given that he evaded paying $200 million in taxes—but his business partner was not so fortunate. The United States charged Vista Equity cofounder Robert Brockman with hiding an extraordinary $2 billion in income from the IRS. (Brockman, who had been ill for several years, died before trial.)

ROLLUPS

Private equity firms also make money by rolling up small companies in given industries to merge or otherwise control them. For instance, as described in later chapters, firms have bought up local medical practices, with a focus on specialties like dermatology, anesthesiology, and obstetrics and gynecology, all of which offer opportunities for specialty services and large out-of-pocket payments. With such market power, private equity firms may be able to raise prices and cut care for patients. Doctors in private equity–owned dermatology practices, for instance, complained that they were pressured to meet quotas for procedures, sell acne creams and antiaging goods, and make expensive referrals.[118] Others complained that they were forced to have unsupervised physician assistants deliver services that doctors ordinarily would provide.

Outside of physicians' offices, private equity firms are rolling up dentist practices, drug treatment centers, hospitals, board game companies, portable toilet providers, mobile home parks, and veterinary clinics, among many others. By buying up these companies, private equity firms can achieve some operational efficiencies by using common suppliers or services to reduce costs. But they can also use their increased market power to charge more and give less.

Consider the case of cheerleading competitions. Varsity Brands is the country's leading organizer of these events. As alleged in a class action complaint, between 2015 and 2018, Varsity bought its three largest rivals, all of which are now owned by Varsity, which in turn is owned by Bain Capital.[119] By controlling 90 percent of the cheerleading competition market, Varsity gained control over the sport's governing body and now decides which events entitle winners to participate in the country's premier competitions. Varsity also allegedly increased participation fees and made money by, for instance, forcing competitors to wear only Varsity-approved uniforms and equipment and stay only in Varsity-approved hotels. "Cheerleading uniform prices have gone through the roof," one local gym owner complained to the Federal Trade Commission. "Competition costs are so high that many athletes have to quit the sport."[120] Varsity and Bain largely deny the allegations of the class action complaint, and the lawsuit remains ongoing.[121]

Or consider the example of veterinary clinics. Today, just six private equity firms own over five thousand practices or over 10 percent of the whole industry.[122] The result: lower job satisfaction and lower quality of care. Back in 2005, over three-quarters of surveyed veterinarians would recommend the profession. Ten years later, that percentage fell to less than half.[123] After PetSmart, which both sold pets and cared for them, was acquired by a private equity firm, an employee said that he "left this company in early 2015 after being bought by BC Partners. The whole company focus shifted from pets and its employees to making money."[124]

Another veterinarian said, "It's pet-icide...the systematic destruction of pets by corporations for profit."[125] In other words, by
buying up companies, combining them, and reducing competition,
private equity firms are able to raise prices, lower wages, and increase profits for themselves. Whether such rollups specifically violate the antitrust laws, the effects, as described, are apparent in all
these and many other industries.

OPERATIONAL EFFICIENCIES: LAYOFFS, PRICE HIKES, AND QUALITY CUTS

The fundamental promise of private equity is that, through professional management and superior insight, firms can bring operational efficiencies to underperforming companies. But what are
those operational efficiencies?

In practice, they are often layoffs. After KKR, Bain, and Vornado Realty Trust bought Toys "R" Us in 2005, the company
fired thousands of workers.[126] This isn't to say that the actual work
of the company shrank: employees said that the company just required those who remained to take on the tasks of their former
coworkers.[127] "The amount of work was—you couldn't do it," one
former employee told *Retail Dive*.[128] "In the end, I lost my career,
my retirement, and my financial stability that took me 29 years to
build up. At the age of 60 I'm still not able to find a full-time job
18 months after my store closed."[129] Ultimately, Toys "R" Us's private equity owners liquidated the entire company and fired thirty-
three thousand employees.

Toys "R" Us is far from exceptional. Over the past decade,
nearly six hundred thousand people working for retail companies
owned by private equity firms have been laid off, at a time when
the industry added over one million jobs.[130] In large companies, 10
percent of employees tend to lose their jobs within two years of a
private equity firm's acquisition.[131]

At the same time, private equity firms often cut the quality of
the products their companies sell. For instance, Eileen Appelbaum
and Rosemary Batt explain that after Catterton Partners bought

the company in 2005, it shut down the company's plant in Oak-
land. The move cost 230 employees their jobs and increased the
amount of time between when cookies were baked and when they
reached retailers.[132] Suppliers complained that their packages were
no longer properly sealed: "One of my last loads, I got a pallet of
Taffy cookies and they were all open. Unsealed," a former driver
for the company told the *New York Times*.[133] And the company reportedly changed its recipes and started using cheaper ingredients.
"Our cookies turned to crap," said a former employee. "They were
nowhere near as good as they used to be."[134]

With products like cookies, consumers can choose what and
whether to buy. But consider the case of a literally captive audience. As described in Chapter 7, private equity–owned companies make over $40 billion in revenue a year providing services
to prisons, where customers—inmates—have little choice but
to accept the services they're offered.[135] The three largest prison
phone companies, for instance, are all private equity owned and
have charged as much as $25 for a fifteen-minute call.[136] Two of the
largest prison medical care providers are owned by private equity
firms and together have been sued about 1,500 times over just five
years for allegedly inadequate patient care.[137] And several prison
cafeteria companies are private equity owned too. One in particular has been accused of serving meals with maggots, potatoes with
"crunchy dirt," and moldy apple crisp and pancakes.[138]

More generally, from retail to snacks to prison services, the
idea of "operational efficiencies" belies a certain arrogance in the
private equity industry, the idea that in three to seven years, well-
educated dilettantes can run a company better than those who've
often spent a lifetime doing so. "What they thought was that people who live here are stupid, and that's the way they treated us," a
former employee of Payless ShoeSource told the *New York Times*,
after the shoe seller was bought by Alden Global Capital.[139] "It
didn't matter how great you were in your field or what other stuff
you had done, it was, 'You live in Kansas, so you're an idiot.'"[140]
This arrogance—forged in business schools, sharpened by industry conferences and its own propaganda—allows private equity

to convince the world, and perhaps itself, that it really is a "superior form of capitalism" and to disguise the ways it really makes its money.

✳

LEASEBACKS. DIVIDEND RECAPS. Bankruptcies. Forced partnerships. Tax avoidance. Rollups. Layoffs. These are the tools by which private equity makes its money. Dangerous in any hands, they are especially so for an industry that, by its very design, is encouraged to think short term and take huge risks, while sharing little financial responsibility if those risks fail to pay off.

Given this, you may wonder: Are all companies that private equity firms buy doomed to failure? Certainly not. Some companies acquired by private equity grow and prosper, and the industry's advocates point to these successes as evidence of private equity's virtues. But while private equity doesn't doom a company to failure, the chance of failure dramatically increases. Roughly one in five large companies acquired through leveraged buyouts go bankrupt in a decade.[141] This is vastly more than the roughly 2 percent of comparable companies not acquired by private equity firms that do. And even among the many companies that survive, private equity often changes their cultures, from ones focused on the long term to the short, from investment to extraction, and from responsibility to recklessness and, at times, lawlessness.

When private equity firms are appropriately restrained—that is, when they do not act like private equity firms—they can actually do real good. Recall the three fundamental flaws in the industry: firms invest for the short term, they load companies up with debt and extract fees, and they insulate themselves from the financial and legal consequences of their actions. When private equity firms do good, when they improve the performance of the companies they acquire and not just reap financial benefits for themselves, it is usually the result of fixing one or more of these flaws.

Look at Blue Wolf Capital and the Caddo River mill. Blue Wolf is a smaller private equity firm that acquires middle-market businesses in a handful of industries. Unlike most of its competitors, it welcomes engagement with labor, declaring on its website that "forging a constructive relationship between employees and management isn't just good for business—it's the right thing to do."[142] In 2017, Blue Wolf and a consortium of investors bought the abandoned Caddo River lumber mill in Glenwood, Arkansas. The mill had closed in 2010—a victim of the Great Recession and collapsing housing prices[143]—and its failure meant that in a town of just 2,500 people, hundreds lost their jobs.[144] In 2017, Blue Wolf's consortium helped to revive the mill, paying to restore its infrastructure.[145] They reportedly spent millions of dollars on new equipment and, in reopening, hired over one hundred workers who were paid, on average, over sixteen dollars an hour. Retirees from the plant's earlier iteration were rehired: one former employee, who had worked at the mill for a quarter century before it first closed, told the *Arkansas Democrat-Gazette* that getting the call to return was "one of the best days of my life."[146] "You could feel the excitement in town," another former worker said. "With it closed for so long, people just didn't think it would be cranked back up again."[147]

The reopening had ripple effects. City Cafe, which had been closed for years, briefly reopened, where the proprietor hoped that a $7.99 buffet would attract returning millworkers.[148] And the leaders of Blue Wolf showed personal, even emotional investment. Charles Miller, a partner at the firm, said that "I've told anyone who wants to hear it that other than meeting my wife and having my children, this is my greatest accomplishment."[149]

In short, what made Blue Wolf different was that it eschewed most of the fundamental problems of private equity. It bought the company entirely with its own and investors' money rather than, as is so often the case, by loading the mill up with debt.[150] This meant that the business could afford to invest in its own operations, rather than service its loans. After reviving the plant, the firm sold its stake to Conifex Timber for $258 million.[151] But again, unlike so many private equity firms, it remained invested in the project. Though it sold its ownership stake, it remained Conifex's largest minority shareholder and took two seats on the company's board.

This meant that it had an incentive to think beyond its short period of official ownership and was invested in the business's long-term future. Success was not guaranteed—during an economic downturn, the mill had to cut down to a single shift[152]—but the business is now owned by a new timber company,[153] which employs over 150 people at the mill.[154]

These differences changed the perspective of Blue Wolf and, in turn, changed the Caddo River timber mill. All of which is to say that investment—risking money to help businesses grow and prosper—is necessary and helpful. Problems occur when private equity turns from investment to extraction.

The leading private equity firms—Blackstone, Apollo, KKR, and the Carlyle Group and hundreds of other, smaller players such as TPG, Vista Equity, Thoma Bravo, Sun Capital, and Platinum Equity—are all different. Some are more extractive, others less so. Some invest for a quick payout; others are more patient. An indictment against one is not necessarily an indictment against all. But they are all bound, to a greater or lesser degree, by a common business model that is fundamentally dangerous. And each has tens of billions of dollars, often more, to effect its agenda.

Perhaps the tactics and the successes and failures of these companies would be less frightening—eddies in the great river of capitalism—were it not for the populations that private equity firms make their money from. These firms focus much of their labor on extracting money from industries that target the most vulnerable people: single-family rental properties, nursing homes, and prison services, among others. It is to these industries, and the lessons they teach us about private equity's tactics, that we now turn.

CHAPTER TWO

ENDING HOMEOWNERSHIP AS WE KNOW IT

Private Equity in Housing

Stephen Schwarzman's seventieth birthday party was, in a word, spectacular. The CEO of the private equity firm Blackstone had spent a year and a reported $10 million to plan the affair, with help from the same company that did events for Calvin Klein, Madonna, and the billionaire David Koch's own seventieth celebration.

Coming as it did shortly after the 2016 election, the party was something of a refuge for a subset of the American elite. "The world is an uncertain place, a lot of people are unhappy with a lot of other people, there are a lot of things that people are upset about," Howard Marks, the cochairman of Oaktree Capital Management, told Bloomberg. "So it's nice to have an evening where everybody's happy, harmonious, and upbeat."[1]

Harmonious indeed. The six hundred guests included leaders of business, fashion, and art, three cabinet secretaries, and literal and figurative royalty: Princess Firyal of Jordan came, as did the president's daughter and son-in-law, Ivanka Trump and Jared

Kushner.[2] President Trump himself, a close friend of Schwarzman's and a neighbor—his Mar-a-Lago estate was less than two miles from Schwarzman's in Palm Beach—was unable to attend, though the men were already in frequent contact.

Schwarzman's invitations promised what a reporter called "an exotic journey," which in practice meant a goulash of different cultural homages.[3] Schwarzman hired actors—some to wear traditional Japanese dress, others Mongolian, along with real camels—to greet guests as they arrived at his fifteen-thousand-square-foot mansion. A balcony of trapeze artists performed as friends and colleagues crossed over what were ordinarily the estate's tennis courts.[4] Dinner itself was hosted in a specially constructed Chinese temple, where Schwarzman's birthday cake, sculpted to resemble the temple, was served.

After dinner, guests were led to yet another temple, where Gwen Stefani and the cast of *Jersey Boys* performed.[5] Stefani sang "Happy Birthday" and danced (presumably a little awkwardly) with Schwarzman himself.[6] The evening ended with a fireworks display that etched across the skies of the Intracoastal Waterway. As one guest put it, "it really was the party of the century."[7]

How did Schwarzman afford to fete himself in this way, welcoming celebrities to his home and building literal temples to celebrate himself? In part, the answer lies in housing. Over the past fifteen years, private equity firms like Schwarzman's have helped to lead what one commentator called "the biggest land grab since the Manifest Destiny."[8] In 2011, no landlord in America owned more than a thousand single-family home rental properties.[9] By 2013, Schwarzman's firm, Blackstone, bought more than that in a single day, at a cost of over $100 million. One of Blackstone's companies, Invitation Homes, became the largest renter of single-family homes in America.[10] More generally, in just two years, private equity firms and hedge funds bought about 350,000 bank-owned homes[11] and, with the industry's help, between 2006 and 2017, 5.4 million single-family homes transitioned from owner occupied to rentals.[12] Now, nearly a third of all rentals in the United States are single-family homes.[13] These statistics help to explain how

Schwarzman was able to celebrate himself as he did. And they help to explain how the very nature of homeownership in America is changing, and how private equity has helped to lead the way.

✻

IT ALL BEGAN in 2007, when the housing market collapsed. Over the previous years, low-interest loans and the rise of a "shadow" banking system that issued, bundled, and sold risky mortgages led to huge increases in housing purchases and prices. Like all manias, the system depended upon there always being another buyer, one willing to pay more for a house than the last. And eventually, the music stopped.

In a matter of months, communities like Bakersfield, California; Reno, Nevada; and Cape Coral, Florida, were transformed.[14] In Las Vegas, one in twenty homes went into foreclosure. In Tampa, a single judge might have three thousand foreclosure cases on her docket at any given time.[15] And in Stockton, California, white notices on empty houses bore the messages, "This is a bank-owned property" and "Bank-owned: no trespassing."[16] "Whenever you see a brown lawn, it's a foreclosure," a local activist told the *Guardian* as he drove down suburban streets. "Look, three in a row."[17]

As the housing crisis metastasized into a broader banking crisis, the economy was fundamentally shaken. Nearly nine million people lost their jobs.[18] Roughly as many lost their homes.[19] And those who stayed in their houses often did so with mortgages demanding more than their properties were worth.

In the face of this calamity, one institution, more than practically any other, was actually positioned to address it: Fannie Mae. Unlike most centers of power in Washington, Fannie Mae's headquarters at the time sat far from downtown, in an enormous colonial revival building whose brick façade was more reminiscent of a college campus than an ordinary office building. And unlike most centers of power in Washington, Fannie Mae was not technically a government agency but rather an independent government-sponsored entity that operated with the implicit financial backing of the United States. Chartered by Congress during the Great Depression, Fannie's purpose then and now was to stabilize the housing market, by buying up individual mortgages from banks, bundling (or "securitizing") them, and selling them to investors. In buying mortgages, Fannie gave money to banks to issue more loans, which in turn gave more people the chance to buy homes. Over eight decades, under various configurations with the government, Fannie and its sidekick agency Freddie Mac (which was created to spur competition within the mortgage securitization industry) grew enormously, and by 2008, the two owned or guaranteed about half of America's $12 trillion mortgage market.[20]

Fannie and Freddie, almost alone among American institutions, actually had the power to keep people in their homes, by reducing the principal on the millions of mortgages they owned or guaranteed. Doing so would have cut homeowners' monthly bills and, for those whose mortgages were larger than their homes were worth, made it rational for them to stay. Doing so would have also reduced the ripple effect of foreclosures, in which the value of whole neighborhoods fell when a few homes in it were dispossessed.

In fact, the Obama administration did propose a modest version of this idea. Under its Principal Reduction Alternative program, the federal government offered financial incentives to investors to reduce the total amount owed on the mortgages they held.[21] And the Treasury Department offered to extend the program to Fannie and Freddie.[22] But stunningly, Edward DeMarco, the acting director of the agency overseeing both, refused. DeMarco looked like the man he was—a career civil servant—and at congressional hearings, the sharp gaze of his blue, bird-like eyes pierced his rimless glasses. Over and over, DeMarco refused to accept the Principal Reduction Alternative program for the Federal Housing Finance Agency, or FHFA, which oversaw Fannie and Freddie, arguing that to do otherwise would constitute a grave "moral hazard."[23] This was a confusion of the term. Helping homeowners would create a moral hazard only if people knew that buying a home was a risky investment (historically, it had not been) and if they expected a government bailout when their investment soured (there was no reason for them to expect this). But it was clear from DeMarco's public statements that he had a deeper, almost emotional reaction against principal reduction. "Fundamentally, principal forgiveness rewrites a contract," he told the Senate. And rewriting a contract, he said, "risks creating a longer-term view by investors that the mortgage contract is less secure than ever before."[24]

Treasury Secretary Timothy Geithner publicly implored DeMarco to act, estimating that principal reduction during the housing crisis could help up to five hundred thousand homeowners and save taxpayers up to $1 billion.[25] A petition on Change.org called him the "single largest obstacle to meaningful economic recovery."[26] Paul Krugman demanded his resignation. But it was to no avail. Through the entirety of the Great Recession, DeMarco and the FHFA refused to implement the principal reduction program, saying that its "anticipated benefits do not outweigh the costs and risks."[27]

DeMarco went even further, not only refusing to implement principal reduction in his institution but working hard to force others from doing the same in theirs. In particular, local governments in some of the communities hit hardest by the recession considered a radical step: seizing underwater home loans through eminent domain and then helping homeowners refinance those loans at lower prices.[28] DeMarco and his agency acted quickly and took the extraordinary step of using the Federal Register—the official public record of the federal government—to threaten the municipalities. The FHFA said that it had "significant concerns" about the use of eminent domain to reduce mortgage principals and that "action may be necessary" to "avoid a risk to safe and sound operations at its regulated entities and to avoid taxpayer expense."[29] The FHFA invited public criticism of the cities' proposals, which organizations like the Americans for Prosperity Foundation (created by Charles and David Koch) were happy to provide. DeMarco and his allies ultimately prevailed. Just one city—Richmond, California—got close to using eminent domain, and even there the progressive mayor was ultimately stymied. No municipality ever reduced homeowners' principals through eminent domain.

There's little point in speculating about DeMarco's motivations during this time. Like all of us, he was perhaps moved by a mixture of genuine belief and personal interest: after leaving the FHFA, DeMarco became president of the Housing Policy Council, a lobbying organization for America's mortgage lenders and servicers.[30] His precise motivation is irrelevant because the outcome was the same: tens of thousands of people likely lost their homes because the FHFA failed to act boldly, when boldness was needed most.

But while DeMarco and the FHFA were hostile to reducing homeowners' principals, there was one group to whom they showed tremendous solicitude: large investors and, in particular, private equity firms. With the collapse of the housing market, millions of Americans lost their homes, and Fannie and Freddie found themselves owning many of them. Rather than reselling these homes to families, potentially at a loss, the FHFA[31] and Federal Reserve[32] hoped that these houses could be flipped into rental properties, properties that investors, not individuals, could buy. In explaining this position, Ben Bernanke, the chairman of the Federal Reserve, surmised that creditors could potentially make more money by renting rather than selling properties. Bernanke suggested that "involuntary renters" could benefit by buying the homes they rented, though offered little sense as to how, exactly, that would happen.[33]

And this is where private equity enters the story. Historically, single-family homes had not been a part of private equity firms' portfolios: they were too disparate and too small to make much money. But bought in bulk, homes presented an opportunity. Private equity firms could convert the houses into rental properties and then derive a steady cash flow with which to pay the debt used to purchase them. Moreover, homeowners, turned into home renters, were something of a captive audience. While a person might leave a studio or one-bedroom apartment with relative ease, a family could move from a home only with great difficulty. The financial crisis—and the solicitous attitude of Fannie Mae and its regulator—were thus an enormous opportunity for private equity firms. And they acted accordingly.

In 2012, the FHFA launched a series of auctions of foreclosed homes, with the intention that the purchased houses be converted into rental properties.[34] Investors developed new software that estimated the best purchases based on a neighborhood's schools, crime, and nearness to transit, as well as possible maintenance costs. Such software allowed investors to participate in thousands of auctions and identify those properties likely to make the most money.[35]

Additionally, by selling the properties in bundles, the FHFA precluded individual homeowners and likely all but the largest and most sophisticated institutional investors from participating.[36] And that is precisely what happened. In the FHFA's first round of auctions, Colony Capital, a private equity firm run by Tom Barrack (a close friend of Donald Trump's who chaired his inaugural committee), bought 970 properties in California, Arizona, and Nevada.[37] Barrack later called his investment strategy "the greatest thing I've ever done in my professional life."[38]

Barrack had reason to be jubilant. Buyers for Barrack's Colony and Stephen Schwarzman's Invitation Homes,[39] along with their peers, fanned across America to purchase dozens and hundreds of houses at a time. At times, the fevered activity felt like it was from another century. At the Gwinnett County courthouse in Georgia, for instance, buyers paid for foreclosed homes on the spot, and Colony's employees brought an actual box full of cashier's checks—$3 million in total—to the courthouse steps.[40] "Game on," said Colony's bidder as the auction began.[41]

Fannie's solicitous support for the single-family home rental industry didn't stop with its pilot project. In 2012, Fannie entered into a joint partnership with Barrack's Colony to operate, lease, and manage a portfolio of over a thousand homes, primarily in Arizona, California, and Nevada.[42] Colony agreed to pay Fannie $35 million, and in exchange, Fannie agreed to give Colony 20 percent or more of the cash flow generated from the properties.[43] Colony said that it expected to make a million dollars a month from the deal.

Fannie Mae was especially kind to Stephen Schwarzman's firm Blackstone and its portfolio company, Invitation Homes. In 2017, Fannie agreed to "secure" a $1 billion loan for Invitation. Under the deal, Invitation borrowed the enormous sum from Wells Fargo, and Fannie in turn agreed to pay Wells Fargo if Invitation ever defaulted.[44] There was little obvious reason for Fannie—which operates with the implicit financial backing of the government—to enter into the deal, and a consortium of 136 nonprofits opposed it.[45] But it proceeded, nevertheless, allowing Invitation to borrow money at a lower rate and thus acquire more houses to rent. In other words, having refused to do all it could to help people keep their homes, Fannie was now using all its powers to help private equity firms buy those homes up.

Ultimately, the magnitude of these companies' acquisitions was astounding. As mentioned above, in just two years, private equity firms and hedge funds bought about 350,000 bank-owned homes, and by 2015, the number of single-family home rentals had grown by nearly three million.[46] "We recognized the unique opportunity created by the housing crisis," an executive from Barrack's company triumphantly declared, "and acted upon it in a bold way."[47]

✳

WHAT WAS IT like to live in one of the hundreds of thousands of homes converted into rental properties by Invitation Homes, Colony, and other private equity–owned firms?[48] In a word: hard.

For one thing, living in a single-family home rental tended to get more expensive each year, given that such homes were often excluded from local rent control laws. In Los Angeles, more than three-quarters of surveyed residents of rental homes reported rent increases, which averaged over $2,000 annually, or roughly 9 percent more than the year before.[49] In large cities—often those that had been hardest hit by the Great Recession—the increases were even larger: 9.3 percent in Las Vegas, 10.6 percent in Tucson, 12.2 percent in Phoenix.[50] To the working-class families that lived in these homes, these were devastating increases: "For me to work

12–14 hour days and barely have enough to pay increasing rents to a multi-billion dollar Wall Street giant, it's like sharecropping all over again," said a tenant of one of Colony's subsidiaries.[51]

Moreover, rent captured only part of the cost of living in these homes. Companies like Invitation and Colony loaded up tenants with fees to extract more money from them. Invitation, for instance, charged utility expenses back to renters, as well as a $9.95 conveyance fee for each bill.[52] It added landscaping fees, pool fees, pet fees, and "smart lock" fees.

Many of these were legal, but some may not have been: class action lawsuits in Texas and California alleged that Blackstone's Invitation charged illegal, excessive late fees to its residents.[53] As of December 2022, the Texas case remains ongoing, but the court in California declined to certify the class of plaintiffs and dismissed the action. It did so in part because the lead plaintiff had signed his lease with Invitation's predecessor companies, which Invitation absorbed through various acquisitions.[54] In other words, the companies' various mergers with one another had the incidental effect of insulating them from liability for their alleged past wrongdoing.

Despite all these expenses, tenants weren't getting much in return. Private equity landlords often placed the burden of maintaining their properties on their residents, either in ordinary lease agreements or in dodgy rent-to-own programs.[55] In such programs, tenants were given the option to buy the properties they rented. But in return, the tenants, not the landlords, were required to make major repairs. It's hard to track the scope of these efforts, but anecdotally, the *New York Times* reports that "few rent-to-own agreements end in actual purchases," and in fact, rent-to-own arrangements are illegal in some states.[56]

When tenants fell behind on their expenses, they faced firms' aggressive and slapdash tactics for collecting money, which ranged from degrading to devastating. Among other things, tenants complained that debt collectors placed menacing phone calls and ruined their credit. After one tenant fell behind on rent, Invitation Homes wrapped caution tape around their house, presumably to shame the tenant into payment.[57] Another found herself bouncing between

Waypoint (owned by Blackstone and Colony at various times) and its debt collector over a previously unknown—and potentially erroneous—$8,000 charge.[58] Neither would take responsibility for correcting the debt, and as a result, "[n]obody would rent to me," the tenant said.[59] "I had to find a co-signer to help me buy a house because they ruined my credit from that $8,000 charge."[60]

And when collections didn't work, there were evictions. Lots of them. A study by the Federal Reserve Bank of Atlanta found that, in a single year, Colony sent eviction notices to nearly one-third of its tenants around the city, far more than any other company.[61] Corporate landlords—those that owned fifteen or more homes in Fulton County—were 68 percent more likely than smaller property owners to file eviction notices, even controlling for property, tenant, and neighborhood characteristics.[62] In some zip codes, over 40 percent of all rental households got an eviction notice, and over 15 percent received a judgment or were forcibly removed. African Americans and women were especially likely to be evicted.

Yet such evictions may have been preferable for some residents of private equity–owned homes, for many of those who stayed faced threats to their health. There was, for instance, the problem of lead, which, when exposed to children, can cause cognitive deficiencies, developmental delays, reduced academic performance, seizures, coma, and death. Researchers in Detroit found that children living in homes owned by large investors (those with fifty or more properties) were significantly more likely to have elevated concentrations of lead in their blood than were other children.[63] There was also the problem of mold, which, indoors, can induce asthma attacks.[64] Thirteen percent of surveyed residents in Los Angeles, for instance, complained of mold in their building.[65]

Here, the story of Monica Lisboa is instructive because it illustrates both the health problems in these buildings and how private equity–owned companies responded.[66] In 2013, Lisboa rented an apartment in Florida operated by the private equity–owned Colony American Homes. As alleged in her subsequent lawsuit, when

Lisboa and her family moved in, she noted a "musty odor" that she assumed would fade with time. It did not, however, and over the months and years that followed the smell grew more intense. Lisboa and her son began to experience rashes, nausea, itchy eyes, headaches, vomiting, and trouble breathing.

Eventually, Lisboa found significant patches of black mold in the property, which she reported to Colony, but which she alleged Colony ignored.[67] Lisboa then paid for her own do-it-yourself mold test, which revealed toxic levels of black mold spores. This finally prompted Colony to hire its own testing company, but when Lisboa sought the results, the testing company said that Colony had instructed it not to release them. Instead, Colony itself allegedly told her that the test results showed that there was no mold on the property. If Lisboa's complaint is accurate, either the testing company had grievously erred, or Colony was lying to Lisboa.

Not trusting Colony, Lisboa reported she paid for yet another test—this one by a professional—who confirmed that there were, indeed, toxic levels of mold on the property.[68] As all this was happening, Lisboa's son had a seizure and had to be hospitalized. There, the doctor said that her son's health issues were caused by toxic mold exposure. But incredibly, while Lisboa and her son were at the hospital, she said she received a phone call: it was Colony, inquiring about her rent payment.

Eventually, according to her complaint, Lisboa and her children had to flee the property to protect themselves.[69] Yet even after they left, and even after Colony was put on notice of the dangerous mold levels in the house, Colony filed an eviction against Lisboa. Colony largely denied Lisboa's allegations, but the ultimate truth of the matter was never resolved: the company settled the case out of court without any admission of wrongdoing.

Lisboa's story is illustrative because it shows how apparent corporate neglect can lead to crises and how distant companies can ignore those crises to their tenants' detriment. Neglect was endemic to the private equity business model, whose focus on short-term profits necessitated abandoning the long-term care of its properties and residents. Or as one resident of another private equity–owned home put it, "Living in a Waypoint property has been an actual nightmare. No family should have to pay to live like this."[70]

✳

LOOKING MORE BROADLY, it's worth asking whether private equity firms are actually worse than other landlords. Most of us remember when a building super never returned our calls or refused to repair a sink. These mom-and-pop landlords are not saints; quite the opposite. But private equity firms have something that smaller landlords do not: billions of dollars. And they have put that money to use lobbying against broader tenant protections.[71]

For instance, in 2014, Starwood Waypoint Homes, alongside Blackstone's Invitation Homes, created the National Rental Home Council, whose agenda included plans to fight further control initiatives.[72] A few years later, Blackstone and Invitation spent millions of dollars to defeat Proposition 10 in California, which would have allowed localities to decide whether rent stabilization laws should extend to single-family homes. The law, if passed, would have been transformative, as about 45 percent of residents in California rent their properties and about a quarter of tenants nationally spend more than half their income on rent.[73] Extending tenant protections to single-family homes—or even giving cities the opportunity to do so—would have been a crucial respite for these people. But naturally, this posed a threat to the business model of private equity firms and the companies they owned. And so, Schwarzman's Blackstone and its portfolio company, Invitation Homes, contributed nearly $7 million to oppose the measure.[74] Much of this money went to the No on Prop 10 PAC,[75] whose ads featured a narrator proclaiming, over pictures of concerned California residents, that the proposition would put "unelected bureaucrats in charge of what you can and can't do with your own home" and would make housing "even more expensive for renters."[76] Opponents of Proposition 10 spent $72 million campaigning against it, more than double what its supporters spent in its favor.[77] Unsurprisingly, the proposition failed.

This sort of influence—the scale of money spent, the focus and organization of the group that spent it—simply would not be possible among more dispersed owners. By concentrating economic power, private equity firms centralized their political power and codified their influence to the detriment of the many tenants who were giving them money in rent and fees every month. Moreover, private equity firms' power—the power that comes from their size—is only growing. In 2016, Tom Barrack's Colony American Homes merged with Starwood Waypoint. The merged company in turn was bought by Blackstone's Invitation Homes in 2017, forming a behemoth single-family home rental operation.[78] Blackstone took Invitation public that year and then, in 2021, bought another home rental company for $6 billion.[79] The result was that more homes were being turned into rentals, and those rentals were owned by ever-larger and more powerful companies.

Private equity firms also got in the business of not just buying single-family home rentals themselves but of also providing the financing for smaller investors to do the same. KKR invested in a company that financed home flippers.[80] Blackstone, meanwhile, created a program to lend to smaller landlords to buy up single-family homes and rent them.[81] This gave Blackstone an opportunity to profit off of rented homes, even those they did not own. And these programs ensured that more homes would be rentals and that there would be more institutional owners—big and small—naturally allied with one another to protect their incomes, often at the expense of their tenants.

There is another sense in which private equity owners were worse than mom-and-pop landlords, namely, that by their very scale, they managed to transform the nature of housing in America. As mentioned above, between 2006 and 2017, 5.4 million single-family homes transitioned from owner-occupied units to rentals.[82] Single-family home rentals now account for more than half of the national rental market.[83] And now, investors buy one in seven homes for sale in large metropolitan cities.[84] Private equity firms account for only a fraction of these sales: for instance, Invitation Homes, previously owned by Blackstone, owns about seventy-five thousand houses.[85] But while private equity firms

are responsible for only a minority of purchases, they are the crucial innovators and partners with the government in spurring this
broader trend.

It is also important to understand where this is happening. Cities hit hardest by the Great Recession saw the largest increase in
rentals.[86] In fact, private equity firms concentrated their acquisitions not just on specific cities but on specific neighborhoods or
what one executive called "strike zones."[87] In one Atlanta zip code,
for instance, Blackstone's Invitation Homes bought 90 percent of
the homes sold over a year and a half.[88] This should be no surprise:
these were the places where Fannie Mae owned foreclosed homes,
which Fannie auctioned off to investors in the process that started
the entire rental boom. But it meant that the people who lost the
most during the Recession were the ones who regained the least
in the years that followed. In fact, according to one credit rating agency, Colony's tenants were typically former homeowners
themselves, people who could no longer afford a home but who
often retained some ties to the neighborhood.[89] By concentrating their purchases—by exercising control over local markets—
private equity firms made it difficult for people to leave. Or as
Jennifer St. Denis, a single mother and renter in Atlanta, told the
Mercury News, "At this point I'm stuck in a renting pattern because rent increases keep going up and moving out is expensive."[90]
She noted that Invitation owned most of the homes in the area that
she would want to live in anyway.

The effect was that, quite simply, fewer people own homes. In
the early 2000s, over 70 percent of households owned their own
houses. Today, that number is around 63 percent, levels not last
seen since the 1980s.[91] For African American and other minority
communities, the percentage is vastly lower: Black homeownership rates, for instance, have returned to what they were in the
1960s.[92] The change is also particularly dramatic among young
people. In 1960, 44 percent of people aged twenty to thirty-four
owned a home. In 2017, barely a quarter did.[93] This is not a change
in preferences—two-thirds of renters said that they would own a

home if they could[94]—but a change in means. "It's creating a greater divide between the haves and have-nots," one analyst told *Vox*. "Homeowners are getting sizable wealth gain. Renters are getting left out."[95]

✳

A RECURRING DEFENSE of private equity is that its use of debt and its short-term focus necessitate excellence and that the sheer intelligence of its leaders improves outcomes for companies. But the industry's foray into aspects of the housing market suggests otherwise. Consider the case of the private equity firm Fortress and its rollup of the mortgage-servicing industry. Mortgage servicers are, in essence, debt collectors: they ensure that homeowners pay their mortgages and pursue foreclosures when they don't. It's an appealing industry for private equity, as it provides a steady cash flow and a captive audience, given that mortgages are often sold from one company to another, and borrowers have no real ability to choose their servicer. Lone Star Capital, Bayview Asset Management, Selene Investment Partners, and Fortress Investment Group all bought up mortgages to service, either directly or through portfolio companies.[96]

Fortress is instructive here. In 2006, just before the housing crisis, the firm bought a mortgage servicing company, which it renamed Nationstar.[97] Consistent with private equity's model of short-term success, Nationstar's—and Fortress's—strategy was one of aggressive expansion, and in the years after the Great Recession, the company bought billions of dollars of mortgages that others no longer wanted to service. It bought whole companies like Greenlight Financial Services[98] and Residential Capital[99] and over $200 billion worth of mortgages from Bank of America.[100] By 2020, it serviced three million loans, with an unpaid principal of about $500 billion.[101] It was the largest nonbank mortgage servicer in the United States and the third largest mortgage servicer overall.

But this aggressive growth, intrinsic to the private equity business model, came at a price: Nationstar struggled with the basic tasks of servicing its mortgages, a fact alleged over and over in media reports and in lawsuits. In 2016, for instance, the *New York Times* reported that Nationstar repeatedly lost customers' files and recorded inaccurate information for others.[102] According to the *Times*, Nationstar often failed to detect its own errors until after foreclosure processes had already begun. (Nationstar's CEO, Jay Bray, defended the company's actions, saying that "[w]e are proud of the work we've done to improve the customer experience.")[103] The following year, the inspector general for the Great Recession bank bailout reported on Nationstar's failure to properly administer the government's Home Affordable Modification Program, or HAMP, which helped struggling borrowers to reduce the principal on their mortgages. "Nationstar has one of the worst track record[s] in HAMP," the inspector general wrote.[104] The company's rule violations "have been widespread spanning multiple quarters. Nationstar has shown little improvement and, even appears to be getting worse."[105] Among other things, the inspector general found that Nationstar wrongfully denied homeowners' admission into HAMP, wrongfully kicked other homeowners out, and reported homeowners as delinquent on their mortgages, when, in fact, they were not.

The errors got more serious. In 2020, without admitting wrongdoing, Nationstar settled lawsuits with all fifty states, the District of Columbia, and the Consumer Financial Protection Bureau to resolve allegations of the company's widespread abuse and incompetence.[106] According to the bureau, it was as if Nationstar failed nearly every aspect of the mortgage servicing industry. The company allegedly foreclosed on borrowers, even after explicitly promising it would not, while the borrowers' loan modifications were under review. It failed to pay people's property taxes on time, and as a result, borrowers faced late penalties. It required borrowers to pay for private mortgage insurance longer than they needed to. And it unilaterally—and improperly—increased borrowers' monthly payments. Heartbreakingly, as alleged, Nationstar even foreclosed on some borrowers whose payments were impermissibly increased.

Rather than litigate, Nationstar settled with the federal and state governments and agreed to pay $73 million to more than forty thousand homeowners.[107] In a separate settlement, the company agreed with the Department of Justice to give over $40 million to another twenty thousand borrowers whose accounts were mishandled during their personal bankruptcies.[108]

But these fines couldn't undo the damage that Nationstar—and Fortress—caused. In Texas, Normie and Derrick Brown got a temporary restraining order against Nationstar to avoid what they believed was a wrongful foreclosure.[109] But Nationstar proceeded with the foreclosure anyway and held an auction for the house even before the court's restraining order was set to expire. Nationstar removed the case to federal court and closed on the sale before the new judge could rule. The Browns lost their house. "You think all you have to do is show them where they did you wrong, and basically justice will prevail," Mr. Brown told the *New York Times*. "That wasn't the case."[110]

Why did Nationstar make so many mistakes? Why was it sued by all fifty states and the federal government? The simplest answer is the most likely: because of its aggressive acquisition campaign, Nationstar apparently didn't have time to properly manage the thousands of mortgages it bought. This worked fine for its private equity owner Fortress: having bought the company in 2006 for $450 million, it sold the business in 2018—when it still held a nearly 70 percent stake—for $3.8 billion.[111] But this growth was a disaster for the literally tens of thousands of people who were harmed, and sometimes devastated, by the company's apparent mismanagement. And this growth was inherent in the business model of Fortress and others, which frequently depended on quickly buying and rolling up companies. Disasters such as private equity acquisition of Nationstar and the resulting fiasco undercut the narrative that private equity owners, through incentives or sheer intelligence, make companies and customers better.

✻

FINALLY, PRIVATE EQUITY'S foray into housing illustrates one more aspect of the industry, namely, its frequent focus on businesses that target poor people. For an industry built to make money, why target people with the least? Because poor and working-class people often lack alternatives to what they buy, and this gives private equity firms the chance to raise prices or cut quality with impunity, knowing that their customers have few alternatives. Nothing illustrates this more clearly than private equity firms' purchase of mobile home parks.

Historically, mobile homes offered pockets of affordability in an increasingly unaffordable housing market. Over nearly two decades, beginning in 1990, the United States actually lost four million units of low-cost housing.[112] By 2019, however, the median home was unaffordable to the average worker in three-fourths of the country.[113] In this environment, mobile homes offered a rare escape from these crushing expenses: used units could cost as little as $10,000, and residents generally made less than $50,000 a year.[114] Fannie Mae called them "one of the few sources of naturally occurring affordable housing" in America.[115]

But mobile homes weren't affordable by accident. The industry was historically run by family businesses that, while far from altruistic, were generally invested for the long term and free from the demands created by short investment horizons and heavy debt loads, which enabled them to keep prices low. But in the last decade, big companies came in, and that started to change. Already by 2013, investors spent $1.2 billion buying mobile home parks; by 2020, they spent $4.2 billion.[116] Private equity firms like Apollo,[117] Carlyle,[118] Stockbridge Capital,[119] Centerbridge Capital,[120] TPG,[121] Blackstone,[122] and Brookfield Asset Management[123] invested in mobile home parks or bought them outright. And as these investors came in, costs for residents began to rise: over a five-year period, the average price of a mobile home increased 35 percent, to more than $61,000.[124]

These were ideal businesses for private equity. They offered steady cash flow with little responsibility: unlike apartments or even single-family home rentals, private equity owners weren't responsible for the upkeep of the houses themselves, just the surrounding community. And the costs of that upkeep—utilities and so forth—could often be pushed onto residents.

Moreover, mobile home owners faced a number of disadvantages relative to those who owned traditional homes. For one thing, they paid two fees for the privilege of residence: a mortgage on the property itself and rent for the lot on which the property sat. For another, they tended to have higher interest rates on their mortgages, meaning that they had to pay more just to get the same equity in their homes. And in fact, the very term *mobile home* was something of a misnomer. Many were attached to concrete foundations[125] and moving them could cost $10,000 or more. As a result, owners rarely did. Private equity firms depended on this fact to increase rents and fees without consequence.

Unsurprisingly, these private equity firms often made terrible owners. After Sunrise Capital Investors bought a park in Akron, Ohio, it tried to double residents' lot rents.[126] The company's plans would "economically evict many of our neighbors," a resident wrote (residents eventually succeeded in stopping the increase).[127] After TPG bought a community in Urbana, Illinois, one resident managed to negotiate a payment plan with the property manager. But "[e]ven a good manager can't change the company wide policies that are aiming to make as much money off of all of us as possible," she told the Private Equity Stakeholder Project.[128] And after Stockbridge Capital bought a park outside Nashville, neighbors complained that the company failed to pick up couches and trash left lying in common areas, while it simultaneously threatened eviction for residents who were just six days late in their rent.[129] "They're almost like slumlords," one resident told the *Washington Post*. "If you point something out, they're just like...whatever. They just want the rent."[130] In essence, private equity firms' innovation was to realize that, because mobile homes were anything but mobile, real money could be squeezed from Americans who had the least.

A particularly wrenching aspect of these increased costs was that they actually took money from residents in two ways. *First*, residents paid the lot rents themselves. *Second*, by raising lot rents, firms made the homes less attractive to future buyers, draining the equity that residents had put into their own houses. In fact, for every $100 increase in rent, homes lost an estimated $10,000 in value.[131] It was an economic pincer move, taking both residents' income and their wealth.

Importantly, the government helped. In 2016, Fannie Mae helped to provide $1 billion in financing for Stockbridge Capital's Yes! Communities. The loan helped Yes! buy up more mobile homes and, crucially, did not limit how much or how often the company could raise rents on the properties it bought.[132] Two years later, Fannie Mae provided $200 million in financing for TPG Capital to buy dozens of mobile home parks itself.[133] George McCarthy, an affordable housing advocate, told National Public Radio that "what's ironic about it is that one of the missions of Fannie Mae and Freddie Mac is to help preserve affordable housing. And they're doing exactly the opposite by helping investors come in and make the most affordable housing in the United States less affordable all the time."[134] To its credit, Fannie subsequently set for itself the goal of financing more mobile home sales to nonprofits, and adding resident protections to future loans.[135] But the scale of its aspirations was small: it aimed to make just three nonprofit deals in 2022, for instance.[136]

Considering all this, it is helpful to see how private equity ownership worked in one specific mobile home community: Plaza Del Rey, in Sunnyvale, California. Sunnyvale sits in the center of Silicon Valley, and its largest employers include Google, Apple, Lockheed Martin, and Amazon. In 2015—the year that the Carlyle Group bought Plaza Del Rey—a typical home in the city cost well over $1 million.[137] In such an environment, the mobile home park offered a pocket of affordability in a community of extraordinary expense, a place where middle- and working-class people could live and get to nearby jobs. For four decades, the park was owned by a single family, until 2015, when the granddaughter sold it to Carlyle for over $150 million.[138] Residents already covered the utilities, property taxes, and cost of upkeep. But within its first year as owner, Carlyle raised rents 7.5 percent, the largest increase in the park's forty-seven-year history. For new residents, Carlyle raised lot rents to $1,600, nearly 40 percent more than the park average.[139] This didn't just hurt people who moved in: it made it harder for existing owners to sell, eviscerating the equity in their homes that they might have built up.

As reported by the *Los Angeles Times*, residents resisted but were infuriatingly outmatched. Some collected cans to pay to meet with a lawyer: after a morning of collection, they raised $46.55: "Enough to pay for a third of an hour with an attorney!" one of them exclaimed.[140] Others protested to the city council, where one of Carlyle's managing directors spoke against them. "We are opposed to rent control in any form and do not believe it furthers the objectives of the city or owners in the long term," the Carlyle executive exhorted.[141]

The council, perhaps fearful of any action that might dampen investment in the city ("The city council expressed no interest in helping us," one resident complained[142]), never imposed any rent control. But it did facilitate a negotiation between Carlyle and the residents, the result of which was a nominal limit on rent increases for those residents who signed on. Yet according to Fred Kameda, a resident familiar with the deal, the rent that Carlyle could charge for new lots was unaffected. This meant that residents would still potentially lose equity in their homes and still struggle to sell them. "Basically we didn't do a very good job negotiating," Kameda said.[143] "However we had no—how would you say it—leverage."[144]

Kameda suspects that Carlyle's real intention was not simply to raise rents but to push out residents and transform the whole park into higher-density and much more profitable housing. Despite Carlyle's protests to the contrary, there was some limited evidence to support the theory. Forty miles away, Carlyle had tried to evict owners in another mobile home park it bought and turn the properties into more profitable rentals.[145] And as part of its deal with Plaza Del Rey residents, Carlyle negotiated the right to make the first offer on homes that went up for sale, setting itself up to do the same there.[146] If that was Carlyle's intention, it never succeeded, though it still managed to make a fabulous profit. In 2019, four years after buying Plaza Del Rey, Carlyle sold the park to another investor for $237.4 million. Carlyle managed to make a 58 percent profit on the deal.[147]

Though Carlyle left, the problems didn't stop for Plaza Del Rey's residents. The new owner increased rents for incoming residents to $2,380, rendering homes, according to existing owners, "unsellable."[148] Residents held protests and met with Representative Ro Khanna, though the new owner barred TV and newspapers from covering Khanna's visit to the residents. "It's outrageous that they didn't allow the press to listen to the residents' concerns,"[149] Khanna said, adding—perhaps aspirationally—that "we don't live in an oligarchy where private equity gets to destroy our communities."[150]

Ultimately, the city imposed a memorandum of understanding that set limits on rate increases for both new and existing owners.[151] But this fell short of an actual rent stabilization ordinance, which already existed in a half dozen nearby towns. Instead, residents had to proactively sign the memorandum, and under it, the new park owner could still substantially increase rates for new mobile home owners.[152]

The whole experience was illustrative. Carlyle was able to turn an extraordinary profit on an investment, not by making a better company but by increasing the costs for those least able to pay. Residents protested, but their protests were largely ineffective, with a local government agonizingly slow to act. And in large part, residents didn't move because they couldn't. By increasing rents—and making properties less attractive to new buyers—Carlyle actually made it harder for existing owners to leave.

It was a cruel system, cruel for everyone except Carlyle and its investing peers. "I think they were carpetbagging scumbags," one resident said of Carlyle.[153] "They don't realize that these are peoples' homes," said another to a local news station. She added, poignantly, "We're not just numbers on a spreadsheet."[154]

✳

PRIVATE EQUITY FIRMS' adventures in housing illustrate the industry's worst tendencies. They bought up hundreds of thousands of homes, raised prices, and reduced quality. They did not demonstrate particular skill in administration, as the follies of Nationstar illustrate. But they did demonstrate enormous political strength, as shown by their defeat of Proposition 10 in California. Finally, they targeted, not those with the most money in America, but those with the least. Nowhere was this clearer than in the case of mobile home parks. And all of this was accomplished with the active support of the government, whose sponsored entity, Fannie Mae, helped to start the fevered rush to acquire homes. We seem, in other words, to be bringing this on ourselves. In so doing, we help to fund the lives and lifestyles of men like Stephen Schwarzman, whose seventieth birthday was described earlier. His "party of the century," with its actors and camels, singers and temples, was all made possible, in large part, by the housing industry he helped to transform.

CHAPTER THREE

PROFITING OFF BANKRUPTCY

Private Equity in Retail

Do you wonder why so many businesses around you are closing and why retail spaces so often seem unoccupied? The common refrain is that Amazon and other online sellers have displaced physical stores and rendered them irrelevant. This is partly true, though it is only part of the story. Another part is that private equity firms are buying up stores that, collectively, employ millions of people and are often driving those stores into bankruptcy. Some of this is simple mismanagement. But some of it is deliberate, for, as the pages below describe, often these firms win in the bankruptcy process when so many others—the companies they buy, the creditors they use, and the employees they pay—lose. All this exacerbates inequality, by shifting money from workers to executives, and from retailers to financiers. And it's happening all the time.

The case of Toys "R" Us is illustrative. The children's superstore looms large in many of our childhood memories, as it has for generations of grown kids. Its founder, Charles P. Lazarus, started the business in his parents' bicycle shop[1] as Children's Bargain Town,[2] a place where parents of the exploding baby boom could buy cribs and other children's furniture. Over time, Lazarus realized that though parents needed to buy cribs just once, they needed to buy toys constantly. In 1957, he launched the first Toys "R" Us in Rockville, Maryland, with its trademark backward "R," written as a child might.

Lazarus built his stores like giant supermarkets, and an early advertisement promised "unlimited quantities" of toys, with "trailer loads arriving continuously."[3] Where other businesses had small showrooms and limited inventory, Toys "R" Us promised to rarely, if ever, run out of the toys that kids loved. And the company's early adoption of computer inventory systems allowed it to know what kids wanted before other companies did.[4]

In time, Toys "R" Us became a national icon. Generations of children remember its advertising jingle, "I don't wanna grow up, I'm a Toys 'R' Us kid," or the Super Toy Run on Nickelodeon, where contestants could win a five-minute shopping spree in the store. In 2001, it opened a giant flagship in Times Square, with an enormous indoor Ferris wheel, life-sized Barbie Dreamhouse, and twenty-foot animatronic T. rex.[5]

It's true that Toys "R" Us was slow to adapt to online retailing, and it committed an unforced error by partnering with Amazon in its first big push into e-commerce.[6] The project helped Amazon learn how to sell products to children, and Toys inadvertently surrendered its competitive advantage. Nevertheless, the company had over $11 billion in revenue[7] when, in 2005, it was purchased by a trio of private equity firms: Bain, KKR, and Vornado.

This is where the troubles began. The firms bought Toys "R" Us for over $6 billion, most of it with debt that Toys—not its purchasers—would have to pay.[8] And the cost of servicing that debt was enormous: about half a billion dollars a year on interest alone,[9] not to mention millions in various fees that the company would need to pay its new owners.[10] This sucked money away from the company that could have been spent making the expensive— and necessary—transition to online retailing.

At the same time, under the private equity firms' ownership, the company bought several competitors, including FAO Schwarz and K-B Toys. For each acquisition, Toys "R" Us paid the private equity firms a transaction fee, which together totaled over $100 million.[11] On top of this, Toys paid Bain, KKR, and Vornado regular management fees—costs for the privilege to be owned by them—and interest on debt that it owed the firms directly. In total, the Private Equity Stakeholder Project estimates that over thirteen years, Toys "R" Us paid Bain, KKR, and Vornado $464 million.[12]

Along the way, the private equity firms drew down the company's assets. Before it was purchased, Toys "R" Us had over $2 billion in cash and cash equivalents. By 2017, the year of the bankruptcy, it had less than one-sixth that.[13] Ann Marie Reinhart, who worked at Toys for twenty-nine years, said that the private equity purchase "changed the dynamic of how the store ran."[14] According to employees, benefits were cut, as were jobs, and the employees who remained had to take on more responsibilities. Stores became shabby as the ordinary work of maintaining a big business—polishing floors, sweeping parking lots, and so forth—grew infrequent.[15] The fans, girders, and lights of the stores, where dust accumulated, were cleaned less often. And the company fell behind on its internal information technology, a part of the business where it had once excelled.

The heavy debt and the flow of cash to the private equity firms made it impossible for Toys to make necessary changes. In 2014, the company announced a TRU Transformation initiative, to improve the in-store and online shopping experience, create exclusive partnerships with toy makers, and reduce costs.[16] But it wasn't enough, and in 2017, the company filed for Chapter 11 bankruptcy.

At the time, many commentators blamed Amazon. But this was, at best, only part of the story. Toys' sales remained steady, even during the Great Recession, and in the year before it filed for bankruptcy, its $11 billion in revenue[17] accounted for an estimated one-fifth of all toy sales in the country.[18] The problem wasn't market share; the problem was the debt. By 2017, Toys' payment on the interest alone nearly matched its entire operating income: the company had $460 million in operating income and $457 million in interest expenses.[19] Without money, the company couldn't make the necessary investments to compete online, couldn't hire the best people, and couldn't keep its stores clean.

In the bankruptcy process, there were clear winners and losers. One of the winners was the Toys' CEO, David Brandon, who thrived as the company struggled. Brandon was an ally of the company's private equity owners—Bain had previously chosen him to run Domino's Pizza, another of their investments[20]—and at Toys "R" Us, he was treated extraordinarily well. As subsequently alleged by a class of Toys' creditors, while the CEOs of comparable companies were typically paid around $1.1 million and the ninetieth percentile were paid $1.56 million, Brandon was paid more than twice that: $3.75 million.[21] He spent that money well. For a while, he lived in a luxurious building on New York's Billionaire's Row,[22] in an apartment with a listed rent of $45,000 a month.[23] And in 2016, he paid over $15 million for a penthouse on the Upper East Side, with terrace views of Central Park.

As his company collapsed, Brandon sought to secure his financial future. The challenge, according to subsequent litigants, was that Toys' lawyers had advised Brandon that his bonus likely would not be approved once the company filed for bankruptcy.[24] So he ordered that bonuses for himself and other top executives be paid three days before then.[25] Brandon ultimately had the company pay him $2.8 million, with similar payouts for other top executives.[26]

Having secured his bonus, Brandon allegedly lied about it. According to subsequent plaintiffs, Beth Burns, an employee at Babies "R" Us in Nashua, New Hampshire, wrote to Brandon after her store was selected for closure. Brandon had promised all of the laid-off employees a severance but then, a week later, retracted the offer. Burns wrote to Brandon and asked him to "please re-think your decision to hand out to the Executives and leave your devoted Associates with nothing."[27] Brandon personally wrote to Burns that "I did want you to know that there have not been millions of bonuses paid to the executives at our company despite what you may have heard."[28] Bonuses at the company were tied to financial performance, he explained, and "based on our performance the past several years, there have not been—nor will there be—any bonuses paid to executives or anyone else given the current financial condition of our company."[29] Brandon, it appeared, was not telling the truth: he was going to be paid millions of dollars and had spent much energy designing his exit package to avoid the restrictions of the bankruptcy laws. Having secured his financial future, Brandon was apparently unwilling to admit as much to his employees.

Beyond Brandon, another winner was Toys' law firm Kirkland & Ellis, which had established itself as the dominant force in large corporate restructurings.[30] In bankruptcy, lawyers are often paid first, the assumption being that they would refuse to work for a failing company without a guarantee that they would be compensated while doing so. But Kirkland's fee here was enormous: it made $56 million for its work[31] or nearly $1,000 an hour.[32] By comparison, according to the tracking service Payscale, the average retail department supervisor at Toys "R" Us made just $12 per hour.[33]

The losers in this process were Toys "R" Us's employees, who got just $2 million in severance.[34] The employees, according to one of their lawyers, had been promised $80 to $100 million in severance pay to work through the busy holiday season,[35] but in bankruptcy, employees were "unsecured creditors" and had little leverage to demand what they were owed. Ultimately, while the CEO received a $2.8 million exit package, employees received severance packages amounting to about $60 per person.[36] The money was little more than "schmuck certificates," according to one of their lawyers, Jack Raisner: about enough for a family meal at Arby's.[37] "For these people, it was devastating," he said.[38] "That'll pay my phone bill," Michelle Perez, a mother with two young children, complained to CBS.[39] "This has really shown how the bankruptcy system is broken," she said.[40]

The final loser in the bankruptcy was Toys "R" Us itself. Toys filed for Chapter 11 bankruptcy, where companies are meant to rehabilitate themselves by discharging some of their debts, rather than Chapter 7 bankruptcy, where companies are shut down and their remaining assets sold to creditors. Toys initially planned to keep operating and was in negotiations to do so, according to one of the company's financial advisers.[41] But a hedge fund called Solus Capital Management owned a key part of Toys "R" Us's debt. It, along with four other debt holders, decided that they were better off if Toys liquidated—that is, if it stopped working entirely and sold itself for parts—than if Toys continued to operate as a business. The debt holders were able to force the issue and shut the company down. Solus reportedly made money on the transaction— and thirty-three thousand people lost their jobs.

How about the private equity firms themselves? KKR claimed to have lost millions of dollars on the deal.[42] But while KKR's various investors may have lost money, the firm itself likely profited. An independent analysis by Dan Primack at *Axios* estimated that KKR, as well as the other private equity investors in the deal, all profited through the millions in management and advisory fees that they bled out from Toys "R" Us over more than a decade of ownership.[43] Subsequent litigation by Toys' creditors revealed that the firms allegedly received $70 million more than even Primack estimated.[44] In other words, KKR and its private equity peers likely did well for themselves, despite protests to the contrary.

At the end of the bankruptcy process, Mary Osman, a former Toys "R" Us employee in Boardman, Ohio, told activists that "I can't find another job at my age—no one will hire me. I dedicated my life to Toys 'R' Us and today I'm left with nothing."[45] Debbie Mizen, a former employee in Youngstown, Ohio, said that "[a]fter devoting 31 years to a company, I have lost not just my job but my financial stability. My only option is to work very physically demanding jobs earning far less than what I worked so hard to achieve." She added, "I deserve better, and so do my coworkers."[46]

✳

TOYS "R" US is just one part of a larger story of enormous advances by private equity firms into the retail industry. Retailers are attractive targets. They own their own property, which can be sold and leased back, and have lots of cash flow, which can be used to pay debts. Collectively, private equity firms have become some of the biggest employers in the country and now own retailers that employ over 5.8 million people.[47]

The problem is that private equity firms have, by and large, done a poor job managing these companies or at least keeping their workers employed and paid. On average, retail companies acquired by private equity experienced a 12 percent drop in employment, and workers' wages tended to fall even as productivity rose.[48] This has both hurt companies and exacerbated inequality.

This decline is at odds with the overall trend in retailing. While over a ten-year period, private equity firms and hedge funds were responsible for an estimated 1.3 million direct and indirect retail job losses, over the same time, the industry as a whole added 1 million jobs.[49] In 2016 and 2017, over 60 percent of the jobs lost in retail were at companies owned by private equity firms.[50] Fully 70 percent of the retail stores that closed in the first quarter of 2019 were owned by such firms.[51]

The businesses they have controlled—and often bankrupted—are ones you likely recognize: Aeropostale, American Apparel, Charlotte Russe, Fairway, Gymboree, Hot Topic, J.Crew, Mervyn's, Neiman Marcus, Nine West, Payless ShoeSource, PetCo, PetSmart, RadioShack, Sports Authority, Sears, Staples, Talbots—plus dozens more.[52] And these closures affect those people in America with the least power. A quarter of retail workers live at or near the poverty line.[53] In some sectors, like retail clothing, the vast majority of employees are women, and a near majority are people of color. As stores close, these people lose their jobs. Localities lose their tax base, and businesses continue to concentrate.

Private equity firms will be quick to say that this is, in a sense, inevitable. With the rise of online shopping and Amazon, the argument goes, traditional retailers are doomed. Not so. Though Amazon is enormous, it occupies only 10 percent of overall retail in America,[54] and hundreds of traditional retailers, like Macy's, Target, and Walmart, have successfully pivoted to e-commerce.[55] Moreover, these companies have something that Amazon, with the exception of its Whole Foods subsidiary and various smaller experiments, does not: physical stores. The combination of on- and offline retailing is something that can help traditional sellers meaningfully compete with Amazon.

But to make this move to e-commerce, retailers need money, and lots of it, to build the infrastructure necessary to sell online. Private equity's business model makes it difficult to meet this challenge. Acquired companies are often saddled with debt, which they must service, on top of management and transaction fees that they may owe to the private equity firms. These costs give retailers little money to invest in themselves. "You need so much money to keep the stores open, so much money to keep the inventory flowing," Marigay McKee, the former president of Saks Fifth Avenue, told the *New York Times*. "Most P.E. firms don't want to make investment before they start seeing the return."[56] "To keep up with everybody's switch to online purchasing, there really needed to be some big capital investments and changes made," Elisabeth de Fontenay, a professor at the Duke University School of Law who specializes in corporate finance, added to the *Times*, "and because these companies were so debt strapped when acquired by private equity firms, they didn't have capital to make these big shifts."[57]

Sometimes the problem was simply that private equity firms understaffed their stores. For instance, after BC Partners bought PetSmart in 2015, it bragged on its website that it increased the company's profitability by "improving corporate efficiency."[58] But in practice, according to employees, this meant dramatic layoffs, which left stores dangerously understaffed.[59] As detailed by Vice News, this had a particularly gruesome effect. With too few employees to transport animals that died at the store, carcasses of dead animals literally piled up in PetSmart freezers across the country. One employee shared a photo she said was filled with two months' worth of dead animals; another employee said their store had a freezer with ten months'. A third employee said that, for lack of time, she would simply throw bodies away. "Sometimes I was doing it weekly because we didn't have staff to take a vet trip to properly dispose of them so I was instructed to dispose of them myself," she told Vice.[60] (A spokesman for PetSmart denied to Vice that the store's standard of care had declined, while a law firm representing the company wrote to the publication that "PetSmart holds the health and well-being of its associates, customers, and pets as its top priority.")[61]

It wasn't just the dead bodies. Employees complained that PetSmart regularly denied veterinary care for sick pets because of the cost.[62] According to PETA, the company even gave bonuses to managers who kept animal care costs low. One employee told Vice that "I loved PetSmart, but ever Since BC partners took over, they don't care about animals or employees or their safety."[63] Another former employee added, "I ended up getting diagnosed with PTSD—PTSD tied to animals. I felt immense guilt. I wouldn't let myself sleep. I felt selfish going to bed. But at my job, animals passed away so often, you couldn't do anything."[64]

At other times, private equity firms simply hired the wrong people. In 2012, Golden Gate Capital and Blum Capital bought the discount shoe seller Payless.[65] As described in a detailed profile in the New York Times, through a series of owners, Payless tumbled through bankruptcy three times in four years. Part of the problem was that for every one dollar in profit Payless made, more than a dollar went to its private equity owners and another quarter went to its lenders. This made the company susceptible to crisis when, for instance, a work slowdown by longshoremen left Payless's shoes waiting on boats for several weeks. But part of the problem was who these owners put in charge. After Alden Global Capital (which describes itself as a hedge fund but engages in private-equity-like buyouts) bought Payless out of bankruptcy, it installed as CEO, not an executive from footwear, fashion, or even retail, but an investment banker: Martin R. Wade III. Payless middle management felt that Wade and his team treated them with contempt: "They became convinced that, 'You guys don't know what you're talking about,'" one former midlevel employee told the Times.[66] And yet, despite their inexperience, the new management enthusiastically pushed its own ideas, such as a plan to buy millions of World Cup–themed flip-flops. The problem was that the sandals didn't arrive until after the World Cup had ended and even then often with flags of countries like Mexico and Argentina, where Payless had no stores. Ultimately, the company had to sell the flip-flops at a deep discount. Another idea was to shift quality inspections from a dedicated facility to individual factories. As a result, Payless received many shoes that were defective in various ways: size six shoes labeled as size three, for example. A former employee said that "missing one shoe can wipe out whatever you think you're saving."[67] Ultimately, Payless returned to bankruptcy and closed all its stores in the United States. (In a statement to the *New York Times*, Golden Gate Capital said that "[w]hen we exited Payless, we left it with a right-sized store footprint and meaningful earnings opportunities for future owners.")

At other times, private equity firms forced retail stores into partnerships with some of its other portfolio companies. For instance, as described in an earlier chapter, Sycamore Partners repeatedly forced the retailers it owned, like Talbots and Aeropostale, to work with its chosen wholesale supplier. Such "synergies" may have benefited Sycamore, which stood to make money whether or not its retailers actually sold their goods. But deprived of the opportunity to choose the suppliers that offered the best products at the lowest costs, the retailers lost.

These are examples of private equity wrecking the companies they ran by underinvesting in the retail stores they owned, by playing matchmaker between portfolio companies, or through sheer mismanagement. But there is a deeper truth: in many cases, private equity firms want these companies to fail, or to at least go bankrupt, in order to get rid of unwanted debts. And here, private equity's true advantage—its ability to navigate the bankruptcy code—comes into view. Bankruptcy is an opaque, enormously complex process and one where great lawyering (though not necessarily great business acumen) is rewarded. Private equity firms thrive in this part of the law, and they have certainly been rewarded.

So it was with Friendly's, the ice cream and diner chain in the American Northeast. Friendly (the "s" was added in the 1980s), was started as an ice creamery in Springfield, Massachusetts, by two brothers at the height of the Great Depression.[68] Curtis and Prestley Blake began their business with a $547 loan from their parents and ran the operation as a family affair: their mother made the syrup that was a key ingredient for their coffee-flavored ice cream.[69] When they closed their shop each evening, one brother would stay through the night to make ice cream for the following day, while the other would go home and sleep. The ice cream maker would retire in the morning for a few hours' rest, then return at noon to begin serving the afternoon customers.[70]

The Blake brothers' competition across town sold two scoops of ice cream for ten cents, and so the brothers charged a nickel.[71] On their first night in business, a line formed out the door that kept them operating until midnight. They sold 552 cones and made $27.

Their work paid off: from their first store they expanded to a second[72] and then to a third. They began offering classic American food—hamburgers and so forth—in addition to their ice cream offerings, which eventually included their famous Fribble milkshake.[73] When the United States entered World War II, the brothers closed their shops, saying that they would reopen "when we win the war"[74] and returned in triumph, adding stores in the years and decades that followed.

In 1979, the Blake brothers, by then in their sixties, sold Friendly to the Hershey chocolate company.[75] Hershey then sold the business to a wealthy restaurateur, who in turn took the company public in 1997. But the chain suffered without its original owners: restaurants became shabby, and menus became stale.[76] One writer observed that the restaurants had "deteriorated to the point where the physical plant itself is downright depressing and as such overshadows the food and service" and that there was an "apparent disconnect between the colorful stream of marketing material pumped out from corporate and the reality of each dated Friendly's location."[77]

In 2007, Sun Capital, co-led by Marc Leder, bought Friendly's for $337 million.[78] Unsurprisingly for those familiar with Leder and Sun Capital, they were unable to bring back the spark that once made Friendly's so successful. In fact, they made the situation considerably worse, by piling debt onto Friendly's that the chain struggled to service[79] and by executing a sale-leaseback on the chain's headquarters and 160 of its restaurants.[80]

In 2011, Sun Capital finally pushed the company into bankruptcy. Here, the private equity firm showed its real skill, for while Sun Capital was unable to run an ice cream chain, it was able to perform an extraordinary sleight of hand that allowed the firm to keep control of Friendly's while sloughing off the company's pension obligations onto a quasi-government agency.

To start, Friendly's successfully petitioned to have its case administered in the Delaware bankruptcy court, a district whose judges were generally predisposed to rule for companies over their creditors in legal disputes.[81] Ordinarily, Friendly's would have filed in Massachusetts—it was headquartered there—but several of its subsidiaries were chartered in Delaware, which gave the company a sufficient jurisdictional hook to have the whole case managed in this preferred venue.

Then, Friendly's lawyers (Kirkland & Ellis, the same firm that represented Toys "R" Us) convinced the court to expedite the bankruptcy process through a 363 sale, named for the relevant section of the bankruptcy code.[82] Usually, a restructuring bankruptcy builds toward a "plan of reorganization": a comprehensive agreement between the company and its creditors about which debts will be paid and which will be discarded, as the business returns to normalcy. A 363 sale abandons this plan of reorganization in favor of a quick auction of some of the business's assets or, more aggressively, of the entire business itself. The winner of the auction typically acquires the assets or business "free and clear" of their outstanding debts.

The auction also largely removes discretion from the bankruptcy court. One judge complained that in such auctions, "the judge is reduced to a figurehead" and "might as well leave his or her signature stamp with the debtor's counsel and go on vacation."[83] In other words, by successfully proposing a 363 sale, Friendly's lawyers were able to take control of the bankruptcy process and largely choose who would buy the company's assets.

And here's where private equity showed its genius. Sun Capital, through Friendly's, proposed to sell the business to . . . itself. One of Sun Capital's subsidiaries was Friendly's owner. But another Sun Capital subsidiary was its largest lender[84] and had loaned Friendly's $152 million, which had blossomed to $268 million with interest.[85] Another affiliate provided $71 million to keep Friendly's in business through bankruptcy (what's known as debtor-in-possession financing).[86] Sun Capital proposed to reacquire Friendly's by forgiving these debts, a tactic known as credit bidding.

The 363 sale allowed for other companies to bid on Friendly's, but most everyone else was at a huge disadvantage. Sun Capital was proposing to buy Friendly's by forgiving debt—debt that was unlikely to be paid in full—while other potential buyers would need to pay actual money for the company. Moreover, Sun Capital was allowed to bid both the principal and interest for the company, meaning that it paid just $152 million for a possible $268 million bid. Nobody else could hope to pay so little for so much.

And nobody did.[87] The auction for Sun Capital, which was to be held at Kirkland & Ellis's New York office,[88] was canceled for lack of interest.[89] Sun Capital's affiliate was able to acquire Friendly's without so much as a fight.[90]

Reading the court documents, there is an absurd sense in which Friendly's—and Sun Capital—talk about themselves in the third person, as if they were completely unrelated. To take one example of many, in an early filing, Friendly's lawyers said that a "bidder" already expressed interest in buying Friendly's, an encouraging sign and one that might incline the court toward approving Friendly's requested auction process. But the lawyers added only in a footnote that the bidder was an affiliate of Friendly's existing owner, Sun Capital.[91] This wasn't necessarily dishonest, but the effect was to make it seem like Friendly's contemplated a genuine sale to a third party, rather than a reshuffling of Sun Capital's ledgers.

But why go through this whole process at all? Why would Friendly's declare bankruptcy, just to be sold from one Sun Capital fund to another? The answer was simple: pensions. At the time of bankruptcy, Friendly's had $115 million in pension liabilities.[92] By selling Friendly's to one of its affiliates, Sun Capital was able to re-acquire its own company free and clear of those liabilities. Instead, they were transferred to the Pension Benefit Guaranty Corporation. The PBGC was chartered by Congress to rescue under-funded pension plans and paid for itself in part through insurance premiums that healthy pension plans paid to it.[93] But it was always meant as the destination of last resort, not as a convenient sucker for strategic bankruptcy reorganizations.

And so the PBGC objected to Friendly's plan, correctly observing that "each and every party to this bankruptcy...is an affiliate of Sun Capital Partners, Inc."[94] The PBGC argued that Sun Capital's loans to Friendly's should probably be treated as equity—that is, further investments by the owner of the company—rather than as debt. This mattered because in bankruptcy a party can't credit bid equity, and if the court granted the motion, Sun Capital would have to wager cash for the company like most everyone else. The PBGC also requested procedures that would encourage the winning bidder to assume the obligations of the company's pension plan. But the court denied both these requests.[95]

The PBGC didn't bother to make the more aggressive argument that the entire 363 sale process was invalid here. Such sales require good faith on the part of the buyer and seller, which can be undermined by collusion between the two.[96] It seems unlikely that the court would have accepted this aggressive position, given that it rejected the PBGC's more modest argument that Sun Capital's debt should be treated as equity. But it could have been worth-while to ask for discovery on whether—and to what extent—Sun Capital's various affiliates communicated with each other and with their parent company before, during, and after the bankruptcy process.

Regardless, Sun Capital was able to reacquire Friendly's free and clear of its pension obligations, without spending anything more than the money it lent its own portfolio company. Pensioners were the obvious losers in this process, who risked having their payments cut (the PBGC observed over the previous decade that it had been forced to cut $70 million in benefits to employees after 363 sales by debtors owned or controlled by private equity firms).[97] Pension plans for more responsible companies lost too: they would have to pay the costs, through increased premiums to the PBGC, that Sun Capital was unwilling to.

Many of Friendly's existing employees lost as well. Sixty-three restaurants closed as part of the bankruptcy process,[98] and the *Albany Times Union* reported that at the Friendly's in Latham, New York, employees hugged at the end of their final shift. While a company spokesperson said that Friendly's would hire as many workers as possible, one employee questioned whether there would be enough open positions to hire the more than twenty coworkers at the Latham shop alone.[99]

Friendly's itself was also a loser. In 2016, Sun Capital sold the company's ice cream manufacturing unit, along with its trademark, to Dean Foods for $155 million.[100] But the core restaurant business never improved. Over the decade, the company lost nearly 70 percent of its locations, which went from over 500 to just 130.[101] Finally, in 2020, Friendly's fell into bankruptcy again. This time, an affiliate of a restaurant franchising company agreed to purchase the business for just $2 million.[102]

The final losers were the brothers who started Friendly's, Curtis and Prestley Blake. Curtis died at age 102 in 2019; Prestley at 106 in 2021. Both men—the men who closed their business during World War II until "we win the war"—lived long enough to see their creation collapse at the hands of Sun Capital. But Sun Capital's cofounder Marc Leder demonstrated no comparable patriotism or seriousness of purpose. When asked about Friendly's collapse and his arguable manipulation of the bankruptcy law, he said simply, "We don't make the rules."[103]

✻

WHAT SUN CAPITAL accomplished was far from unique. Over fifty companies owned by private equity firms have pushed their pension plans onto the PBGC.[104] But the result in Friendly's seems almost farcical: why would a court allow a private equity firm to do-si-do a company from one affiliate to another, shaking off pension obligations in the process? Some of it may simply be that private equity firms remain ahead of regulators and courts. Josh Gotbaum, a former head of the PBGC, complained that "in many cases financial institutions and financial markets have outstripped both the law's ability to comprehend them and bankruptcy courts' ability to preserve fair treatment of other constituencies in the face of them."[105]

But much of this may also have to do with private equity firms' ability to choose their venue. In 1979, Congress revised the bankruptcy code to give companies wide latitude to choose where to declare bankruptcy.[106] Several jurisdictions became the courts of choice for distressed companies and the lawyers who represented them: initially New York and Delaware (where the Friendly's case was filed) but increasingly White Plains, Houston, and the Eastern District of Virginia (where the Toys "R" Us case was filed). Today, more than 90 percent of the country's big bankruptcy cases happen in these five districts.[107] In these jurisdictions, according to UCLA law professor Lynn M. LoPucki, courts showed solicitude toward large corporations, their financiers, and their lawyers over ordinary lenders.[108] Preferred courts let attorneys charge higher fees, relaxed conflict of interest standards, and indemnified lawyers and financial advisers from wrongdoing.[109] According to LoPucki, the jobs of executives, "including those who led their companies into financial disaster," were secured, and executives were even allowed bonuses in bankruptcy, on the theory that their skills were never more necessary.[110] This solicitude ultimately hurt creditors and the bankrupt companies themselves. Firms reorganized in Delaware failed significantly more often than firms organized elsewhere, suggesting that lax standards led to reorganization plans that were unrealistic or impossible to achieve.

A body of academic literature has explored why courts competed like this. Perhaps judges in these favored districts tried to bring in business to the local bankruptcy bar by developing the law to favor the executives and lawyers who chose where to file.[111]

Perhaps they desired the prestige and challenge that came with handling the biggest cases with the most talented litigators. Or perhaps more anodyne personal preferences in the law explain their rulings. Regardless of the specific motivation, it's clear that a handful of courts are predisposed to the sorts of arguments that firms like Sun Capital make. And it's also clear that companies like Sun Capital have the ability to choose their court in a way that, say, criminal defendants cannot.

The accommodation afforded companies filing for bankruptcy can reach almost absurd proportions. The department store Belk, which was purchased by the private equity firm Sycamore Partners, substantially completed its bankruptcy—a process that could ordinarily take months[112]—in a single day. Belk was based in North Carolina and incorporated in Delaware but filed in Houston by establishing a subsidiary corporation there, forcing the subsidiary into insolvency and bringing the parent business into bankruptcy with it.[113] Belk's attorneys—once again, the law firm of Kirkland & Ellis—filed a reorganization plan the evening of February 23, 2021. The court approved the plan at 10:08 a.m. the next day, apparently accepting Belk's argument that it had already negotiated a settlement with its creditors.

With an almost literal rubber stamp over the agreement, the court had no real way to confirm this assertion, or inquire whether, as may well have been the case, Belk strong-armed its creditors into agreeing to a plan they didn't know they could contest. Nor was it able to interrogate the decision by Belk's board to allow Sycamore to remain in control of the company (likely it was because the board itself was chosen by Sycamore).[114] Nor did the court control how much in fees Kirkland extracted through the process: as Professor Lynn LoPucki explained, the court file approving the bankruptcy had no information about how much work Kirkland did in preparing the bankruptcy petition. In so doing, without violating any law, Kirkland essentially bypassed the system for court approval of bankruptcy attorney fees.

The Office of the US Trustee, the branch of the Department of Justice charged with ensuring the fair application of the bankruptcy code, objected, arguing that the speed of the whole endeavor violated due process.[115] The court entered the judgment anyway. It wasn't corruption, but it wasn't what Congress intended with the bankruptcy code, either, and it gave the process—and Belk's creditors—short shrift.

This drift in the bankruptcy code helps to explain why so many of the retail companies that private equity firms bought went bankrupt, namely, that doing so was a good deal for private equity. It wasn't exclusively, or even primarily, that Amazon destroyed their businesses. It was that private equity firms loaded these companies with debt, made the pivot to online commerce impossible, then found ways to avoid their creditors through the opaque and shifting bankruptcy process. And this drift helps to explain the fundamental mystery: how private equity firms continue to expand and profit in retail, even as the companies they buy wither and die.

✳

COMPANIES' PREFERENCE FOR certain courts, and those courts' preference for certain companies, means that employees must increasingly turn to tools outside of the bankruptcy process to get fair compensation. And that's what happened with Ann Marie Reinhart and Toys "R" Us. As described in the introduction, Reinhart began working as a part-time cashier in 1988 and joined full-time as a supervisor after both her children entered school.[116] With it, she got health insurance. "Back then, Toys 'R' Us was very good to all of us," Reinhart told the *Progressive*. "It let me be the mom that I wanted to be."[117]

Reinhart ultimately worked at the company for twenty-nine years.[118] She stayed with the company through the frantic holiday rushes. "Almost the entire month of December, I didn't see my husband," she said.[119] "He got up early for work. I would come home and he would be sleeping. Then, he would leave for work and I would be sleeping."[120] She stayed after an angry customer threw a Green Power Ranger action figure at her head (she still had a scar). She stayed when she moved her whole family from Long Island to

Durham, North Carolina, transferring to a new store. But when Toys "R" Us went under, she did too.

After she was laid off, Reinhart became active in the Dead Giraffe Society, a Facebook group of former Toys "R" Us employees named for the company's mascot, Geoffrey the Giraffe.[121] With the assistance of the organizing group United for Respect, Reinhart and others began to advocate for better treatment of the company's former workers. They met with members of Congress, who, at their urging, wrote to Bain, KKR, and Vornado and demanded to know why their employees hadn't been paid severance.[122] They convinced Senators Cory Booker and Robert Menendez, along with Congressman Bill Pascrell, to protest with them.[123] They held a march through Manhattan, carrying a coffin for the mascot Geoffrey,[124] and rallied outside the penthouse home of the CEO, David Brandon.[125]

But most importantly, they started meeting with the private equity firms' investors. Across a dozen states, they met with fourteen pension funds,[126] and at their urging the Minnesota State Board of Investment suspended investments in KKR until it investigated the Toys "R" Us employees' claims.[127] More than any statement from a member of Congress or bad publicity from a protest, it was this threat of the loss of money that forced private equity firms to change.

In November 2018, KKR and Bain announced a $20 million settlement fund for former employees.[128] This was nothing compared to the $250 million that the private equity firms that bought Toys received in advisory fees alone.[129] Payments to the employees ranged from a few hundred dollars to $12,000 per worker.[130] The settlement wasn't enough: worker advocates said that former employees were owed more than three times that amount.[131] But KKR and Bain weren't legally required to give more, and the settlement occurred outside the bankruptcy process. In fact, it was ten times the size of what Reinhart and others were able to get through litigation. In other words, though the settlement wasn't enough in employees' eyes, it was so much more than what they could have expected through bankruptcy. It showed that outside advocacy and agitation—quite simply, embarrassing companies into action and threatening their access to pension fund money—could serve as an interim substitute, however insufficient and incomplete, for the bankruptcy system.

The announcement of the severance fund "rejuvenated me," Reinhart said. "It's a win for us, and it's a win for any other retail worker that this happens to in the future."[132] Though Reinhart and her fellow activists didn't get what the Toys "R" Us employees deserved, they got the employees more than they could have expected and more than they could through litigation alone. In this way, Reinhart showed a path for how workers might fight for themselves—through protest and pressure on investors—as private equity firms continue their march across the retail industry.

Reinhart began to organize more broadly. She trained former employees at Sears, Payless, and Gymboree to fight for their own severance payments.[133] She advocated in Congress for the Stop Wall Street Looting Act, which would curtail some of private equity's worst excesses. And she campaigned for a fifteen-dollar minimum wage.[134]

Reinhart lived barely long enough to see her own accomplishment. She struggled to find work with health insurance after she was laid off[135] and for a time was forced to choose between her asthma medication and her husband's diabetes medication.[136] Eventually, she went to work at the Belk department store—ironically, the same store purchased by private equity and put through bankruptcy in a single day.[137]

Reinhart died in early 2021 from COVID-19.[138] But before her death, about her organizing, Reinhart said, "Nothing but good has come out of it for me."[139] In an obituary in the *New York Times*, Alison Paolillo, who worked with Reinhart, said that "[s]he was our voice.... She fought for us."[140] United for Respect called her "a working class hero of our time."[141]

CHAPTER FOUR

DEADLY CARE

Private Equity in Nursing Homes

Perhaps more than any other person, David Rubenstein illustrates private equity's entwining of money and power, and how the latter can legitimize how the former is made. Rubenstein, the cofounder of the Carlyle Group, is now a billionaire many times over. But he came from modest means. His father worked for the postal service while his mother stayed at home, and he grew up a studious, only child, a Jewish kid in Baltimore at a time when the city was rigidly divided along religious and ethnic lines.[1] Though he was a shy boy, Rubenstein had a knack for making powerful connections. In high school, he became friends with the star quarterback and found a mentor in a Baltimore judge who ran a boys club.[2] After law school he worked to become a protégé of former Kennedy adviser Ted Sorensen[3] and later worked as legal counsel for Indiana senator Birch Bayh, who was running in the Democratic primary for president at the time.[4] When Bayh lost, Rubenstein managed to jump over to the campaign of the man who won the nomination, Jimmy Carter, and became close with one of Carter's chief advisers, Stuart Eizenstat.[5] Thanks to his connections, when Carter won, he was appointed deputy domestic policy adviser to the president. He was twenty-seven.

At the White House, Rubenstein had an almost monk-like aura. Quiet, serious, reluctant to take credit for himself, he worked harder than anyone.[6] He ate dinner from the vending machines and planned meetings with union leaders, helped to oversee the Democratic party platform, and shaped the federal budget.[7] A picture in the National Archives shows Rubenstein outside the White House, wearing a dark suit with wide lapels. His thick black hair swoops down over his forehead, and he looks past the camera with an awkward smile mixed with concern.[8]

Rubenstein looked forward to a promising future at the White House. But, for him, tragedy struck: in 1980, Carter lost reelection in a landslide. Rubenstein was out of a job, a Carter insider in Washington at a time when no one had much use for such insiders. He struggled to find work—he eventually found a job with a moderately prestigious law firm[9]—and settled into the lifestyle of that common figure in Washington: the former government official, peddling his wares in private practice.

But Rubenstein's quiet, studious persona hid a deeper, burning ambition. He found himself unsuited to the practice of law and yearned for something more rewarding, in every sense of the word. In 1987, he and four acquaintances joined together to form an investment firm.[10] They named themselves the Carlyle Group, after the white-marbled New York City hotel.[11] At first, they didn't know what their business would be: their initial success was in selling the tax losses of Native Alaskans to corporations seeking write-offs, the benefit of a government loophole that Congress quickly closed.[12] But in 1989, Rubenstein discovered his core idea when he hired Frank Carlucci, the former secretary of defense to Ronald Reagan, to serve as the firm's vice chairman.[13] The diminutive, angular Carlucci exuded power—he had previously served as national security adviser, deputy secretary of defense, and deputy director of the CIA—and he brought to the firm a vast network of connections that Rubenstein and his colleagues lacked.

One of their first victories with Carlucci was a deal to help Prince Al-Waleed bin Talal of Saudi Arabia invest $500 million in Citicorp, a coup for Carlyle that stunned the other, vastly larger and more established institutions of high finance.[14] In another deal, Carlyle bought the airline food service company Caterair and, at the suggestion of a Republican political operative, brought George W. Bush, the then flailing son of the current president, George H. W. Bush, on its board.[15] Caterair would later collapse, but the investment proved a successful one for Carlyle: the elder Bush, apparently convinced by his former secretary of state Jim Baker,[16] later agreed to travel the world on Carlyle's behalf as a paid speaker.[17]

What Rubenstein discovered in Carlucci and those who followed was an alchemy of money and power: by hiring well-connected former government officials, he could find new deals and new money, as investors wanted to spend time with these people and learn what they might not from the *Wall Street Journal* or *New York Times*. Over the years, Carlyle built a stable of extraordinarily powerful figures to work on its behalf: not only former president George H. W. Bush but also former British prime minister John Major, former secretary of state James Baker, former White House budget chief Dick Darman, former SEC chairman Arthur Levitt, and former FCC chairmen William Kennard and Julius Genachowski,[18] among others.

With its connections, Carlyle prospered. Its assets under management—the amount of investor money it controlled—rose from $5 million in 1987[19] to $14 billion in 2003[20] and then to an astounding $376 billion in 2022.[21] The company, alone or with others, bought and sold Hertz, Dunkin' Brands, Getty Images, and the consulting firm Booz Allen Hamilton, among many others.[22] And Rubenstein, the quiet scholar, became rich. He bought the home next to his own in Bethesda and converted it into a guesthouse. He built a ten-thousand-square-foot chalet in Colorado and a vacation home big enough for thirty people in Nantucket (Presidents Biden, Carter, and George H. W. Bush all, at various times, stayed overnight as his guests).[23] By 2021, he was worth over $4 billion.[24]

As Rubenstein grew in wealth and stature, he modeled himself as something of a "thinking man's" titan of industry. While other billionaires shed their power suits and, in California, donned jeans and T-shirts, Rubenstein continued to wear pinstripe suits, Hermes ties, and what a reporter described as a "substantial watch."[25] He possessed an exceedingly dry, self-deprecating sense of humor and a level of self-awareness perhaps unexpected from a billionaire (regarding private equity, he says, "I like to say it's the highest calling of mankind, but nobody agrees"[26]). He read several books a week[27] and began hosting an interview program on Bloomberg TV[28] and a podcast with the New York Historical Society.

As he grew older, Rubenstein became a philanthropist, devoting special attention to patriotic causes. He bought original copies of the Declaration of Independence and the Emancipation Proclamation and lent them to various museums.[29] He donated millions to repair the Washington Monument and millions more to refurbish Monticello.[30] He became chairman or trustee of the Kennedy Center, the National Gallery of Art, and the Library of Congress.

He also developed into a fixture in Washington. Photos document his upward trajectory: there he is shaking hands with Paul Ryan.[31] There he is, in a tuxedo, conferring with Dr. Anthony Fauci.[32] There he is standing for a portrait with Sally Field, Mike Pompeo, and, strangely, Big Bird at a Kennedy Center event.[33] His hair is white now, but he still looks past the camera with that awkward smile of concern, just as he did as a young Carter staffer forty years before.

All this socializing had a purpose. As previously explained, private equity firms need lots of money to buy companies. Only a small portion of that money comes from the firms themselves; a much larger portion comes from investors who are, figuratively, along for the ride. While others at the firm actually ran the business, it was Rubenstein's job to bring that investment money in, which is what he did by meeting with the very rich, charming them, gossiping with them, and going around the world to meet them: Rubenstein estimated that he traveled three hundred days a year.[34] By 2017, his last year as co-CEO—he now serves as cochairman of the board—Carlyle had $195 billion in assets under management, raised from investors like the ones Rubenstein feted.[35] Rubenstein, with all his networking, cultivated these investors and brought in the money Carlyle needed to buy companies.

In a deeper sense, all of Rubenstein's ventures fed into a single, larger project: creating an aura of respectability for himself and, even more importantly, for Carlyle. With his now vast network, Rubenstein and the former government officials he employed assured investors that the money they spent with Carlyle was safe. And his public philanthropy sent a message that the money they gave him, if far from charitable, was at least estimable. If a single firm employed so many former leaders in government, if the leader of the firm spent so much of his time giving his money away, surely an investment with them was money well spent.

But how exactly were Carlyle—and Rubenstein—making their money? The firm made hundreds of deals in a range of industries, but it is worth considering just one: its acquisition of the nursing home chain HCR ManorCare. The deal is worth considering because it shows many of the tactics—sale leasebacks and transaction fees, leverage and layoffs—that Carlyle often used to make money at the expense of its portfolio companies. And it is worth considering because it shows how so many of those people with whom Rubenstein met and who gave his firm money were, knowingly or not, subsidizing what many viewed as the plunder of the nursing home industry.

*

NURSING HOMES HAVE a fraught history. They are the descendants of English almshouses: homes administered by local governments for the very sick, the very poor, and the very old. Because almshouses took on those people whom family members would not or could not care for, their operations were, unsurprisingly, generally shabby. In time, "old age homes" developed as an alternative in America. Often run by private charities, rather than public governments, they tended to care for what were then called the "worthy poor": old people as opposed to, say, drunks.[36] The Social Security Act of 1935 hastened the growth of this private industry by withholding direct payments to people living in public almshouses, so that these latter facilities could not take residents' money. The move decimated the sad almshouse industry, but it had another, perhaps unintended effect: it created a huge pool of government funds that could be spent on care for the elderly, one that new, for-profit companies were eager to access. The Medicare and Medicaid Acts of 1965 expanded this opportunity when they offered payments directly to institutions willing to care for the sick and old.

This is how the nursing home industry developed: a jumble of nonprofit and for-profit institutions vying for the elderly and the government money that accompanied them. The business went through cycles of reform and regression, as exposés revealed the squalid conditions of various facilities, which were alternately shut down, reformed, or forgotten. In the 1990s, cheap money led to industry consolidation, as individual institutions were rolled up into larger chains.[37] Today in America, there are about fifteen thousand nursing homes who together house about 1.3 million residents.[38]

This is where Rubenstein's Carlyle Group stepped in. In 2007, Carlyle bought HCR ManorCare, then the second-largest nursing home chain in America.[39] Carlyle entered the industry at an auspicious time. The country was aging, and the need for nursing homes was growing. Research in one state found that facilities tended to have between 19 and 22 percent profit margins.[40] Moreover, ManorCare itself was a sensible investment. The company had operated since the late 1950s[41] and for much of its history ran better-than-average homes marketed to people who did not need to rely on Medicare or Medicaid for payment.[42] "They're the cream of the crop in the industry," one analyst told the *Washington Post* midway through the company's history.[43] The company was profitable the year before Carlyle bought it, and when Carlyle made the acquisition, an analyst explained that "the basic fundamentals... [of ManorCare] are very good."[44] Given this—the strength of the industry and the strength of ManorCare—what happened next was all the more tragic.

As described in the introduction of this book, most of the $6.1 billion that Carlyle paid for ManorCare—$4.8 billion—was borrowed, while the firm and its investors put up the remainder. Carlyle's first major move, in 2010, was to sell ManorCare's real estate to another investment firm for over $6 billion.[45] ManorCare then rented back the facilities that it once owned. This was the sale-leaseback tactic, described in Chapter 1, that is a hallmark of so many private equity deals. As Peter Whoriskey and Dan Keating of the *Washington Post* later recounted, by selling ManorCare's real estate, Carlyle was able to recover the money that it had put into the deal.[46] In other words, with this sale alone, Carlyle had basically broken even and still owned an enormous nursing home chain.

But selling ManorCare's property put a terrible strain on the business. ManorCare needed real estate to operate, and with the sale, ManorCare was obligated to pay nearly half a billion dollars a year in rent to occupy the buildings it was already using.[47] On top of this, under the terms of the deal, ManorCare was still responsible for paying the buildings' insurance, upkeep, and property taxes. This meant that ManorCare now had all the obligations of owning its properties, with all the costs of renting them.

Carlyle extracted money from ManorCare in other ways too, including a $61 million transaction fee for buying the business itself.[48] It also took about $27 million over nine years in advisory fees: fees that ManorCare paid for the privilege of being owned by Carlyle. Like the sale-leaseback, these too are common tactics of the private equity industry writ large.

Unsurprisingly, the business suffered. After the sale of its property, ManorCare made hundreds of layoffs. It instituted cost-cutting programs, and some of its nursing homes were unable to afford their rent. Health code violations rose 26 percent between 2013 and 2017, three times faster than at all other nursing homes.

Despite ManorCare's cost cutting and the real estate sales that Carlyle directed, by 2018, the company was over $7 billion in debt.[49] Like most private equity deals, this was debt that Manor-Care, not Carlyle, owed, and as mentioned, Carlyle itself had quickly recouped its own investment in the firm. And so, without money, the company filed for bankruptcy in 2018 and was ultimately sold to a nonprofit.[50] The speed of this destruction was almost impressive: ManorCare had operated since the 1950s, and

Carlyle drove it into bankruptcy in barely a decade. But despite the pace of this gutting, Carlyle itself profited from the project. It made back the money it invested through the sale-leaseback, plus millions more through transaction and advisory fees. Which is to say that the firm made money despite the fact that—or perhaps because—it devastated the business it owned. And it suggests that Carlyle's investors—the men and women whom David Ruben-stein charmed with his stable of former government officials— were funding ventures far more destructive and distasteful than they perhaps even realized.

✳

MANORCARE IS NOT isolated. Rather, it is illustrative of private eq-uity's larger role in the nursing home industry. Between 2004 and 2008, four of the five largest nursing homes—Genesis Health-Care, Golden Living, Sava Senior Care, and ManorCare—were acquired by private equity firms.[51] All of them executed sale-leaseback agreements like ManorCare. All of them faced similar allegations of mismanagement and abuse.[52] And amazingly, all of them were charged by the Department of Justice for fraud.[53] (Genesis, Golden Living, and Sava paid settlements ranging from $613,000 to $53 million without admitting wrongdo-ing, while the Department of Justice dropped its prosecution of ManorCare.[54])

The appeal of nursing homes to these firms was obvious. Nurs-ing homes had lots of cash flow, often coming from reliable gov-ernment sources like Medicare. Additionally, nursing homes often had physical assets—buildings and so forth—that could be sold for profit. The problem was that, as numerous studies demonstrated, private equity firms ignored the fundamental tenets of work in nursing homes. In general, nursing homes offer better care the more time caregivers spend with residents and the better trained those caregivers are.[55] Private equity firms disregarded both these basic elements of care. One study found that private equity owners, on average, cut the number of staffing hours at nursing homes.[56] This made it more likely that elderly people, left unattended, could injure themselves, soil themselves, or develop bedsores: all issues that, unaddressed, could be deadly. Another study found that private equity firms shifted to lower-skilled workers, relying less on registered nurses, who must have associate's or bachelor's degrees, and more on licensed practical nurses, who need only a simpler, one-year certificate.[57] Perhaps as a result of both trends, private equity–owned facilities tended, more than others, to rely on antipsychotic drugs to control their residents.[58] Such drugs can make patients more docile, acting as a crutch when homes are understaffed. But they can also increase older users' risk of death and are thus generally disfavored.

The consequences of these actions in aggregate are almost difficult to comprehend. In 2021, researchers at the Universities of Chicago and Pennsylvania, as well as New York University, compared the short-term mortality of residents in homes owned by private equity firms with that of residents in other facilities. What they found was astounding: private equity ownership was associated with over twenty thousand premature deaths in nursing homes over twelve years.[59] Such a figure may be hard to absorb, but it is important to remember that each of those twenty thousand people had, at one point, family, friends, people whom they loved and who loved them in turn.

Moreover, residents in private equity–owned nursing homes particularly suffered during the pandemic. A study of facilities in one state found that residents and staff in such homes were more likely to get COVID-19 and were more likely to die from it than were those in other for-profit, nonprofit, and public facilities in the state.[60] Around the country, private equity–owned homes frequently experienced the largest outbreaks in their cities or states, many of which were particularly acute: at one facility, for instance, nearly three-quarters of patients were infected and eighteen died.[61]

Outcomes were bad for residents but also for employees. Already, nursing work is difficult, in part because so many patients need help being lifted or moved, and dangerous, because some patients may be violent.[62] In fact, registered nurses and nursing assistants have among the most musculoskeletal injuries of any profession, and nursing assistants in particular are injured more often than are police, correctional officers, and even construction workers.[63] But with cost cutting, private equity firms exacerbated caregivers' already difficult work. In addition to increased risks for COVID, Milly Silva, a union representative, told Congress that nursing home staff were forced to pay for shampoo and soap for residents when their facilities would not do so.[64] One caregiver reportedly complained that her facility stopped training its staff as soon as a private equity firm bought it; another "would break down crying" because there were just two nursing staff to care for fifty residents during the height of the pandemic.[65] No wonder then that there were, according to Silva, "astronomical annual turnover rates" in the industry overall: 128 percent nationally and over 300 percent in some institutions.[66]

Finally, despite the harm to residents and workers, private equity–owned homes actually cost more, not less, for patients and taxpayers. The same academics who estimated twenty thousand premature deaths found that fees, lease payments, and interest payments by nursing homes all increased after being bought by private equity firms, while cash on hand declined.[67] Meanwhile, the amount billed to patients increased by 11 percent. The vast majority—90 percent—of this was paid by taxpayers through Medicare.[68]

✳

GIVEN THESE OBVIOUS and deadly failings, one might expect that private equity firms would taper their investment in nursing homes for fear of regulation or litigation. But this wasn't the case. In fact, in 2020, when COVID-19 outbreaks and deaths in nursing homes were the stuff of national headlines, firms spent over $1.5 billion buying facilities, an increase of more than $1 billion from the year before.[69]

Why would private equity firms rush into such a deadly business, a business that firms had a demonstrated history of making worse? Likely in part because they knew that the government was largely unwilling or unable to police nursing homes'—and their private equity owners'—worst abuses. The industry is regulated at both the federal and state level: the federal government sets minimum standards of care, while states add their own requirements and typically inspect nursing homes to ensure, in theory at least, that their facilities meet those requirements.[70] Through these inspections, state surveyors issue "deficiencies"—notices of failures to follow federal or state guidelines—which are categorized as "harm" or "no harm" depending on whether a resident has been hurt by the violation. With enough harm deficiencies, a nursing home can be fined and, if repeated, shut down.[71]

The problem is that state regulators often refuse to say that violations harm residents, even when those harms are obvious.[72] This is bad for residents of all nursing homes but is particularly dangerous for those who live in facilities owned by private equity firms, where such harm is much more likely to occur. For instance, Illinois inspectors said that no one was harmed when inadequate housekeeping led to a maggot infestation on a resident's scrotum.[73] Inspectors in Wisconsin said that no harm resulted when a resident broke a femur.[74] And inspectors in California said that a resident's "avoidable" accident, which resulted in "screaming, pain, and [a] broken shinbone," caused no harm.[75]

Why are regulators so scared to call these incidents of harm what they are? At a narrow level, nursing homes tend to have many chances to challenge harm deficiency designations,[76] which may discourage inspectors from bothering to issue designations that will be litigated in court. As one inspector told the New York Times, "I feel sometimes the things I cite don't mean anything because it gets tossed out at the state level.... Sometimes it makes you wonder why we spin our wheels on a problem."[77] More importantly, when a nursing home does receive sufficient harm deficiencies and is shut down, it may fall into the hands of the state government, which may be charged with managing the facility. This is an expensive and difficult responsibility, which the state may be ill equipped to handle,[78] and as such, there is a strong incentive for surveyors to treat nursing homes lightly.

At a more general level, inspectors may hold back their harshest judgments because nursing homes are a force in government. The industry's primary advocacy organization has given over $18 million in federal contributions and spent over $52 million lobbying, including $5 million in the 2022 election cycle alone.[79] Over the years, large, private equity–owned chains like Genesis, ManorCare, and Golden Living spent millions more on contributions and lobbying.[80] "The nursing home lobby is so well funded," Charlene Harrington, a professor at the University of California San Francisco School of Nursing and expert on nursing homes, told the Intercept, "and it's so hard to make changes because of these political contributions."[81] This power is felt in the conciliatory approach that state regulators have taken toward the industry. Inspectors in Pennsylvania, for instance, were instructed to be "kinder and gentler" to nursing homes, while those in Arkansas said that they were discouraged from issuing severe citations.[82] Inspectors in Oklahoma even referred to nursing homes, rather than the patients they serve, as their "clients."[83] "They're just not that interested in regulating," Harrington said in another interview.[84] "And they don't want to pick a fight with these big companies."[85] This aversion to action affects all nursing home residents, but it is particularly concerning for residents of private equity–owned homes, where there are far greater mortal dangers.

Given this general reluctance by regulators to regulate, the task of protecting residents has often fallen to plaintiffs' lawyers like Ernie Tosh. Tosh is a big man, with a beard and straight, gray hair that goes down to his shoulders. He listens to Swedish death metal in his leisure time, and in his low, soft voice, he teases and praises his colleagues and brings detail and profanity to his commentary on the industry. With some technical skills, Tosh built a database of nursing home companies on which many other lawyers relied. But more than his spreadsheets, people value his personality and his easy, warm nature. "Ernie's superpower is bringing together people who need to know each other," one lawyer, Nicole Snapp-Holloway, said.[86] "If you don't like Ernie, something's wrong with you."[87]

Tosh had been suing nursing homes for years, representing residents who'd been wronged, as well as their families, and who hoped to recover some damages for the harm that they experienced. In theory, the money that people like Tosh collected from homes would make it rational for facility owners to provide decent care. But, unsurprisingly, nursing homes made it exceedingly hard to get such money. "We can't get jack shit in a civil case," Tosh said.[88] "We've been actively litigating nursing home cases for 25 years, and the quality of care has gotten worse. Clearly we are not having an impact."[89]

Why was this so? For one thing, nursing homes—including private equity–owned homes—conceal their assets through shell and related companies.[90] Like *matryoshka* nesting dolls, nursing home chains have built layers of companies on top of individual nursing homes, obscuring their ultimate owners and making it harder for plaintiffs to collect money. They also outsource their services to related companies that their parent companies also control.[91] Thus, a nursing home might have one company for its real estate, another for its staffing, another for its equipment, and so on. On paper, it would appear that the nursing home itself is cash strapped, paying most of its money to these related companies. But ultimately, all of the different companies would be controlled by the same parent company, which reaps the combined profits as if running the nursing home directly. Academics found that the use of these shell companies exploded in just a few years.[92] Nearly three-fourths of nursing homes in the United States now use "related parties" to take money from their core nursing homes.[93] "[M]oney is siphoned out to these related parties," Ernie Tosh told the *New York Times*. "The cash flow gets really obscured through the related party transactions."[94] Unsurprisingly, facilities that use related companies have, on average, lower staffing, more complaints, and higher rates of patient injuries than those that do not.[95]

These tactics obscure the assets of nursing homes and make them look poorer than they really are. By doing so, nursing homes make it harder for plaintiffs to find those assets and harder for them to win those assets in litigation. The industry has even said as much. At a 2012 conference for nursing home executives, a presentation slide titled "Pros of Complex Corporate Structure" stated that "many plaintiffs' attorneys will never conduct corporate structure discovery because it's too expensive and time consuming."[96] "There's a game that's played, that if you don't sue the right entities, your family is out of luck," one plaintiffs' lawyer told the *Naples Daily News*. "You have to then start trying to chase the money."[97]

These tactics to hide assets have been extraordinarily successful. For instance, after plaintiffs in one suit obtained a $110 million verdict against two private equity–owned nursing homes in Florida, the nursing homes simply shifted their liabilities to a related company that had no assets, while creating a solvent nursing home chain that was nominally protected from judgment.[98] The result was that the plaintiffs had a judgment to collect money from a company that, on paper at least, had none. Despite the seemingly obvious game to avoid paying, more than a decade after the case began, the litigation remains ongoing.[99]

Nursing homes also get help from the government to stop plaintiffs from getting damages. For instance, private equity–owned Genesis HealthCare allegedly required its residents to sign arbitration agreements before coming to their facilities.[100] Under these agreements, residents and their families consented not to go to court in the case of injury or wrongful death but instead bring their disputes to arbitrators paid for by Genesis itself. (For its part, Genesis claimed it merely offered the arbitration agreements, rather than required them.) It should be no surprise that families recovered less, if at all, when using arbitration. In fact, the American Association for Justice, a professional organization for plaintiffs' lawyers, found that over a five-year period consumers brought just sixty-two cases against nursing homes to the leading arbitration firms.[101] Of these cases, consumers won monetary awards in just four of them.

In 2016, the Obama administration issued a rule banning the use of arbitration agreements at nursing homes. But the industry's lobbying organization, on whose board sat various representatives of private equity–owned nursing facilities,[102] took swift action. It and a state affiliate in Mississippi sued to enjoin the rule before it went into effect. Within a few months, a federal judge ruled in favor of the nursing homes, concluding that the executive branch lacked the authority to promulgate such a rule. Three years later, the Trump administration finalized its own rule, largely allowing nursing homes to use arbitration agreements with residents.[103] In essence, this just reaffirmed what the nursing homes were doing. The next year, a district court upheld the validity of the rule.[104] Given the Supreme Court's favorable attitude toward forced arbitration, the outcome was unsurprising, but the decision made it harder for the Biden administration or any other to contain the use of arbitration agreements in the future.

But arbitration agreements were just the beginning, as the nursing home industry's greatest accomplishment was, in the wake of the pandemic, to create broad legal immunity for itself. COVID-19 laid bare the inadequacies of so many nursing homes. According to Lori Smetanka, executive director of the advocacy organization National Consumer Voice, many facilities had relied on residents' family members to provide unpaid care. With the arrival of the pandemic, those family members were, by and large, unable to visit, a fact that, according to Smetanka, exposed how so many homes were inadequately staffed. Suing these homes for negligent COVID-19 infections would have been a powerful incentive for nursing homes to improve their staffing and quality of care. But that's not what happened. Instead, with extraordinary speed, thirty-eight states enacted liability shields that largely prevented people from suing nursing homes for deaths and injuries resulting from their handling of the pandemic.[105] Several of these passed at the public urging of the nursing home industry association's state affiliates; others presumably passed with their more subtle support.

Moreover, just three of the laws specifically restricted their scope to harms resulting from exposure to the coronavirus, according to the National Consumer Voice. So laws nominally passed to insulate nursing homes from liability for COVID-related deaths—already a questionable goal—in fact gave them broader and, in some cases, permanent, protection from lawsuits.

These liability shields have had entirely predictable results. For instance, when Carol Ballard's daughter tried to visit her at a facility operated by the private equity–owned Genesis HealthCare, she found Ballard collapsed on the floor in front of her wheelchair.[106] Ballard had apparently been infected with COVID-19 and passed away the next day. Ballard wasn't alone: fully one-third of residents in the facility died of the virus. Yet there was little that Ballard's daughter could do to hold Genesis responsible for the outbreak, as the state's governor had signed a broad immunity shield just the day before. Ballard's family had no way to hold Genesis accountable, or even to investigate through litigation if Genesis had been negligent or responsible for the widespread outbreak in its facility. "Even with a history of these nursing homes having problems, why was immunity put in place?" Ballard's daughter asked the *Washington Post*. "I'm not looking for money. I'm looking for somebody to be held accountable."[107] (A spokesman for Genesis HealthCare told the *Post* that "we understand how difficult a time this has been" but that "the experience we have had with our families . . . has been overwhelmingly positive.")[108] With broad immunity, there was little chance that there would ever be such accountability for the facility or its private equity owner.

The nursing home industry has essentially shielded itself from serious oversight or litigation, which in turn has made the industry even more attractive to private equity firms. As Ernie Tosh, the plaintiff's lawyer, said, "We are just a cost of doing business."[109] This is evidenced by the fact, as mentioned above, that private equity investment in nursing homes actually increased during the pandemic, a time when the industry should have been in greatest peril. But insulated from liability and the consequences of their own actions, it was also a time of enormous opportunity for private equity firms.

✳

THE CASE OF Angela Ruckh and Consulate Health Care illustrates how difficult it is to recover damages from nursing homes, especially those owned by private equity firms. Consulate, owned by Formation Capital, was a massive nursing home chain with over ten thousand employees in twenty states.[110] It also had a terrible record of care. In Florida, where Consulate ran one out of every nine nursing homes, more than half of its facilities had just one or two stars on the federal government's five-star rating system. (This was quite an indictment, given that the government's rating system was notoriously easy to game.)[111]

Ruckh was a nurse with over twenty years' experience at the time her case was filed, and for five months in 2011, she worked at two facilities owned by Consulate.[112] As alleged by Ruckh, the conditions in the homes she worked at were abysmal. The facilities were understaffed, and at one point, according to her complaint, Ruckh saw a resident with an untreated wound. Beside the resident was a nurse's note: "dressing not done—too much to do—not enough time to do it."[113] At other times, according to Ruckh, residents were denied critical care because they were on Medicaid,[114] which provided less money for services than did Medicare or private insurance. At least twice, state regulators found deficiencies with Consulate's care so serious that they had the opportunity to shutter the chain.[115] For instance, separate from the incident Ruckh already described, staff failed to treat a resident's surgical wound for over two weeks and gave the resident drugs instead when she cried in pain.[116] Another time, Consulate allegedly failed to report an instance when a patient with severe dementia was found performing oral sex on another patient. Instead, the facility's director of nursing declared the dementia patient to be a consenting adult. These were far from the only violations, yet the state refused to close any of Consulate's facilities.

The private equity–owned Consulate wasn't just delivering poor-quality care; it was also committing fraud. In particular, it was overcharging the government for services that were unnecessary or that never happened. So Ruckh sued under the False Claims Act, a federal law that empowered whistleblowers to sue for the misuse of government money: in this case, from Medicare and Medicaid. The case was complicated, as Consulate disguised the wealth of its nursing homes using many of the tactics described earlier.[117] For instance, it organized its nursing homes into individual companies making their finances appear shaky, while paying rent, management, and rehabilitation fees to companies affiliated with Consulate or Formation.[118] Moreover, represented by various elite law firms—Baker & Hostetler; Akin Gump Strauss Hauer & Feld; and Skadden Arps[119]—the nursing homes moved to dismiss the case and objected to various discovery motions. This resulted in an enormous delay: the case did not go to trial until 2017, six years after the litigation began. For over twenty days, a jury heard about the nursing homes' alleged fraudulent practices and, after deliberation, found the homes guilty. The jurors returned a stunning verdict: nearly $350 million in damages.

Then, something unusual happened. Nearly a year after the trial, the district court judge vacated the jury's decision—what's called "judgment as a matter of law"—concluding that Ruckh had failed to show that the alleged losses were material or that the nursing home acted with sufficient knowledge that what it was doing was wrong.[120] The court also found that Ruckh failed to demonstrate that the nursing homes' management company was liable for the actions of the individual homes.

In other words, Consulate and its private equity owners were insulated from the actions of the individual homes. It was a stunning loss, and Ruckh appealed. Another year and a half passed, and finally an appellate court largely reversed the judge's findings.[121] In the main, it reinstated the jury's verdict against the companies, though reduced the damages claim, from nearly $350 million to about $257 million.[122] Ruckh had won, but the time elapsed was extraordinary: it had now been nearly ten years since she had first filed her complaint.[123]

And this is where Ruckh's story took a turn. Within weeks of the jury's verdict being largely reinstated, the private equity–controlled nursing homes declared bankruptcy.[124] And in bankruptcy, the nursing home was able to discharge almost all the damages that

Ruckh had won. In the end, Ruckh and the Department of Justice settled for just $4.5 million in damages, with three-quarters going back to the government and one-quarter going to Ruckh.[125] It took ten years, and Ruckh got $1 million for fraud that cost taxpayers $80 million.[126] And the private equity company that owned the nursing homes—Formation—continues to thrive, with $2 billion in assets under management and investments in nearly two dozen companies.[127] Considering all that had been invested in the case, it was a stunning loss. But it was also a guide. Smetanka of the National Consumer Voice said, "We're really worried that this is going to become the playbook for other companies."[128] Smetanka added that Formation's nursing homes weren't even banned from getting funds from Medicare or Medicaid.[129] For private equity firms, she said, "Their real focus is on going in, getting what they can from the facility, and turning it over."[130] Formation's victory would make it easier for it, and all other private equity firms, to continue doing just that.

✳

WHAT CAN BE done? The short answer, explained more in Chapter 12, is that regulators must be made accountable to residents themselves, not the organization controlling nursing homes. Those who've been harmed at facilities must be allowed to seek justice in court. To help accomplish this, regulators can require nursing homes to meet minimum staffing requirements and disclose their ultimate parent owners. State legislatures can repeal their liability shields and narrow the scope of arbitration agreements, even in the face of a hostile Supreme Court on the latter issue. And state attorneys general can investigate the worst-performing homes. But these institutions will act only if people force them to.

And it is worth doing so. As cases like ManorCare and Consulate illustrate, nursing homes expose private equity's worst tendencies. With a captive market, firms can—and reportedly do—gut homes' assets and eviscerate their quality of care, resulting in quite literally tens of thousands of deaths. And with a sclerotic regulatory bureaucracy, firms have little reason to change. Disaster is not guaranteed, but without oversight, it becomes more likely. These allegations of mismanagement and neglect put a disquieting color on all the money that David Rubenstein raised for investments like these and reveal the irony of his quip that private equity was the "highest calling of mankind."

CHAPTER FIVE

MAKING IT ALL WORSE

Private Equity in Health Care

If you are an American, there is an exceedingly good chance that you are worried about the cost of your health care. About four in ten of us have medical debt, and about the same number have delayed their own health care for fear of its price.[1] Fully a quarter of Americans say that they or a family member has skipped medications, cut back on necessary prescription drugs, or delayed buying medicine simply because of their costs.[2] These costs keep rising: the growth in health care spending in America vastly outpaces inflation and today takes up about a fifth of our entire economy.[3]

There are many reasons for the rising cost of health care in this country. But one of them is private equity, which spent over $150 billion in 2021—the most recent year for which there is data—acquiring companies in every part of the industry.[4] By buying and combining competitors, firms have been able to raise prices, lower pay for employees, and decrease the quality of care for patients.[5]

Consider the case of dermatology. The business caters to wealthier clients who, one might think, would be somewhat insulated from private equity's whims. Not so. In less than a decade, private equity firms bought 184 dermatology practices and 381 clinics.[6] The results were, at times, disastrous.

For instance, as reported by Heather Perlberg of *Bloomberg Businessweek*, after Audax Group bought the dermatology chain Advanced Dermatology and Cosmetic Surgery, it limited the purchase of basic supplies, which, one doctor alleged, left his office without gauze, antiseptic solution, or even toilet paper.[7] Audax also allegedly imposed a scorecard system to give offices money when they met daily and monthly financial quotas. At U.S. Dermatology Partners, another major private equity–owned dermatology chain, a doctor complained that the corporate office switched, without consulting medical staff, to a cheaper brand of needles.[8] The needles, the doctor claimed, were unreliable and often broke off inside patients' bodies. Elsewhere, firms gamed procedures and staffing: several practices had to send patients home with open wounds, only to recall them the next day for stitches, a tactic that allowed the practices to recoup more from insurers. Other practices, according to doctors and staff, were forced to rely increasingly on physician assistants over doctors for various tasks, which resulted in assistants missing potentially deadly skin cancers. Perhaps these tactics were profitable, but they were not good for patients. As one doctor observed to Bloomberg, "You can't serve two masters. You can't serve patients and investors."[9] (Audax and Advanced Dermatology Partners declined to comment to Bloomberg about the article.)

Despite this cost cutting, money did not necessarily flow to doctors. While older physicians could profit by selling their practices to private equity firms,[10] younger doctors who remained often found that they were overburdened and underpaid relative to their more senior colleagues. One dermatologist told MedPage Today that many of his fellow practitioners "have expressed an outright refusal to work for private equity–backed dermatology groups."[11] Consequently, job postings now frequently advertise that their offices are "NOT Private Equity" in their titles.[12]

But it's not just dermatology: all kinds of physician practices are being bought by private equity firms. Anesthesiology, cardiology, oncology, radiology, pediatrics, urgent care, mental health, dentistry, obstetrics and gynecology, and so many others. Private equity firms are buying clinics in these fields and more, and all at an extraordinary pace.[13] While comprehensive statistics are hard to collect, researchers at the Brookings Institution estimate that private equity firms have bought over 1,200 clinics across a range of specialties in little more than a decade.[14] Yet even this number considerably understates private equity firms' role in health care more broadly, as they have bought not just medical practices but also companies providing pharmaceuticals, medical devices, information technology, insurance, and others.[15] Together, firms have spent more than half a trillion dollars buying up health care companies around the world in just a decade.

Why are private equity firms spending so much in health care? A few reasons. Many companies in the industry offer steady cash flows through reliable programs like Medicare and Medicaid. Firms can use these cash flows to pay down the debts they use to buy businesses. Additionally, many health care companies have, for better or worse, loyal customers (think about the challenges of finding an in-network radiology clinic, for instance, or a therapist you like). As a result, firms can often raise prices or cut services without necessarily losing business. Finally, many health care companies, which offer similar services across disparate geographies, are ripe for consolidation through rollups. By buying competitors, private equity firms make it easier to raise prices and cut costs without consequence. Such rollups are not unique to private equity, but private equity firms, with their need for short-term profits and their insulation from legal consequences, are particularly disposed toward them. And the consequences of these rollups are vividly on display in two areas: hospitals and emergency rooms.

Private equity firms have long been attracted to hospitals. In 2004, for instance, Blackstone acquired a majority interest in Vanguard Health Systems,[16] a chain of hospitals in Arizona, California, Illinois, and Texas.[17] In 2006, a consortium of firms, including KKR and Bain Capital, bought the chain Hospital Corporation of America for $33 billion,[18] in what at the time was the largest leveraged buyout in history.[19] And in 2010, Cerberus created the Steward Health Care Network, which, with over thirty hospitals in nine states[20] and $6.6 billion in annual revenue,[21] became one of the largest hospital chains in the United States.[22] All three companies subsequently rolled up additional hospitals into the companies they acquired.[23] Once they did, the private equity firms executed many of the tactics that are now familiar. Blackstone did a dividend recapitalization of Vanguard and then sold it to another company, which subsequently struggled to service the debt.[24] Bain charged over $100 million in management and transaction fees to the Hospital Corporation of America.[25] And Cerberus did a sale-leaseback of Steward's real estate.[26]

Steward in particular illustrates the consequences of using private equity tactics on hospitals. As reported by Bloomberg, after Cerberus executed its sale-leaseback on Steward, the hospital chain sat "on a financial knife's-edge."[27] So, using proprietary software to predict staffing needs, Cerberus fired over five hundred employees. Predictably, this resulted in a shortage of nurses and other aides. Staff were frequently forced to work overtime on top of already draining twelve-hour shifts. And nurses had less time to care for patients. Steward's intensive care patients received, on average, four fewer hours of nursing care every day than did patients at other, similarly sized hospitals. "Frequently, I'm not performing the job up to standard," one nurse told Bloomberg.[28] "I feel like I'm failing my patients."[29] But it wasn't the nurses' fault: it was Cerberus's policies that led to the short-staffing.

Cerberus's underinvestment led to predictably bad outcomes. Steward had higher rates of patient falls than other, similarly sized hospitals, as well as higher rates of infection. One nurse wrote that patients had to wait in hallways when there were no available beds. Other nurses said that they were forced to work overtime, even after their twelve-hour shifts ended. When a mouse got trapped in an electrical transformer at one of Cerberus's hospitals, the facility was left without power for thirty-eight hours. To cope with the crisis, hospital workers had to move COVID-19 patients from their own wing to the main intensive care unit, where they were separated only by a wheeled privacy screen, a solution so ineffectual as to be almost insulting. "They're pretty much all about the money," one nurse told Bloomberg about Cerberus.[30] "They made that clear over and over again over the last 10 years. Their M.O. is take care of corporate first."[31] This was true: although Steward's situation was financially precarious, Cerberus more than made back its investment.

If Cerberus's—and private equity's—rollup of hospitals led to dire consequences, the situation was even worse with emergency medicine. Emergency care is particularly attractive to private equity because of its "inelastic" demand: people rarely choose where to get shot, for instance, or when to have a heart attack. They therefore tend to go to one of several nearby hospitals. Increasingly, these hospitals are staffed by one of two companies, Envision and TeamHealth, which are owned by KKR and Blackstone, respectively.[32] Over many years, these companies executed a dramatic rollup strategy to buy and combine companies that staffed emergency rooms with doctors. By 2018, about two-thirds of emergency rooms outsourced at least some of their staffing to a third party,[33] many to companies like Envision and TeamHealth. The problem was that the two private equity–owned companies often failed in the basic task of ensuring that the hospitals they serviced had the doctors and supplies they needed.

Consider the case of Dr. Raymond Brovont, who was employed by Envision's predecessor, EmCare, as the director of an emergency room in Overland Park, Kansas. EmCare had a long history with private equity: the firm Onex bought the company in 2004 and took it public the next year, though continued to own a majority of shares.[34] Clayton, Dubilier & Rice bought the business in 2011[35] and took it public once again, though the company kept a substantial stake in the company until 2015 and kept affiliated directors on the board until 2017.[36] Finally, KKR bought the business's parent, now named Envision, in 2018.[37]

As medical director at Overland Park, Brovont worked under a number of private equity owners and investors and quickly felt that EmCare had dangerously understaffed his department. For most of the day, just one doctor was on call to treat patients in both the pediatric and ordinary emergency rooms. Yet at the same time, the hospital required an emergency doctor to attend to any code blues, situations in which a patient's heart or lungs stopped working.[38] This could occur anywhere in the hospital, and when it did, it often meant that the emergency room had quite literally no doctor available.

Brovont feared that this short-staffing violated the law, as well as the standards set out by the American College of Surgeons.[39] And so he complained and ultimately organized a meeting between his emergency room doctors and an EmCare executive, Dr. Patrick McHugh. McHugh listened to the doctor's complaints but offered an astoundingly tone-deaf reply. He wrote to all emergency room physicians, noting that for the hospital chain, "many of their staffing decisions are financially motivated. EmCare is no different."[40] "Profits are in everyone's best interest," he added. "Thank you as well for respecting my request to refrain from publicly voicing your concerns/objections until we are given a fair opportunity to address them."[41] In his email, McHugh even included links to EmCare's stock and financial information. His comments were refreshingly honest, but they laid bare the basic problem: EmCare was apparently making decisions that affected patients and was doing so, it appeared, out of a desire for profits alone, untempered by, for instance, medical judgment.

After the meeting, no changes were made.[42] Brovont raised the issue several more times with the EmCare executive, to no effect. And so Brovont wrote a formal letter, endorsed by all the physicians in the emergency department, complaining about the understaffing crisis. He never received a response, only a terse shot from the EmCare executive in the hallway: "Why would you ever put that in writing?"[43] Six weeks later, Brovont was fired.

Brovont eventually sued the EmCare subsidiaries who employed him for wrongful termination.[44] In the course of litigation, it was revealed that Brovont's firing "petrified" the other doctors and created a "weird cult of coercion" and silence on the code blue policy.[45] Eventually, and encouragingly, Brovont won nearly $26 million for his firing, including substantial punitive damages.[46] After the judgment, however, the hospital declined to say whether it had actually changed the understaffing policies that Brovont had complained about.[47]

The debacle with Brovont was illustrative, but it wasn't isolated. Like EmCare, Blackstone's TeamHealth fired an emergency room physician—Dr. Ming Lin—after he complained about his hospital's inadequate COVID-19 protections. In particular, Lin sent a letter—and posted its contents on Facebook—to the hospital's chief medical officer, recommending that staff have their temperatures taken at the beginning of their shifts and that patients be triaged in the hospital parking lot.[48] He also criticized as "ludicrous" the hospital's practice of testing patients for COVID only after a prior influenza test proved negative.[49] Doing so needlessly exposed both patients and doctors to increased risk, he argued. Shortly after Lin published his complaint, TeamHealth terminated Lin's shifts with the hospital, telling Lin that while the company believed that his comments were "intended to be constructive... unfortunately it is not possible for you to return" to work.[50] Ultimately the ACLU chose to represent Dr. Lin in a wrongful termination lawsuit, characterizing the matter as one of free speech. TeamHealth denied that it had fired Lin and told NBC that it offered to place him "anywhere in the country"; the litigation remains ongoing.[51]

Cases like Brovont's and Lin's occurred because they were fundamental to Envision's and TeamHealth's business model under private equity ownership, the whole point of which was to reduce the amount of money spent on doctors and services in emergency rooms. This reached absurd proportions when, for instance, both companies cut hours for emergency room doctors during the early months of the COVID-19 pandemic.[52] Because doctors were paid by the hour, this also, in effect, cut their salaries, a fact that TeamHealth initially denied. "[T]o see TeamHealth blatantly lying is infuriating," one doctor told ProPublica.[53] Infuriating, perhaps, but not surprising. Private equity firms bought these companies on the explicit promise of cost cutting: when it bought Envision, KKR said that it would focus on "operational improvement initiatives," while when it bought TeamHealth, Blackstone said that it was attracted to "near-term cost reduction opportunities."[54] These were euphemisms for budget cuts, and it should be no surprise that the firms followed through on their promises.

These companies' practices, including their use of surprise billing, which is discussed in later chapters, put a tremendous strain on doctors. One clinician who worked for TeamHealth told ProPublica, "This is not what I signed up for and this isn't what most other ER docs signed up for. I went into medicine to lessen suffering, but as I understand more clearly my role as an employee of TeamHealth, I realize that I'm unintentionally worsening some patients' suffering."[55] Robert McNamara, a former president of the American Academy of Emergency Medicine, said that working for these companies "tears at your soul."[56] Yet, he added, "It's pretty hard to get a doctor to speak up against these corporations... because they fear about being blacklisted."[57]

✳

THE BASIC LOGIC of private equity drove these disastrous outcomes in dermatology, hospitals, and emergency medicine. But sometimes, the relentless pressure to increase profits and cut costs shoved these companies into allegedly illegal conduct. In 2017, for instance, EmCare settled a case with the Department of Justice over allegations that it improperly referred patients to hospitals in exchange for kickbacks.[58] Under the alleged scheme, a chain of hospitals made bonus payments to EmCare's physicians in exchange for increasing the number of patient admissions, as Medicare generally pays three times as much for inpatient care as it does for outpatient care.[59] If substantiated, this was risky conduct. People ought to be admitted to hospitals only when truly necessary, given the danger of infection and medical misadventure.[60] EmCare agreed to pay nearly $30 million to resolve the allegations.[61] But it was unclear how much these fines mattered. One industry analyst, Sheryl R. Skolnick, wrote that investors "seem to think that D.O.J. investigations, qui tam suits and allegations of serious Medicare fraud are simply a cost of doing business."[62]

EmCare wasn't alone. In 2021, UnitedHealthcare sued Blackstone's TeamHealth for "upcoding," that is, using billing codes unjustified by the underlying medical distresses. In a battle between a health insurance company and a private equity–owned physician staffing firm, it was hard to say that there was a clear hero. And TeamHealth gave as good as it got, successfully suing United for underpaying on thousands of claims.[63] Yet according to United, for example, TeamHealth charged $1,712—and billed the case as one of "particularly high complexity"—to treat someone who came to the hospital with indigestion from eating a chili dog (he was prescribed Maalox and sent home).[64] According to United, TeamHealth upcoded tens if not hundreds of thousands of claims, which resulted in overpayments in excess of $100 million.[65] But for a case that began in 2021, over actions allegedly taken years before, trial was set for 2024.[66] In other words, it would take years to litigate the truth of the matter.

Finally, in 2020, another Blackstone-owned health care company, Apria Healthcare Group, agreed to pay tens of millions of dollars for allegedly billing the government for ventilators that were never used. Under Medicare, the government provided higher reimbursement rates for so-called noninvasive ventilators: those that could be worn like a mask, rather than, say, inserted down patients' throats with tubes.[67] As alleged by the Justice Department, Apria Healthcare moved aggressively to sell these devices, so aggressively, in fact, that it billed the government for ventilators it knew were not being used. Having been found out, Apria agreed to pay $40.5 million without admitting wrongdoing.[68] But such a settlement was little more than a rounding error for Apria and its private equity owner. In 2020, Blackstone did a dividend recapitalization of the company, making nearly five times what Apria paid to the government for its wrongdoing.[69] Recall that with a dividend recapitalization, a private equity firm makes its portfolio company borrow money to pay the private equity firm. It's like using someone else's credit card, and because private equity firms tend to lose only a little money if the company fails but gain disproportionately if the company succeeds, it almost always makes sense for the firm to do this. Here, Blackstone forced Apria to borrow $410 million to pay Blackstone.[70] In 2021, Apria went public, netting its owners an additional $170 million, of which Blackstone received a substantial percentage. Also that year, the Trump administration removed Apria's noninvasive ventilators from the government's competitive bidding process, a move that could have raised device prices by more than a third.[71] Finally, to save costs, Apria fired respiratory specialists who were necessary to make sure that patients were using the ventilator machines correctly.[72] All of which is to say that the fines levied on Apria were likely far too small to constrain its alleged behavior. They were, to borrow a phrase, simply a cost of doing business.

Surveying all this alleged wrongdoing, it's worth noting that the few plaintiffs who litigate their cases to trial may take years— and spend millions of dollars—to do so. As a result, most plaintiffs, including the government, tend to settle and often without requiring defendants to admit their own guilt.[73] While this may save time and money, it prevents the development of any useful case law that future plaintiffs can cite. And in either case—resolution by trial or by settlement—the amounts that defendants pay typically are simply too small to be anything other than a distraction for most wrongdoers.

With these limitations in bringing fraud cases, some doctors are taking the issue on themselves and challenging the legality of the very business model of companies like Envision and TeamHealth. Both companies are owned by private equity firms—KKR and Blackstone, respectively—neither of which are run by physicians. But state "corporate practice of medicine" laws nominally prohibit people other than doctors and institutions other than hospitals from owning medical practices.[74] These laws capture the reasonable notion that medical practices should be owned by those who actually understand medicine and who are driven by professional obligations and duties of care over and above a simple desire for profit.

In general, private equity firms circumvented these laws by establishing intermediate "physician management" companies that bought the assets of the offices they acquired and by setting up separate service agreements to employ the doctors at those practices.[75] In states where corporate practice of medicine laws are more strict, private equity firms established new businesses run by "friendly" or "captive" physicians allied with the firms.[76] These arrangements potentially circumvented state laws, but left the private equity firms—who now owned the assets of the clinics, and essentially employed the physicians who work there—effectively in charge of the practices they bought.

State medical licensing boards, who are, by and large, charged with policing violations of the corporate practice of medicine laws, should have stopped this. But Dr. Robert McNamara, the former president of the American Academy of Emergency Medicine, complained that they were slow to do so. Perhaps it was simply a failure to understand the issue or their own authority; perhaps it was a fear of causing controversy. Whatever the result, according to McNamara, it fell to others to enforce the law.

And so, in 2020, the American Academy of Emergency Medicine (AAEM) sued Envision for violating the corporate practice statutes. As alleged by the Academy, Envision created hundreds of subsidiary medical groups, each run by a doctor, to manage its many practices. But according to AAEM, these medical groups were "a mere front" for Envision itself.[77] In fact, just a single doctor served as the CEO of potentially hundreds of these companies.[78] And this doctor, Envision ensured, had no actual authority over the businesses he ran: he was restricted, for instance, in his ability to issue dividends, create new stock, or sell the medical group.[79]

But as AAEM alleged, Envision controlled, not just business decisions, but medical ones too; through a series of "best practices," "red rules," and "evidence-based pathways" it promulgated protocols that described how to treat patients.[80] Envision also used "benchmarking" reports to compare doctors' performance to the company's standards, as well as "practice improvement feedback" to "educate" doctors on clinical decisions.[81] In effect, according to

AAEM, Envision was "rendering physicians as mere employees, and diminishing physician independence and freedom from commercial interests."[82]

Envision's management would be fine—perhaps even helpful— if decisions were made by medical professionals. But the AAEM alleged that this was not the case. In filing the case, the academy's president said in a statement that emergency room patients "deserve treatment by a board certified emergency physician whose fiduciary duty is to place the patient's medical needs above all else, and not by a private equity or lay corporation whose fiduciary duty is to place profit before the patient."[83] The litigation remains ongoing.[84]

✱

THE CASE AGAINST Envision is not a panacea because it attacks just one part of private equity's entry into health care. But it gets to a fundamental issue, namely, that health care decisions should be motivated by need and knowledge, not by profit. Private equity firms' desire for money is not unique in our health care industry. Yet the crushing logic of their business model, with its relentless focus on short-term profits, brings out many of the industry's worst tendencies. How might these broader harms be addressed? One possibility is plain: the antitrust laws.

As mentioned, private equity firms often buy companies— dermatology clinics, for instance, or emergency room staffing firms—through rollup strategies, by which they purchase several similar businesses and combine them into one. The purported reasons for these rollups are efficiencies of scale. For example, a private equity firm can consolidate billing, records, and marketing operations of several clinics, allowing doctors to focus on the practice of medicine. This may be so, but there are other reasons too. By building larger practices, private equity firms and their companies can negotiate higher rates from patients' insurance companies and from uninsured customers. And by buying up many competitors, firms can lower the quality of their care without consequence, knowing that patients will struggle to find alternatives.

These are precisely the sorts of harms that the antitrust laws were meant to protect against. In particular, Section 7 of the Clayton Act prohibits acquisitions that may lessen competition by, for instance, raising prices for consumers, reducing pay for workers, or gutting the quality of care. As far back as a decade ago, as many as a fifth of physician markets were already so consolidated that further acquisitions would presumptively violate the law.[85] Since then, private equity rollups have only grown more ambitious. While the specific facts of each rollup matter, the trends suggest that those empowered to enforce the antitrust laws—most prominently, the Department of Justice and Federal Trade Commission (FTC)—could and should focus their attention on ensuring compliance with those laws.

But for the most part, they have not done so. The federal government does not appear to have challenged a single physician practice rollup, likely because the agencies were unaware that they were even occurring (private equity firms and other purchasers only report proposed acquisitions above a certain size).[86] But the government rarely challenged the acquisitions that it did know about, too. When the hospital chain Community Health Systems bought one of its largest rivals, the FTC required that it divest just two hospitals.[87] When Cerberus's Steward Health Care Network bought its own rival for nearly $2 billion, it required no divestitures at all.[88] And when Vanguard bought the Detroit Medical Center, the Commission allowed the acquisition and, in fact, did so on an expedited basis.[89]

In short, because of private equity, patients at hospitals with fewer competitors faced worse health outcomes, while families paid thousands more to medical monopolies than they would have in more competitive markets.[90] And people who went to physician practices and hospitals rolled up by private equity firms experienced all the harms—understaffing, increased costs, and insufficient care—described above.

Why did this happen? The simple answer is that the antitrust laws have been under a sustained assault for two generations, the result of which is that it has become increasingly difficult for the enforcement agencies to stop the sorts of rollups that private equity firms are now engaged in.

This was not always the case. The nation's primary antitrust law, the Sherman Act, was passed as a "comprehensive charter of economic liberty"[91] and, in fits and starts, protected America from the domination of great trusts, conglomerates, and monopolies. At the turn of the last century, Theodore Roosevelt wielded the statute to splinter J. P. Morgan's Northern Securities railroad trust and break up John D. Rockefeller's Standard Oil. His successor, William Howard Taft, brought even more cases than Roosevelt, dissolved the "sugar trust," and moved to end the U.S. Steel monopoly.[92] President Wilson signed successor legislation, the Clayton Act, which brought necessary scrutiny to mergers and acquisitions. And Franklin Roosevelt, through the great assistant attorney general Thurman Arnold, brought nearly as many cases as his predecessors combined.[93] Arnold's strategy to "hit hard, hit everyone and hit them all at once"[94] helped to simultaneously lower prices for consumers and increase production and employment, laying the foundation for an economic expansion after World War II broadly shared with the growing middle class.

By the 1960s, antitrust law, or at least the subset of law concerned with acquisitions, was strong and simple. The Department of Justice and FTC's merger guidelines—the agencies' statement to the world about which acquisitions they would and would not tolerate—laid out clear concentration thresholds above which further acquisitions would almost always be prohibited. This wasn't to say that companies couldn't get bigger, but they would have to do so through organic growth and competition on the merits, rather than by simply buying up competitors.

Unsurprisingly, the broader business community despised this approach and set out to remake the laws to its benefit. In this effort, businesses found an eager intellectual defender in Robert Bork, the pugnacious, oddly bearded professor at the University of Chicago. In his academic articles and enormously influential 1978 book *The Antitrust Paradox*, Bork set out to deconstruct America's antitrust laws. He argued that the statutes were drafted narrowly to maximize "consumer welfare," which in practice meant low-ering prices. (This ignored their other purposes, including pro-tecting small businesses, workers, and democracy itself from the too-strong influence of big corporations.)[95] Bork pushed to permit most predatory pricing schemes, where companies underpriced their rivals to drive them out of business. He claimed that tacit collusion—the process of a few firms raising their prices in coordina-tion without explicitly agreeing to do so—probably never actually occurred. And most importantly, he argued that mergers between competitors should generally be allowed and that so-called con-glomerate mergers—acquisitions in disparate industries, like those that private equity firms make—should be permitted entirely.[96]

Intellectually, Bork was not alone. He was joined, with vary-ing levels of nuance and agreement, by University of Chicago professors (and later judges) Richard Posner and Frank Easter-brook, as well as Harvard professors Donald Turner and Phillip Areeda. Harvard professor and later Supreme Court justice Ste-phen Breyer was also an occasional fellow traveler. These men cast a skeptical eye on antitrust enforcement generally and believed that the harm of overenforcement vastly outweighed the risks of underenforcement.[97]

Financially, too, Bork was not alone. In 1976, the Law and Economics Center, funded by corporate donors,[98] began holding an annual economics institute for federal judges,[99] where it spread a conservative doctrine on antitrust. By 1990, 40 percent of sit-ting federal judges had completed its flagship program,[100] despite apparent conflicts of interest: multiple judges who attended the course heard antitrust cases involving companies who sponsored the classes they took.[101] Nevertheless, the program survived and continues to operate today.[102]

Meanwhile, big companies had the money to litigate Bork's novel claims in court.[103] Eventually, Bork and his corporate allies got their way. In 1979, one year after the release of *The Antitrust Paradox*, the Supreme Court endorsed Bork's dubious proposition that "Congress designed the Sherman Act as a 'consumer welfare prescription.' "[104] In 1986, the Court said that tacit collusion could not violate Section 1 of the Sherman Act, and raised the standards for proving explicit collusion cases.[105] In 1993, it neutered most predatory pricing claims by requiring plaintiffs to show that defendants would likely recoup the costs of their predatory schemes, a virtual impossibility to prove.[106] And gallingly, in 2004, Justice Scalia essentially endorsed the concept of monopoly, writing in *Verizon v. Trinko* that "it is an important element of the free-market system. The opportunity to charge monopoly prices—at least for a short period—is what attracts 'business acumen' in the first place; it induces risk taking that produces innovation and economic growth."[107] No wonder then that the government often struggled to bring successful cases against merging companies.

Antitrust enforcers suffered their own structural problems during this time as well. Enforcement agencies remained persistently understaffed,[108] and they had little insight into smaller acquisitions—for instance, rollups of physician practices—that fell below the reporting thresholds set by statute. The result was that the Justice Department and FTC were simply unaware that many of these acquisitions were even occurring.

But antitrust enforcers got in their own way, too. The Justice Department and FTC's merger guidelines in the late 1960s set clear standards for when they would challenge proposed acquisitions, based on the number of competitors remaining in the market.[109] Importantly, the guidelines largely rejected mitigating "efficiencies" that might justify these acquisitions. This was so, the guidelines explained, because efficiencies could "normally be realized through internal expansion" and because there were usually "severe difficulties" in identifying and measuring those efficiencies.[110] The idea motivating the guidelines at the time was simple: big companies could get bigger, but they would have to do so on their merits, not simply through acquisitions.

In 1982, the Reagan administration revised the merger guidelines to add a number of exceptions to this framework. Among other things, where it was easy for new competitors to enter the market, or where competitors' products were highly differentiated, the enforcement agencies announced that they were less likely to challenge proposed mergers.[111] Subsequent revisions in the 1980s and 1990s to the merger guidelines across administrations added further complications and exceptions and raised the ceiling under which mergers would be presumptively permitted.[112] By 2010, the guidelines made an about-face on their earlier incantation, cheering that efficiencies were "a primary benefit of mergers" and that mergers could "result in lower prices, improved quality, enhanced service, or new products."[113] Far from rejecting speculative efficiency arguments, the guidelines now begged for them.

Three things resulted from all these changes. *First*, by raising the concentration thresholds, the merger guidelines treated a vast new swath of mergers as presumptively procompetitive. *Second*, by encouraging efficiency arguments and allowing a host of other exceptions, the enforcement agencies put judges in the impossible position of balancing harms and benefits that were both qualitative (for instance, hypothesized price increases or decreases) and quantitative (for instance, increased or decreased innovations). *Third*, by complicating the merger analysis, the enforcers encouraged more reliance on expert economists, whose work judges were ill-equipped to evaluate. Faced with complications, exceptions, and complex economics, judges were prone to figuratively throw up their hands and permit mergers that, under earlier versions of the guidelines, ought not to have been allowed. And knowing all this, enforcement agencies became less likely to bring actions in the first place: from 2015 to 2019, antitrust enforcers blocked just three of the seventy-five largest acquisitions.[114] With so many ways to lose a case, the Department of Justice and FTC spent enormous resources preparing the cases they did bring, meaning that they tended to file just a few health care cases—if that—each year.[115]

The result was that antitrust law became a shadow of what it once was. The consequences surround us. Today in America, there are just four leading airlines.[116] There are three cell phone companies.[117] There are two leading drug stores.[118] Plausibly no one benefited from this decline of antitrust more than the private equity industry, particularly in health care. Concentration didn't cause all the problems in the health care system, but it certainly contributed to them. And this concentration wasn't an accident: we let it happen.

Thankfully, this may be starting to change. The department and FTC are working to revise the tangled merger guidelines. Both offices are now led by officials who believe in aggressive antitrust enforcement, and both are taking aggressive action to prevent rollups in the health care industry. The FTC, for instance, has successfully challenged four large hospital mergers, including the acquisition of Steward Health Care Network (once owned by Cerberus) by HCA Healthcare (once owned in part by KKR).[119] The Department of Justice, meanwhile, sued to block UnitedHealth Group's $13 billion acquisition of Change Healthcare, a company owned in part by Blackstone.[120] (The department lost that case at trial, but merely bringing the case demonstrated a willingness to be aggressive.) Outside of government, these enforcers are supported by a growing chorus of activists and academics who are pushing to rethink the goals of the antitrust laws, away from Bork's cramped vision of "consumer welfare" and closer to the broader reasons for which the laws have traditionally been enforced. It's encouraging; exciting even. But undoing the damage to the law, health care, and elsewhere will take time.

*

HEALTH CARE ILLUSTRATES some of private equity firms' worst tendencies: their focus on short-term profits over long-term care, their disregard for customers and patients, and their general ability to avoid meaningful consequences for their actions. But, however fitfully and incompletely, that may be starting to change. Though we have spent decades crippling antitrust laws, a new generation of enforcers may revitalize the law in health care and beyond. In the meantime, as the state corporate practice of medicine suits show, doctors and patients may be able to challenge some of these acquisitions themselves. These efforts are just beginning. But they point to a way in which the government, patients, and medical professionals, working alone and together, might slow or even stop the private equity industry's takeover of the American health care system.

CHAPTER SIX

THIS TIME WILL BE DIFFERENT

Private Equity in Finance

The chapters thus far have explained how private equity firms have re-shaped the economy, by buying companies and raising prices, cutting jobs, and shifting money from ordinary businesses to themselves. This is the traditional work of private equity. Yet increasingly, firms like Blackstone and Apollo are moving beyond the business of buying and selling companies and into obscure markets like private credit once dominated by the investment banks that started the Great Recession. Yet they are doing so with far less oversight than those investment banks ever faced. To fund their operations, firms are inhaling money from insurance companies and soon from retirement funds, including potentially your own. Some regulators appear to believe themselves powerless to stop this expansion; others are eager to help. Either way, private equity is metastasizing into new businesses and new pools of money. That they are doing this largely without oversight is deeply disturbing for anyone who remembers the Great Recession.

＊

AT THE END of the last century and into the twenty-first, well-known investment banks, like Goldman Sachs, JP Morgan, and

Lehman Brothers, became sprawling financial conglomerates. They still performed the traditional work of advising companies on acquisitions and public offerings. But they also got into the business of trading securities—stocks, bonds, and futures—for their own accounts and bought, bundled, and sold (securitized, in industry parlance) mortgages and other financial products. When the housing market collapsed, the leading investment banks were fundamentally shaken, and those that survived were either bought by or transformed into bank holding companies.[1] In this new form, these firms were more tightly regulated, less free to make loans, and largely barred from trading for their own benefit. They were also subject to potential supervision by the newly created Financial Stability Oversight Council and required to conduct "stress tests"—estimates of how they would handle catastrophic losses—for regulators. A particular indignity to bankers, many of these companies were required for the first time to report aspects of their executives' compensation.

Under this new scrutiny, the investment banks pulled back from many of their riskiest investments. Something needed to fill the void, and that something was private equity. This was possible because private equity firms were far less regulated than were other kinds of firms and often structured their investments as private funds, exempt from the ordinary disclosure requirements that, say, mutual funds had to provide.[2] They also had lower capital requirements—that is, minimum amounts of money to be kept on hand for downturns—than did bank holding companies. And they escaped being designated "systemically important" by the Financial Stability Oversight Council, a move that would have considerably increased regulatory requirements on them.

With comparatively less oversight, the largest private equity firms, like Blackstone, Apollo, KKR, and Carlyle, began to diversify, just as the investment banks had. And just like the investment banks, private equity firms threatened to become too big to fail: that is, to become so large that the government would not tolerate their collapse. They bought real estate and infrastructure.

They launched their own hedge funds and recruited from investment banks, which were forced by regulation to shut down their own operations.[3] And perhaps most importantly, they got into the business of private credit, which, as the name might suggest, is an alternative to the public stock markets. Historically, when a big company wanted to raise money, it did so by issuing stock. In exchange for the obligations of being public—such as filing quarterly and annual financial returns—the company was allowed to broadly solicit money for investments, generally through an initial public offering. But to avoid such burdens, some companies—usually small or midsized businesses—borrowed money on the private credit market from individual lenders, who typically would accept less transparency from borrowers in exchange for higher interest rates.

Because of this looser oversight, over the course of forty years, private credit grew and by some measures eclipsed the public markets. The statistics here are necessarily incomplete, given that private credit is so opaque, but the *Wall Street Journal* reports that assets held by private debt funds—businesses that lent private credit—grew nearly fivefold from 2007 to 2020, to $850 billion.[4] So-called Regulation D offerings—broad solicitations for money, similar to initial public offerings in the public markets—raised over $1.5 trillion in 2019, more than all the money raised through the stock markets in the same year.[5] Meanwhile, as private credit grew, public markets shrank: In 1996, there were over 7,400 companies listed on US stock exchanges. By 2018, there were fewer than half that.[6]

In the wake of the Great Recession, private equity firms became leading lenders of private credit as investment banks receded from the business. Now, Blackstone and Apollo have the largest private credit funds in the world, right after the behemoth Japanese firm SoftBank Group.[7] In fact, for many private equity firms, the actual business of private equity—leveraged buyouts—now makes up only a minority of their business. Ares, a private equity firm created by several Apollo alumni,[8] makes a substantial majority of its business ($262 billion in assets under management) in private credit, while just $31 billion is invested in private equity.[9] Blackstone has nearly as much invested in credit and insurance ($259 billion) as it does in private equity ($261 billion), while real estate, insurance, and hedge funds make up the bulk of its remaining ventures.[10]

The growth of private credit, and private equity's role within it, raises significant concerns. Private borrowers are likely to be smaller, and more indebted, than their public counterparts[11] and are thus more likely to default on their loans. Private lenders, meanwhile, including private equity firms, do not have the capital requirements that investment banks now must have and so are in greater danger of collapsing when borrowers fail to pay their loans. But beyond the individual risks for individual borrowers and lenders, private credit creates broader systemic risks too. According to the *Financial Times*, the ratings firm Moody's, for instance, warned of the "opacity, eroding standards and the difficulty in trading these slices" of debt.[12] For instance, private credit lenders typically sell off chunks of the loans they make to other investors, a process known as securitization. Often, these lenders do not bother to seek grades on the trustworthiness of their debts from ratings agencies like Standard and Poor's or Moody's.[13] When they do, according to investor Dan Rasmussen, they typically rely on second-tier ratings agencies, who are willing to give overly optimistic projections that borrowers will repay.[14] What this means is that other investors might be buying securitized loans that are far less reliable than they think. And while the private credit market is vastly smaller than the US mortgage market, it is growing rapidly, from barely $100 billion in investable money in 2005 to over $900 billion in 2021.[15] In other words, the same dynamic that started the Great Recession may be happening here, albeit at a smaller scale.

Republican and Democratic administrations both worked eagerly for forty years to make possible the growth of private credit and private equity firms' role within it. In 1982, for instance, the Securities and Exchange Commission (SEC) under President Reagan issued Regulation D, through which companies could generally borrow from "accredited investors"—shorthand for wealthy or sophisticated lenders—without registering with the SEC.[16] This created a new class of firms from which companies could borrow money. Then, in 1990, the SEC allowed for the syndication of private capital to certain institutional buyers. Investors could now make loans on the private market and then bundle the promises of payment on those loans and sell them to other investors. This Rule 144A, in essence, created a new, secondary market for private credit.

These regulations were issued under SEC chairmen appointed by Presidents Reagan and Bush, respectively. But Democratic administrations got in on the game too. In 1996, Congress passed, and President Clinton signed, legislation that lifted the requirement that private funds—funds that made loans on the private credit market—be limited to one hundred or fewer investors.[17] This created the opportunity for investors to build vast stores of capital with which to make private loans.[18] The legislation passed overwhelmingly in the House (just eight members voted against it) and by unanimous consent in the Senate.[19] Then, in 2012, Congress passed, and President Obama signed, the JOBS (Jumpstart Our Business Startups) Act, which further expanded the private credit market by permitting borrowers to make general solicitations for money.[20] This meant that private credit sales could be advertised publicly and essentially obviated the purpose of going public. The legislation passed with bipartisan majorities in both chambers of Congress.[21]

The result of all these changes was to make it vastly easier to lend and borrow money outside of the stock market, with vastly less oversight.[22] This is risky for the individual lenders and borrowers, who have less transparency in their transactions and thus likely face a greater risk of default. But this is also risky for the economy overall, as the mistakes that companies make in the opaque private credit market can affect those who had no part in it, such as customers, suppliers, employees, and communities. And with underregulated private equity firms eager to take on this work, it is as if all the risks inherent in the financial system before the Great

Recession are simply moving from one set of institutions—the investment banks—to a new set: private equity firms.

✳

PRIVATE CREDIT IS just one area where firms like Blackstone and Apollo have expanded. The simple fact is that these firms are so much more complex and so much bigger than they were a generation ago. For Blackstone, the diversity of its interests is astounding. It has expanded from private equity to private credit, as well as into real estate and hedge funds.[23] It operates a "life sciences" initiative that invests in nascent medical technologies[24] and manages a separate fund with some $30 billion to spend on infrastructure projects. Almost incidentally, it has even become the largest private sector property owner in America.[25] Similar transformations have occurred at the other leading private equity firms,[26] who now invest in infrastructure,[27] health care,[28] and energy,[29] among so much else. They also create hedge funds[30] and buy and securitize distressed mortgages (exactly the business that overturned companies like Lehman Brothers).[31] The biggest firms don't even call themselves private equity anymore: they are "alternative asset managers."[32]

The risk posed by this expansion is twofold. *First*, with less transparency than other financial institutions, private equity firms may make bigger, riskier bets, whose failures would affect not just them but employees, customers, and communities. *Second*, once they reach a certain size, some private equity firms might become too big to fail, that is, their collapse would be so devastating to the economy that the government would step in to prevent their failure. Knowing this, the biggest private equity firms may be encouraged not to scale back but to take ever-greater risks, assuming that they will be bailed out if those risks fail.

As private equity firms have expanded in every direction, they have become the hot places to work on Wall Street.[33] Before the Great Recession, Goldman Sachs was perhaps the most coveted firm to work for on Wall Street. Now, pay there has fallen in half, and private equity firms like Blackstone have taken its place: one commentator said, "Blackstone remind[s] me of Goldman Sachs in the 1990s—every time you see a new business that is growing, that is where they are."[34]

The statistics bear this out. Nearly a fifth of Blackstone's employees and more than a quarter of KKR's previously worked at Goldman Sachs or Morgan Stanley, while just 1 percent of Goldman Sachs or Morgan Stanley employees previously worked at Blackstone or KKR.[35] In other words, people are leaving banks to go to private equity firms but not the other way around. There's also the matter of pay, from the bottom to the top. New hires at private equity firms may earn double what young employees at the big investment banks might.[36] Meanwhile, the CEO of Goldman Sachs made just under $24 million in 2020;[37] the president of Blackstone received close to ten times that much.[38] And since 2005, nearly two dozen private equity executives have become multibillionaires.[39] None of the CEOs of the largest investment banks save one—Jamie Dimon of JP Morgan Chase—is worth close to that much.[40]

The migration from investment banks to private equity firms means that the great mass of talent in finance is shifting to ever-less regulated and transparent parts of the industry. It means that inequality, as expressed in the extraordinary pay of private equity executives, continues to grow. And it means that these private equity firms are simply getting bigger, with the consequent risks to the economy and the creation of too-big-to-fail firms just discussed. For perspective, KKR had $15 billion in 2005 in assets under management;[41] today, it has $459 billion.[42] Blackstone had $79 billion in 2007;[43] today it has $731 billion.[44] Several firms anticipate having $1 trillion in assets in a few years' time.[45] But to achieve these goals, private equity firms need money—enormous sums of money— with which to invest in their various plans. And with regulators' help, they're getting it, from a perhaps unexpected source: you.

✳

TO FINANCE THEIR expanding operations, private equity firms are buying insurance companies.[46] In 2019, for instance, Carlyle bought Fortitude, a reinsurance company (an insurer for insurers).[47] A few years later, Blackstone bought Allstate Life Insurance.[48] KKR bought Global Atlantic.[49] And Apollo bought Athene.[50] Together, private equity firms spent almost $40 billion buying insurance companies in the United States and today control over 7 percent of the industry's assets, some $376 billion—double what they had in 2015.[51] This means that firms are getting ever bigger, increasing risks to our economy in the ways just described. It also means, as explained momentarily, that people's insurance policies—including potentially your own—may be less safe.

As described shortly, this expansion could threaten people's life insurance policies, including your own, as firms invest people's premiums in possibly riskier assets. Notably, this buying spree was enabled by state insurance regulators, who approved acquisitions of companies domiciled in their states.[52] These regulators, the *Washington Post* reported, frequently received "campaign contributions, lavish dinners and the prospect of future employment" in the industry they regulated.[53] In fact, of over one hundred state insurance commissioners surveyed, more than half ultimately worked for insurance companies after their careers in public service ended.[54] Little wonder, then, that the industry's acquisitions were so often approved.

But why were firms buying these companies in the first place? Like so many other businesses that attracted private equity, insurance offered a steady cash flow. People make premium payments every month that insurers invest, hoping to make the money they need to pay when the policies came due. By buying insurers, private equity firms believed that they invest the insurers' money—in leveraged buyouts, for instance, or in private credit—better than the insurers would themselves. On top of this, firms could charge the insurance companies they owned and, ultimately, their customers, various management fees for sourcing investments.[55] Regarding these increased fees, Larry Rybka, the CEO of private insurance company Valmark Financial, told CNBC that "there's nothing good in this for the policyholder."[56]

Private equity's appetite for risk attracted it to insurance for another reason, namely, that it could engineer them to hold ever-fewer reserves and give the money to the private equity firms. By law, insurers have to keep money in reserve—capital requirements are set by state regulators—to pay out their benefits. But private equity firms have set up complicated schemes to avoid these restrictions. In particular, several created reinsurance companies—insurers for insurers—in Bermuda, and sold US policies to them.[57] Bermuda has lower taxes and, crucially, lower capital requirements, which allow the private equity firms to use more of their policyholders' money as they choose.[58] This means that private equity firms have more to invest from policyholders than do traditional insurance companies. But it also means that they have less cushion with which to absorb losses if those investments fail. Unsurprisingly, this poses huge risks for policyholders and governments. With lower capital reserves, private equity–owned insurance companies are more likely to fail if their investments do, and with private equity firms shoveling their money into riskier ventures, that failure is becoming more likely. Private equity firms' "focus is on maximizing their immediate financial returns, rather than ensuring that promised retirement benefits are there at the end of the day for policyholders," said Ben Lawsky, the former superintendent of New York State's financial regulator.[59] "This type of business model isn't necessarily a natural fit for the insurance business, where a failure can put policyholders at very significant risk."[60]

Apollo Global Management and the insurance company it helped to create, Athene Holding, illustrate many of the problems. Apollo was, in many ways, culturally ill suited to run a staid insurance company. Profiles of Apollo tended to describe it as "bare-knuckled," "cutthroat," and "rough-edged," adjectives describing a culture at odds with the quiet, conservative business of taking premiums and paying out policies.[61] It was the kind of place where an employee who failed to respond to a boss's Saturday morning emails might get a follow-up "?" ten minutes later,[62] where employees worked twenty-hour days,[63] and where, when one of the firm's original founders finally resigned, employees hummed "Ding-Dong! The Witch Is Dead" from *The Wizard of Oz*.[64] Moreover, it was a place riven with controversy. In 2020, the *New York Times* revealed that Leon Black, Apollo's cofounder and CEO, had paid the financier and sex offender Jeffrey Epstein $158 million for supposed tax and estate planning services.[65] As reported in Bloomberg, Black was not accused of being involved in Epstein's criminal activities, and an internal investigation by an independent law firm found no connection between Black and Epstein's illegal activity. Observers were incredulous, however, at the purported justification for the payments, given that Epstein, in fact, had no tax or estate planning training.[66] The next year, a former model accused Black of sexual assault and sued him for defamation.[67] Black countersued and alleged that the woman's case was, in fact, orchestrated by another cofounder—Josh Harris—who sought to steal his job. The whole crisis resulted in both Black and Harris leaving the firm they founded and suggested that Apollo was, in culture and values, a poor fit for an industry—insurance—that rested on caution, conservatism, and good judgment.

Nevertheless, Apollo became a private equity leader in the insurance industry, beginning with its decision, in 2009, to provide funding to create Athene. Athene's business model was, in a sense, simple: it would buy the policies that other insurers no longer wanted or the pension obligations that companies could no longer afford. It would then invest the money that policyholders and pensioners gave them every month or year into investments that, it hoped, would earn more than it would have to pay when those policies came due.[68] Over a decade, Athene bought up plans and whole insurers, and took on the pensions of companies like Lockheed Martin[69] and JC Penney.[70] At the same time, Apollo became increasingly entwined with the insurer: by 2021, Athene provided Apollo with 40 percent of its assets under management—that is, the money it could use to invest in projects—and 30 percent of its revenue from fees.[71] That year, Apollo decided to buy a majority stake in Athene outright.

Athene and Apollo's operations raised a number of concerns. For one, Athene's business model was predicated on earning more

money than other insurers in large part by buying "alternative assets" like Apollo's own private equity and debt funds.[72] These were
more profitable than other staid investments. But they were also
riskier. And the insurance industry, perhaps more than virtually
any other, feared risk.

For another, according to Tom Gober, an independent forensic account who focused on fraud in the insurance industry,[73]
Athene dramatically increased its liabilities—that is, its obligations
to policyholders—without increasing its surplus: the excess of its
assets over its obligations. Between 2020 and 2021, the company's
liabilities increased by nearly $30 billion to $105 billion. At the
same time, its surplus declined from 1.7 percent of liabilities to 1.2
percent.[74] This was exceedingly small: according to Gober, an insurance company's average surplus was over 5 percent and could
go as high as 25 percent.[75] This meant that only a small percentage of Athene's investments needed to sour before, legally, the state
would be required to take it over.

Finally, according to Gober, Athene "ceded," or sold, over $50
billion in liabilities to its own offshore affiliates. Generally, offshore affiliates existed in jurisdictions where accounting standards
were looser and capital requirements were lower.[76] This meant that
a large portion of Athene's business was managed in places that
likely allowed even riskier investing strategies than those permitted in the United States.

Together, this meant that, under Apollo's watch, Athene was
allegedly investing in riskier assets, while keeping ever less capital on hand if those investments soured. At the same time, it was
moving more of its business offshore, where even riskier behavior
was allowed. While this did not spell disaster, it certainly increased
the chances that disaster could occur. And it was all overseen by a
company—Apollo—whose culture was wildly at odds with that
of the insurance industry.

So what would happen if Athene, or any private equity–
owned insurance company, collapsed? State guaranty organizations
would, as their names suggest, guarantee insurance policies up to a
certain point. But these insurers do not cover the entirety of claim

holders' policies—generally they pay only up to $300,000[77]—and variable annuity programs (those whose payments fluctuate with the performance of their investments) are not covered at all.[78] Moreover, guaranty organizations are funded with payments by other insurers. So, when an insurance company fails, it is the more responsible, surviving insurers who must pay the costs. This means that while private equity firms such as Apollo use insurance companies like Athene to extract fees and fund various investments, if those investments sour, it will be others—other, more responsible companies, and other, unsuspecting policyholders—who will bear the cost.

✳

BUT INSURANCE WAS only a small part of private equity's quest for more assets. The industry also lobbied—successfully—to access 401(k) funds, including, possibly someday, your own. This change matters because the money that private equity firms need to finance their acquisitions and other endeavors has traditionally come from the very rich, from endowments and sovereign wealth funds, and from pension funds. But in recent years, the industry largely exhausted these resources.[79] In search of new pools of money, firms looked to 401(k) funds. Such funds historically had not invested in private equity, as courts and regulators were generally skeptical about the appropriateness of such investments for retirees. For unlike stocks and bonds, investments in private equity funds were generally "illiquid"—that is, they could not be withdrawn whenever people needed them. Private equity firms also often charged high fees that were difficult to comprehend, and potentially, their investments were riskier than those in the stock market.

Nothing categorically prevented managers of retirement funds from investing in companies like Blackstone and Carlyle, but few did, for fear of being sued over investments gone bad. To get 401(k) money, private equity firms needed help from the government to insulate these funds from lawsuits. And that's exactly what they did, with the help of two men—Eugene Scalia and Jay Clayton—who served as secretary of labor and chairman of the SEC, respectively, during the Trump administration.

Scalia is the son of the late Supreme Court justice and inherited his father's abiding support for big corporations. At the law firm of Gibson Dunn, which primarily defended large companies, Scalia's clients included Bank of America, Goldman Sachs, Facebook, and Walmart.[80] He developed a particular specialty defending businesses in suits brought by their employees and the government. Among other accomplishments, he defended UPS from a lawsuit brought by workers injured on the job[81] and represented SeaWorld in a lawsuit by the government after one of its whales killed a trainer. He was well compensated for this work and earned over $6 million in the roughly year and a half before President Trump nominated him to serve as secretary of labor.[82] Once in government, Scalia continued to be a fierce advocate for companies and against employees: among other things, he reduced COVID-19 reporting requirements for companies[83] while at the same time opposing extended unemployment benefits for workers.[84]

Scalia's partner in government, Jay Clayton, was a corporate lawyer before President Trump appointed him chairman of the SEC. Like Scalia, Clayton represented big businesses, though his practice skewed toward dealmaking on behalf of finance and private equity firms.[85] And like Scalia, Clayton was rich: he enjoyed membership in the Philadelphia Cricket Club (the nation's oldest country club),[86] invested with a half-dozen leading private equity firms,[87] and, with his wife, accumulated assets worth between $12 and $47 million.[88] Lastly, like Scalia, Clayton advocated for business while in government. During his tenure as chairman, the SEC's enforcement actions dropped dramatically: in one year, it brought just thirty-one insider trading cases, the lowest level since 1996.[89] "That means they're not trying," Bartlett Naylor of Public Citizen told NPR. "That means they told the cops to go play canasta instead of doing their job."[90]

Clayton fought to expand private equity's access to ordinary investors' money. In an interview with, of all people, the cofounder of the private equity firm the Carlyle Group, David

Rubenstein, Clayton enthused about the idea of giving private equity firms access to retirees' funds. "[R]etirement money in the defined-contribution [i.e., 401(k)] plan doesn't have the same investment opportunities that a defined-benefit [i.e., pension] plan has, even though they're both retirement dollars," he complained.[91] Rubenstein, in what looked a lot like lobbying out in public, agreed: 401(k) managers should probably be allowed to invest some money in private equity firms, he said, even if some of the money was "lost or didn't do as well."[92]

And so Clayton worked with Scalia to give firms like Rubenstein's Carlyle access to ordinary investors' money.[93] In 2020, with the support of both Clayton and Scalia, the Department of Labor issued a letter that generally permitted funds that managed 401(k)s to invest part of their clients' assets with private equity firms.[94] The letter didn't change any laws or regulations, but it endorsed fund managers' decisions to invest in private equity. With the government's imprimatur, this alone essentially insulated funds from lawsuits by ordinary people if and when their investments ever went bad.

The letter was a huge boon to private equity. At the time it was issued, the industry had about $4 trillion in assets under management;[95] 401(k) funds had about $6 trillion.[96] Even if the industry got only a small fraction of that money, it would expand firms' total assets under management dramatically. Years earlier, Stephen Schwarzman of Blackstone had gushed that "in life you have to have a dream," and "one of the dreams" was to access ordinary investors' money.[97] That dream was now a reality. The industry's lobbying organization said that the letter would "give more hardworking Americans expanded access to private markets."[98] Scalia observed that it "helps level the playing field for ordinary investors,"[99] and Clayton enthused that the letter would give "Main Street investors" a "choice" to invest in the private markets. Consumer groups were far less sanguine. "Secretary Scalia is still working for his former clients," Barbara Roper of the Consumer Federation of America complained.[100] "This is a multipronged attack on Americans' retirement security."[101] With the danger posed by private equity—its illiquidity, its fees, and its volatility—she was likely right.

Clayton and Scalia were well compensated after their government work. Within months of leaving office, Clayton was appointed to the newly created position of lead independent director at Apollo Global Management.[102] Shortly thereafter, as Apollo's CEO and chairman Leon Black was consumed by scandal, Clayton was named to replace Black as nonexecutive chairman of the company.[103] Scalia, meanwhile, returned to his old law firm, Gibson Dunn, where he cochaired its regulatory practice[104] and continued to write about his passion: cutting unemployment benefits for workers.[105]

✳

WHAT WILL HAPPEN now that private equity has all this money? *First*, people's retirement accounts may be less secure. Investments in private equity firms are simply less transparent than those in, say, public companies. Our history of financial crises teaches that opacity inevitably leads to riskier investments, and risky investments, by definition, sometimes fail. *Second*, with more cash but not necessarily more companies to buy, private equity firms may compete more vigorously on the same deals. The value of a business is often determined in part by a "multiple" of its cash flow: a business might be worth three, four, or five times however much it makes in a year. Competition among firms has increased these multiples to such an extent that, by 2020, average deal valuations were twelve times the common measure of cash flow, higher than the previous peak in 2007.[106] Private equity firms are also just buying worse companies. In 2019, for the first time ever, a majority of private equity investments went to unprofitable companies. With these companies forced to service the debt that private equity firms load onto them, this will all increase the odds that the companies themselves will fail.

More generally, private equity firms will continue to take on many of the tasks that investment banks had before the Great Recession. With ever more money under their management to finance their various adventures, this poses systemic risks for the economy. But unlike the Great Recession, private equity firms may have externalized many of the risks they create. If one of their businesses fails, private equity firms may lose their management fees and their investment in the company. But the majority—likely the vast majority—of the losses will be absorbed by employees, investors, and lenders,[107] since private equity firms generally aren't liable for the debts of their funds. The result: in a future financial crisis, the companies that private equity firms own may fail, but the private equity firms themselves may survive and even thrive.

There are things that can be done to reverse this. To push companies out of the private credit markets and toward the public markets, the SEC can revise Regulation D, which permits broad solicitations of private money, and Rule 144A, which permits the resale of private debt. To reduce risks to retirees and investors, the Department of Labor can rescind its letter granting private equity firms access to 401(k)s, and state regulators can reject future private equity acquisitions of insurance companies. To its credit, the Biden administration added a follow-up letter, generally limiting private equity investments to those 401(k) managers that already had experience working with private equity.[108] But the new letter contained loopholes so large that Bloomberg concluded that "the fundamentals of the [original] letter remained untouched."[109]

More systematically, the Federal Reserve, alongside other regulators, should prohibit the banks they regulate from making loans to private equity firms that would result in excessive leverage to companies. The Financial Stability Oversight Council, part of the Treasury Department, should designate the largest private equity firms as systemically important, subjecting them to greater oversight. And state insurance regulators should cast a skeptical eye upon further acquisitions of insurance companies by these firms. Together, these actions would contain the metastasization of private equity to disparate industries and limit the damage that such expansion might cause.

We have to move quickly. As private equity firms get used to the rules promulgated by the Trump administration, it will become harder and harder to undo them. It is possible to do so and prevent private equity firms from repeating the mistakes of the investment banks a generation ago. But we have to act now.

CHAPTER SEVEN

CAPTIVE AUDIENCE

Private Equity in Prisons

America's prisons are increasingly operated by private equity firms. If you're incarcerated today, the food you eat at the cafeteria or buy at the commissary may be served by the Keefe Group or Trinity Services Group, both of which are owned by the private equity firm H.I.G. Capital.[1] If you call your lawyer or a loved one, you will likely do so on a phone operated by Securus Technologies (owned by Platinum Equity),[2] ICSolutions (H.I.G.),[3] or Global Tel Link (American Securities).[4] If you get sick, the care you receive may be administered by Wellpath (H.I.G.)[5] or Corizon Health (Flacks Group).[6] If you're placed under house arrest, the ankle monitor you wear may be operated by an Apax Partners company.[7] And if you are given a debit card with your prison wages upon release,[8] it may be managed by a business owned by Platinum Equity.[9]

Along the way, you may pay thousands of dollars to these companies for the cost of your own incarceration: money to the commissary, money to place a phone call or send an email, money to post bail, and money to access your own wages. You may even pay money for every minute you read an e-book,[10] a sort of proto-privatization of the prison library system.

The story of private equity's privatization of prison services is infuriating in its own right. But it is also illustrative of the industry's broader business model, for it shows how, when facing a captive audience, firms are willing—eager, even—to eviscerate the services they offer, until the companies they buy give the bare minimum required for subsistence and survival, and sometimes less. While this is seen most clearly in the prison industry, private equity's perspective is not exclusive to it. As other chapters explain, it is fundamental to these firms' philosophies to raise prices and cut care to a natural breaking point, and with short investment horizons, they do so with little regard for the long-term consequences. Unfortunately—and here again, prisons are illustrative but not exclusive—this is all happening with the support of local governments, whose contracts with private equity firms save, and often generate, money for police and sheriffs' offices. In fact, local law enforcement agencies have become private equity's strongest advocates, defending the industry and shielding it from scrutiny and regulation. The entwining of private equity and government is not unique, but in prisons, it finds its nadir.

As for the incarceration industry itself, this trend is without meaningful precedent. In America, we have a long history of debtors' prisons: punishments for those who could not pay their debts and deterrents for those who might be similarly situated. These were in time replaced with the civil bankruptcy code, which allowed people to discharge their debts without going to prison.[11] We also have a dark history of convict leasing, where prisoners— overwhelmingly African American men—were lent out as labor to private companies.[12] But only rarely have we actually charged prisoners for their own incarceration, as most inmates lacked the ability to pay for their imprisonment.[13] Yet now, that is precisely what we are doing, with prisoners' and their families' money going not primarily to the government but to companies and, in particular, to companies owned by private equity firms.

These firms are attracted to prison services for a number of reasons. *First*, prison services tend to offer steady cash flows through government contracts, which private equity firms are adept at landing. *Second*, these businesses service a literally captive audience—prisoners—who will tolerate, because they must, steep price increases and deep quality cuts. In other words, prison services can be gutted, largely without consequence. *Third*, prisons are run by government agencies that can be co-opted to become firms' allies and advocates. To emphasize, while these traits attract private equity to prisons, they exist in so many other industries described in this book: health care, housing, nursing homes, and so much else. In other words, what private equity firms do to prisoners, they may someday hope to do to you.

✳

THE MOST PUBLIC part of this story has been private equity firms' purchase of prison phone companies. (Unless otherwise indicated, I use the terms *jail* and *prison* interchangeably, though jails are typically where people are held after being newly arrested, while awaiting trial, or to serve short sentences. Prisons are generally where people convicted of crimes serve their sentences.) For decades, inmates were generally allowed only a few collect calls a year, until 1973, when the Federal Bureau of Prisons recommended expanding inmates' access to phones, citing evidence of increased recidivism among people who were isolated from their families and communities.[14] Federal prisons loosened their restrictions on calls, followed by state and local facilities, and for a decade, prisoners were able to reach their loved ones at rates comparable to those on the outside, as billing was handled by AT&T. But after the breakup of America's telephone monopoly and a favorable deregulatory ruling from the Federal Communications Commission (FCC) in the early 1990s,[15] companies like Sprint and MCI entered the prison communications business, followed by smaller, niche competitors,[16] like Securus Technologies and Global Tel Link. Under their contracts, governments didn't pay these companies for their services. Rather, it was the opposite: the companies paid the prisons for the privilege to operate the phone systems and made their money by charging prisoners for their calls. This created a perverse incentive system: prison phone companies were encouraged not to lower their rates but to raise them so that correctional facilities got as much money as possible.[17]

At this point, private equity got in the game, attracted to an industry with steady cash flows and a literally captive audience. In 2004, H.I.G. Capital bought the company that became Securus,[18] which it sold to Castle Harlan in 2011,[19] who sold it to ABRY Partners in 2013,[20] who sold it in turn to Platinum Equity in 2017.[21] Similar dances occurred with the other leading phone companies: Global Tel Link (now ViaPath Technologies) is now owned by the private equity firm American Securities,[22] and ICSolutions was most recently owned by H.I.G. Capital.[23]

This was a great deal for prisons, which were allegedly offered as much as 94 percent of the revenue that phone companies made from inmates' calls.[24] With prisons and companies aligned, costs for inmates spiraled. Many states charged $12 or more for a fifteen-minute call,[25] and in one Arkansas jail, the cost reached nearly $25.[26] Companies also charged various fees for users to pay their bills by credit card, to pay by phone, to process bills, and to variously create, maintain, or close accounts.[27] One former inmate told the *Detroit Free Press* that he spent $3,000 on calls over just five months to keep in touch with his family and maintain a rental property business.[28] "Life didn't stop because I was in jail," he said.[29] Another limited his calls to only the most urgent situations, going months without talking to his four- and five-year-old children so that his family could afford childcare and other expenses. "The longer you've been in prison, the more distant you become to the outside world," yet another former inmate told The Verge.[30] "People can't afford you anymore."[31]

Moreover, the costs of these calls were borne largely by those least able to pay. Family members—women in particular—overwhelmingly shouldered the burden of prison phone calls, and one-third of these family members went into debt to pay for them.[32] "It's death by a thousand pennies," one woman, who founded a support group for incarcerated family members, told the *Nation*. "Most people around here just don't have a lot of pennies to spare."[33]

This was all in contrast to the people who profited from these calls. It is worth spending a moment to focus on just one: Tom Gores, whose private equity firm, Platinum Equity, owns Securus. Gores is an American success story, a child of immigrants who formed Platinum Equity by cold-calling businesses to ask if they had divisions they wanted to sell off.[34] He bought his first business for $200,000 and flipped it to profitability in six months.[35] Over the years, Gores purchased dozens of companies, including the *San Diego Union-Tribune*,[36] the textbook publisher McGraw-Hill,[37] and the yearbook and class ring company Jostens.[38] Along the way he became fabulously rich, and his 90,000-square-foot office in Beverly Hills featured marble and mahogany paneling, paintings by Joan Miró and Alexander Calder, and a courtyard fountain.[39] In 2016, he bought a home in Los Angeles for $100 million,[40] whose structures covered two acres and in which a single bedroom spanned 5,300 square feet, about twice the size of an average American home.[41] The estate had two outdoor pools (and inside, a water wall flowing into a third), a hair salon with manicure and pedicure stations, and a theater with a dedicated valet entrance.[42]

In 2017, shortly after buying his mansion, Gores, through his firm, bought Securus for $1.5 billion.[43] His purchase would have likely generated little interest—another private equity billionaire buying another prison services company—were it not for the fact that he'd also bought the Detroit Pistons a few years before. Gores apparently was not an adept manager, as he traded young players who would succeed elsewhere for established ones who nevertheless failed to win the Pistons a title.[44] But Gores did demonstrate genuine empathy and support for the community. He donated $10 million to address the Flint water crisis.[45] He moved the team from suburban Auburn Hills back to downtown Detroit.[46] And after the killings of Breonna Taylor, George Floyd, and Ahmaud Arbery, Gores issued a statement in support of racial justice and committed to specific local initiatives.[47]

In light of these actions, his purchase of a prison phone company—one that profited from a criminal justice system that disproportionately affected people of color—seemed wildly hypocritical. And here, Bianca Tylek and her organization, Worth Rises, were able to capitalize on this hypocrisy. Tylek was a criminal justice reform advocate who founded Worth Rises after graduating from law school in 2016. She had spent the first part of her career working for Morgan Stanley and Citibank, and the way her conversation was littered with profanity was evidence of her time in the finance industry. Her experience also meant that she was perhaps uniquely capable among activists of understanding private equity and its weaknesses. "In banking, I learned a skill set to build companies that I now use to dismantle them," she said.[48]

In 2018, Worth Rises successfully pushed the FCC to block Securus's proposed acquisition of one of its last remaining competitors, ICSolutions. The group argued that the merger would result in just two companies controlling 90 percent of the prison phone market and would "lead to fewer options for facilities and higher rates for the end consumers, [namely,] those with incarcerated loved ones."[49] The FCC apparently agreed, and forced Securus to abandon the deal.[50]

Worth Rises then turned to lobby Platinum Equity's investors, exploiting a quirk in the industry that made private equity more susceptible to influence than, say, most public companies, whose investors tend to be dispersed. If you have a 401(k), for instance, your money may be invested in hundreds of different businesses. In contrast, private equity firms typically draw from a smaller number of large institutional investors, often public pension funds, and these pension funds allow public comments before making investment decisions. Worth Rises seized on this fact and lobbied three large pension funds that were considering investing with Platinum Equity. In a major victory, one of them—Pennsylvania's public employee fund—chose not to invest a reported $150 million with the private equity firm.[51] Dave Fillman, the chairman of the fund's board, said that "I've been on this board for about 20 years, and I've never seen the amount of negative press on a firm that I've seen here today."[52] He said he feared Platinum would invest in some other "messed up" company "that we're not going to know about."[53]

The public pressure campaign continued. In September 2020, Worth Rises and another nonprofit wrote a letter to the Los Angeles County Museum of Art, opposing Gores's membership on the museum's board.[54] After some hemming and hawing, Gores resigned. A few months later, the organization took out a full-page ad in the *New York Times*, addressed to the commissioner of the NBA and the league's various owners, asking, "If black lives matter, what are you doing about Detroit Pistons owner Tom Gores?"[55] Gores said of the ad, "it hurts,"[56] and later conceded that the prison telephone business should probably be run by nonprofits.[57] It was an understandable but hollow statement, given that Gores was perhaps the only person in the world capable of making that happen.

And so, Worth Rises and other advocacy organizations continued to push their agenda at the local level and in the courts. San Francisco,[58] New York,[59] and Connecticut[60] all passed bills to make phone calls free for inmates, all at Worth Rises's urging. At the same time, the nonprofit Justice Catalyst and a coalition of other groups sued Securus and Global Tel Link in federal district court, alleging that the companies conspired to raise prices. (The defendants largely denied the allegations and the litigation remains ongoing.)[61] Separately, hundreds of lawyers sued Securus for illegally recording privileged phone calls.[62] Communications between lawyers and their clients generally are constitutionally protected, but 750 attorneys in and around Kansas alleged that Securus had a widespread policy of recording their conversations with inmates. Securus and a private prison operator ultimately agreed to settle the case for $3.7 million, while similar lawsuits began in Maine, Texas, Kansas, and California.[63]

Faced with all this pressure, over the course of 2020, Gores and Securus announced a number of new measures. They would give away $3 million to reduce recidivism and improve prisoner reentry,[64] they would continue to reduce the cost of calls,[65] and Gores himself would give away his personal profits from the company.[66] Gores told the *Detroit Free Press*, with considerable self-importance, that "ultimately it'll be a blessing that I'm in there and that somebody cares about what's happening."[67] But Tylek responded, "We're not asking you to come save people; we're asking you to stop taking from them."[68] She added, "So before you can argue that you want to do something good and all these things, you have to stop doing the harm that you're trying to unwind. Those two things can't operate in the same space."[69] Thus far, Gores hasn't heeded Tylek's direction: he has not yet sold Securus—now rebranded Aventiv Technologies—nor has he shut it down. It remains, as of this writing, a part of Platinum Equity's portfolio.[70]

＊

THE GRASSROOTS EFFORTS to lower Securus's outrageous prices were heartening, but they were necessitated by a twenty-year, largely unsuccessful movement to regulate these companies at the federal level. In 2001, a group of inmates and their family members sued the leading prison phone companies, including the company that became Securus,[71] alleging that their high costs violated inmates' constitutional rights.[72] Later that year, a court ruled that the lawsuit was premature and that the plaintiffs would need to first seek redress through the Federal Communications Commission. But under President Bush's appointees, the FCC took no action, and for years the matter lingered, until finally Barack Obama was elected president and appointed Mignon Clyburn as a new commissioner. Clyburn was one of the few African American members in the commission's history, and after meeting with activists, she took a particular interest in the issue of prison phone call costs. It took barely half an hour, she said, to convince her of the importance of the matter, which disproportionately affected families of color and which later she described as a "tax on pain."[73] Prison phone systems, she said, were "the smartest, most evil way to make money."[74]

Clyburn pushed the FCC to regulate the cost of prison calls, a move that, unsurprisingly, Securus and its peers opposed. They were joined in opposition by the National Sheriffs' Association, which represented a powerful constituency. "Who is going to go against the sheriffs of these counties?" asked Clyburn.[75] "Who is going to go against the wardens?"[76] In comments to the FCC, the sheriffs threatened that taxes could rise if rates were reduced, or that prison phone calls could be banned entirely.[77] It did not need to be said—though, inexplicably, the sheriffs said it—that they received financial benefits from their arrangement with the companies.[78] (Even today, the Sheriffs' Association lists Global Tel Link—now Viapath Technologies—as one of its "Diamond Level" corporate partners, which entitles it to a private dinner with the association's executive committee and a reception with its board of directors.)[79] In other words, the Sheriffs' Association took Securus's money and became one of its most vocal and powerful advocates.

Yet even in the face of all this lobbying by law enforcement and the phone companies, in 2013 Clyburn convinced her fellow commissioners to place strong limits on the rates for such calls.[80] Under the new rules, collect calls would cost twenty-five cents a minute. It was an enormous accomplishment and one that the phone companies and their allies in state government sued to stop. But before a court could even reach a decision, Donald Trump was elected president and appointed a former Verizon lawyer, Ajit Pai, as chairman of the FCC. One week later, in a highly unusual move, Pai said that the commission would refuse to defend much of its own regulation.[81]

Pai's decision was controversial: in private practice, Securus had been one of his clients,[82] and in 2017, as chairman, he voted to approve Platinum Equity's acquisition of the company.[83] (Later, Pai left the commission to work for another private equity firm.[84]) Clyburn called Pai's decision not to defend the rule "one of the most painful times of my life."[85] Without the government to argue for its own proposal, an appeals court held that the FCC lacked the authority to regulate intrastate prison phone calls, rendering the rule largely toothless.[86] Clyburn said the decision marked "a sad day for the more than 2.7 million children in this country with at least one incarcerated parent."[87]

In 2021, with a newly reconstituted commission under President Biden, the FCC voted unanimously to lower the rates for interstate—as opposed to intrastate—calls.[88] But because the vast majority of prison calls are reportedly made in state,[89] the action affected only a portion of the business of these companies. Meanwhile, members of Congress proposed legislation to regulate intrastate calls,[90] but the bills have languished in committee.

Looking back on the whole reform effort, Clyburn lamented the entrenched forces, including local law enforcement, who defended the current system. "There are just too many critical people that are being enriched," she said.[91] "There is a dependence on this flow of income. Those who have become dependent on it are not going to give it up."[92] The whole saga showed how hard it was to regulate these companies at the federal level and explained why activists focused so much on action by states and cities. A sclerotic administrative process, a skeptical court, and occasionally industry-friendly leadership all make it exceedingly difficult to enact national reforms.

Finally, the story shows how prison phone companies and local law enforcement allied with one another in a mutually beneficial financial partnership, a story that continues today. In recent years, Securus and Global Tel Link have expanded to sell video teleconferencing services to prisoners. In theory, this could have been a boon to inmates, who now could talk to loved ones who couldn't visit in person. But unsurprisingly, these companies demanded extraordinary sums for their services. Securus's subsidiary, JPay, for instance, charged $12.95 for a half-hour call in Washington state.[93] Prisoners there earned between 36 cents and $2.70 per hour,[94] meaning that a single thirty-minute call could cost nearly a week's wages.

Not that inmates had much of a choice. For a time, in its contracts with law enforcement, Securus required that prisons using their teleconferencing service actually stop in-person visits.[95] In Keene, New Hampshire, for instance, when the local jail signed a teleconferencing contract with Securus, it agreed to ban all in-person visits with family members.[96] One mother described the process of going to the jail to "visit" her son, not directly in person or even separated by plexiglass but through a small screen. During the visit the sound often failed and the video frequently froze. "I can't stand it, because he's on the screen in front of me, and I can't touch him," she told NPR.[97]

Under heavy criticism, in 2015, Securus struck this term from its contracts, and delegated the decision to local authorities.[98] But the local authorities had the same incentives as Securus because they were getting a slice of the money coming from the teleconferencing services. So even after the company stopped demanding that prisons end in-person visits, according to the nonprofit news organization The Appeal, prisons continued to do so voluntarily.[99] The companies and prisons, it seems, had fully allied with one another to the harm of inmates and their families.

These stories were upsetting, but they were not isolated to prisons, as firms like Platinum Equity and H.I.G. cut the quality of care and otherwise mismanaged other companies in their portfolios. For instance, as detailed in Chapter 8, Platinum's portfolio company, Transworld Systems, was fined millions of dollars for mishandling students' loan accounts. H.I.G. Capital, meanwhile, paid nearly $20 million to resolve claims that a mental health company it owned provided services with unlicensed and unqualified staff.[100] Increasing prices and slashing the quality of the services their companies provided was central to these firms' business models. And if their tactics in prison services seemed extreme, it was only because inmates had even less ability to fight back than did, say, student borrowers and mental health patients.

※

PHONES ARE JUST one star in the constellation of private equity's rollup of prison services. For example, H.I.G. Capital's portfolio companies Keefe Group and Trinity Services increasingly provide the food that inmates eat in cafeterias and commissaries. While these companies offer their services across the country, it is instructive to look at the experiment in just one state: Michigan. There, the government moved to privatize its prison food services in 2013,[101] and in 2015, contracted H.I.G.-owned Trinity Services to provide meals. It was quickly apparent that the quality of the food that Trinity offered was appalling. On at least three occasions, Trinity served food with maggots in it, and other times served food contaminated with mold and "crunchy dirt." One former Trinity employee, Steve Pine, said that he was fired for refusing to serve about one hundred bags of rotten potatoes.[102] "It was the most disgusting thing I've seen in my life," Pine told the *Detroit Free Press*. "You could smell them...they had black and green mold all over them."[103] Another former corrections officer told Salon, "It was a human atrocity against the inmates, in my opinion." He added, "The rotten garbage that was being served, plus the way they were allowing it to be prepared. It was an atrocity."[104]

However terrible the food was, at times, there wasn't enough of it.[105] Under its cafeteria contract, Trinity was paid based on the number of prisoners in the facilities rather than the number of meals it served.[106] In theory, this saved effort in tracking how many meals were served. But it also subtly changed Trinity's incentives, for it meant that even if the meals were so bad that prisoners would not or could not eat them, the company would still be paid. Through another portfolio company, Trinity's private equity owner also owned the contract for the commissaries, where prisoners paid for food and supplies. Together, this created a perverse incentive system to reduce the quantity and quality of cafeteria meals in order to push inmates to pay for commissary food. As such, inmates complained to Detroit's *Metro Times* that Trinity wasn't serving food with the minimum calories required by law.[107] "[W]hen a person goes hungry," said one inmate, "the only thing it does is make them angry."[108]

Prisoners' complaints about the food actually helped to incite a prison riot, in which inmates started a fire, smashed windows and sinks, and barricaded themselves into their housing areas.[109] Officers with pepper bomb–loaded guns were sent to quell the uprising, reportedly the first time the state had to quash a riot since 1981. The riot cost the Michigan government about $900,000.[110] And these weren't the only problems with Trinity. The company had enormous staff turnover—one Trinity employee was fired for having sex with an inmate—and over one hundred of its other employees were placed on "stop orders" for violating prison rules.[111] Ultimately, Michigan's governor announced that the state would no longer rely on Trinity for food services.[112] The experiment with private equity–owned privatization of prison food in that state had failed.[113]

Michigan wasn't the only state that used Trinity. In Arizona, the company allegedly served meat marked "not fit for human consumption."[114] The meat, supposedly turkey, had already turned green, and one inmate told the *Phoenix New Times* that "[w]e would constantly be gagging from the smell that seeped out."[115] In Ohio, Trinity reportedly served chicken labeled "for further processing only."[116] In Utah, it served food with maggots, mold, and dirt.[117] And in Atlanta, where Trinity provided food services, prisoners complained about being severely undernourished. One inmate said that he regularly ate toothpaste and toilet paper to ease his hunger pangs.[118] Another repeatedly filed a complaint with a single word: "Hungry."[119] In a system that served only two meals a day, several inmates said that they lost twenty pounds or more over just a few months.

In all these cases, the basic logic of private equity applied: with a captive audience and steady cash flows, firms' portfolio companies could serve, quite literally, inedible food without consequence. Of course, private equity firms and their businesses might be more responsible if they faced legal consequences for their actions, and lots of prisoners have sued to stop various mistreatments. But the law has developed in ways unfavorable to prisoners and favorable to governments and prison service companies. For one thing, the Prison Litigation Reform Act required prisoners to exhaust their administrative remedies before bringing their challenges to court,[120] a long and potentially fruitless process. For another, a forgiving body of case law has developed for prison food providers, which allows that "isolated incidents" of rodents or insects appearing near food do not violate the Eighth Amendment's ban on cruel and unusual punishment.[121] Moreover, to successfully sue the companies (as opposed to individual employees), prisoners must generally show that the companies were, in effect, acting as arms of the state[122] and that they had unconstitutional policies, as opposed to merely the occasional impermissible incident.[123] Finally, to recover damages not just from the companies but their private equity owners, plaintiffs must often show that a given company and private equity firm are so intertwined that their "separate personalities do not exist," a difficult proposition to prove.[124]

The cumulative effect of these decisions was to make it enormously difficult for prisoners to successfully sue and recover damages for atrocious, unsafe, or insufficient food. This difficulty became a near impossibility when trying to hold private equity owners responsible as well. Without the possibility of consequences, firms had no incentive other than to provide the worst food at the cheapest prices to prisoners. It saved money, and no matter the harm to people, the private equity firms themselves would be fine.

More than food, private equity's flaws were most concerning in their acquisitions of prison health care companies. The industry owed its modern genesis to the Supreme Court, which, in its 1976 decision *Estelle v. Gamble*, established prisoners' constitutional right to health care. That case concerned J. W. Gamble, a Texas inmate who was injured while working on loan at a local textile mill.[125] Gamble's doctors gave him painkillers for the injury but failed to perform an X-ray, and when Gamble refused to work further, was moved to solitary confinement. Gamble protested his treatment in a case that wound its way to the Supreme Court and argued that his inadequate care was an unconstitutional violation of the Eighth Amendment's prohibition on cruel and unusual punishment. The Supreme Court agreed and announced that the "deliberate indifference to serious medical needs of prisoners" violated the Constitution. Gamble's case thus created a legal minimum of care for prisoners in America (Gamble himself did not benefit, as a lower court found that his care was not so poor as to justify compensation. He was later murdered by a fellow prisoner). But correctional facilities struggled to adapt to this constitutional guarantee of basic health care, and after the widespread closure of mental health hospitals in the 1990s and 2000s, many people who would have wound up in such facilities went to jail.[126] Increasingly, prisons turned to private companies to offer health care services, and by 2018, 62 percent of surveyed jails used some sort of private health care service.

Today, the two leading correctional health care companies—Wellpath and Corizon Health—are owned by private equity firms (H.I.G. Capital and BlueMountain Capital Management, respectively). Wellpath cares for about 250,000 prisoners, and Corizon has responsibility for 180,000.[127] As with phone and food services, these companies have disastrous contractual incentives. They are often paid a flat rate based on the number of prisoners in a facility and are thus incentivized to keep costs low. Unsurprisingly, there are any number of examples of these companies badly mishandling or ignoring prisoners' health problems, with horrible results. In Arizona, for instance, a fifty-nine-year-old inmate allegedly died after nurses ignored his cries for help, even while "weeping lesions" on his body were covered with flies.[128] At the time, the state's prison health care services were administered by Corizon.[129] Another inmate wrote a "notice of impending death" when his cancer went untreated,[130] also by Corizon.[131] "Now because of there [sic] delay, I may be luckey [sic] to be alive for 30 days," he wrote.[132] He was dead in a month. Another lawsuit alleged that a prisoner died in 2017 from a rare fungal infection (Corizon managed his care).[133] The inmate allegedly suffered a "staggeringly slow, physically and mentally excruciating death."[134] (Before trial, Corizon successfully had the case dismissed by disqualifying the expert witness for the inmate's mother, making her unable to prosecute her claim.)[135] In New York's Westchester County, a thirty-six-year-old man died of a heart attack after a nurse for Correct Care Solutions (the predecessor to Wellpath) said that he was faking his symptoms.[136] And in another case involving Correct Care Solutions, a mentally ill woman alerted staff that she was having contractions. Staff failed to come to her aid, and she was forced to give birth in her cell, alone.[137]

Overall, Corizon and Wellpath were sued about 1,500 times in just five years,[138] not just for individual harms like the ones above but for broader systemic failings too. In Maine, for instance, a class action lawsuit alleged that Wellpath treated just 3 of the more than 580 inmates who were diagnosed with hepatitis C, a disease that can damage and eventually destroy liver function.[139] Instead, Wellpath and the department of corrections had an apparent policy, not of preventing the disease's progression but of treating only those people who already showed signs of extreme liver damage. The state ultimately settled the class action lawsuit and agreed to treat all inmates who suffered from the disease. Elsewhere, in Pierce County, outside Seattle, Washington, prison officials alleged that medical professionals employed by the private equity–owned Correct Care Solutions were not, in fact, licensed to practice in the state and "had to be escorted out of the jail by corrections staff."[140] Insufficient management and inadequate training "resulted in literally weekly turnover," according to the county.[141] The company even lacked enough medications to treat patients, with a nursing director announcing a "drug holiday" for a week.[142] A jury eventually awarded the county nearly $2 million for the company's negligence.[143]

But if private equity–owned health care companies weren't doing a good job, why were they so dominant? In essence, these companies' real product may not be their health care services but the indemnification they provide state and local governments.[144] Corizon and Wellpath widely agree to defend prisoners' claims against them, relieving governments of some of the burden of costly litigation. These companies often rely on the same law firms for their defenses[145] and so can bring to bear a national litigation strategy against individual defendants. The likely result: more wins, fewer losses, and less litigation for governments to worry about. As Todd Murphy, the business development director for one of Wellpath's predecessor companies,[146] put it, "the biggest thing we do is indemnify the county against risk and reliability, [and] do everything we can to keep them out of trouble."[147]

And if private equity firms insulate governments from legal liability, they also insulate themselves too. In one case, for instance, an incarcerated man died of sepsis while under the general care of

Wellpath.[148] When his estate sued Wellpath's owner, H.I.G. Capital, for wrongful death, H.I.G. successfully had the case against it dismissed.[149] The court determined that even if H.I.G. "acquired, controlled, managed, and directed Wellpath," that alone would be insufficient to hold the private equity firm liable, as the one was not the "alter ego" of the other.[150] If such a conclusion seems confusing, it was: the decision was the sort of legal sleight of hand that made no sense except perhaps to the lawyers who performed it. But it also showed how private equity firms were insulated from the consequences of their own actions and had little, if any, incentive to improve the quality of their care, even when lack of care proved deadly.

✻

FINALLY, AS PART of their rollup, private equity firms are expanding their carceral reach beyond prison itself and into prison release cards. These are debit cards that facilities give inmates when leaving jail or prison, in theory holding the money that the inmates brought with them, that they made inside, or that the facilities gave them. But multiple lawsuits allege that the business model of these companies was largely to extract fees from prisoners. For instance, one plaintiff, Jeffrey Reichert, was arrested for driving while intoxicated.[151] When he was detained, the local jail confiscated the $177.66 he had in cash. He spent just four hours in detention but upon his release was not given his money back. Instead, he was given an ironically named Access Freedom debit card.[152] Reichert quickly found that the card, which he had not previously agreed to take, was slowly draining him of his money: there was a weekly maintenance fee, an inquiry fee to check the balance, and an issuer fee to withdraw funds.[153] This, it turned out, was company policy: the Keefe Group, which issued the card and which was owned by H.I.G. Capital, charged fees for card activity, for card *inactivity*, to request too much money, to ask about how much money there was to request, to replace a card, and to close the account. "Clearly, these cards are designed to make it impossible to avoid fees," wrote Lauren Sanders of the National Consumer Law Center.[154] A portion of the case was settled, and Keefe agreed to pay a percentage of the fees it took from prisoners, but much of the litigation remains ongoing.[155] Additionally, the Consumer Financial Protection Bureau (CFPB) eventually fined JPay, which issued many of these cards and which was owned by Tom Gores's Platinum Equity. The CFPB said that JPay's tactic to attach fees to credit cards after people were released from prison was abusive.[156] In the settlement, JPay agreed to give the former prisoners $4 million and pay a penalty of $2 million, as well as limit the fees that it would charge in the future.[157]

While such litigation and regulation is welcome, it appears simply to be the cost of doing business for the companies themselves, as private equity firms continue to invest in prison services. The reason why goes back to the kinds of businesses that Tom Gores and his peers buy. Platinum Equity's website advertises that it seeks companies with "[l]ong-term customers and stable revenue."[158] So it is with prisons, where a loyal customer base is guaranteed and where customers are certain to provide Platinum with a stable source of revenue. Moreover, it's an industry where prisoners have little power to protest declining product quality or increasing prices. Finally, it is an industry where private equity can form alliances with state and local governments and turn them into effective advocates for the status quo.

In this sense, private equity's excursion in prison services is less unique than it is illustrative: in industries where consumers have limited options, private equity firms will raise the prices and gut the quality of their services until people very nearly reach the breaking point, and firms do this with the government's help. In this way, what firms do in prisons is no different than what they do in civilian health care, housing, and nursing homes. The only difference is that in these other industries, the actions of private equity happen on a far grander scale.

But if there is reason for fear, there is also reason for hope. People like Bianca Tylek and Mignon Clyburn have, in fits and starts, been able to shame, litigate, regulate, and legislate against companies like Securus and Platinum Equity and, however incompletely, slow their growth. Where courts blocked substantial reform at the federal level, activists pushed change locally. Where private equity firms were unwilling to divest from the industry, they convinced institutional investors not to invest in the private equity firms themselves. Their strategy is a multifront attack on prison services, and it is one that can serve as a model for activists in other industries as private equity firms spread ever outward.

PART II

HOW THEY GET THEIR WAY

CHAPTER EIGHT

SUING THEIR OWN CUSTOMERS

Private Equity in the Courts

When private equity firms buy companies, they sometimes get in the business, not of making new products or services, but of suing their own customers. This opportunity to target people—especially poor and working-class people—often seems like the very reason that some firms buy businesses. When they do, they benefit from a small mountain of favorable case law, and where favorable laws do not exist, they spend enormous sums to create them. Yet when customers try to seek some measure of justice for themselves, they are often stymied, by arbitration agreements, by limitations on suing investors, and by a host of other legal decisions that make it hard for ordinary people to get redress. It is as if private equity firms and their allies have built a justice system to their liking. Now the rest of us must survive within it.

Consider when, in 2016, Mariner Finance allegedly sent Leticia Castellanos, unprompted, a check for $2,539.[1] Castellanos hadn't asked for the money; Mariner had just sent it. According to Castellano's subsequent complaint, the only thing she needed to do was endorse the check and in so doing agree to pay Mariner a little under a hundred dollars a month for a little over three years. The check was, in fact, a loan, with a 25 percent interest rate. Though Castellanos lived in the gentrifying Fells Point neighborhood of Baltimore, she herself made just $800 a month. A hundred dollars was more than she could afford, but to cover emergency repairs to her boiler, she endorsed the check anyway.

As she subsequently alleged, after Castellanos made several payments, Mariner reached out to her to discuss the terms of her loan.[2] But rather than finding a way to accommodate Castellanos's fixed income, Mariner convinced her to borrow more money, this time over $3,000. Most of that went back to Mariner to cover her existing debt. But oddly, the loan also included payments for multiple insurance policies—a life insurance policy, a "Non-filing" policy to protect Mariner if Castellanos's collateral was no good, and an "Accidental Death–Dismemberment–Loss of Sight" policy—that Mariner said it would buy for her.[3] It was unclear whether Castellanos ever asked for any of these things. Of the more than $3,000 that she borrowed in this second loan, the vast majority went back to Mariner for the unpaid balance of her account and for Mariner's insurance. Less than one-tenth went back to Castellanos.

Unsurprisingly, given the size of the loan and her modest income, Castellanos reported that she fell behind on her monthly payments.[4] So Mariner sued to collect the debt in Maryland state court, seeking interest and late fees.[5] With the assistance of a law firm specializing in consumer protection,[6] Castellanos counter-sued, alleging fraud, usury, and violations of Maryland's debt collection and consumer protection acts, among other harms.

And here, things took a turn for the worse for Castellanos. Knowingly or not, when she signed the terms of her second loan, she agreed to a broad arbitration provision, which committed her to resolving any disputes she had with Mariner at an arbitration firm of the company's choosing.[7] But fiendishly, Mariner was not similarly bound: the company could use the machinery of the state court system to garnish her wages and seize her assets.[8]

So Mariner moved to have Castellanos's case pushed into arbitration. Castellanos opposed, arguing through her lawyer that

Mariner couldn't have it both ways, litigating its own claims against Castellanos while defending against hers in arbitration.[9] But the case law simply was not on her side. The local judge, citing the US Supreme Court, noted a "strong federal policy favoring arbitration."[10] It found no problem with the double standard of this particular agreement: Castellanos, the court held, was bound to pursue her claims in arbitration, while Mariner could continue to collect its debt through the state court system. With Castellanos compelled to arbitrate her claims, in a system where plaintiffs must often agree to silence about the outcomes of their disputes, the ultimate outcome of her fight with Mariner never became public.[11]

Mariner Finance, which sent Leticia Castellanos that first check, is owned by the private equity firm Warburg Pincus.[12] Warburg's president, Timothy Geithner, was once President Barack Obama's treasury secretary. Mariner isn't quite a payday lender: it's an "installment" lender whose loans are a little larger and whose repayment periods are a little longer than those of its more notorious cousin. Nevertheless, Mariner is one part of a small army of lending companies targeting working-class and poor people that private equity firms have purchased in recent years. Among others, Friedman Fleischer & Lowe bought Speedy Cash.[13] Diamond Castle Holdings bought a controlling interest in Community Choice Financial.[14] Blackstone bought Lendmark Financial Services LLC.[15] And Lone Star Funds bought DFC Global.[16] The list goes on.

Payday and installment lending is an ideal industry for private equity. It provides a stable cash flow and a captive customer base that has little alternative but to keep using its product. The loans that so many people receive from payday lenders aren't used to buy real-world necessities but to service prior loans. In fact, the Consumer Financial Protection Bureau (CFPB) found that over 80 percent of payday loans were renewed or refinanced within two weeks.[17] For the vast majority of these "loan sequences," the principal on the most recent loan was the same or larger than the principal on the first, meaning that for the duration, the borrower was paying only interest and fees to the lender, rather than escaping the debt.

While payday lending is an ideal industry for private equity, private equity in turn exacerbates the industry's worst tendencies. Consider two payday lenders: Advance America, which is independently operated, and ACE Cash, which is owned by a private equity firm, JLL Partners.[18] Advance is the larger of the two,[19] but between 2012 and 2022, it had fewer than 700 complaints filed against it to the CFPB.[20] In contrast, ACE, the smaller, private equity–owned company, had 1,800 complaints, more than twice as many.[21] Among other things, borrowers alleged that people collecting debts for ACE called their family and work,[22] threatened prosecution,[23] and attempted to collect on loans never made.[24] ACE ultimately entered into a $10 million settlement with the CFPB over substantially similar allegations.[25] But ACE wasn't alone. After Blackstone bought Lendmark in 2013, for instance, complaints against it rose every year.[26] It seemed that the logic of private equity, with its focus on quick profits and limitations on private equity firms' own liability, pushed these companies into actions that were cruel and, in the case of ACE, allegedly illegal.

But in addition to making payday lenders worse, private equity firms also made them more litigious. In 2012, the year before Warburg Pincus bought Mariner Finance, the company was a plaintiff in just 240 state cases. By 2018, that number had risen to over 2,000, an eightfold increase.[27] The contrast was even more dramatic with OneMain Financial, which Fortress Investment Group bought in 2015.[28] The year before the acquisition, OneMain brought 406 state cases. The year after the acquisition, it brought 1,200. Three years later the number increased over 10,000.[29] These dramatic increases suggested that private equity firms saw legal action as an effective way to wring more money out of people who received the loans and perhaps even built it into their business plans when buying these companies. For upon winning a judgment, lenders could garnish their customer's wages and deplete their bank accounts, often simply by completing a form provided by the court and serving it on the borrower's bank or employer.[30] Suing their customers wasn't an aberration: it appeared to be a business strategy.

In contrast, as Leticia Castellanos's story illustrates, where consumers tried to sue these lenders for violations of, say, state consumer protection laws, they were often compelled into arbitration, where private companies, not courts, resolved their disputes. This was bad for a number of reasons. To start, plaintiffs often had to pay a filing fee—one that could go to several thousand dollars[31]—just to bring their claims. And when they did, their cases were litigated before arbitration companies who were typically paid for by the defendant business. A large body of research[32] has shown that these companies, knowing who paid their bills, typically sided with the defendants that fronted for their services. In the rare arbitrations in which consumers actually won, they were often bound by nondisclosure agreements that prevented them from publicizing their victories and notifying people like them of the opportunity to sue. At the same time, victorious plaintiffs in arbitration did not develop any precedential case law—as they might through ordinary litigation—that fellow consumers could rely upon.

These basic injustices could have been resolved through regulation. Toward the tail end of the Obama administration, the CFPB proposed a rule that would require lenders to confirm that borrowers could plausibly pay back the money they received,[33] as opposed to simply servicing the debt in perpetuity. This would have helped to end the cycles of debt that so many consumers faced, reducing the chance for subsequent litigation. The rule also placed some limits on lenders' ability to take money from borrowers' bank accounts to repay debts.[34]

The CFPB finalized the rule in 2017, at the outset of the Trump administration. But the payday lending industry—supported, in part, by private equity firms—brought its enormous litigation and lobbying effort to bear upon the regulation. To start, the Community Financial Services Association of America, which included numerous private equity–backed lenders,[35] sued the CFPB, arguing that the bureau lacked the authority to promulgate the rule. The groups succeeded in repeatedly delaying the rule's implementation.[36] Meanwhile, Community Choice Financial (owned by the private equity firm Diamond Castle Holdings) retained the services of President Trump's former campaign manager Corey Lewandowski, who went on television to advocate that Trump fire the CFPB's director, Richard Cordray.[37] Under pressure, Cordray resigned[38] and was ultimately replaced by former congressman Mick Mulvaney, who had been publicly contemptuous of the whole organization and who had called it a "sick, sad joke."[39] Private equity–backed lenders also lobbied generously during this time. ACE Cash Express, owned by JLL Partners, spent $390,000 in 2018 alone.[40] Lendmark Financial Services, owned by Blackstone, spent $400,000.[41] Mariner Finance, owned by Warburg Pincus, spent nearly $100,000.[42] And OneMain Financial, owned by Fortress Investment Group, spent $1 million.[43] Their spending was successful. In 2020, the CFPB rescinded the core provisions of the rule, including the provision that payday lenders prove customers' ability to repay their principals (rather than merely servicing the debt). This left essentially just the limitations on how often lenders could try to take money from delinquent borrowers' accounts.[44]

A similar assault—this one in Congress—occurred when the CFPB issued a rule prohibiting financial institutions from forcing consumers into arbitration agreements like the one that bound Leticia Castellanos.[45] The bureau's rule did not sit well with Arkansas senator Tom Cotton, who said it "ignores the consumer benefits of arbitration and treats Arkansans like helpless children, incapable of making business decisions in their own best interests."[46] Unstated was that consumers rarely, if ever, had a choice to opt out of arbitration. Also unstated were the tens of thousands of dollars that payday lenders had donated to Senator Cotton himself.[47] Executives at Blackstone, which owned the payday lender Lendmark, were particularly generous: more than a half dozen of its executives, including its president, Stephen Schwarzman, donated to Cotton and his campaign funds.[48]

Cotton was joined in opposition by the Trump administration's Treasury Department and Office of the Comptroller of the Currency, the latter of which regulated national banks. The Treasury Department issued a fevered report saying that the prohibition on forced arbitration would raise costs for consumers.[49]

The comptroller, meanwhile, fretted that the rule could result in "potentially ruinous liability" for lenders.[50] (The comptroller apparently failed to appreciate the argument that it would be "ruinous" to hold lenders fully responsible for their actions in court.) Armed with these regulators' support, in 2017, allies of the finance industry introduced resolutions under the rarely used Congressional Review Act, which allowed Congress to rescind recently implemented regulations.[51] The resolution passed both chambers and was signed by President Trump. Afterward, Senator Cotton released a statement calling the repeal "good news for the American consumer."[52] That election cycle, Cotton received $1.8 million from the finance industry.[53]

The effect of all of this was that the courts continued to operate just as companies like Mariner Finance would prefer. Mariner could force people like Leticia Castellanos to arbitrate their claims, while pursuing its own claims against borrowers in court. When it did, Mariner added a cruel twist: it would require borrowers to pay the cost of Mariner's own attorneys. "That really got me," one borrower who was obligated to pay Mariner over $500 for the company's own lawyer told the *Washington Post*.[54] The whole court system, it seemed, was built for companies like Mariner and not for people like Leticia Castellanos.

✳

PRIVATE EQUITY'S FORAY into payday lending is just one instance of the industry's expansion into areas where firms have profited, not by improving the businesses they buy but by suing their customers. This makes sense for private equity firms, whose short-term investments preclude the sorts of actions that would build long-term trust and engagement with customers. Take, for instance, Southeastern Emergency Physicians. Southeastern is a physician staffing company that makes money by assigning doctors to hospitals and other medical facilities. In 2017, Blackstone bought Southeastern and its parent company.[55] Shortly thereafter, Southeastern's litigation docket exploded. Between 2017 and 2019, Southeastern filed 4,800 lawsuits against patients for unpaid bills in the Memphis metropolitan area alone. In the first half of 2019, it sued more patients than three of the largest regional hospitals combined.

Southeastern's explosion in litigation is directly correlated with Blackstone's purchase of the company. The year before Blackstone bought it, Southeastern filed a comparatively modest 798 lawsuits in Shelby County.[56] The year after, it filed more than double that. Meanwhile, former call center agents were instructed not to raise with patients the possibility of charity care, the common—and required[57]—practice of forgiving debts for those who cannot afford to pay. "A lot of times, a patient would call in and say, 'Hey, can you give us a discount?'" a former TeamHealth employee told NPR. "But we had to say, 'No, I can't do that,' because we weren't allowed to say, 'Well, did you apply for charity care at the hospital?'"[58] (After its tactics were publicly reported, TeamHealth said that it would no longer sue patients.)[59]

It wasn't just health care. The student loan collector Transworld Systems, for instance, supported tens of thousands of lawsuits against borrowers.[60] After the private equity firm Platinum Equity bought the company in 2014, the CFPB received over 4,600 complaints about it.[61] As alleged, Transworld sued people for debts that it couldn't prove that they actually owed and pressured its employees into signing affidavits saying that they knew debts were legitimate, when in fact they had no such knowledge. In 2017, the CFPB fined the company $2.5 million for these illegal practices.[62] But the bureau has yet to collect, as given the complicated ownership structures of student debt, Transworld now contests whether it actually agreed to a valid settlement.[63] Years after the CFPB issued its fine, the litigation remains ongoing. Meanwhile, Transworld has continued to prosper and expand, buying numerous other debt collection companies.[64]

Private equity–owned businesses pursue similarly litigious strategies in other industries, such as single-family home rentals,[65] nursing facilities,[66] and mobile homes.[67] These are not, as noted earlier, necessarily industries with wealthy customers or clients. In fact, some of them cater to the poorest people in America. Why, then, do private equity–owned companies focus on suing these customers? Because they are the ones least able to fight back. Defending against a collection action is a costly exercise, affirmatively suing these companies for wrongdoing even more so. Customers of these businesses do not have much money and are far less able to defend themselves than are wealthier clientele in other industries, who might be able to hire lawyers or at least devote the time to fighting unjust tactics.

✳

IN THE PURSUIT of their own customers, private equity firms have both created and benefited from changes in the law and the legal profession. First among these was the general reshaping of corporate law in favor of private equity. Big law firms like Kirkland & Ellis and Paul Weiss used to make their money primarily from litigation, while transactional work—the business of helping companies organize, issue stock, and buy and sell one another—formed a rump of the overall revenues of these forms. In time, these roles shifted, with the largest law firms making most of their money from transactional work: that is, helping businesses buy one another, go public, form investment funds, and so forth. And for some firms, that transactional work came ever more often from private equity.

Take Kirkland & Ellis. The firm had many of the leading lights of conservative litigation, including partners Bill Barr, Ken Starr, and Paul Clement. In 2010, however, a transactional lawyer—Jeff Hammes—took over as chairman of the firm's global management executive committee.[68] Within a decade, three-quarters of Kirkland's business was transactional work, a big part of which came from private equity, as the firm serviced over 450 different firms.[69] "[P]rivate equity has become a massive asset class," one partner told the *Financial Times*, "with a demand for legal services that is diverse and deep."[70] Kirkland was smart "because we realised how damn good that business was."[71]

Similar transformations occurred at other big law firms, many of which developed dedicated practice areas for private equity.[72]

Quinn Emanuel, for instance, claimed that it had over 250 lawyers working in its private equity litigation practice group.[73] Sidley Austin, meanwhile, bragged about its "strong relationships
with an extensive network of government lawyers and enforcement officials" who could provide "credibility" to private equity
firms facing regulatory issues.[74] Other firms similarly staffed up.
The consequence of this was that private equity firms generally
had access to some of the best-paid lawyers in the country for their
highest-stakes matters.

As law firms changed, so did the law itself, in particular, laws
insulating private equity firms from the legal consequences of
their actions. Consider the case of Annie Salley, discussed earlier
in the introduction. Salley was in her early seventies when she was
admitted to the Heartland nursing home in Hanahan, South Carolina. Heartland was owned, through a series of shell companies,
by HCR ManorCare and, in turn, by several funds controlled by
the private equity firm Carlyle Group.[75] As previously discussed,
Carlyle bought ManorCare by loading the company up with debt
and selling its property. The move left the company cash strapped,
the natural consequence of which was to cut the quality of care.

This had disastrous consequences for Salley. With urinary
tract infections, arthritis, and foot pain, Salley struggled to get
herself to the bathroom.[76] But as subsequently alleged by her estate, with inadequate staffing at the facility, Salley was forced to do
so herself, the result of which was that one evening she fell and hit
her head on a bathroom fixture. After the accident, nursing home
staff reportedly failed to perform a head scan and did not refer her
to a doctor, even though Salley exhibited confusion, "thrash[ed]
around," and vomited.

As her estate alleged, Salley was eventually ejected from the
nursing home—her family was unable to afford the copay on
her insurance—and was shortly thereafter taken to a local hospital, where doctors discovered severe bleeding in her brain.[77] The
blood was allegedly several weeks old (presumably from the fall
in the nursing home) and had pushed her brain to one side of her
head. Surgeons attempted to relieve the pressure by drilling into

her head but were unsuccessful, and Salley died of subdural hematoma: that is, pooling of blood in the skull.

Salley's estate eventually sued the nursing home, as well as its ultimate parent company, Carlyle. But Carlyle moved to dismiss the case against it and, in so doing, performed several legal sleights of hand. For one thing, Carlyle argued that it didn't actually own ManorCare or its facilities. Rather, it claimed, it simply advised a series of funds that did. For another, Carlyle refused to participate in any discovery about its control over the facility in which Salley was injured. But it did produce affidavits from Carlyle and Manor-Care executives asserting that the firm had no responsibility for the "policies or procedures" at Salley's facility, nor did it have "responsibility or involvement" with its "day-to-day operations."[78] This allowed Carlyle to shape the facts of the case in its favor, without giving the lawyers for Salley's estate the opportunity to respond.

Although this was brought as a "motion to dismiss," in which Salley's estate was entitled to all reasonable inferences in its favor, the court granted Carlyle's motion. It held that the estate had not "alleged specific facts that support a claim that Carlyle actually did control the budget of Heartland."[79] Moreover, the court held, "it would be a far stretch for the court [to] infer this fact based solely on alleged ownership of a sixth-tier subsidiary."[80] Of course, it was hard for plaintiffs to allege specific facts because Carlyle moved to dismiss the case before discovery began. The nursing home was a sixth-tier subsidiary—a common tactic in the industry that obscures ultimate ownership and responsibility,[81] of which the court was presumably unaware. Ultimately, Salley's family was unable to collect any money from Carlyle for the death of their mother. The case was settled with ManorCare and its affiliates for an undisclosed sum and without an admission of wrongdoing.

Salley's case showed how private equity firms managed to avoid legal liability for their actions. It was also a relatively simple case to dispose of—just a matter of crafting a motion to dismiss. In contrast, the case of Scott Brass showed how far and how long a private equity firm would go to insulate itself from the consequences of its actions. Scott Brass was not a person but a company,

an industrial metal manufacturer based in Rhode Island.[82] Sun
Capital bought the business in 2007, and like so many of the firm's
other acquisitions, the company quickly fell into bankruptcy.[83] In
the wreckage, the employees' pension fund tried to hold Sun Capital liable for its underfunded benefits.[84] But Sun Capital refused
and in 2010 sought a judgment in federal court that it was not responsible for these debts.

The subsequent litigation was tortuously long. After over two
years of argument, the district court held that Sun Capital was not
a "trade or business" as required under the relevant statute and
therefore could not be held liable for the pension.[85] A year later,
the First Circuit reversed the decision.[86] Four years after that, the
district court found that Sun Capital's various funds could be held
liable for the debt.[87] But Sun Capital again appealed, on the rather
facile argument that investors were generally responsible for pension debts only when they owned 80 percent or more of a company and that, in fact, two separate Sun Capital funds owned Scott
Brass: one with a 70 percent stake, the other 30 percent.

In 2019, the appellate court sided with Sun Capital and against
the employees. On the merits, the decision was likely incorrect.
Nevertheless, Sun Capital won an important victory. The process
had taken nine years over what was, for Sun Capital, a pittance:
$4.5 million.[88] In fact, it's plausible that Sun Capital actually spent
more than that litigating the issue, but the case was a model for
how private equity firms could avoid liability for underfunded
pensions. And it demonstrated how far a firm would go to protect
the principle that it should not be held responsible for the consequences of its actions.

*

WHILE PRIVATE EQUITY firms worked hard to insulate themselves
from legal liability generally, two other, broader developments
in the law helped the industry: the fall of class action lawsuits and
the concomitant rise of forced arbitration.

With class actions, one or a handful of plaintiffs can bring suit
on behalf of all similarly situated people: say, all the residents in a

nursing home chain or all the purchasers of a defective product. These class actions are necessary when it would be unaffordable for each person to bring suit individually. By allowing plaintiffs' lawyers to recover a contingency on the total amount awarded, class actions make it possible—and rational—to recover for these sorts of ordinary harms.

But class actions have been under sustained assault for over forty years. From the Reagan administration onward, conservative administrations appointed judges hostile to class action lawsuits.[89] Meanwhile, with far more money than their opponents, the corporate defense bar had the resources to challenge nearly every facet of class action case law. This pincer move had its intended effect, as increasingly conservative judges, faced with the opportunity to do so, desiccated class actions. Among other things, judges required plaintiffs to prove ever more of their case ever earlier in litigation.[90] They raised the standards for certifying classes. And they rejected proposed settlements between purported classes and defendants.

At the same time, courts increasingly blessed the use of forced arbitration agreements. As noted earlier, since the 1980s, the Supreme Court has repeatedly expressed a "federal policy favoring arbitration" and directed that these agreements be enforced as corporations had written them.[91] As with class actions, an increasingly conservative judiciary blessed ever more lopsided arbitration agreements that favored companies over consumers and employees. In 2011, for instance, the Supreme Court held that federal law preempted any state statutes that would require agreements to allow plaintiffs to arbitrate in groups, like in ordinary class actions.[92] In 2013, it held that arbitration agreements could be enforced even when they would make it economically impossible for plaintiffs to pursue their claims.[93] And in 2018, the Court held that employees could be compelled into arbitration and waive their right to join class actions as a condition of employment.[94]

The result was an explosion in the use of arbitration agreements. In the 1990s, about 2 percent of companies used arbitration with their nonunion employees; by 2019, more than half did.[95] In

2020, over two-thirds of popular brands surveyed by Consumer Reports, from GE and Kenmore to Sony, Bose, Microsoft, LG, Samsung, and Dell, used mandatory arbitration clauses to manage disputes with their own customers.[96] And, as intended, almost no one used these agreements. Of the over 800 million consumer arbitration agreements in effect in 2018, only 6,000—less than 1 percent of 1 percent—actually resulted in arbitration.[97] Even among the infinitesimally small number of cases brought, people rarely won. The Consumer Financial Protection Bureau found that when customers brought arbitration disputes over financial products, for instance, they succeeded barely more than a quarter of the time, and recovered just thirteen cents for every dollar in damages claimed.

Private equity firms benefited from both of these trends. As previously discussed, portfolio companies in the payday loan, nursing home,[98] and single-family home rental[99] industries all forced their customers to use arbitration agreements, to the enormous detriment of people like Leticia Castellanos. At the same time, they have successfully defeated class action lawsuits against themselves and their portfolio companies. To take just one example, in Kentucky, beneficiaries of the state's pension fund filed a class action lawsuit against KKR and Blackstone, alleging that the firms breached their fiduciary duties by selling the pension fund financial products with onerous, hidden fees.[100] It was a dangerous case for the private equity firms, as the plaintiffs alleged billions of dollars in damages. And so KKR and Blackstone filed an unusual "writ of prohibition" with the state appellate court, arguing that the plaintiffs had no standing to sue. The appeals court and, subsequently, the Kentucky Supreme Court agreed. Because the pension plan had not yet collapsed, the court held, the plaintiffs could not sue;[101] their allegations were "too speculative and hypothetical" for the court to consider.[102] This was a devastating loss for pensioners in Kentucky. But as Blackstone's lawyers noted, its impact was larger, given the rise in lawsuits filed by beneficiaries of underfunded pensions across the country.[103] The case showed how private equity firms both benefited from existing case law and worked to shape their own, neutering class actions as a tool for justice along the way.

❋

WHAT CAN BE done so that private equity firms do not enjoy such lopsided advantages in our justice system? To start with, plaintiff-side lawyers need to understand and explain how private equity firms are often intimately involved in the management of their portfolio companies. Most judges simply do not know what private equity firms are or how they work. Showing that firms like Carlyle and Sun Capital don't just invest in but also shape the strategy of their portfolio companies may help plaintiffs to extend liability to private equity firms.

At the same time, we're seeing a variety of new tactics emerge to protect consumers, even under increasingly hostile case law. One is mass arbitration. To make arbitration agreements seem fair, defendant companies often agreed to pay the costs of any case.[104] Effectively foreclosed from pursuing class actions, a few enterprising law firms took these companies at their word and brought hundreds or thousands of individual arbitration claims, the costs of which companies had to bear. This gave plaintiffs, for the first time, some negotiating leverage with these businesses. Mass arbitrations have been brought against companies as diverse as Uber, Amazon, DoorDash, Intuit, Buffalo Wild Wings, and FanDuel, the latter two of which were owned or invested in by private equity firms.[105] And when companies have tried to wriggle out of their agreements, courts have held them to their word. When DoorDash, for instance, tried to renege on paying thousands of arbitration fees, the presiding judge wrote that its employees were exercising "the remnant of procedural rights left to them."[106] DoorDash's "hypocrisy" in refusing to pay, the judge wrote, "will not be blessed."[107]

Faced with the first serious challenge to the architecture of arbitration, companies are regrouping to reduce what leverage consumers have gained. DoorDash, for instance, reconfigured its employee contract to significantly slow the pace at which cases are reviewed, to the detriment of plaintiffs. The defense-side law firm Gibson

Dunn, meanwhile, has recommended that businesses no longer pay for the cost of arbitration and instead force plaintiffs to pay when arbitrators deem claims frivolous.[108] Demonstrating enormous chutzpah, companies are trying to make these changes retroactively. And they are also creating "batching" mechanisms to force individual plaintiffs into class action–like procedures in arbitration.

Yet even if mass arbitrations lose their potency, plaintiffs are finding other ways to challenge private equity's conduct. One nascent possibility is to pursue lawsuits for breach of fiduciary duty. The directors who sit on corporate boards typically have various duties of loyalty and care to the companies they oversee; in essence, they cannot be negligent or ransack a company for their own gain. But when private equity firms buy companies, they often install their own employees or allies on their boards. These directors may act in the interest of their private equity employers over the businesses they oversee, approving exorbitant management fees, for example, or agreeing to sell businesses for less than their worth. When they do so, board members may violate their fiduciary duties, and the people harmed by their actions—creditors, employees, even customers—may sue to stop them.

We've seen a handful of cases like this succeed. In 2013, for example, the private equity firm Sycamore Partners bought the Jones Group, a manufacturer of several then popular shoe lines, including Nine West, Anne Klein, and Gloria Vanderbilt.[109] The Jones Group's board approved its sale to Sycamore, even though the deal resulted in debt levels for the company higher than what its own investment bankers said it could sustain. After the merger, Sycamore's executives decided to sell some of the company's most promising businesses to their own affiliates. They did so at a price well below the businesses' market values and well below what the Jones Group had paid for them just a few years before.[110]

The move helped to destroy the company, which filed for bankruptcy in 2018.

Ultimately, a consortium of the old Jones Group's creditors sued the company's former board of directors and others, alleging, among other things, a breach of fiduciary duty. Judge Jed Rakoff,

a sort of liberal lion of the Southern District of New York, point-
edly refused to dismiss their claims. Judge Rakoff found that the
directors had failed to conduct a reasonable investigation into
whether the sale to Sycamore would render the company insol-
vent.[111] It was a technical, narrow ruling, but it showed how people
might sue board members of other companies who approved similarly disastrous sales to private equity firms. This was a lightning
bolt within the industry. Law firms sent out hurried client alerts.
And the finance commentator William Cohan wrote in his article
for the *New York Times,* "The Private Equity Party Might Be Ending," that, given the chance that officers and directors could now
be held liable for private equity firms' most brazen actions, "[t]he
days of just selling a company to the highest bidder regardless of
the consequences—might just be over."[112] The defendants, perhaps
realizing what the case had revealed, quickly settled the matter.[113]

The suit showed what was possible: private equity–appointed
board members could finally perhaps be held legally liable for
decimating companies. Of course, there are challenges to bringing these sorts of suits. Corporate directors are generally insulated
from liability by the "business judgment rule," which typically
protects executives' decisions made in good faith.[114] And executives have learned, in advance of major sales, to get materials from
their financial advisers assuring them of the reasonableness of their
actions.[115] But private equity firms are getting increasingly bold,
and their acquisitions increasingly financially unreasonable: as far
back as 2014, 40 percent of private equity deals used debt in excess
of what the Federal Reserve considered financially sustainable;
that number has likely increased considerably.[116] These sorts of decisions can ruin companies and careers, but potentially they can be
challenged under the law.

❋

THE AMERICAN JUSTICE system today is tremendously solicitous
and supportive of private equity. Firms have built whole businesses not on raising the quality or reducing the costs of their
products but on simply suing their customers. They've spent

enormous sums to insulate themselves from the legal consequences of their actions, and they've both benefited from and shaped the law on class actions and arbitrations to their own benefit.

But we can do something about this. Plaintiffs' lawyers can educate judges on just how private equity firms work. Mass arbitrations can be a tool for fighting inequity. So too may be suits for breaches of fiduciary duty. There are creative ways in which private equity firms may be held responsible for their actions. All we need are the lawyers to act.

CHAPTER NINE

PRIVATIZING THE PUBLIC SECTOR

Private Equity in Local Government

In 2014, Middletown, Pennsylvania, was in trouble. The small borough was tens of millions of dollars in debt to service its water and sewer system and employee benefit program.[1] In addition, its pension obligations to retired police were rising.[2] Middletown was unlikely to grow its way out of the problem, as its population had been declining for decades.[3] Moreover, the per capita income ran thousands of dollars below the national average,[4] and in a borough of nine thousand people, less than one-fifth of residents had bachelor's degrees and nearly one in six people lived in poverty.[5]

In 2014, the city's leaders hit upon an idea, one that had been pursued with apparent success by other cash-precarious towns: lease the water system. For an upfront payment and some annual revenue, Middletown would let a company manage its water utilities and collect fees from its citizens. The company the town chose was Middletown Water Joint Venture LLC, led by the private equity firm KKR. It was a "good decision" for the "long term," according to city council member Ben Kapenstein.[6] "I think the citizens got a good deal," he said.[7]

It did, indeed, seem like a good deal for Middletown. KKR was offering to make essential investments in the city's water system, federal funds for which had dried up long ago. And even though KKR would be paying for those investments, Middletown would continue to own the infrastructure: the project was merely a lease to the joint venture. KKR promised, in general, not to raise rates for four years, after which it would be allowed to do so only at a certain percentage above inflation.[8] And most importantly, Middletown was getting money—tens of millions of dollars upfront and hundreds of thousands of dollars every year[9]—to deal with the city's debt and pension liabilities.[10]

But if the deal seemed too good to be true, it was, of course. The joint venture was not initially allowed to raise rates—in general. But in fact, it could do so if demand fell below a threshold, one that was pegged to the city's water consumption in a year of particularly high demand.[11] When, unsurprisingly, residents' water use fell below that peak, the operating company assessed a 11.5 percent rate increase.[12]

In a place like Middletown, where incomes were not high, these increases were not affordable. On Facebook, Jackquline Foster wrote that "Middletown is just becoming to[o] expensive," and that she was "barely surviving now being a single mom of 3."[13] Sheila Hinkson commented, "guess I cut the cable off and forget the Internet[,] not to mention doctor co-pays etc. . . . Maybe even have to take a bath every other day? When does it stop?"[14] Tom Buck complained—accurately, as it turned out—that "we can post and bitch all we want on Facebook but that won't change a damn thing."[15]

It became increasingly clear that the operating company and KKR had simply out-negotiated the small city of Middletown. One of the members of the lease exploratory committee—a city council member—was just four years out of college.[16] In subsequent litigation, the city said that the companies foisted the loophole that allowed the rate increases in the final days of negotiation, a tactic that the city perhaps did not understand at the time, and certainly did not address.[17] Ultimately, recognizing its own error, Middleton sued to get out of the contract but without success. The city's primary argument—that KKR and its operating partner could not have actually intended these enormous rate increases—was weak, and the defendants were represented by Allen and Overy, one of the largest law firms in the world.[18] The judge dismissed the city's case,[19] and the lawsuit proved to be another instance in which the city was simply no match, strategically, for KKR.

KKR and its operating partner, eventually named Suez, were great at negotiating the deal but bad at running the system. In 2018, Suez alerted residents that one of its disinfection systems had failed and urged them to "BOIL YOUR WATER BEFORE USING."[20] The company's advisory assured residents that they should not be concerned, even if "the water is yellow," though they directed residents to disinfect their water even for tasks as small as brushing one's teeth. Yet Suez declined to provide bottled water to residents. Meanwhile, KKR sold its 90 percent stake in the project to another private equity firm, tripling its money in under four years.[21] The town, it appeared, had been played.

The situation was even worse in Bayonne, New Jersey, which had taken a similar deal with KKR and its operating partner a few years before. In announcing the agreement, the parties made big promises. A law firm hired by the water authority estimated that the city could save over $35 million over forty years.[22] The CEO of the operating company extolled "KKR's long-term vision," which, he said, "brings credibility to address America's water challenges."[23] The Clinton Global Initiative even featured the partnership as an innovative new business model in its annual meeting.[24]

In announcing the deal, Bayonne officials promised a four-year rate freeze, but unsurprisingly, that never happened. Because the city had guaranteed revenue to KKR and its operating partner and because people were using less water than expected, rates increased substantially almost every year.[25] Moreover, Bayonne agreed to pay for any major infrastructure repairs itself and, if it needed any money to do so, to borrow specifically from KKR.[26] In other words, the deal was almost comically lopsided. Yet despite the talk of KKR's "long-term vision," within a few years, the firm sold its stake to another private equity firm, in the same deal in which it offloaded its investment in Middletown, for $110 million.[27] It nearly tripled its money on the Bayonne project.[28]

In the aftermath of the deal, citizens of Bayonne tried to find ways to escape their forty-year contract, or at least live under it. "I've become the water nazi," one resident told the *Hudson Reporter*, "telling my family: 'You've got two minutes in the shower.'" "I buy flowers that require little water because I don't want to use my water," she added.[29] A third resident complained that she had been charged $900 for a single three-month period. "There is no water being used other than our faucets and our toilets and our shower," she told the *Jersey Journal*. "I don't know how to handle this."[30] Liens against properties for unpaid water bills rose dramatically.[31]

But there was little that residents, or Bayonne, could do. After hiring a law firm to review its contract, the city found that the only way it could escape its forty-year agreement would be to buy the parties out, for hundreds of millions of dollars. This was an unaffordable proposition. And so, while KKR left the deal after just a few years, having made tens of millions of dollars, Bayonne was saddled for decades with an agreement that its residents simply could not afford. Bayonne, like Middletown, had been played.

*

THE DISASTERS IN Middletown and Bayonne are part of a much larger story about how the basic facets of government are increasingly being privatized, with the aid of private equity firms. For a variety of reasons, since the 1970s, the government has invested ever less, as a percentage of our economy, in infrastructure.[32] At the same time, states and localities, which bear primary responsibility for education and emergency services, faced a pincer move of declining federal aid and laws that limit their ability to raise taxes.[33] As a result, many infrastructure projects were never funded, and governments have struggled to find ever more creative ways to continue their basic functioning.

Private equity firms stepped in to fill this gap. Often through dedicated infrastructure funds, firms invested in the projects to keep America running: Carlyle bought into electric vehicle charging stations.[34] KKR bought oil and gas distributors.[35] Riverstone Holdings bought power plants.[36] And Blackstone invested in cell phone towers.[37] With a "huge funding gap" in infrastructure, one Carlyle executive observed, there was an opportunity for private equity firms to fund essential assets for "providing drinking water, power, roads, and airports."[38] An executive at KKR said, "We are slowly starting to see more cities looking at these partnerships given all the fiscal pressures they're facing."[39]

Beyond traditional infrastructure, private equity firms bought businesses that offered services once provided primarily by the government, including ambulance companies and firefighting departments, 911 dispatch services, and technical colleges. In all these industries, the basic business model of private equity, which demanded short-term results while insulating firms from the consequences of their actions, yielded all the predictable disasters. But these disasters had particular poignancy because the people betrayed, overcharged, and underserved were simply using the services they had the right to expect from their government. In other words, they had no other choice.

✳

TO BEGIN, PRIVATE equity firms bought—and hobbled—one of the leading providers of 911 dispatch services. In 2006, the private equity firms Thomas H. Lee Partners and the Quadrangle Group bought the West Corporation, an operator of customer call centers.[40] Among other things, West nominally provided routing services for 911 dispatch, ensuring that local calls went to the right departments. The problem was that, under its new ownership, the company repeatedly failed in this basic task, leading to widespread failures and thousands of calls that never reached emergency dispatchers.

In 2014, for instance, West suffered a six-hour outage that affected eleven million people, or 3 percent of the entire country.[41] Over six thousand calls never reached a dispatcher, and for a time, virtually the entire state of Washington was without a working

911 system. The FCC fined West $1.4 million, which agreed to implement a compliance program.[42] In August 2018, a "human error" made by a West employee resulted in nearly 700 calls in Minnesota not connecting.[43] West agreed to pay the FCC a fine and, again, implement a compliance plan.[44] In December of the same year, West failed once more, with a thirty-seven-hour outage that resulted in nearly 900 calls not being routed.[45] And then again in 2020, West, now named Intrado, had an outage in fourteen states for over an hour, in which 135 calls failed to reach their dispatchers.[46] It agreed to pay $1.75 million and, yet again, implement a compliance program.[47]

Were the company's cascading failures the fault of its private equity owners? Plausibly, yes. Under their ownership, the company experienced dramatic layoffs. In 2006, when it was first bought, West had 29,000 employees.[48] By 2016, its last year as a public company, it had fewer than 11,000.[49] Additionally, according to Reuters, the company "grappled with a debt pile of more than $3 billion,"[50] which by necessity made it harder for the business to invest in its own operations. Meanwhile, as reported by Fitch Ratings, the company identified $125 million in "cost savings," which is to say, budget cuts.[51] The consequence of these three things—large layoffs, borrowing, and budget cuts, all hallmarks of private equity ownership—was that the company had fewer people and less money to invest in the actual operations of the business. Inevitably "human error" and the failure of a basic social service became all the more likely.

✳

THE 911 DISPATCH was just one small part of private equity's expansion into emergency services; the far larger part was its acquisition of ambulance companies. It may be surprising to learn that ambulances were once free, overwhelmingly provided by the government—especially for younger people who have only known the prohibitive costs of calling an ambulance. In fact, in 1988, a national survey of cities found that not one had privatized its ambulance services.[52] But in the 1990s, amid municipal budget cuts and a growing distrust in government, that began to change. By 1997, 16 percent of cities had privatized their ambulance services.[53] By 2012, nearly 40 percent had.[54] If localities were looking to sell their ambulance operations, private equity firms were looking to buy them, as people who called emergency services were willing to pay perhaps enormous sums to save their own lives. So, over the course of fifteen years, Patriarch Partners, Warburg Pincus, Clayton, Dubilier & Rice, and KKR, among other firms, all bought ground ambulance companies.[55] KKR and American Securities also bought the largest air ambulance companies—those that delivered patients by helicopter and plane—which, together with one other firm, controlled two-thirds of the industry.[56]

The results were upsetting and unsurprising. As reported by the *New York Times*, within three years, a quarter of the twelve ambulance companies recently bought by private equity firms went bankrupt. By comparison, none of more than one thousand other, nonprivate equity–owned companies that the paper tracked failed over the same period of time. When one private equity–owned ambulance company, TransCare, went bankrupt, fully 30 percent of its ambulances were not operating. Some vehicles had brakes that didn't work, while others took upward of four hours to get started. "You really had to become a MacGyver in the field," one former employee told the *Times*.[57] Response times at another ambulance company, Rural/Metro, slowed after it was bought by the private equity firm Warburg Pincus, and during some crises, the company simply had no ambulances to dispatch.

While quality suffered, private equity firms kept companies focused on their priority: profits. Rural/Metro, for instance, pushed its employees to get patients to sign documents, even in times of dire need, so that the company could bill them. "Almost always, if the patient is alert, they will be able to sign" release documents, a poster hung in Rural/Metro ambulances and fire stations explained.[58]

While private equity firms cannot bear the full blame for rising costs, over the past five years—a time when the industry continued to invest in ambulances[59]—costs for consumers rose 23 percent, such that, before insurance is paid, a single ride now costs, on average, nearly $1,300.[60] At the same time, nearly half of all rides now result in surprise medical bills for privately insured patients, a tactic particularly favored by private equity firms.[61] Among air ambulances, a single ride in a private equity–owned plane or helicopter now costs, on average, $48,000, nearly $20,000 more than with a nonprivate equity–owned company.[62] Private equity firms cannot fully explain the rising costs for ambulances, but the costs they impose have become so ingrained in our social consciousness that the industry, in essence, helped to transform an essential service into a luxury, and an unaffordable one at that.

Beyond ambulances, at least two private equity firms are bringing these same innovations to fire departments, which similarly command a captive—and potentially lucrative—consumer base. In 2011, Warburg Pincus bought Rural/Metro, which KKR in turn bought in 2018. Rural/Metro contracted with cities to provide fire services and solicited individuals for subscriptions in smaller communities, often in the arid Southwest.

The company also put out fires for nonsubscribers but at an enormous cost. To take just one example, in 2013, Justine and Kasia Purcell's mobile home in Maricopa County, Arizona, burned down.[63] The couple was away from home at the time, preparing for the birth of a child, and arrived only to see firefighters put out the remnants of their house, which was totally destroyed. Some of those firefighters were from Rural/Metro, and though they were unable to save the Purcells' home, the company billed them for nearly $20,000. Later, a spokesperson for Rural/Metro told Huff-Post that the Purcells "knew they had an obligation/option to pay our annual subscription" and had "elected to ... roll the dice that they would not have a fire—they lost."[64] Such stories are not isolated. Reporters for the *New York Times* spoke with more than a dozen people who had been sued by Rural/Metro for putting out fires. One couple, the Addies, who similarly lost their mobile home to a fire, were sued for about $7,000. To save money to pay off the debt, Mr. Addie said, "We just eat two meals a day instead of three."[65] (In contrast, Henry Kravis, the cofounder of Rural/Metro's private equity owner, KKR, is worth just shy of $10 billion.[66])

The stories above—on water utilities, ambulances, and fire departments—tell some simple truths about the effect of the private equity business model. In each industry, firms found cities and states that, starved of revenue, were willing to give up their responsibilities for fiscal reprieve. And in each, firms found a captive audience—citizens and residents—that had little choice but to pay the prices charged. The money these people paid did not go to local governments to help in the basic project of caring for one another. Instead, it went to firms that were motivated not by the public good but by private desires. People can demand these services back and force governments to reclaim the responsibilities they lost. But the cost, in money, time, and political effort, will be enormous.

✳

FINALLY, PRIVATE EQUITY firms are turning to higher education, the result, once again, of government underinvestment. Historically, the task of funding public colleges fell primarily to the states.[67] But over the last two decades, and in particular after the Great Recession, local investment in higher education fell dramatically, while federal investment failed to fully make up the difference.[68] State schools faced significant budget shortfalls and, in response, most raised tuition.[69] Community colleges were particularly hard hit and, for the first time, turned to tuition as a major source of revenue, which increased substantially.[70] This meant that community and public colleges were no longer seen as an obviously affordable path to higher education. This also meant that they had fewer resources to make the kinds of changes, such as night classes and flexible start dates, to meet students' changing needs. Enter for-profit colleges, who were able to turn their enormous marketing teams to steer students to their programs who, in another era, might have gone to public institutions of higher education. Underfunded community colleges were slow to adapt to the lives and needs of their students, while for-profit enrollment officers (i.e., salespeople) were there to help people navigate the system in a way that publicly funded schools didn't.

Such for-profit colleges were ideal acquisition targets for private equity firms: they had lots of cash flow, a consumer base that, once enrolled, would struggle to leave, and enormous revenue from the government in the form of student loans and grants. So when enrollment in for-profits rose dramatically in the 2000s (particularly after the Great Recession), private equity firms began an aggressive push into the industry. Warburg Pincus helped to create Ashford University. KKR and its allies bought Laureate Education. Landmark Partners, with others, bought the Education Corporation of America. And Apollo Global Management bought the University of Phoenix. In all, the Private Equity Stakeholder Project identified over fifty acquisitions of for-profit colleges.[71]

The industry that private equity entered had a miserable reputation and deservedly so. For every dollar of tuition they received, for-profits spent just 29 cents on instruction, compared to 84 cents at private colleges, and $1.42 at public universities.[72] Students who attended for-profit bachelor's programs left, on average, with $14,000 more debt than their peers in nonprofit colleges.[73] And while for-profits enrolled just 8 percent of students, they accounted for 30 percent of student loan defaults.[74] Most importantly, students who attended could expect to earn well below what their peers at public schools made, and at least one study found that graduates of for-profit colleges were no more likely to be hired than candidates who attended no college at all.[75]

But if it were possible, the outcomes at private equity–owned schools were even worse than at ordinary for-profits. Research found that students at these schools paid higher tuition and left with more debt.[76] They were less likely to graduate, less likely to pay off their loans, and less likely to earn as much as their peers at ordinary for-profits. Private equity firms invested less in faculty and more—much more—in sales even than did other for-profits. As a result, they siphoned students away from nearby community colleges. And all the while, they were more likely to be investigated by the government, mostly for recruiting violations, such as misrepresenting student loan terms, graduation rates, and employment outcomes.

The case of Ashford University is instructive. Ashford began as the Franciscan University of the Prairies,[77] a small college run by nuns[78] whose campus in Clinton, Iowa, sat just off the Mississippi River. In 2005, the private equity firm Warburg Pincus—now run by President Obama's former treasury secretary, Tim Geithner—funded a handful of executives from the University of Phoenix[79] to buy the school, sever its affiliation with the Catholic Church, and repurpose it as a for-profit college, which they renamed Ashford University.[80] By doing so, the executives inherited the college's accreditation, which gave it access to federal financial aid.

With accreditation, Ashford's new leaders were able to explode enrollment. When they bought the college in 2005, it had just 332 students.[81] Six years later, it had over 83,000, almost all of them enrolled in the school's online program. In just a few years, Ashford became the second-largest degree-granting college in the country, and its revenue grew from $7.9 million in 2005 to $968 million in 2012.

But Ashford, it turned out, was allegedly little more than a scheme to extract money from its students. At a time when the school had over seventy thousand enrollees, its online degree program allegedly had just seven full-time faculty.[82] A study led by Senator Tom Harkin found that in 2011, the school had over 1,700 recruiters, but one—just one—employee devoted to helping its graduates find jobs.

Unsurprisingly, students had terrible outcomes. One former student complained, "I've gotten my resume updated numerous times, I've applied to well over 100 jobs, and years later I still don't have a job in my field."[83] Another said, after failing to find a job, "I have given up hope and I feel like I wasted 4 years and all that money for a useless paper that hangs on my wall."[84] According to the California attorney general, an alumni survey conducted by Ashford itself found that over half of its respondents were either unemployed or working in a field unrelated to their degree.[85]

Separate studies reportedly found that barely a quarter of students enrolled in bachelor's degree programs graduated within six years, while just 10 percent of students enrolled in associate's degree programs graduated within three.[86] As alleged in the same lawsuit, three years after leaving, less than a quarter of students had paid any money toward the principal balance of their loans.[87]

An education at Ashford was almost worthless; it was also overpriced. The four-year cost of an online bachelor's degree, including tuition, fees, books, and supplies, was over $60,000.[88] By comparison, the average cost of attending a local public four-year college in person, including room and board, was less than half that amount.[89]

And yet, Ashford enrolled tens of thousands of students through an extraordinarily aggressive, highly successful, and potentially illegal sales campaign. As the California attorney general subsequently alleged, Ashford's salespeople, misleadingly called enrollment advisers, university advisers, or admissions counselors,[90] told prospective students that federal financial aid would cover the entire cost of their attendance and, in fact, that surplus aid could be spent on cars and vacations. They said that the credits earned from other schools would transfer to Ashford. And they promised that entirely unrelated programs would help students achieve their ambitions: one recruiter, for instance, allegedly told a student that a program in acupuncture, reiki, and traditional Chinese medicine would help him to become a biochemist. "They lied about the costs. . . . The tuition and fees were outrageous. . . . So many lies," said one student.[91] Another student added, "I didn't realize how disregarded this degree [from Ashford] would be until I couldn't find a job."[92]

Recruiters also trapped students into enrolling. One of their alleged tactics was to promise that federal financial aid would cover the cost of attendance but that any award letters could be sent only after students enrolled.[93] Students would receive their letters months after classes started, discovering then that they might in fact owe thousands of dollars themselves. At that point, the students could withdraw or continue, but they would be obligated to pay Ashford either way. This left students trapped. By the time of the California lawsuit in 2017, students owed billions of dollars to the government in loans and hundreds of millions to Ashford itself.[94]

The salespeople were themselves under tremendous pressure. Managers allegedly forced people to stand at their desks when they missed sales targets and prodded them to make bets on one another's performances.[95] One manager had a "Guess Who" game where she showed her team's metrics and asked people to guess who had gotten each. Another saved the key cards of fired admissions staff on a key ring, which she would rattle in front of salespeople to remind them of what would happen if they failed to meet their targets. Because of these tactics, one director of admissions—that is, one of the salespeople—at Ashford said, "you stop thinking of these students as people, you start putting numbers on people.... Your entire day was consumed with a number so that you wouldn't get in trouble."[96] Ultimately, California succeeded in its lawsuit against Ashford, which the court ordered must pay $22 million for defrauding students.[97]

In short, Ashford preyed upon students' dreams: the dreams of an affordable, accessible education that, due to declining government investment, was ever harder to obtain. Ashford was in part able to accomplish this—to create the patina of legitimacy—because of its real estate. Recruiters were able to say that the school had a beautiful campus and a tradition dating back to 1918, and that students were simply enrolling in an online program from a reputable university, one in which the instruction would be just as good as that delivered to the school's in-person students.[98] But there were vanishingly few such students. In fact, the school shut the physical location entirely in 2015.[99]

Various government agencies investigated Ashford, but none succeeded in closing it. *First*, Senator Harkin's investigation into the for-profit college industry generally and Ashford specifically found that spending on instruction there fell from $5,000 to $700 per student after Warburg Pincus's allies bought the college.[100] Meanwhile, more than twice as much money went to profits and

nearly four times as much went to recruiting as went to actual
teaching. Senator Harkin also revealed that Andrew Clark, the
chief executive of Ashford's parent company, made $20.5 million
in a single year, more than twenty times that of his counterpart
at Harvard.[101] "I think this is a scam," Senator Harkin said, "an
absolute scam."[102] *Second*, in 2016, the Consumer Financial Protection Bureau fined Ashford's parent company tens of millions of
dollars for offering private loans to its students, which the company's salespeople said students could pay off for as little as $25 per
month.[103] This was false, and the bureau required Ashford to give
millions back to the students it misled. *Third*, in 2018, the Iowa
attorney general settled with the college for, among other things,
charging students in the middle of courses a surprise "technology
fee" of $900 to $1,200. Ashford agreed to return over $7 million
back to students.[104] *Finally*, there were other investigations by the
Massachusetts, North Carolina, and New York attorneys general,
as well as the US Department of Justice, the Department of Education, and the Securities and Exchange Commission.[105] But none of
these investigations succeeded in closing Ashford, which was ultimately sold to the University of Arizona.[106]

The private equity firm Warburg Pincus was central to the
school's whole project. In its prospectus to launch as a public company, Ashford's parent gloated that the private equity firm had
started the business, alongside the college's management team.[107]
After the company went public in 2009, Warburg retained two-
thirds of the company's common stock[108] and held two seats on the
company's seven-person board, while a third was held by a former employee of Warburg's.[109] As the attention on Ashford turned
sour, Warburg appeared to—but did not in fact—cut ties with the
school. In particular, after Senator Harkin's deeply embarrassing
hearing on the company, Warburg filed papers to sell its stake in
the business[110] (at the time it owned 65 percent of the company[111]).
But it didn't actually divest, at least not meaningfully, because six
years later, it remained the company's largest shareholder. Finally,
in 2017, thirteen years after its initial investment, Warburg sold
its stake in the company[112]—and only then after another scandal

over whether the school could accept money from the Department of Veterans Affairs.[113] Now, while Warburg Pincus prominently discusses many of its investments on its website, there is literally no reference to Ashford University on it.

But this makes sense. Ashford made hundreds of millions of dollars in profits.[114] Though the terms of Warburg's investment are not public, a portion of this money likely went to the private equity firm as the company's earliest investor and biggest shareholder. Why would it need to advertise this fact? Warburg got everything it needed.

*

THE STORY OF Ashford University illustrates what could happen when private equity got in the business of higher education. But there were so many other schools owned by private equity firms and so many other problems. For instance, graduates at the Austin campus of Southern Careers, owned by Endeavour Capital, earned nearly $5,000 less than the average Austin resident with only a high school diploma.[115] Three years after leaving school, less than a fifth of students there had paid back any of their federal student loans. More generally, students at private equity–owned for-profits were less likely to graduate and held more debt than students even at other for-profits.[116]

Moreover, not just Ashford, but other private equity–owned schools engaged in deception. For example, Education Management Corporation, owned at various times by Goldman Sachs's private equity arm, Providence Equity Partners, and Leeds Equity Partners, agreed to pay nearly $100 million to settle claims that it engaged in an illegal student recruiting scheme.[117] Education Affiliates, meanwhile, owned by JLL partners, agreed to pay $13 million to settle claims that it violated the False Claims Act and submitted false student loan applications to the Department of Education.[118]

Some private equity–owned schools even exceeded Ashford in certain ways, by, for instance, abandoning their students midway through the school year. Vatterott College, for example, owned by TA Associates, shut down on a day's notice.[119] Education Corporation of America, supported by Willis Stein & Partners, shut down with similarly little advance warning. This dizzying abandonment, perhaps more than anything, showed that these schools were interested in taking from, rather than educating, the students who enrolled with them.

These disastrous outcomes were so common because the problems of for-profit colleges and the problems of private equity compounded upon one another. If for-profit colleges were, by definition, concerned primarily with making money, private equity firms exacerbated that perspective by loading companies up with debt, extracting fees, and demanding returns in just a few short years. If for-profits insufficiently considered the needs of students, private equity firms made the problem worse, knowing that they were unlikely to be held legally liable for the consequences of their own actions.

But private equity wasn't alone. Allies in the federal government didn't just allow for-profit colleges to flourish: they overwhelmingly subsidized them. For example, between 2006 and 2016, Ashford got between 80 and 87 percent of its money from the federal government, primarily through federal student loans and grants.[120] This was not unusual: on average, over 80 percent of revenue from private equity–owned for-profits came from the government.[121] In fact, the industry's reliance on these loans and grants was so intense that the Department of Education had a rule that no more than 90 percent of colleges' revenue could come from it. (For-profits circumvented the rule nevertheless: Southern Careers Institute, owned by Endeavour Capital, actually got 98 percent of its revenue from the government.)

The government tried to constrain some of the industry's worst instincts but with limited success. In 2014, the Obama administration issued the "gainful employment" rule. Under it, colleges whose students generally had debt payments more than 12 percent of their incomes could lose their access to federal financial aid.[122] Though the rule took years to implement, it had an effect: colleges shut down some of their worst-performing programs and instituted tuition freezes.[123] Several private equity–owned for-profits failed under the rule, including programs at the University of Phoenix (owned by Apollo Global Management),[124] the Fortis Institute (owned by JLL Partners), and Brightwood College (owned by Landmark Partners and Vision Capital).[125] Apollo said that it would close programs likely to fail under the rule,[126] Fortis eventually shut down some campuses,[127] and Brightwood College eventually closed entirely.[128]

Implementing the rule was a tortuous process, however. The drafters took eight years to research the issue and considered 190,000 public comments.[129] Along the way, they faced $16 million worth of industry lobbying, spent particularly to hire Democrats close to the White House.[130] And after the rule was implemented, Congress and the courts were aggressively pushed to stall or stop it. For instance, House Education Committee chairman John Kline, who subsequently received over $100,000 from the for-profit industry, held a hearing called "The Gainful Employment Regulation: Limiting Job Growth and Student Choice" and claimed that the regulation would hamper the creation of career training programs and stifle job growth.[131] Meanwhile, after winning an injunction against an earlier version of the rule in 2012,[132] for-profit trade associations brought lawsuits in New York and Washington, DC. Both suits ultimately failed,[133] but it took years for the courts to resolve the matter.

Although the rule survived these legal changes, once Donald Trump was elected president, his administration acted quickly to undo it. In particular, President Trump's secretary of education, Betsy DeVos, was an advocate for for-profits and delayed the rule, suspended it, and proposed rewriting it, before ultimately rescinding it in 2019.[134] Along the way, her department acknowledged that doing so would cost the government $6.2 billion over ten years.[135] The Biden administration ultimately vowed to revive some version of the rule but chafed at simply returning to the old one, which it said was now technically outdated, and actually went to court to prevent it from being implemented.[136] All of which is to say that, nearly a decade after the rule was first promulgated, for-profit colleges and their private equity owners are not bound by any gainful employment regulation.

Under Secretary DeVos—a longtime advocate for the for-profit industry who herself invested in private equity[137]—the government found other ways to support the for-profit industry. DeVos disbanded the team that was investigating fraud at for-profit colleges.[138] She restored recognition for the accrediting body that oversaw several collapsed for-profits, and she hired several for-profit allies to work in her administration, including a former executive at Warburg Pincus's Ashford University, Robert Eitel, who worked at the Department of Education for a time without even leaving his old job.[139] With Eitel at the department, DeVos worked to dismantle another Obama-era regulation on for-profits, the "borrower defense" rule, which allowed students to discharge their debts when colleges lied about their job placement rates or otherwise broke state consumer protection laws.[140] Under the Obama rule, students received, on average, $11,154 in relief.[141] Under DeVos's replacement rule, they received $523.[142] The Biden administration announced plans to review DeVos's rule, but like so many other federal regulations, doing so could take months or years.

In short, the government subsidized the for-profit college industry but did little to constrain its predation. It was an industry that preyed upon people's dreams. But it was an industry that existed in large part because the government at the local and state level was unable to help people realize those dreams themselves. States' relative decline in higher education funding and the inability to compete with for-profit marketing meant that students moved from public universities and community colleges to for-profits. And throughout, private equity firms were ready to fund the entire endeavor, making an already predatory industry worse.

✳

IN THE STORIES above—in infrastructure, emergency services, and higher education—private equity is both a symptom and a cause of the problem. Though the basic logic of private equity made life worse for people who depended on running water, reliable ambulances, and affordable education, private equity only entered these businesses because governments chose to reduce their commitment to residents. For those who have pushed the philosophy that private industry in general—and private equity in particular—can always provide better and cheaper services than the government, these stories are a painful rebuttal. And for those of us who have lived with the consequences of that ideology, they show that we can demand that our governments do better. As explained later in Chapter 12, we can sue to stop private equity's predation in these industries. We can return the basic responsibilities of infrastructure and emergency services to our local governments. And we can demand that these services be affordable. That our governments once took on these responsibilities as a matter of course shows that, in fact, they can do so again.

CHAPTER TEN

THE INDUSTRY'S STRONGEST ADVOCATES

Private Equity in Congress

Private equity is a force in Congress. Since 1990, the industry has given over $896 million to congressional candidates and members.[1] This distribution of money has been bipartisan, with Republicans getting more—but just slightly more—than Democrats.[2] But this money tells only part of the story of the industry's influence. As noted earlier, private equity firms are populated with people who once held the most powerful positions in government. In addition to cabinet secretaries, generals, and two Speakers of the House (Paul Ryan and Newt Gingrich), any number of former congresspeople and senators now lobby on behalf of the industry[3] and several serve as their advisers or board members.[4] Perhaps even more importantly, the industry offers a home not just for former leaders in government but for their staff too. The lobbying disclosure forms for the largest firms are filled with the names of former government employees: former chiefs of staff and counsels, former legislative directors, and former special assistants.[5] This means that when someone in government is lobbied by a private equity firm, the person doing the lobbying may be a friend or a former boss. It also means that those currently in government know that, quite likely, they have a home to go to when their time in public service comes to an end.

As a result, private equity has become one of Congress's most important constituents. Through its money and connections, the industry has worked its unpopular will on Congress to enact surprise medical billing. It protected its preferred tax benefit, the carried interest loophole, despite its astounding unfairness and a fifteen-year campaign to end it. It extracted money from Congress during the pandemic. And it evaded oversight when firms, however inadvertently, damaged our national security. Quite simply, Congress works for few constituencies harder than it works for private equity.

All of the issues just mentioned are concerning, but it is the first—surprise medical billing—that tends to touch Americans most directly. For instance, Drew Calver was forty-four years old when he had his heart attack.[6] Perhaps even more than most cardiac episodes, it was unexpected: Calver was a healthy high school teacher and swim coach and had competed in an Ironman Triathlon just a few months before. As he collapsed onto his bedroom floor, Calver called out to his young daughter and used the voice recognition feature on his phone to send a text message to his wife, who was at the grocery store at the time. Ultimately, a neighbor got to Calver and took him to a nearby hospital. Doctors implanted stents in his clogged artery the next day.

As reported by Kaiser Health News and NPR, Calver recovered, but at a terrible financial cost. The hospital charged him $164,941, of which he was personally responsible for over $100,000,[7] despite the fact that Calver had insurance and that he even had the wherewithal to ask from his hospital bed whether it could cover the cost of his care (he was assured it would). But while his insurance company nominally agreed to pay for his operation, it and the hospital failed to settle on a price. The hospital, managed in part by the private equity–funded HCA Healthcare, billed Calver for the extraordinary remainder. "I can't pay this bill on my teacher salary," Calver said, "and I don't want this to go to a debt collector."[8]

After Calver's story was reported, the hospital that treated him dramatically lowered the amount it demanded.[9] But he was lucky; few people in America can expect national coverage for their own billing crises. Unfortunately, Calver's crisis is achingly typical. In a country where two-thirds of bankruptcies are the result, in part, of medical emergencies,[10] almost two in five Americans are "very worried" about receiving surprise medical bills.[11] These typically occur when a patient seeks treatment at a hospital or clinic that is nominally within their insurance network but is cared for by a doctor who is not and so is billed at an out-of-network rate.[12] Nearly one in five emergency room visits and one in six hospital stays result in such a surprise bill.[13] The problem is particularly acute for ambulances. Fully half of emergency ground trips result in out-of-network charges, and about two-thirds of trips on air ambulances—helicopters and planes—are out-of-network for the patients they carry, at an average cost of over $36,000 for each helicopter ride.[14]

Private equity firms are responsible for much of this. Doctors once worked directly for hospitals or on individual contracts.[15] But in time, and as discussed previously, these hospitals shifted to rely on physician staffing companies to populate their facilities. Physician staffing companies often depend on creating surprise, out-of-network bills for the patients in their care. And in the last decade, private equity firms bought them up. As described in Chapter 5, in 2016, Blackstone bought TeamHealth,[16] with over twenty thousand employees,[17] and in 2018, KKR acquired Envision,[18] with over seventy thousand.[19] The private equity owners loaded up both these businesses with debt, which together provided staffing for about a third of all emergency rooms.[20] At the same time, some of the same private equity firms bought up ground and air ambulance companies. KKR bought Air Medical Resource Group[21] and American Medical Response;[22] American Securities bought Air Methods;[23] and Patriarch Partners bought TransCare,[24] among other acquisitions.

Little good came from private equity firms entering the market. Researchers at Yale found that after Blackstone-owned Envision took over staffing at nearly two hundred emergency rooms, most—and in some extraordinary cases, all—of their bills became out-of-network surprises.[25] "I discovered a pattern of inflated bills and out-of-network bills," one doctor at such a hospital told the *New York Times*.[26] "What they are doing is egregious billing."[27] On average, emergency room patient costs increased 83 percent after the company took over.[28] "It almost looked like a light switch was being flipped on," said one of the researchers.[29] (In a statement to the *Times*, Envision's subsidiary EmCare called the study "fundamentally flawed and dated.")[30]

This seemed like precisely the kind of issue that Congress should solve, and at the end of the last decade, there was broad, bipartisan support for action: 90 percent of Democrats, 75 percent of independents, and 60 percent of Republicans wanted the government to prohibit surprise medical bills.[31] The key issue for Congress, however—beyond whether to act at all—was whether to set bill prices through benchmarking or through arbitration. Under benchmarking, out-of-network bills would be set at, say, the median price that insured patients paid. So, for example, if the average in-network patient paid $2,500 to treat a broken arm, an out-of-network patient would be billed the same. Under arbitration, the provider—often the staffing company like Envision or TeamHealth—and the insurer would go before a third party to determine a "fair" price. This way an arbitrator would decide, considering various factors, how much a patient should pay to mend a broken arm. Benchmarking was simpler and cheaper and would more likely have lowered health care costs. Arbitration was more complicated and less likely to do so. To the extent that they were willing to accept any legislation, staffing companies and their private equity owners preferred the latter proposal.

In 2019, despite all the ordinary dysfunction in Congress, committees in both the House and Senate neared agreement on a compromise solution.[32] Under it, small bills would be benchmarked to the in-network rate, while large bills would go to arbitration.[33] Even the White House had apparently agreed to the plan. It actually looked like something might happen. But for the private equity–owned staffing companies, this was an existential fight. State-level legislation had reduced out-of-network billing by more than a third in New York.[34] Similar federal legislation could be mortally damaging to TeamHealth and Envision, both of whom, thanks to their private equity ownership, were billions of dollars in debt.[35]

And so staffing companies and their private equity owners spent money—lots of money—to kill the bill. A mysterious group called Doctor Patient Unity, later revealed to be funded by Blackstone's Envision and KKR's TeamHealth, spent $54 million to oppose surprising billing legislation.[36] Their ads said that the bill was the "first step toward socialists' Medicare-for-all dream" and was an effort by big insurance companies to "profit from patients' pain."[37] The group was also unusually aggressive in whom it targeted. For instance, it deluged Senator Tina Smith with $2 million in attack ads, even though she supported the softer arbitration, as opposed to benchmarking, proposal (Senator Smith said that she thought the ads were "designed to intimidate us" into dropping the legislation entirely).[38]

And Doctor Patient Unity wasn't the only private equity–affiliated group agitating against change. Physicians for Fair Coverage, a half dozen of whose corporate board members were funded by private equity firms,[39] spent $4 million in just three months.[40] Their ads claimed that surprise billing legislation "would cut money that vulnerable patients rely on the most" and that "seniors, children and Americans who rely on Medicaid would be hurt."[41] (The ad, in addition to being wrong, was a non sequitur: surprise billing legislation was completely unrelated to Medicaid.) A third group, American Physician Partners, hired three lobbying firms and a former congressman to make their case in Congress.[42] The organization was affiliated with several staffing companies funded by the private equity firm Welsh, Carson, Anderson & Stowe.[43]

Ultimately, a more direct touch solved private equity's problem: Blackstone, which owned TeamHealth, gave Representative

Richard Neal, the chairman of the powerful Ways and Means Committee, over $31,000.[44] And so, in December 2019, just as Congress was finalizing compromise legislation, Neal and a colleague introduced a competing proposal that appeared to rely on arbitration alone. Neal's proposal wasn't even an actual bill—it was a one-page description of a potential bill—but it was enough to shatter the fragile coalition that supported compromise legislation.[45] One Republican aide told *BuzzFeed News* that "there is extreme frustration. This was the deal. It was vetted. It was signed off on. It was approved. The White House endorsed it."[46] And yet, the deal was dead.

The next year, Congress tried again, and again, Representative Neal almost killed the bill.[47] Only after repeated intervention by Speaker Nancy Pelosi did Congress, remarkably, manage to pass any legislation.[48] But the bill that passed was weaker than the benchmarking proposal, weaker even than the compromise legislation that had been proposed the year before. Instead, all types of medical bills would be pushed into a complicated dispute resolution process that could result in arbitration: essentially, Representative Neal's proposal. And once there, arbitrators were circumscribed in what they could consider in determining a fair price and could not, for instance, consider the cost that Medicare or Medicaid paid for similar procedures,[49] something that would likely have saved people money. Additionally, surprise bills from ground ambulances—bills that averaged $1,200 per ride,[50] often from private equity–owned companies—were excluded from the legislation entirely.[51]

The bill, undoubtedly, was progress: most Americans would not experience surprise medical bills in the way that they had before. But by resorting to arbitration, Congress failed to actually address the exorbitant prices that companies like Envision and TeamHealth threatened. Those prices would likely be absorbed into higher insurance premiums, which, in turn, would be passed on to consumers. That TeamHealth praised the legislation upon passage[52] was a sure sign that the problem remained.

Even after Congress passed the bill, private equity's lobbying didn't stop. In 2021, the Biden administration issued a rule to implement the legislation. Private equity–owned providers, however, apparently felt that the regulation would sway arbitrators toward awarding too-low fees. And so, in November of that year, 150 members of Congress sent a letter to the relevant agencies, urging them to weaken the rule.[53] The letter's lead authors all received large donations from Blackstone, KKR, and private equity–backed physician staffing companies.[54] And they weren't alone. Senators Bill Cassidy (who, in the 2020 election cycle, received over $57,000 from KKR and over $13,000 from Blackstone)[55] and Maggie Hassan (who received $12,000 from a private equity–funded staffing company)[56] wrote their own letter.[57] So too did Representatives Kevin Brady ($14,000 from Blackstone)[58] and Richard Neal ($31,800 from Blackstone).[59]

The letters weren't just nudges to the regulators; they were a way to shape the history of what Congress intended with the legislation. This proved quite useful when several providers sued to enjoin the rule. In their opening brief, the companies actually cited Brady and Neal's letter to argue that the Biden administration had misinterpreted Congress's intent in writing the regulation.[60] The letters were, in effect, tools to rewrite congressional history. And private equity, having largely won in Congress, was now using that history to win further advances. The industry was relentless, and it was enormously successful.

*

IF PRIVATE EQUITY exercised power in Congress to protect its ability to issue large medical bills, it demonstrated overwhelming—and overwhelmingly successful—force to protect its prized tax benefit: the carried interest loophole. As explained in Chapter 1, private equity firms were historically compensated on a 2-and-20 model: every year, they would take 2 percent of the assets they managed and 20 percent of the profits they earned past a certain threshold. The 2 percent of assets was taxed as ordinary income, while the 20 percent was taxed at the lower capital gains rate. Intuitively, this seemed unfair. Though private equity executives were earning income just as most people did, much of the money they made was taxed at a far lower rate than for the rest of us. This trick was what became known as the "carried interest loophole."

In 2006, Victor Fleischer, then a professor at the University of Illinois, brought this loophole to national attention in an unexpectedly popular law review article.[61] Fleischer's point was that by taxing a large part of private equity executives' compensation as capital gains, rather than as ordinary income, many executives in the industry could have lower effective tax rates than did ordinary Americans. A decade and a half later, the news that the very rich may pay relatively little in taxes is no surprise, but at the time, it was a revelation. Multiple members of Congress introduced bills to close the loophole, and then Senator Obama campaigned against the tax preference.[62]

But then Blackstone staffed up.[63] In 2007, the firm and its companies spent over $5 million on lobbying—more than five times what it spent the year before—to employ dozens of former staffers and a couple congressmen. By 2011, Blackstone's spending rose to over $8 million annually. (Carlyle, KKR, and Apollo also spent millions on lobbying during this time.)[64] And with that spending came results: none of the reforms introduced in Congress, or proposed by the president, went anywhere. After becoming president, Obama tried repeatedly, in 2011[65] and again in 2015,[66] to create momentum on the issue but failed each time. Toward the end of the Obama administration, Steve Rosenthal of the Tax Policy Center reflected that the private equity industry had "tied up the Congress for six or seven years." Remarking as one might about a bank heist, "[i]t's really phenomenal," he said.[67]

The industry would tie up Congress for many more years. President Obama's successor was generally regressive on most tax issues, but he had a curious distaste for carried interest. As a candidate, Trump claimed that the loophole had "been so good for Wall Street investors and for people like me but unfair to American workers" and promised to eliminate it.[68] Multiple times, the president reportedly tried to close the loophole as part of his 2017 tax cut package, and multiple times he was rebuffed. The about-faces in Congress during this time were almost comical. In late

November 2017, for instance, Susan Collins proposed to pay for an expanded child care tax credit by closing the carried interest loophole.[69] But just one day after she made the proposal, two Republican officials (one of whom—Drew Maloney—later left to run the private equity industry's main lobbying arm) said that she had retreated on carried interest. As if in reward for her reversal, Collins subsequently became a major recipient of private equity donations: KKR and Blackstone numbered among her largest contributors,[70] and Blackstone's Stephen Schwarzman personally gave $2 million to a super PAC that supported her.[71]

Faced with a strong constituency in Congress for protecting the tax benefit, Treasury Secretary Steve Mnuchin—an investor who subsequently formed his own private equity fund[72]—fashioned a compromise of sorts. Under it, carried interest treatment would apply to the profits of assets held longer than three years; less than three years, and profits would be treated as ordinary income.[73] The problem was that private equity firms typically held their investments for far longer than that, meaning that vanishingly few private equity firms would actually be affected by the change. The deal "was structured by industry to appear to do something while affecting as few as possible," said Victor Fleischer, the law professor who first brought attention to the issue.[74] As if to cement the tight bond between Mnuchin and private equity, the next year, his key legislative adviser left to run the industry's lobbying association.[75]

With Trump having failed to meaningfully address the loophole, the task fell finally to his successor. President Biden initially proposed, as part of his first budget, to raise the capital gains rate and eliminate the carried interest loophole for people with very high incomes.[76] But as his proposal wended its way through Congress, it grew weaker.[77] By the fall of his first year as president, the carried interest solution was reportedly no longer a part of his budget negotiations.[78] "This is a loophole that absolutely should be closed," Jared Bernstein, one of the president's senior economic advisers, told CNBC.[79] But "when you go up to Capitol Hill and you start negotiating on taxes, there are more lobbyists in this town on taxes than there are members of Congress."[80] This was true: there were over 4,100 lobbyists registered to work on tax issues, or about 7 for every 1 member of Congress. Moreover, while the administration was pushing to close the carried interest loophole, lobbying by private equity firms surged: Carlyle spent over $3 million in 2021, KKR over $4 million, Blackstone over $5 million,[81] and Apollo over $7 million.[82] Apollo alone employed the former general counsel to the House Republican caucus,[83] a former senior adviser to a past Speaker of the House,[84] a former chief of staff to another Speaker,[85] and a former US senator, among more than a dozen other former officials.[86]

Eventually, even the modest increase in the capital gains rate that Biden proposed failed. Senator Kyrsten Sinema conditioned her support for President Biden's revived Build Back Better legislation, by then renamed the Inflation Reduction Act, on making no modifications to the carried interest loophole. Looking at her contributors, this was unsurprising. By year-end 2021, two of Senator Sinema's top five donors were private equity firms; a third was Goldman Sachs.[87] Meaningful tax reform and a final fix for the carried interest loophole never stood a chance, it seemed.

Incredibly, in the debate over the legislation, private equity managed not just to protect its tax advantage but gain a new one. The Inflation Reduction Act established a corporate minimum tax for companies making over $1 billion in revenue a year. A key question was whether private equity firms and their portfolio companies would be considered together or apart for the purposes of calculating such revenue. This mattered, as it would mean that most private equity firms' portfolio companies would be subject to the minimum tax. But if they were exempted, it would give firms an advantage over other acquiring firms, as it would mean that the acquired companies might avoid paying a minimum rate.

As the legislation was considered on the floor, members of Congress rejected dozens of amendments, including amendments to extend the child tax credit, to cover dental, hearing, and vision benefits under Medicare, and to expand access to free preschool.[88] One of the few amendments they did approve was one to clarify that companies owned by the same investor—for instance, a private equity firm—would not be considered together for purposes of the minimum tax.[89] In short, private equity firms not only protected their preferred tax advantage, the carried interest loophole; they actually gained a new one. Yet again, the industry's allies in Congress delivered for private equity as they did for few others.

*

PRIVATE EQUITY'S FIGHTS to protect surprise medical billing and the carried interest loophole illustrate the industry's effectiveness in Congress in scuttling legislation and avoiding taxation. But private equity firms have also been effective in convincing Congress to, quite simply, give them money. For instance, at the outset of the pandemic, the industry received over $5 billion in federal assistance, in part through programs meant to help small businesses.[90] This might not have been so objectionable—COVID didn't distinguish between corporate ownership structures—except that the private equity firms whose companies received this money held over $908 billion in reserves. This meant that private equity firms, which might otherwise have had to spend their own money rescuing their portfolio companies, could simply do more deals instead. And that's exactly what happened: the ten firms that received the most bailout money did 230 leveraged buyouts in just nine months.[91] More importantly, this also meant that private equity firms could appropriate bailout money from their portfolio companies. For instance, businesses that Apollo, Blackstone, Carlyle, and KKR owned together got $1.8 billion in aid in 2020. But that year, those same firms extracted $5.4 billion in management fees from their businesses. In other words, with hundreds of millions of dollars flowing from Congress to their companies, private equity firms were able to take that money—and more—for themselves.

At the same time, private equity firms convinced the Department of Health and Human Services to give them more than $1.5 billion in no-interest loans through programs that Congress greatly expanded during the pandemic.[92] KKR and its subsidiaries, for example, got nearly three hundred loans that totaled more than $60 million, even though the firm itself had over $58 billion in reserves. Apollo Global Management and its subsidiaries, meanwhile, received at least $500 million, despite the fact that Apollo had $46 billion in cash on hand.[93] These loans were initially due within seven to twelve months, when, in October 2020, Congress further delayed repayments.[94] This free money was unnecessary for the private equity firms but allowed them to finance their various adventures free of charge. Not without reason, two Apollo executives said that the pandemic was a "time to shine."[95]

How did the industry accomplish this? The path is not perfectly clear, though it is worth noting that eighteen private equity firms and the industry's trade association together spent $32 million on lobbying in 2020.[96] These firms further disclosed that they lobbied on the CARES Act, Congress's primary emergency legislation during the pandemic.[97] While it is difficult to know what happened in the meetings their lobbyists had with legislators, it seems clear that private equity spent large sums of money to get even more money from the government.

*

CONGRESS HAS THE responsibility not just to legislate but also to investigate and oversee. Its various committees have the power to compel testimony and the production of documents, to issue reports, and to ensure that issues of national importance are receiving their due. But just as private equity got its way in legislation and appropriation, it managed to avoid Congress's tools of oversight. Here, the case of SolarWinds is instructive. That company sold software to help companies manage their computer networks, and its products were enormously popular: the company reportedly had over 320,000 customers[98] and contracts with the government worth $230 million. "We manage everyone's network gear," SolarWinds CEO once boasted.[99]

In 2016, the private equity firms Silver Lake and Thoma Bravo bought SolarWinds for several billion dollars.[100] Thoma Bravo's basic strategy was simple: buy and combine companies, increase their prices, and cut costs by hiring employees in other countries.[101] These moves were typically accompanied by layoffs, often of 10 percent or more of a company's employees.[102] And that's largely what happened with SolarWinds. The company bought up several competitors[103] and moved some of its software development to Belarus.[104] According to the *New York Times*, "every part of the business was examined for cost savings and common security practices were eschewed because of their expense."[105]

With an obsession over savings, SolarWinds allegedly neglected its own security. One former employee claimed that the company internally relied on older operating systems and web browsers that were more vulnerable to attack.[106] Plaintiffs in a class action lawsuit said that the company failed to create a password policy or cybersecurity training for its employees.[107] And a cybersecurity researcher discovered that the company accidentally published—and failed to take down for over a year—the password to its update server, from which customers downloaded its software.[108] (Almost comically, that password was "solarwinds123.")[109] Allegedly, the company even advised customers to disable their own antivirus tools before installing SolarWinds software,[110] a recommendation that put its own users in danger.

Allegedly, this neglect was no accident. In 2017, a cybersecurity adviser for the company met with SolarWinds executives and implored them to improve their internal security. Failure to do so, he warned, would be "catastrophic."[111] But under Silver Lake and Thoma Bravo's management, SolarWinds apparently declined to follow his advice. As alleged in a subsequent lawsuit, one participant said that the CEO "won't like spending that kind of money" to make internal reforms.[112] The adviser resigned in protest and subsequently said that a major breach of the company was inevitable.[113]

That's precisely what happened. Sometime in 2019,[114] hackers affiliated with Russia's intelligence service managed to embed malicious code into the software update for one of SolarWinds's most popular products.[115] Over the course of several months, thousands of customers downloaded the infected software,[116] through which the hackers were able to steal users' credentials and access ever more sensitive parts of their victims' networks.[117] Hundreds of businesses and at least a half-dozen federal agencies were infected.[118] Many of the details of the hack remain secret, but the government revealed that, at the very least, the intruders were able to access the emails of senior officials at the Treasury Department[119] and prosecutors at the Justice Department.[120] One government official called it "the worst hacking case in the history of America."[121]

It's hard to say that Thoma Bravo and Silver Lake's cost cutting inevitably led to the attack, just as it's hard to say that the budget cuts at Carlyle's nursing homes inevitably led to more accidents and deaths. But the drive to cut costs, to increase profits over long-run sustainability, permeated the company's culture. And the particular decision to shift software development to Eastern Europe, where Russia had deep connections, potentially exposed Solar-Winds to just this sort of attack.[122]

Congress could have done something, and to its credit, it tried. At least five committees—the Senate Committee on Intelligence, the House Committees on Oversight and Reform and on Science, Space and Technology, and both chambers' committees on homeland security—held hearings, jointly or individually, on the attack.[123] They heard testimony from current and former employees, from government officials, and from various experts. But missing from these hearings was testimony from executives at SolarWinds's actual owners, Silver Lake and Thoma Bravo.[124] In fact, while the Congressional Record during this time had nearly fifty references to SolarWinds, there was not a single reference to either private equity firm.[125] Silver Lake and Thoma Bravo, as owners of the company, were a crucial part of the story, but Congress never got their testimony and perhaps never even tried. This was made more galling by the fact that the two firms sold $280 million in stock just six days before the company revealed that it had been hacked.[126] The move saved the private equity firms $100 million in losses.[127] It was also, potentially, illegal, as selling stock based on "confidential corporate"—that is, insider—information is generally prohibited, and the Securities and Exchange Commission opened an investigation. That Silver Lake and Thoma Bravo potentially broke the law to avoid paying a financial price for their behavior was another reason to demand the companies' testimony. But Congress never did.

✳

PUBLIC RECORDS FROM this time do not show that Thoma Bravo or Silver Lake lobbied to avoid congressional testimony. Rather, the truth may be simpler and sadder: it simply did not occur to members of Congress to investigate these firms' roles in the crises just described. The lack of understanding of private equity, as well as Congress's innate chumminess with the industry, meant that these firms just don't receive the scrutiny that other risks to national security pose. But this failure to oversee suggests that if ignorance, not influence, is to blame, then there may be a chance for Congress, properly informed, to investigate some of the problems posed by private equity. In particular, the legislative branch may be uniquely positioned to examine one sprawling problem, alluded to in the previous example: private equity's ties to foreign governments.

Private equity firms make no secret of the fact that they take money from foreign countries and investors. But the extent of the industry's entanglement may be greater than is commonly understood. To take just one example, Blackstone has established numerous connections with America's fickle allies, like Saudi Arabia, and outright adversaries, like China and Russia. When Blackstone went public in 2007, for instance, China's sovereign wealth fund bought an enormous stake in the company,[128] just below that which triggered a review by the US government for national security concerns.[129] The purchase was apparently the first time that China invested its foreign reserves in something other than US treasuries[130] and, according to Stephen Schwarzman, required the personal approval of Premier Wen Jiabao.[131] In turn, Blackstone invested in various businesses in China[132] and, among other assets, sold the famous Waldorf Astoria hotel to a Chinese investment firm.[133] Perhaps as a result, the *Washington Post* said that Schwarzman had "one of the closest relationships to Beijing of any American executive."[134]

At the same time, Blackstone developed ties with the Russian government, at least for a while. In 2011, Schwarzman, along with several other private equity executives, joined the international advisory board of the Russian Direct Investment Fund, which married private and government money for development projects inside the country.[135] The partnership was short-lived, however: after Russia invaded Crimea in 2014, Schwarzman and others' names were removed from the fund's list of advisers,[136] and the following year, the Obama administration sanctioned the fund as punishment for Russia's actions.[137]

Finally, Blackstone cultivated ties to Saudi Arabia. Schwarzman spent years courting the country's de facto leader, Crown Prince Mohammed bin Salman,[138] meeting with him repeatedly and at one point hosting him for lunch in Schwarzman's Manhattan apartment.[139] In 2017, as part of President Trump's first state visit to the Saudi kingdom, Blackstone announced that the country would give the firm up to $20 billion to invest in infrastructure projects, primarily in the United States. Afterward, Schwarzman showered praise on the work of the young prince, telling CNBC, "It's sort of extraordinary what's going on in Saudi Arabia...you see economic growth and other good things happen when you have intelligent, informed, reform-oriented governments."[140] He added, "As an outsider, this is like a case study. And it's happening so fast and is so bold."[141] Perhaps this was true, though as Schwarzman was potentially aware, at the same time the crown prince was also arresting his critics[142] and holding some of the country's elite hostage.[143]

After Saudi operatives killed dissident journalist Jamal Khashoggi, Blackstone distanced itself visually, but not financially, from the country. In 2018, Schwarzman declined to attend Saudi's Future Investment Initiative, the "Davos in the Desert" of figurative and literal potentates.[144] But his company did not back out of its financial partnership with the country,[145] and ultimately, Blackstone abandoned even the optical illusion of distance: in 2021, Schwarzman returned to the Davos in the Desert event, where he spoke about women's empowerment at his firm.[146]

Perhaps these connections would not be so concerning were it not for the fact that Schwarzman played such a substantial role in shaping policy during the Trump administration. Schwarzman spoke with the president and his advisers frequently,[147] and Treasury Secretary Steven Mnuchin said that he talked to Schwarzman more than nearly any other business leader.[148] On matters of foreign policy, the Trump administration treated Schwarzman as a private diplomat. He served as an interlocutor between China's President Xi Jinping and Trump and advised Trump on a summit between the two at Mar-a-Lago.[149] He publicly nudged Trump not to declare China a currency manipulator and—after making eight trips to China in a single year on behalf of the administration—helped to negotiate a trade agreement between the two countries.[150]

This may or may not have been a good deal for America, but it almost certainly was a good deal for Blackstone. Reduced tariffs could potentially help the firm's industrial investments, as could a repeal prohibiting foreign ownership of Chinese financial services firms[151] in China could create new investment possibilities. And the mere fact of consultation mattered. Going back to Blackstone's deal with Saudi Arabia, that country reportedly considered working with several investment firms but chose Blackstone only after Schwarzman started advising Trump.[152] Schwarzman's proximity to power was an asset.

Blackstone's disquieting relationships with foreign policy adversaries and its leader's role in shaping American policy should be concerning for us all. And Blackstone's combination of foreign investment and domestic influence, while illustrative, is hardly exhaustive. The industry's connections to foreign governments are worthy of investigation, understanding, and perhaps, someday, legislation.

In this sense, Congress is uniquely positioned to act. Private equity's entanglement with foreign governments does not appear illegal. As such, the government's law enforcement agencies are largely irrelevant. Meanwhile, the arms of our foreign policy—the State Department and Defense Department, for instance—do not generally perform these sorts of reflective, searching inquiries that touch as much on life in America as they do abroad. The White House itself is so thinly staffed and lacks the subpoena power to compel testimony that would be necessary to investigate the issue. That leaves Congress, which has the broad purview to investigate people and companies. It has the power to compel testimony. And crucially, it does not need to pass a sixty-vote threshold in the Senate to begin an investigation. All that's required is the majority support of just one relevant committee or subcommittee; the filibuster plays no role here. An enterprising senator or congressperson need only convince a handful of colleagues that this is an issue worthy of their attention. In other words, even in a dysfunctional institution like Congress, action to investigate and constrain private equity's entwining with foreign adversaries might really be possible here.

✳

SURPRISE MEDICAL BILLING, carried interest, COVID funding, and so much else: these issues illustrate Congress's failure to legislate or oversee—and at times, its outright capture by—private equity. But if there is failure in the institution of Congress, there is also opportunity. The disturbing relationship between the industry and foreign adversaries is an issue worthy of Congress's attention and uniquely suited to its scope and powers. Progress is possible, even in the face of dysfunction. All that's needed is a single enterprising congressperson to begin this work.

PART III

HOW TO STOP THEM

CHAPTER ELEVEN

WHAT WE MUST DO

So what is to be done? I hope that the chapters thus far have convinced you that private equity firms are transforming America—not for the better—and creating systemic risks for our economy as a whole. I hope too that I have convinced you that these firms have done so not because of great business acumen—most of the people who run the largest private equity firms do not know how to write software, run a factory, or market a product—but in large part because of their ability to find, or create, gaps in our legal system. Finally, I hope that I have convinced you that our various arms of government, from the courts to Congress to our federal and state regulators, not only allowed this to happen but, often, actively encouraged it.

This story feeds into a deeper pessimism in our country. The twenty-first century has been enormously disheartening for most Americans. With the failure of the government to equitably address the Great Recession, its inconsistent and often inept response to the global pandemic, and its inability to address the urgent problems of health care, climate change, economic inequality, systemic racism, and the opioid crisis, there is a reason why public faith in our institutions is abysmal.

With our economy specifically, there is a widespread sense that things have simply stopped working. For most Americans, real wages have barely grown in two generations, while for the very rich they have doubled, and for the exceedingly rich, tripled.[1] Despite the commitment of over $4 trillion in emergency stimulus funds over the past fifteen years, household wealth for most Americans has yet to return to its pre–Great Recession high (this, of course, has not been true for the wealthy).[2] Meanwhile, businesses in increasingly concentrated industries have used the pandemic to raise prices for consumers and increase profits for themselves. But it isn't just that the economy feels unfair; it feels like it's breaking down. Manufacturing—the part of our economy that actually builds things—continues to shrink, while finance continues to grow.[3] We need banks and investors to provide capital and build businesses, but we do not need to give them as much power as they have today: research shows that American finance has long since exceeded the size at which it begins to hurt, rather than help, our growth.[4] Anecdotally, it feels like everything's getting a little worse: our products are lower quality, our stores are understaffed. Private equity is not the whole of this story, but by draining productive companies of their assets, it is a part. The question becomes ever more urgent: Can we still make things as a country? Can we still care for ourselves?

Commentators have looked abroad and backward to see where America might be going. Perhaps, some argue, America in 2023 is Japan in 1993. There, banks, often enmeshed in conglomerate *keiretsu* not unlike our own private equity firms, drove a speculative real estate bubble to absurd proportions.[5] When the bubble burst, the banks and *keiretsu* needlessly prolonged the survival of various zombie companies in order to hide their own financial risk.[6] Businesses moved production overseas and replaced their workforces with temporary employees who had less job security and fewer benefits.[7] Productivity collapsed, and unemployment exploded.[8] The government, which had been slow to recognize the crisis, ultimately spent enormous but insufficient sums on stimulus, creating a huge public debt. In the ensuing "lost decades," Japanese citizens disengaged from politics, and voter participation plummeted to levels more like those in America. Less than a fifth of Japanese people now believe that their children will be better off than themselves,[9] almost identical to public polling here.[10] Perhaps America is bound for similar years of twilight.

Or perhaps, more darkly, America in 2023 is Germany in 1933. There, giant corporations—in particular, the chemical manufacturer IG Farben—supported the Nazis at crucial moments and helped bring Hitler to power. Farben, for instance, made a massive contribution to the Nazis on the day of the Reichstag fire and spread the party's propaganda through its company-owned newspapers.[11] Once installed, Hitler made the corporations a part of his engine of war. Farben in particular ran a concentration camp at Auschwitz, and two dozen of its executives were ultimately tried at Nuremberg. Perhaps, some might argue, America is headed toward similar democratic collapse, enabled by its corporate elite.

Or perhaps—and this is my hope—America in 2023 is America in 1903. The turn of the last century was a time of renewal after two generations of darkness. After America abandoned the commitment of Reconstruction in 1877, most citizens lived in fear and misery. In the South, a dual campaign of white terrorism and voter suppression destroyed biracial state governments and reestablished rule by white elites. "Black Codes," blessed by President Andrew Johnson, criminalized the existence of "idle," "vagrant," or "undomiciled" African Americans and forced them into prison or labor much like the slave conditions they had escaped.[12] In the North, the fortunes of men like J. P. Morgan and James J. Hill were built on railroads, while over two hundred thousand mechanics and laborers died in their repair shops and on the tracks themselves. At a time when New York millionaires hosted literal treasure hunts on their country estates, burying diamonds in the lawn for friends to find with golden trowels, the *New York Times* and *Harper's Weekly* lobbied for a constitutional amendment to *take away* the right to vote from middle-income and working-class residents.

Government in the Gilded Age did not simply stand idly by: it was an advocate and defender for racial and economic elites. The Justice Department largely abandoned any attempt to stop white terrorism in the South,[13] while the Supreme Court interpreted the

Fourteenth Amendment to make it largely powerless to stop racial segregation. As monopolies formed in the steel, tobacco, and oil businesses, the Court also ruled that the new antitrust laws were powerless to stop manufacturing monopolies but could be used to break up labor unions. State courts, meanwhile, invalidated employee protections and anticompany store laws. And the US Supreme Court, in its famous *Lochner* decision, nullified a law limiting some workers to sixty-hour workweeks for violating their "liberty of contract."[14] The governor of New York at the time said it most truly when he declared, unironically, that "in America the people support the government; it is not the province of the government to support the people."[15]

And then, slowly, fitfully, with terrible defeats and disappointments, something changed. The rural Grangers and populists and, later, urban progressives led multiple movements to remake America. In the twenty years from 1901 to 1920, they started the first antitrust movement and broke up the steel, tobacco, sugar, and oil monopolies. In Congress, they established eight-hour workdays for interstate rail workers[16] and empowered the government to set fair railway rates.[17] They created regional banks to lend to farmers[18] and postal banks for others to save.[19] In the states, they passed factory safety laws[20] and worker compensation laws.[21] Localities established clean air ordinances,[22] and Congress created the national parks system.

For farmers, the rural Grange movement bought cooperatively owned machinery and grain elevators.[23] For workers, Congress prohibited discrimination against rail workers who joined unions and in 1912 created the Department of Labor.[24] To reduce inequality, the country passed a constitutional amendment to authorize a graduated income tax. To expand democracy, progressives successfully forced the direct election of senators and the president and passed the Nineteenth Amendment, which granted suffrage to women.

These were flawed movements. The vision of progress that these groups held largely excluded African Americans and immigrants. Yet, on balance, they remade America for the better and laid the social and organizational foundation for the New Deal a generation later. Arguably, the post–Second World War boom, which brought about the greatest middle-class prosperity in American history, happened because of the work that began at the turn of the century.

History here has a funny rhyming quality. When Stephen Schwarzman held an opulent sixtieth birthday party with hundreds of guests and video tributes to himself,[25] he did so at the Park Avenue Armory, which—perhaps unknown to Schwarzman or his guests—was built a century earlier by Gilded Age barons in part to defend against mobs of laborers.[26] Meanwhile, Schwarzman's Park Avenue apartment was once owned by John D. Rockefeller Jr., son of the creator of the Standard Oil Monopoly.[27] Schwarzman quite literally inhabits the role of a Gilded Age tycoon. And just as those tycoons were eventually tamed—the Standard Oil monopoly was splintered, the masses that the volunteers of the Park Avenue Armory feared eventually organized into unions—so too it can happen here.

All of which is to say that our country is not necessarily doomed to follow the path of others. America has experienced a first Gilded Age, yet with successes and setbacks and through shifting coalitions and years of effort, ordinary people remade the country. We can do so again. We are aided, ironically, by the fact that the victory of private equity over our economy was not an accident; it was the result of deliberate choices we made. If we once chose to let private equity win, we can reverse that choice, constrain the industry, and make room in our economy and our lives for more productive businesses, ones that actually build things and solve problems for consumers.

To do that, we need to make dozens of changes to our laws and regulations, changes that fall into three groups. *First*, we need to constrain private equity firms' abuses in specific industries by, for instance, setting minimum standards of care in nursing homes and ending contracts with private prison health care and cafeteria providers. *Second*, we need to change the incentives that drive private equity's worst excesses. In particular, we need to change our laws to make private equity firms consider the long-term effects of their actions, to stop firms from loading up the companies they buy with debt and extracting fees, and to stop them from dodging the legal consequences of their actions. *Finally,* we need to reduce the systemic risks that private equity poses to our economy overall, in particular through its expansion into insurance, retirement funds, and private credit. The chapter that follows describes these reforms in detail.

These are changes we can accomplish through regulation, litigation, and, if possible, legislation. But to do so, we must confront the reality that one branch of the federal government—Congress—has proven largely incapable of solving the greatest challenges of the past quarter century. As the previous chapters have, I hope, demonstrated, the courts, federal regulators, and state and local governments are not absolved here. But only Congress can write national legislation for the good of ordinary Americans, and for the most part, it has not done so. Consider some of the biggest crises facing America: the opioid epidemic, climate change, a broken immigration system, and economic inequality, to name just a few. These problems have been with us for generations, and yet, despite a handful of bills passed—most recently, the Inflation Reduction Act, which would offer incentives to reduce greenhouse gas emissions—Congress has proven largely unable to solve any of them. This is not necessarily because of a deeper division in our country. Large majorities of Americans, for instance, support gun control, climate change legislation, and a public health care option. In fact, majorities of Republicans support these measures too.[28] The problem isn't a deep division in our country on these issues; the problem is that Congress is largely unable to reflect the popular will, in particular when doing so would constrain the power of big businesses. It will be particularly hard to take action on private equity, whose firms have donated enormous sums to members of Congress and on a bipartisan basis. Blackstone, for instance, and its affiliated donors (employees and so forth) gave $38 million in just one election cycle and to both Democrats and Republicans. Overall, the industry gave over $200 million in the 2020 election cycle alone.[29]

Someday this may change. Congress may reform itself by, for instance, eliminating the filibuster, resuscitating its professional staff, and empowering its committees over its party leadership. Politicians responsive to widespread popular support for action on inequality may come into office. The institution may live up to its best ideals and rein in the excesses of corporate power while it addresses our climate crisis, passes comprehensive immigration reform, and finally confronts the raging opioid epidemic.

Perhaps. But we cannot wait for that to happen. Instead, we must use the other levers of power over private equity: federal agencies, courts, investors, and state and local governments.

Through federal agencies, we can address many of private equity's abuses in specific industries and contain some of the more dangerous tactics—dividend recapitalizations, for example—that drive the industry's worst behaviors. The Department of Health and Human Services, for instance, can impose minimum staffing criteria at nursing homes. The Department of Labor can effectively block private equity firms from accessing individuals' 401(k) savings. And the Federal Reserve can designate firms as systematically important and subject them to greater regulatory oversight.

Through the courts, we can stop some of the gaming that allows private equity to take all the benefits of its risk taking while experiencing none of the harms. The government or private litigants, for instance, can pierce the corporate veil that, in specific cases, insulates firms from the liability of their portfolio companies. Antitrust enforcers like the Department of Justice, Federal Trade Commission, and state attorneys general, as well as individuals, can investigate and sue to stop private equity rollups of various industries.

Through investors, we can shape private equity firms' behaviors. Worth Rises's successful effort to stop or slow public pension investments in private equity firms buying prison phone companies is a useful model. Where firms are acquiring particularly odious businesses, public pension funds can be pressured not to invest.

Finally, through the states, we can stop abuses in some of the most predatory industries in which private equity invests. States can, for instance, end contracts with for-profit prison health care and phone services companies. They can enforce corporate practice of medicine laws to stop the rollup of physician practices. They can end the most abusive arbitration agreements and outlaw the most predatory debt collection practices. And they can ensure basic protections for tenants in single-family home rentals and limit corporate ownership of these properties.

Perhaps most importantly, through states we can regulate the fundamental shortcomings of the industry. Private equity firms are often short-sighted, extractive, and insulated from the consequences of their actions. States can change that. Within certain constitutional limits on how much they can regulate actions beyond their borders, states can likely limit how much debt locally headquartered companies can take on in the process of being acquired. They can ban the use of dividend recapitalizations and sale-leasebacks for the same. And they can update their own liability laws and hold firms responsible for what they do. In the absence of congressional action, states can be some of the most powerful forces for reform.

To accomplish this, we do not need, as some might suggest, to rethink the entirety of the finance industry or overthrow capitalism itself (if such a thing were possible). No, the changes we need are not small, but they are not utopian either. We just need to make private equity firms, simply put, boring. The essential work of providing capital, both public and private, for businesses to grow and prosper should and will continue. But if we're successful, private equity firms will not be so readily able to extract money from captive companies. Instead, that money will go to productive businesses, which will be able to reinvest in infrastructure and employees, research and marketing. Rather than money flowing to the very richest among us, it will—at least potentially—go to useful endeavors. In the process, we will relearn how to make things. We will build a better economy for all.

To do all of this, we'll need to organize ourselves.

We'll need better reporting on private equity. Some of this will come from traditional news outlets, but nonprofit and volunteer organizations can play an important role here too. The Prison Policy Initiative, for instance, has done excellent reporting on private equity's purchase of prison phone services. Other industry-specific efforts would help enormously. We'll also need databases of private equity portfolio companies, their owners, and the institutional investors that support the private equity firms themselves. This will give activists areas on which to focus. And we'll need to better understand—and publicize—which firms are giving money to which politicians and when the latter are acting on the former's behalf.

We'll also need a way to channel popular energy. Groups like the Private Equity Stakeholder Project, Americans for Financial Reform, the American Economic Liberties Project, and the Open Markets Initiative are already doing important advocacy work. These organizations should consider campaigns to encourage people to get involved in federal rulemaking. Agencies like the Securities and Exchange Commission and the Consumer Financial Protection Bureau are doing important work, but it is often difficult for people to understand those efforts, much less comment on them. Advocacy organizations can help to clear the fog. These groups should also find a way to include people in the litigation process. Too often, public interest litigation is filled with dry briefs, devoid of human context. Organizations should find ways to include people in cases, through affidavits and testimony, which will help judges and clerks understand the human component of the decisions they make.

Finally, we'll need allies. Private equity firms will spend enormous sums to protect their interests. But we have the advantage of having more people. We'll need to build partnerships with other groups—social justice organizations, unions, small businesses, plaintiff-side law firms, and religious groups—who have experienced the effects of private equity firms' injustice firsthand. We'll need to educate one another on how private equity firms affect our specific areas of concern and share tactics (for instance, on how to hold firms legally accountable for the actions of their portfolio companies) that will be of interest to us all. We'll also need to run for office. Yes, advocates for economic justice need to win the Congress and presidency, but we also need to populate legislatures and city councils: as mentioned, much of the engine for action here will, for years to come, be at the state and local level. We also need public-spirited public servants. As someone who has worked in government several times, I can attest both to the importance of line-level government employees and to the need for people in government who care about, and can fight on behalf of, ordinary people.

So what can you do? Here, let me speak personally for a moment. My first job in the Department of Justice was in the National Security Division and specifically in the office that advised the White House on the legality and advisability of various national security policies. I held that job at the tail end of the Obama administration and into the Trump administration. As relevant here, for several months, my office was intimately involved in debates over the Trump administration's travel ban, which barred transit from several majority Muslim nations. It was a horrifying experience, and for several months, in meetings and memos, I and others tried to stop the various iterations of the ban from being issued or to have countries taken off the list. I was obviously unsuccessful in that effort and left the office shortly after the ban was issued, which the Supreme Court subsequently upheld. Nevertheless, throughout that process, I remember feeling strengthened knowing that my objections were supported by people—millions of people—outside the Department of Justice. The literal protests in the street gave me, a junior lawyer in a quiet office, the strength to make my complaints to more senior and powerful people.

All of which is to say that protest has an effect. In big departments and agencies, it can give career staff the courage to argue their points. In courts, it can alter and expand what judges and clerks consider possible options. The effects of protests might not always be visible, the strand connecting outburst and action not always clear, but I can say that they have an effect because they had an effect on me.

So, I encourage you to make your voice heard, at whatever level of volume you can. Tweet your outrage if you have a

moment. Volunteer your time or money to any of the organizations mentioned in this book, or find one that works on your
specific area of interest if you can (there are so many great local
groups working on, for instance, housing justice, eldercare, and retail workers' rights). If no organization does what you think needs
doing, start your own. And, quite seriously, run for local office. In
a time when national legislation is infrequent, we need smart people to push state and local lawmaking in the right direction. Your
voice matters.

Most importantly, do not give in to despair or nihilism. Yes,
private equity is part of a larger story of the financialization of our
American economy, a story about how our country has grown
more unequal and unjust. But to believe that our condition is, for
better or worse, inevitable is exactly what the most privileged
among us want you to believe. They want you to think that a better world isn't possible. They want things to stay as they are.

This isn't to say that change is certain, but it is possible. Let's
get started.

CHAPTER TWELVE

AN AGENDA FOR REFORM

The specific reforms in this chapter would rein in private equity's worst excesses. They fall into three groups and are organized by the different institutions that can make them a reality. *First* are reforms that address wrongdoing in specific industries where private equity firms have been active: nursing homes, for instance, and prison services. *Second* are those that would limit private equity firms' ability to engage in specific abusive tactics, like dividend recapitalizations and excessive management fees. *Finally* are those recommendations that would reduce the systemic risks that the industry poses to the broader economy through, for instance, its investment in private credit.

THE DEPARTMENT OF JUSTICE AND FEDERAL TRADE COMMISSION

Investigate rollups. Private equity firms are acquiring individual companies in a host of industries and rolling them up into larger businesses. This is happening to a diverse array of fields: dentist and dermatology practices, portable toilet and puzzle companies, church software providers and veterinary clinics, to name just a few. As these businesses are rolled up, prices are liable to rise, while quality—and pay for employees—is likely to fall. While not every rollup is illegal, in their extreme forms, they may violate antitrust laws, which prohibit acquisitions that may reduce competition.

In addition to investigating rollups themselves, the FTC and Justice Department should engage the states in this process too by more regularly referring matters of local interest to state attorneys general. The agencies should require more information from companies that propose to merge with or acquire one another. In particular, forms that companies submit to the government when proposing major acquisitions should be revised to require private equity firms to better show the investments they have in competing companies. This will make it easier for agencies to identify and stop incipient rollups.

Revise the merger guidelines. The antitrust merger guidelines describe when the Justice Department or FTC will typically intervene to stop proposed acquisitions. These have become baroque documents with too many exceptions that permit what once would have been impermissible acquisitions. Fortunately, under new and assertive leadership, the Justice Department and FTC are revising these guidelines. The agencies should return to the framework of the earlier 1968 guidelines, which offered clear direction for when mergers would be permitted and offered few exceptions that would cloud the agencies'—and courts'—analyses.

Investigate interlocking directorates. Private equity firms often place their allies on the boards of the companies they buy. Ordinarily this is fine, but private equity firms may violate antitrust laws if they install their representatives on the boards of competing companies. Such "interlocking directorates" are generally illegal because they could facilitate collusion between companies. The FTC and Justice Department should investigate these interlocks to ensure that private equity firms do not have so easy a mechanism to coordinate collusion among the companies they invest in.

Prohibit and prosecute tacit collusion. As private equity firms engage in rollups, it becomes easier for the remaining companies to engage in "tacit collusion," the practice by which companies can raise prices in coordination without an explicit agreement. Though rarely used, the FTC has broad authority to stop this.[1] The commission should prosecute the worst tacit colluders directly or promulgate a rule to stop the practice in general. Either strategy would make it harder for private equity firms to profit off of rolling up and concentrating industries.

Investigate prison health services. Prisoners are guaranteed a minimum quality of health care under the Eighth Amendment's prohibition against cruel and unusual punishment. But private equity firms' acquisition of leading prison health care companies led to a marked deterioration in the quality of care for inmates: as described in an earlier chapter, one female inmate was forced to give birth alone in her cell, for instance, while another prisoner died after his weeping lesions went untreated.[2] The Justice Department's Civil Rights Division, specifically its Special Litigation Section, should investigate these companies to determine whether they are violating prisoners' constitutional rights.

At the same time, the Justice Department should investigate private equity firms' acquisitions of prison food services, which have had similarly disastrous results. Inmates, as noted earlier, allegedly have been forced to eat meat labeled "not fit for human consumption,"[3] for instance, while others ate toothpaste to stave off hunger pangs or shivered at night with hunger, given that portions were so small.[4] The department should investigate these practices for similar constitutional violations.

Fairly enforce the bankruptcy code. Private equity firms have successfully used the bankruptcy code to discharge employees' pension obligations while retaining control of the companies they buy. (Josh Gotbaum, the former head of the Pension Benefit Guaranty Corporation, called this "pension laundering.")[5] They have done so in part by relying on "363 sales," which expedite the bankruptcy process at the expense of other lenders, and "credit bids," which, in essence, allow private equity firms to buy companies at a discount.

The United States Trustee Program, a part of the Department of Justice, is tasked with ensuring the equitable enforcement of the bankruptcy code. The trustees should file amicus briefs in high-profile bankruptcies arguing for limitations on 363 sales and credit bids. The trustees should also push to ensure that private equity firms do not slough off their pension obligations through the bankruptcy process. The trustees are well respected in the bankruptcy courts; their voice could make a difference.

Help to pierce the corporate veil. Private equity firms are often insulated from the wrongdoing of their portfolio companies, even when the firms themselves were responsible for or even directed that wrongdoing. The challenge for plaintiffs is to pierce the corporate veil, a legal argument that courts are often reluctant to accept. Plaintiffs would be aided if the Department of Justice—likely through the Consumer Protection Branch or the Fraud Section of the Commercial Litigation Branch of the Civil Division—joined a handful of plaintiffs in amicus briefs to help clarify that a private equity firm should not be insulated from liability where a company's misdeeds were directly caused by the firm's actions.

DEPARTMENT OF LABOR

Reverse private equity access to 401(k)s. The Trump administration issued a directive allowing 401(k) asset managers to invest in private equity funds. This will increase risks for ordinary retirement savers, while giving private equity firms access to trillions of dollars they do not need. This will also likely encourage private equity firms to pay yet more money for the companies they buy. These companies, loaded with debt, will then increase the systemic risk to the economy as a whole. The loophole enabled by this directive is unnecessary and should be eliminated. The Biden administration, thankfully, has started this effort, though it continues to permit a potentially large subset of 401(k) managers—those that also manage pension plans—to continue to invest in private equity.[6] The administration should complete the job and fully prohibit private equity firms from accessing 401(k) funds.

Clarify that the WARN Act applies to private equity firms. The Worker Adjustment and Retraining Notification

(WARN) Act requires that companies provide advance notice to their employees when contemplating major layoffs and provides damages to employees when their employers fail to do so. This statute is often violated, but the case law is muddled as to whether liability under the act extends to private equity owners of companies. The Department of Labor should help clarify through amicus briefs that, in fact, the act applies to private equity.

CONSUMER FINANCIAL PROTECTION BUREAU

Revive the payday lending rule. Private equity firms have bought up payday lenders. Toward the end of the Obama administration, the Consumer Financial Protection Bureau proposed a rule that would require these lenders to estimate that borrowers could actually repay the loans they were offered.[7] This mattered because the overwhelming majority of payday borrowers are trapped in lending cycles they cannot escape, in which they pay exorbitant fees and interest. The Trump administration largely gutted this rule, leaving only limitations on how often payday lenders could take money from borrowers' bank accounts. The CFPB should revive and expand the earlier, 2016 rule, which, fortunately, it is already considering doing.[8]

Revive the financial institution arbitration rule. Payday lenders have achieved a frustrating double standard: borrowers agree to pursue their own claims in arbitration but grant lenders the ability to prosecute their debts through the state court system. This standard, unsurprisingly, has been disastrous for borrowers, who, in pursuing arbitration, must often front unaffordable filing fees. In 2016, the Obama administration issued a rule to limit financial institutions' use of forced arbitration agreements. The Trump administration and Congress rescinded the rule using the Congressional Review Act. That act prohibits the CFPB from simply reintroducing the rule,[9] so the bureau should consider a more tailored regulation—one that prohibits the litigation-arbitration double standard just described—which might survive both congressional and judicial scrutiny.

Investigate usurious rates of prison release cards. Private equity firms have bought up companies that offer "prison release cards." These cards—essentially debit cards—are given when prisoners are released from jail or prison and contain the money they brought with them or earned while incarcerated. But usurious fees—for withdrawals, balance inquiries, and card activity and inactivity—make this little more than a way to steal former inmates' money. The CFPB has done important work investigating whether the fees charged by one company (JPay) violated the Electronic Funds Transfer Act.[10] The bureau should conduct an additional, larger investigation of the industry as a whole.

DEPARTMENT OF HEALTH AND HUMAN SERVICES

Impose staffing minimums and ban arbitration agreements at nursing homes. Private equity firms have been buying up thousands of nursing homes and generally gutting the quality of their care. Under the supervisory authority of the Center for Medicare and Medicaid Services, or the Occupational Health and Safety Administration's authority to regulate workplace safety, the Department of Health and Human Services should require a baseline level of nursing home staffing—likely 4.1 hours per resident per day[11]—that is generally recognized as necessary for residents' safety. Fortunately, the Biden administration has begun a process to set minimum staffing levels; it should complete that effort.[12] Similarly, the Obama administration in 2016 issued rules to largely ban arbitration agreements for nursing home residents. The Trump administration largely gutted this rule, allowing forced arbitration agreements in almost all circumstances. The 2016 rule should be revived.

Require reporting on the ultimate parent entity of nursing homes. Private equity firms often obscure their ultimate ownership of nursing homes to avoid legal liability. The Center for Medicare or Medicaid Services has regulations that require homes to disclose any investors with a 5 percent or greater ownership stake.[13] These regulations should be updated to require nursing homes to identify the ultimate parent entities of the investors, as well as the ultimate parent entities of the contractors that they use (nursing homes often obscure their wealth by paying money to contractors that they themselves own). This information should be made public so that the families of those who die in nursing homes know whom to sue.

FEDERAL COMMUNICATIONS COMMISSION

Make interstate prison calls free or at-cost. Private equity firms have bought up the leading prison phone companies and charged exorbitant rates. With new legislation signed in early 2023, the FCC finally has renewed authority to regulate interstate, as well as intrastate, prison phone services. Given the positive demonstrated effects of allowing prisoners to communicate with their families, the commission should use this authority and follow the path of several cities to make these calls free or at-cost.

Prohibit replacement of free in-person meetings with for-pay teleconferencing meetings. Prisons are increasingly replacing spaces for in-person visits with private equity–owned videoconferencing systems. This would not necessarily be a bad thing except that the private equity firms that own these prison teleconferencing systems are charging exorbitant fees. The result is that, increasingly, prisoners must pay to see their own family members. The FCC should use its regulatory authority over phone systems, if possible, to mandate that prisons that adopt these videoconferencing systems not replace in-person visits and make videoconferences free or at-cost.

DEPARTMENT OF EDUCATION

End abuses of for-profit colleges. Private equity firms are buying up the booming industry of for-profit colleges. From 2000 to 2010, undergraduate enrollment in for-profit colleges quadrupled.[14] The results have been disastrous. Private for-profit colleges enroll just 10 percent of students but account for half of student loan defaults. Average tuition at a for-profit is $10,000 higher than at a public community college. And graduates of for-profits typically earn less than graduates of public or non-profit colleges.

The Obama administration imposed a "gainful employment" rule, which cut federal spending when schools' graduates were unable to meet certain debt-to-earnings ratios. The Trump administration rescinded this rule. The Department of Education should reinstate it and expand the regulation to consider the outcomes for nongraduates as well.[15] The Trump administration also weakened the "borrower defense" rule, which created a process for canceling student debt when students were defrauded by schools. This too should be reinstated.

The Department of Education should also fix the so-called 90/10 rule, which generally requires that no more than 90 percent of students' tuition come from government sources but which historically excepted military funds, such as those from the GI Bill. The result has been that for-profit colleges particularly target veterans for enrollment,[16] who complain that college salespeople contact them dozens of times a week, often falsely describing themselves as "Pentagon Advisors" whose school is "Pentagon-approved."[17] In fact, almost one-third of GI Bill funds go to for-profit colleges.[18] Legislation in 2021 aimed to close that loophole by extending the 90-10 rule to all federal benefit programs, including military ones. The Department of Education, in drafting regulations to implement the new law, should confirm that it does.

The department also needs to hold executives accountable when for-profit schools shut down. The Center for American Progress proposed the innovative idea of conditioning the receipt of federal aid on for-profit school executives agreeing to hold themselves liable for school failures.[19] Money paid in salaries and bonuses should be clawed back to reimburse students who were cheated out of proper educations and who had nothing to do with the schools' mismanagement.

Finally, the government should make public data on graduate earnings and loan repayment rates for each for-profit college so that students can make informed decisions about the risks of attending for-profit schools.[20] Publicity is not a panacea, but if students are aware of schools' actual costs and likely outcomes, they may be more likely to enroll in nonprofit universities and community colleges.

SECURITIES AND EXCHANGE COMMISSION

Reduce the size, and increase the transparency, of private credit. Private equity firms are lending money to companies through the "private credit" markets, which function as something of an alternative to the stock markets, albeit with far less transparency. With less visibility, companies are more likely to take on too much debt, creating a bubble that may, like all bubbles, eventually burst, to the detriment of companies' consumers and workers. To push borrowers back to the public markets, the SEC should narrow Regulation D by limiting the size of private offerings, which function as an alternative to IPOs. The SEC should also reform Regulation 144A to limit the ability of private equity and other firms to pass off the debt they lend to other investors, a process known as syndication that gives firms an incentive to make loans, with little care to their quality. If possible, the SEC should require firms that seek private credit above a threshold size to publicly disclose certain facts about themselves, such as their level of indebtedness. To the extent that private credit is replacing the public market, the SEC should bring similar transparency to it.

Bring necessary transparency to the industry. The Dodd-Frank Act requires private equity firms to file a document—Form PF—with the SEC, which provides general statements about the firms' leverage and liquidity.[21] As currently designed, however, this form is not particularly informative and should be revised to collect much more information. For instance, rather than general statements, each firm should provide specific data on executive compensation, the companies the firm has invested in, and the level of indebtedness of those companies. Additionally, each firm should report generally accepted measures of revenue and income (the industry's preferred metric, "internal rate of return," has been shown to be liable to gaming). Finally, each firm should report on how much it has lent and borrowed through the "private credit" market, an emerging source of funds that poses systemic risks to the economy.

Establish fiduciary duties and fee disclosure requirements for private equity firms. Various professions have fiduciary duties, such as candor and loyalty, which generally require those professionals to be honest with their clients and to put the interests of their clients ahead of their own. Private equity firms, however, can often contract with their investors to slough off these duties, in essence preventing institutions that invest in them from suing when they act against those investors' interests.[22] Thankfully, the SEC has proposed a rule clarifying that private equity firms can no longer abandon their fiduciary duties[23] and must also disclose the fees they charge to investors.[24] The commission should complete this important process.

Prohibit incentive-based pay when companies engage in immediate dividend recapitalizations, lay off masses of workers, or abandon pensions. Section 956(b) of the Dodd-Frank Act directs federal agencies to "prohibit any types of incentive-based payment arrangement, or any feature of any such arrangement, that the regulators determine encourages inappropriate risks by covered financial institutions."[25] To the extent possible, the SEC should issue a rule barring incentive-based pay at private equity firms when their portfolio companies engage in dividend recapitalizations, mass layoffs, or abandoned pensions within the first several years of ownership. The rule should also ban pay when firms demand excessive management or transaction fees from their portfolio companies. Doing so would contain the excessive risks that private equity firms often place onto the economy.

INTERNAL REVENUE SERVICE

End the carried interest loophole. Many private equity executives pay lower tax rates than ordinary Americans, thanks to the 2-and-20 model, explained in Chapter 10. For close to fifteen years, however, Congress has struggled to close the loophole through legislation. Professor Victor Fleischer, who first popularized this issue, proposes that the IRS use its existing statutory authorities to issue a rule to eliminate this loophole.[26] Doing so would be far simpler than waiting another generation for legislative action and would dramatically reduce the incentives for private equity to engage in risky dealmaking.

Investigate management fee waivers. As just mentioned, private equity firms tend to be compensated on a 2-and-20 model, with variable tax rates. Private equity firms are increasingly creating complicated ways to have the 2 in the 2-and-20 model treated as capital gains too, using what are called management fee waivers. These waivers may often violate the tax code, but the IRS rarely investigates them, in part, perhaps, because the IRS never finished rulemaking to clarify which kinds of waivers are illegal. The agency should finish this rulemaking process and investigate the most egregious waiver schemes.[27]

Shift enforcement to the largest tax abusers. Many if not most private equity firms organize themselves as partnerships. The United States loses an estimated $75 billion per year from investors in partnerships who fail to report their income accurately.[28] Yet despite such widespread violations, these legal structures are exceedingly unlikely to be audited. In fact, people earning less than $25,000 are three times as likely to be audited as are partnerships. This is a terribly inefficient allocation of resources. Understanding that audits of partnerships are more complicated, the IRS should find ways to shift its enforcement resources to these vastly more important and, for taxpayers, costly, tax avoidance schemes.

FEDERAL RESERVE

Limit bank lending to overleveraged private equity portfolio companies. The Federal Reserve can play an important, perhaps crucial, role in regulating the banks that lend to private equity firms and the companies they buy. Back in 2013, the Fed and other bank regulators issued informal guidance, generally recommending that companies not borrow more than six times their annual cash flow.[29] This guidance was widely ignored, and by 2021, a third of all US loans sold to investors exceeded this threshold.[30] This creates huge risks for the companies that private equity firms buy: debt sucks money away from companies' operations and makes them vulnerable to collapse in slight downturns. To the extent possible, the Fed, alongside other bank regulators, should prohibit banks from making loans to private equity firms that would result in excessive leverage for companies. In the meantime, the Fed should revise its nonbinding guidance and more aggressively investigate those banks who flout it.

FANNIE MAE AND FREDDIE MAC

Protect tenants in private equity–owned rental properties. Government-sponsored entities like Fannie Mae and Freddie Mac helped to drive single-family properties to private equity firms. These same organizations can now help to protect consumers, by selling distressed properties they own to institutional investors only when those investors agree to basic tenant protections,[31] such as caps on fees, limits on rent increases, and rights of first refusal for tenants to buy these properties. Fannie and Freddie should also set internal preferences to sell to nonprofits and other mission-driven developers, who are less likely to take advantage of tenants.[32] To their credit, both Fannie and Freddie have started to prioritize some of these issues,[33] but they must dramatically increase their ambitions.

TREASURY DEPARTMENT

Designate the largest private equity firms as systemically important. In the wake of the Great Recession, Congress created the Financial Stability Oversight Council to monitor incipient risks to the economy and designate systemically important businesses to heightened oversight. The Obama administration identified a handful of such businesses, while the Trump administration attempted to undo much of that work.[34] The council should designate the largest private equity firms as systemically important to the financial system. Doing so will subject them to greater reporting requirements and potentially help curtail their most dangerous practices, such as loading up the companies they own with excessive debt.

STATE AND LOCAL GOVERNMENTS

Prohibit dividend recapitalizations and other abuses. In the absence of action by Congress, states can play perhaps the most important role in limiting private equity firms' abuses. As described throughout this book, private equity firms suffer from three core problems in their business model: they invest for the short term, load companies up with debt and extract fees, and insulate themselves from legal liability. States can address all three of these issues. They can require that private equity firms buying businesses headquartered within their borders hold those businesses for a meaningful period of time. They can require that firms not load up local companies with debt, not extract unreasonable fees, and not engage in tactics like dividend recapitalizations and sale-leasebacks, which often eviscerate companies' assets. And they can reform their "corporate veil" statutes to make it possible to hold firms responsible for the consequences of their actions.

Such actions will no doubt be subject to legal challenge. But states shape their own liability laws, regulate in-state companies, and even in certain circumstances impose laws that have effects beyond their borders. In a world where congressional legislation is unlikely, states may be the most powerful institutions to constrain the actions of private equity.

Investigate rollups. As described above, private equity firms are rolling up a huge range of industries. States, through their attorneys general, have the authority to enforce the antitrust laws and stop these abuses. To do so, they will need better information about acquisitions that are occurring. States should require companies to submit to them the same information they submit to the federal government about large proposed transactions and require independent reporting on smaller transactions that are nevertheless important, such as rollups in the medical profession. Washington and Connecticut already require reporting like this on significant health care mergers.[35] Other states should do the same.

Strengthen corporate practice of medicine laws. Private equity firms are rolling up medical practices in part because they have been able to circumvent state corporate practice of medicine laws. To make this possible, firms are appointing figurehead physicians to "run" these companies, when, in fact, it is the firms themselves that allegedly do so. States should update their laws that prohibit this "corporate practice of medicine" to more clearly ban this behavior and prevent medical decisions from being made by nonmedical professionals.

End contracts with abusive prison service companies. Private equity firms have bought numerous prison services, from cafeteria and commissary providers to health care companies and prison release card servicers. Previous chapters document the overwhelmingly negative result—far worse than what would likely happen if the states were in charge of these services. States and localities should end their contracts with private equity providers of these services and do this work themselves. By removing the profit motive for these services, governments will eliminate the incentive that drives down the quality of care in each industry and may ultimately save themselves money.

End surprise billing for ambulances. Congress passed legislation to deal, in part, with the scourge of surprise medical billing. But the legislation did not address surprise billing by ground ambulatory services.[36] States, many of whom independently adopted their own legislation on the issue, should ban surprise billing by these ambulance companies.

Ban abusive arbitration agreements. Private equity firms have imposed arbitration agreements in a range of industries in which they have been active: nursing homes, payday lending, for-profit colleges, and others. The Supreme Court has circumscribed states' ability to regulate these agreements, but there is still some room to maneuver. California, for instance, prohibited employers from forcing employees to sign arbitration agreements as a condition of their employment. The Supreme Court may yet invalidate the legislation, but in late 2021, the Ninth Circuit upheld it.[37] Vermont, meanwhile, proposed legislation banning "unconscionable" arbitration agreements, such as those that would require fees greater than those for a court proceeding.[38] The bill was ultimately vetoed,[39] but it, along with model legislation proposed by the National Consumer Law Center,[40] could serve as a template for other states.

Stop abusive debt collection practices. Private equity firms are buying up payday and installment lenders. States can update their sometimes comically out-of-date lists of personal property exempt from collection: until 2011, for instance, Massachusetts protected two cows, twelve sheep, and two swine from being taken by debt collectors, but only a car worth up to $750.[41] Updates will ensure that borrowers can keep essential assets—cars, phones, and so forth—that are necessary to work and survive. States can also prohibit the abuse of arrest warrants in civil cases and cap the statute of limitations on collecting consumer debts. Importantly, states can limit how aggressively debtors can garnish low-income people's wages, leaving a minimum for how much must be kept in people's bank accounts.[42] Finally, states can require creditors to have actual documentation that the debts they seek to collect are valid and properly transferred to the companies trying to collect the debts,[43] something, incredibly, that often does not happen.

Protect tenants in private equity–owned rental properties. Private equity firms are buying up single-family homes and flipping them into rental properties. States and cities should make sure that these residents are adequately protected. For instance, governments should extend rent control and tenant protection laws to single-family rental homes (California and Oregon have already done this[44]). They should limit how many properties a single owner can have and impose a residential vacancy tax for corporate property owners, to discourage owners from strategically keeping properties empty.[45] Governments should also stop selling foreclosed homes in bundles, a practice that ensures that only institutional investors can buy these properties.[46] And they should ban hidden fees that drive so much of private equity firms' income from rental properties. Disclosure laws here are not enough: governments should cap how much a corporate landowner can make from fees as a percentage of rental income.

Corporate control of the rental properties is also distorting the market: in 2021 alone, asking rents for houses rose 13 percent over the year before.[47] Building more properties is important, but in a market increasingly controlled by large investors, it is also necessary to impose limits on rent increases for some properties: Oregon, for instance, limits rent increases to 7 percent above the local rate of inflation; California, 5 percent.[48] Tenants should also be given a right of first refusal to buy properties they rent. Washington, DC, Portland, and Baltimore have already adopted this;[49] others should follow their lead.

End abuses of for-profit colleges. As discussed above, private equity firms are investing in for-profit colleges, which often have abysmal graduation and job placement rates while leaving students mired in debt. The Century Foundation has made a number of recommendations for how states can contain the abuses of for-profit colleges.

First, where data shows that for-profit schools are being particularly predatory—for instance, saddling students with unreasonable debt or demonstrating poor graduation or job placement rates—they should be shut down.[50] For-profit colleges already report much of this information to the Department of Education. States should require that the same information be sent to them, so that they can decide whether these schools should continue to operate. Additionally, states should create a private right of action for students to sue schools that have poor student outcomes.

Second, states should ensure that for-profit colleges actually spend money on instruction. For instance, public and nonprofit colleges generally spend over half the money they receive on teaching; for-profit colleges spend less than 10 percent.[51] Each college reports to the US Department of Education how much money it spends on instruction. States should demand this information themselves and require that a minimum percentage be spent on teaching.[52] This may ultimately discourage private equity investment in the industry.

Third, schools that go bankrupt must do so in an orderly way. For-profit colleges often close down unexpectedly, leaving students in the lurch. States should require colleges to close in an orderly fashion, and students shouldn't have to pay money (and in fact, should be refunded) when a school abruptly closes before they get their degrees.[53] Maryland's Disorderly School Closures Act[54] already does this and can serve as a model for other states.

Fourth, for-profit colleges must stop disguising themselves as nonprofits. All nonprofits must file a Form 990 with the IRS to prove that they are not abusing their tax-exempt status.[55] While the IRS should pursue investigations into the issue, the agency's staffing has been gutted. States should require the same information to be sent to them, to conduct their own independent reviews.

Finally, for-profit colleges must stop requiring students to sign binding arbitration clauses. The Obama administration issued a rule to end forced arbitration for students at for-profit colleges, a rule that the Trump administration reversed.[56] While the Department of Education should reinstate the rule, states can accomplish the same by conditioning the grant of any money they send to for-profit colleges on their dropping the use of arbitration agreements.[57]

STATE ATTORNEYS GENERAL AND PRIVATE PLAINTIFFS

State attorneys general and, in many cases, ordinary people can sue to stop some of private equity firms' worst excesses and generally can follow the litigation strategy for the Justice Department and

FTC described above. For instance, attorneys general and private plaintiffs can sue to stop anticompetitive rollups, as well as the interlocking directorates of corporate boards. When harmed, people can also sue for violations of state corporate practice of medicine laws. And both consumers and state attorneys general can sue private equity–owned businesses—for-profit colleges, nursing homes, prison services, and so forth—that violate local consumer protection laws.

Most creatively, people may be able to sue the board members of private equity–owned companies for breaches of fiduciary duty. Board members typically owe duties of care and loyalty to the companies they oversee, and yet many board members are personally divided between the companies they lead and the private equity firms they often work for. When board members authorize dividend recapitalizations, sale-leasebacks, or excessive fees, they may violate their obligations to these companies. Employees at, or customers of, companies gutted by private equity firms should seek to recover damages under this theory.[58]

CONGRESS

More than anything, to address the fundamental problems with the private equity business model, Congress should pass the Stop Wall Street Looting Act. This legislation, introduced by Senators Elizabeth Warren, Tammy Baldwin, and Sherrod Brown, as well as Representatives Mark Pocan and Pramila Jayapal,[59] would give workers higher priority in the bankruptcy process, end the carried interest loophole, and prevent companies from doing dividend recapitalizations within the first two years of ownership.

Congress can also address through legislation virtually all of the regulatory solutions discussed above. It can also fill important gaps that can only be fixed through new laws. For instance, it can condition the receipt of additional stimulus money on not firing workers or engaging in extractive practices like dividend recapitalizations and excessive management fees or executive compensation.[60]

Even if it is not feasible to pass legislation with a sixty-vote majority in the Senate, Congress should launch an investigation into private equity, similar to its high-profile investigation into Big Tech, which produced important revelations about the industry. With subpoena power, Congress will be able to uncover, in ways that ordinary reporting cannot, so much about how private equity firms are making their money. It can also uniquely focus on the concerning ties that many private equity firms have with foreign governments and the extent to which those ties may hurt our economy and our national security.

INVESTORS

Private equity firms get their money through a variety of sources: sovereign wealth funds, high-net-worth individuals, and, most importantly, public pension funds, which provide nearly half of firms' investable money.[61] Most public pension funds have open meetings and invite comments from the public. Following the example of Worth Rises's successful efforts to slow investments in prison phone services, discussed in Chapter 7, activists should use these meetings to stop public pensions from investing in the most predatory private equity firms.

ACTIVISTS

Activists—individuals, nonprofit organizations, academics, and others—play an essential role in building the infrastructure and public pressure for action on the predatory practices of private equity.

First, new or existing groups can connect people agitating for change in disparate industries affected by private equity, such as nursing homes, payday lending, prison services, and medical practices. The specifics of each industry are different, but there is much that these people can learn from one another, including how private equity firms are organized, where they might be vulnerable to lawsuits, when public advocacy campaigns have been particularly effective, and who might join adjacent causes in solidarity. There is much that we can learn from each other, and strength that we can draw on.

Second, these organizations can publish explanations of how the private equity business model affects their area of concern. Plaintiffs can then make better arguments to pierce the corporate veil and hold firms accountable for the actions of their portfolio companies. Publishing a database of the largest investors in private equity firm funds—public pension funds chief among them—will help activists identify which funds they should pressure to divest investments. Highlighting which politicians are getting the most money from private equity firms—information that is publicly available through the nonprofit Open Secrets but that is seldom reported—will be illuminating and informative. Many of private equity's influence campaigns are conducted in the open; all that is necessary is for someone to look.

Third, these organizations can make it easier for people to participate in rulemaking and litigation. Protests matter. So too do comments submitted to regulators and affidavits submitted to courts. The processes for participating in rulemaking and litigation can be obscure, but it is important for people to be a part of them. Citizens can make concrete the harms of decisions that private equity firms, more often than not, would like to be kept obscure and technical. Organizations can help people understand how to participate in these processes and convince them to do so.

Fourth, organizations focused on doing something about private equity plunder can power creative lawsuits, something that government agencies cannot. For instance, activists should work with investors in or former employees of private equity–owned companies to sue for breach of fiduciary duty and work with consumers to bring mass arbitration claims. These kinds of cases require finding private plaintiffs, a task that only activists outside of government can do.

Finally, organizations can pressure public pension funds to divest from private equity firms that engage in particularly odious tactics and pressure nonprofits (for instance, art museums), on whose board many private equity leaders sit, to agitate for change. Public pressure campaigns worked in the prison services industry, and they can work elsewhere too. All that's necessary are the organizations and people to offer focus and momentum.

✳

THE ACTIONS DESCRIBED above would rein in private equity's worst excesses and help to protect consumers, workers, and the economy as a whole. While many are ambitious and time consuming, the risk of inaction is enormous. As described at the outset of this book, left unconstrained, private equity will transform the economy in this decade the way that Big Tech did in the last decade and subprime lenders did in the decade before that.

But if inaction carries enormous risks, action carries enormous opportunity. Americans are a diverse and dynamic people. Limiting private equity—freeing people from these companies' predation and enabling their own entrepreneurialism—could immeasurably improve people's lives and the spirit of our country. The recommendations above are ambitious, but they are all achievable.

A better world is possible. We just need to demand it.

ACKNOWLEDGMENTS

This book relies on the reporting and research of hundreds of journalists, academics, and activists without whose work this project would have been impossible. I am enormously grateful for their research, as evidenced by the hundreds of citations in this book. Where appropriate, I have mentioned specific writers in the text to draw attention to their important work.

The opportunity to write this book has been an enormous gift, and I am grateful to my agent Gail Ross and editor John Mahaney for their faith in an unknown author. Thank you to Ben Wittes and Ganesh Sitaraman for crucial advice and introductions at the outset of the project, and to "Team Plunder"—Amita Chauhan, Zoe Li, Lindsay Maher, and Claire Yang—for exceptional research and revisions. Thank you to Johanna Dickson, Maggie Goodlander, Danielle Hauck, Aaron Hoag, Jonathan Kanter, Dara Kaye, Dave Lawrence, Kelly Lenkevich, Carolyn Levin, Karina Lubell, Kate Mueller, Adam Severt, and Paul Sliker, as well as to my many friends who read chapters and listened to long monologues during this project, including Max Friedman, Ben Heller, Nick Kelly, Leora Kelman, Henry Klementowicz, Paul Kubicki, Nikki Leon, Amy Marshak, Eric Rosenblum, Alan Rozenshtein, Laura Sloan, Alex Statman, and Glover Wright.

Two final notes of gratitude. *First*, to Louis Brandeis, whose book *Other People's Money, and How the Bankers Use It* was the inspiration and lodestar for this project. Brandeis's ideas permeated every part of this effort, and I returned repeatedly to his writings throughout and thought often about how his work a century ago is newly urgent today. *Second*, to my mother, Martha Ballou. She was and is a fierce champion for working people and someone whose moral compass I try to emulate. This book, of course, is dedicated to her.

NOTES

INTRODUCTION: A NEW GILDED AGE

1. Peter Whoriskey & Dan Keating, *Overdoses, Bedsores, Broken Bones: What Happened When a Private-Equity Firm Sought to Care for Society's Most Vulnerable*, WASH. POST (Nov. 25, 2018), https://wapo.st/2TMbMzj.

2. *William Conway, Jr.*, FORBES, https://www.forbes.com/profile/william-conway -jr/?sh=7d8e699f7ae6; *David Rubenstein*, FORBES, https://www.forbes.com/profile/david -rubenstein/?sh=13fecb91792f; *Daniel D'Aniello*, FORBES, https://www.forbes.com/profile /daniel-daniello/?sh=64cf09de6ea9.

3. Whoriskey & Keating, *supra* note 1.

4. *Id.*

5. *Id.*

6. Matthew Goldstein *et al.*, *Push for Profits Left Nursing Homes Struggling to Provide Care*, N.Y. TIMES (May 7, 2020), https://www.nytimes.com/2020/05/07/business/coronavirus -nursing-homes.html.

7. Whoriskey & Keating, *supra* note 1.

8. Complaint, *Salley et al. v. Heartland-Charleston of Hanahan SC LLC et al.*, No. 2:10-cv-791 (D.S.C. Mar. 29, 2010), EB No. 1.

9. Motion to Dismiss at 3, *Salley et al. v. Heartland-Charleston of Hanahan SC LLC et al.*, No. 2:10-cv-791 (D.S.C. June 25, 2010), ECF No. 15-1.

10. Order Granting Motion to Dismiss at 9, *Salley et al. v. Heartland-Charleston of Hanahan SC LLC et al.*, No. 2:10-cv-791 (D.S.C. June 25, 2010), ECF No. 45.

11. Ben Unglesbee, *In Pandemic Era, Private Equity–Owned Retail Is as Vulnerable as Ever*, RETAIL DIVE (July 14, 2020), https://www.retaildive.com/news/in-pandemic-era-private -equity-owned-retail-is-as-vulnerable-as-ever/581252/ (BC Partners acquired PetSmart, Leonard Green acquired J.Crew, and Sycamore acquired Talbots); *KKR to Acquire DTC Pioneer 1-800 Contacts from AEA Investors*, PR NEWSWIRE (Sept. 23, 2020), https://www .prnewswire.com/news-releases/kkr-to-acquire-dtc-pioneer-1-800-contacts-from-aea -investors-301136355.html (KKR acquired 1-800 Contacts).

12. Ingrid Lunden, *Iconic Font Company Monotype Is Getting Acquired by PE Firm HGGC for $825M*, TECHCRUNCH (July 26, 2019), https://techcrunch.com/2019/07/26

/iconic-font-company-monotype-is-getting-acquired-by-pe-firm-hggc-for-825m/; *Monotype*, HGGC, https://www.hggc.com/portfolio/monotype; *Bembo Family*, MONO-TYPE, https://catalog.monotype.com/family/monotype/bembo (the private equity firm HGGC bought Monotype, which licenses Bembo, among other fonts).

13. *Get the Private Equity Data You Need to Fundraise Faster, Invest Smarter and Exit Stronger*, PITCHBOOK, https://pitchbook.com/private-equity-database (identifying over 47,000 businesses in which private equity invests); Vartika Gupta *et al.*, *Reports of Corporates' Demise Have Been Greatly Exaggerated*, MCKINSEY (Oct. 21, 2021) (identifying about four thousand publicly traded companies in the United States).

14. Mark Vandevelde, *How Private Equity Came to Resemble the Sprawling Empires It Once Broke Up*, FIN. TIMES (Oct. 15, 2021), https://www.ft.com/content/2c56a7da-6435-469c-90d8-28e966f20379.

15. Paul J. Davies, *Why Private Equity Risks Tripping on Its Own Success*, WALL ST. J. (Feb. 13, 2018), https://www.wsj.com/articles/why-private-equity-risks-tripping-on-its-own-success-1518518193.

16. *Blackstone Growth (BXG)*, BLACKSTONE, https://www.blackstone.com/our-businesses/blackstone-growth-bxg/.

17. Frank Holmes, *Top 10 Largest Fortune 500 Employers in the U.S.*, FORBES (Oct. 26, 2022), https://www.forbes.com/sites/greatspeculations/2022/10/26/top-10-largest-fortune-500-employers-in-the-us/?sh=57eebb977e36.

18. Eileen Appelbaum & Rosemary Batt, PRIVATE EQUITY AT WORK: WHEN WALL STREET MANAGES MAIN STREET 41, 43–44, 52–53 (2014) (discussing use of debt, short-term investments, limited liability, and fees).

19. Alicia McElhaney, *LBOs Make (More) Companies Go Bankrupt, Research Shows*, IN-STITUTIONAL INVESTOR (July 26, 2019), https://www.institutionalinvestor.com/article/b1gfygl4r8661f/LBOs-Make-More-Companies-Go-Bankrupt-Research-Shows.

20. Jim Baker *et al.*, *Pirate Equity: How Wall Street Firms Are Pillaging American Retail*, CENTER FOR POPULAR DEMOCRACY *ET AL.* 9 (2019), https://united4respect.org/wp-content/uploads/2019/07/Pirate-Equity-How-Wall-Street-Firms-are-Pillaging-American-Retail-July-2019.pdf; Emily Stewart, *What Is Private Equity, and Why Is It Killing Everything You Love?*, VOX (Jan. 6, 2020), https://www.vox.com/the-goods/2020/1/6/21024740/private-equity-taylor-swift-toys-r-us-elizabeth-warren; Rosemary Batt *et al.*, *How Private Equity Firms Will Profit from COVID-19*, AM. PROSPECT (May 7, 2020), https://prospect.org/coronavirus/private-equity-firms-profit-covid-19-j-crew/; Sapna Maheshwari & Vanessa Friedman, *The Pandemic Helped Topple Two Retailers. So Did Private Equity*, N.Y. TIMES (June 18, 2020), https://www.nytimes.com/2020/05/14/business/coronavirus-retail-bankruptcies-private-equity.html; Ben Unglesbee & Nicole Ault, *Is the Road to Bankruptcy Paved by Private Equity?*, RETAIL DIVE (Nov. 9, 2018), https://www.retaildive.com/news/the-road-to-bankruptcy/540617/; Adam Lewis, *Private Equity–Backed Bankruptcies Surged in May, but Future Might Not Be So Bleak*, PITCHBOOK (June 5, 2020), https://pitchbook.com/news/articles/private-equity-backed-bankruptcies-surged-in-may-but-future-might-not-be-so-bleak; Jordan Weissmann, *Why Private Equity Keeps Wrecking Retail Chains Like Fairway*, SLATE (Jan. 26, 2020), https://slate.com/business/2020/01/private-equity-retail-fairway-why.html.

21. *The Forbes 400*, FORBES (2020), https://www.forbes.com/forbes-400/.

22. *GDP (current US$)*, WORLD BANK, https://data.worldbank.org/indicator/NY.GDP.MKTP.CD.

23. Dawn Lim, *Blackstone's Schwarzman Collects $1.1 Billion in Dividends, Pay*, BLOOMBERG (Feb. 25, 2022), https://www.bloomberg.com/news/articles/2022-02-26

/blackstone-s-schwarzman-collects-1-1-billion-in-dividends-pay; Nicole Goodkind, *JPMorgan Shareholders Vote Down Pay Bump for CEO Jamie Dimon*, CNN (May 18, 2022), https://www.cnn.com/2022/05/18/investing/jpmorgan-ceo-pay-shareholders /index.html; *Everything Is Private Equity Now*, BLOOMBERG (Oct. 3, 2019), https:// www.bloomberg.com/news/features/2019-10-03/how-private-equity-works-and-took -over-everything.

24. Jordan Weissmann, *How Wall Street Devoured Corporate America*, ATLANTIC (Mar. 5, 2013), https://www.theatlantic.com/business/archive/2013/03/how-wall-street-devoured -corporate-america/273732/.

25. Elizabeth Warren, *End Wall Street's Stranglehold on Our Economy*, MEDIUM (July 18, 2019), https://medium.com/@teamwarren/end-wall-streets-stranglehold-on -our-economy-70cf038bac76.

26. *Private Equity & Investment Firms: Summary*, OPEN SECRETS, https://www.opensecrets .org/industries/indus.php?ind=F2600&cycle=All.

27. *Timothy F. Geithner*, WARBURG PINCUS, https://warburgpincus.com/team/timothy -f-geithner.

28. *Team*, LINDSAY GOLDBERG, https://www.lindsaygoldbergllc.com/team.

29. *Investment Team*, JAM CAPITAL, http://www.jamcapitalpartners.net/#team-header-1.

30. *Team*, SOLAMERE CAPITAL, https://www.solamerecapital.com/team/.

31. *David H. Petraeus*, KKR, https://www.kkr.com/our-firm/leadership/david-h -petraeus.

32. Zachary Mider & Jennifer Jacobs, *At Cerberus, Feinberg Built a Web of National Security Ties*, BLOOMBERG (Feb. 16, 2017), https://www.bloomberg.com/news/articles /2017-02-16/at-cerberus-feinberg-built-a-web-of-national-security-contacts.

33. *Senator Kelly A. Ayotte*, BLACKSTONE, https://www.blackstone.com/people/senator -kelly-a-ayotte/; Tony Cook, *Evan Bayh's Board Seats Made Him Millions After Senate*, IN-DYSTAR (Aug. 13, 2016), https://www.indystar.com/story/news/politics/2016/08/13/evan -bayhs-private-sector-work-raises-questions/88582174/.

34. *Dan Quayle*, CERBERUS, https://www.cerberus.com/our-firm/leadership/dan -quayle/.

35. Tim Shorrock, *Kushner and Bannon Team Up to Privatize the War in Afghanistan*, NATION (July 14, 2017), https://www.thenation.com/article/archive/kushner-and-bannon -team-up-to-privatize-the-war-in-afghanistan/.

36. *Cutting James Baker's Ties*, N.Y. TIMES (Dec. 12, 2003), https://www.nytimes.com /2003/12/12/opinion/cutting-james-baker-s-ties.html (identifying Baker's employment with the Carlyle Group); Lee Fang, *Homeland Security Pick Gen. John Kelly Fails to Disclose Ties to Defense Contractors*, INTERCEPT (Jan. 17, 2017), https://theintercept.com/2017/01/17 /homeland-security-pick-gen-john-kelly-fails-to-disclose-ties-to-defense-contractors / (identifying John Kelly's employment with DC Capital Partners); Zachary Mider & Jennifer Jacobs, *At Cerberus, Feinberg Built a Web of National Security Ties*, BLOOMBERG (Feb. 16, 2017), https://www.bloomberg.com/news/articles/2017-02-16/at-cerberus-feinberg -built-a-web-of-national-security-contacts (identifying Dan Coats's employment with Cerberus); *John W. Snow*, CERBERUS, https://www.cerberus.com/our-firm/leadership /john-w-snow/; *Former FCC Chairman Kennard to Join the Carlyle Group*, CARLYLE GROUP (May 1, 2001), https://www.carlyle.com/media-room/news-release-archive/former-fcc -chairman-kennard-join-carlyle-group; *Julius Genachowski*, CARLYLE GROUP, https://www .carlyle.com/about-carlyle/team/julius-genachowski; *Ajit Pai*, SEARCHLIGHT CAPITAL, https://www.searchlightcap.com/team/ajit-pai/; *Former SEC Chairman Arthur Levitt to Join the Carlyle Group*, CARLYLE GROUP (May 1, 2001), https://www.carlyle.com/media-room

/news-release-archive/former-sec-chairman-arthur-levitt-join-carlyle-group; *Apollo Appoints Jay Clayton as Lead Independent Director*, APOLLO GLOBAL MANAGEMENT (Feb. 18, 2021), https://www.apollo.com/media/press-releases/2021/02-18-2021-113016273.

37. *US PE Breakdown*, PITCHBOOK (Jan. 11, 2022), https://pitchbook.com/news /reports/2021-annual-us-pe-breakdown.

38. Louis Brandeis, OTHER PEOPLE'S MONEY AND HOW THE BANKERS USE IT 13 (1914).

39. *Id.* at 16 (discussing excessive fees); *id.* at 49 (discussing forced partnerships); *id.* at 75 (discussing decline in product quality).

CHAPTER 1: OTHER PEOPLE'S MONEY, AND HOW THEY USE IT

1. Dan Primack, *How Workers Suffered from Shopko's Bankruptcy While Sun Capital Made Money*, AXIOS (June 11, 2019), https://www.axios.com/shopko-bankruptcy-sun-capital -547b97ba-901c-4201-92cc-6d3168357fa3.html.

2. *ShopKo Through the Years*, POUGHKEEPSIE J. (Jan. 16, 2019), https://www .poughkeepsiejournal.com/picture-gallery/money/2019/01/09/shopko-through-years -bankruptcy-green-bay-stores-headquarters/2526099002/.

3. Jeff Bollier, *"There Were Memories Here": Shopko Store Where Business Was Born Ends 57-year Run*, GREEN BAY PRESS-GAZETTE (Apr. 22, 2019), https://www.greenbaypressgazette .com/story/news/2019/04/22/there-were-memories-here-green-bays-original -shopko-store-closes-bankrupcy-liquidation/3537413002/.

4. *Shopko*, WIKIPEDIA, https://en.wikipedia.org/wiki/Shopko; *List of Former Shopko Stores*, MALLS AND RETAIL WIKI, https://malls.fandom.com/wiki/List_of_former_Shopko _Stores.

5. Erik Gunn, *One Year After Shopko Went Bankrupt*, URBAN MILWAUKEE (Mar. 22, 2020), https://urbanmilwaukee.com/2020/03/22/one-year-after-shopko-went-bankrupt/.

6. *Id.*

7. Jeff Bollier, *Shopko Files for Bankruptcy, Will Close 105 Stores, Including 16 in Wisconsin*, GREEN BAY PRESS-GAZETTE (Jan. 16, 2019), https://www.greenbaypressgazette.com/story /money/2019/01/16/shopko-files-bankruptcy-close-38-more-stores/2551819002/; Sari Lesk, *Shopko to Close All Stores, Liquidate After Unsuccessful Attempt to Find a Buyer*, MILWAUKEE BUS. J. (Mar. 18, 2019), https://www.bizjournals.com/milwaukee/news/2019/03/18/shopko -to-close-all-stores-liquidate-after.html.

8. *Sun Cap Affiliate to Buy ShopKo*, PROGRESSIVE GROCER (Oct. 19, 2005), https:// progressivegrocer.com/sun-cap-affiliate-buy-shopko.

9. Ryan Chittum & Dennis K. Berman, *Spirit Finance to Buy Most of ShopKo's Property*, WALL ST. J. (May 10, 2006), https://www.wsj.com/articles/SB114723045415348642.

10. *Id.*

11. Jeff Bollier, *Shopko Used Borrowed Money to Pay Dividends; Owes Wisconsin $13 Million in Taxes, Fees*, GREEN BAY PRESS-GAZETTE (Mar. 1, 2019), https://www.greenbaypressgazette .com/story/money/2019/03/01/shopko-dividends-under-investigation-also-owes -wisconsin-13-5-million/2906336002/.

12. Primack, *supra* note 1.

13. Bollier, *supra* note 11.

14. *Creditor Data Details—Claim # 345*, KROLL (July 29, 2019), https://cases.ra.kroll .com/shopko/Home-ClaimInfo.

15. *Shopko Timeline of Notable Events, from 1961–2019*, GREEN BAY PRESS-GAZETTE (Jan. 16, 2019), https://www.greenbaypressgazette.com/story/money/2019/01/16/shopko-timeline -notable-events-1961-2019/2540803002/.

16. Primack, *supra* note 1.

17. Jeff Bollier, *Bankruptcy Judge Approves $3 Million for 4,000 Former Shopko Workers Promised Severance*, GREEN BAY PRESS-GAZETTE (Oct. 15, 2020), https://www.greenbaypress gazette.com/story/money/2020/10/15/shopko-severance-bankruptcy-judge-approves -3-million-severance-pay-4-000-workers/3651776001/; WBAY news staff, *Court Approves Severance Pay Settlement for Former Shopko Employees*, WBAY (Oct. 16, 2020), https://www .wbay.com/2020/10/16/court-approves-severance-pay-settlement-for-former-shopko -employees/.

18. *Id.*

19. Gunn, *supra* note 5.

20. *Id.*

21. *Id.*

22. Dana Schuster, *This Party-Boy Investor Throws the Grossest Ragers in the Hamptons*, N.Y. POST (July 2, 2015), https://nypost.com/2015/07/02/the-hugh-hefner-of-the-hamptons -is-back-with-naked-ladies-lasers-and-booze-galore/.

23. PageSix.com staff, *Nude Frolic in Tycoon's Pool*, PAGE SIX (Aug. 7, 2011), https:// pagesix.com/2011/08/07/nude-frolic-in-tycoons-pool/.

24. *Id.*

25. Mark Memmott, *Romney's Wrong and Right About the "47 Percent,"* NPR (Sept. 18, 2012), https://www.npr.org/sections/thetwo-way/2012/09/18/161333783/romneys -wrong-and-right-about-the-47-percent.

26. David Corn, *Secret Video: Romney Tells Millionaire Donors What He Really Thinks of Obama Voters*, MOTHER JONES (Sept. 17, 2012), https://www.motherjones.com/politics /2012/09/secret-video-romney-private-fundraiser/.

27. Alexander Bolton, *Restive GOP Freshmen Eye Entitlement Reform*, THE HILL (Oct. 1, 2016), https://thehill.com/homenews/senate/298792-restive-gop-freshmen-eye-enti tlement-reform.

28. Jeff Stein, *Ryan Says Republicans to Target Welfare, Medicare, Medicaid Spending in 2018*, WASH. POST (Dec. 6, 2017), https://www.washingtonpost.com/news/wonk/wp/2017/12/01 /gop-eyes-post-tax-cut-changes-to-welfare-medicare-and-social-security/.

29. Steve Kadel, *Congressman: Reform Entitlement Programs to Reduce Federal Debt*, TIMES-INDEPENDENT (Apr. 4, 2013), https://www.moabtimes.com/articles/congressman -reform-entitlement-programs-to-reduce-federal-debt-2/.

30. Hannah Hess, *Welfare Reform Act Champion Clay Shaw Dies*, ROLL CALL (Sept. 11, 2013) https://rollcall.com/2013/09/11/welfare-reform-act-champion-clay-shaw-dies/.

31. Nicole Goodkind, *Mitch McConnell Calls for Social Security, Medicare, Medicaid Cuts After Passing Tax Cuts, Massive Defense Spending*, NEWSWEEK (Oct. 16, 2018), https://www .newsweek.com/deficit-budget-tax-plan-social-security-medicaid-medicare-entitlement -1172941.

32. *Individual Contributions*, FEDERAL ELECTIONS COMMISSION, https://www.fec.gov/data /receipts/individual-contributions/?contributor_name=leder&contributor_employer= sun+capital.

33. Wolf Richter, *Another Retail Chain Bought & Stripped Bare by Sun Capital Goes Bankrupt*, WOLF STREET (Jan. 17, 2019), https://wolfstreet.com/2019/01/17/another-retail -chain-owned-stripped-bare-by-sun-capital-goes-bankrupt/.

34. *2021 Highlights*, SUN CAPITAL PARTNERS (2021), https://suncappart.com/wp-content /uploads/2022/03/Sun-Capital-2021-Highlights.pdf.

35. *George Fisher Baker*, WIKIPEDIA, https://en.wikipedia.org/wiki/George_Fisher _Baker; *George F. Baker, 91, Dies Suddenly of Pneumonia*, N.Y. TIMES (May 3, 1931), https://

www.nytimes.com/1931/05/03/archives/george-f-baker-91-dies-suddenly-of-pneumonia
-dean-of-nations.html.

36. Louis Brandeis, OTHER PEOPLE'S MONEY AND HOW THE BANKERS USE IT 116 (1914).

37. *Id.*

38. *Vetrerie Riunite*, SUN CAPITAL, https://suncappart.com/portfolio/vetrerie-riunite/.

39. *West Dermatology*, SUN CAPITAL, https://suncappart.com/portfolio/west-derma
tology/.

40. *Smokey Bones*, SUN CAPITAL, https://suncappart.com/portfolio/smokey-bones/.

41. *Windsor Fashions*, SUN CAPITAL, https://suncappart.com/portfolio/windsor-fashions/.

42. Brandeis, *supra* note 36, at 5, 13.

43. *Baker, George Fisher*, SCOTT J. WINSLOW AMERICANA, https://www.scottwinslow
.com/manufacturer/BAKER_GEORGE_FISHER/2446 (estimating Baker's fortune
at $73.5 million in 1931, or about $1.4 billion in 2022 dollars).

44. *#79 Stephen Schwarzman*, FORBES, https://www.forbes.com/profile/stephen
-schwarzman/?sh=6ee1ffa6234a.

45. Mark Luscombe, *Historical Capital Gains Rates*, WOLTERS KLUWER (Mar. 9,
2022), https://www.wolterskluwer.com/en/expert-insights/whole-ball-of-tax-historical
-capital-gains-rates.

46. Philip Shabecoff, *U.S. Eases Pension Investing*, N.Y. TIMES (June 21, 1979), https://
www.nytimes.com/1979/06/21/archives/us-eases-pension-investing-pension-investments
.html.

47. Ann Crittenden, *Reaping the Big Profits from a Fat Cat*, N.Y. TIMES (Aug. 7, 1983),
https://www.nytimes.com/1983/08/07/business/reaping-the-big-profits-from-a-fat
-cat.html.

48. David Gelles, *Billionaire Confessional: David Rubenstein on Wealth and Privilege*, N.Y.
TIMES (Mar. 12, 2020), https://www.nytimes.com/2020/03/12/business/david-rubenstein
-carlyle-corner-office.html.

49. Stephen Gandel, *3 Reasons the Go-Go '80s Aren't Back on Wall Street*, FORTUNE
(Oct. 20, 2015), https://fortune.com/2015/10/20/wall-street-1980s/.

50. *History of the RJR Nabisco Takeover*, N.Y. TIMES (Dec. 2, 1988), https://www
.nytimes.com/1988/12/02/business/history-of-the-rjr-nabisco-takeover.html.

51. John M. Doyle, *Judge Dismisses Prison Term for Former Milken Associate*, ASSOCI-
ATED PRESS (Sept. 8, 1992), https://apnews.com/article/2efffe6a8df8a34c9e4200ec0473
25ed.

52. *Savings and Loan Crisis*, FEDERAL RESERVE HISTORY, https://www.federalreservehistory
.org/essays/savings-and-loan-crisis.

53. Tom Pratt, *Snapple Insiders to Cash In Part of Huge LBO Windfall*, INVESTMENT
DEALERS' DIGEST (Sept. 20, 1993) https://www.proquest.com/docview/198348759.

54. Antoine Gara, *How Burger King's Brilliant Brazilian Billionaire Turned $1.2B into $22B*,
THESTREET (Aug. 25, 2014), https://www.thestreet.com/markets/mergers-and-acquisitions
/how-burger-kings-brilliant-brazilian-billionaire-turned-12b-into-22b-12856055.

55. James Politi & John Murray Brown, *Houghton Mifflin Agrees $5BN Sale*, FIN.
TIMES (Nov. 29, 2006), https://www.ft.com/content/07a232e4-7f60-11db-b193-00007
79e2340.

56. John Kreiser, *Harrah's Accepts $17.1B Buyout Bid*, CBS (Dec. 19, 2006), https://
www.cbsnews.com/news/harrahs-accepts-171b-buyout-bid/.

57. Sue Zeidler, *MGM Seeks Lenders' OK for Pre-packaged Bankruptcy*, REUTERS (Oct. 7,
2010), https://www.reuters.com/article/us-mgm-restructuring/mgm-seeks-lenders-ok
-for-pre-packaged-bankruptcy-idUSTRE69706320101008.

58. Jeff Spross, *How Vulture Capitalists Ate Toys 'R' Us*, THE WEEK (Mar. 16, 2018), https://theweek.com/articles/761124/how-vulture-capitalists-ate-toys-r.

59. Daniel Rasmussen, *Private Equity: Overvalued or Overrated?*, AM. AFFAIRS (Spring 2018), https://americanaffairsjournal.org/2018/02/private-equity-overvalued-overrated/.

60. BLACKSTONE, https://www.blackstone.com/.

61. *About*, APOLLO, https://www.apollo.com/about-apollo; *see also Google Books Ngram Viewer*, GOOGLE, https://books.google.com/ngrams/graph?content=%22private+equity%22%2C+%22leveraged+buyout%22&year_start=1800&year_end=2019&corpus=26&smoothing=3 (The term *leveraged buyout* rose to prominence in 1987 and immediately declined in use. *Private equity* replaced leveraged buyout as the term of art, peaked in 2009, then similarly collapsed).

62. *US PE Breakdown*, PITCHBOOK 4 (Jan. 11, 2022), https://files.pitchbook.com/website/files/pdf/2021_Annual_US_PE_Breakdown.pdf.

63. *Gross Domestic Product*, FEDERAL RESERVE BANK ST. LOUIS, https://fred.stlouisfed.org/series/GDP (Q4 2022 GDP was about $24 trillion).

64. Dylan Thomas, *KKR Scales AUM in 2021, Targets Private Wealth*, S&P GLOBAL (Feb. 8, 2022), https://www.spglobal.com/marketintelligence/en/news-insights/latest-news-headlines/kkr-scales-aum-in-2021-targets-private-wealth-68795650.

65. *Blackstone Reports Fourth Quarter and Full Year 2021 Results*, BLACKSTONE (Jan. 27, 2022), https://s23.q4cdn.com/714267708/files/doc_financials/2021/q4/Blackstone4Q21Earnings PressRelease.pdf.

66. For simplicity's sake, unless otherwise indicated, references to private equity firms in this book include the funds they manage.

67. Eileen Appelbaum & Rosemary Batt, PRIVATE EQUITY AT WORK: WHEN WALL STREET MANAGES MAIN STREET 2–3 (2014).

68. *Id.* at 3, 7.

69. *Id.* at 72.

70. Victoria Knight, *Private Equity Ownership of Nursing Homes Triggers Capitol Hill Questions—and a GAO Probe*, KAISER HEALTH NEWS (Apr. 13, 2022), https://khn.org/news/article/private-equity-ownership-of-nursing-homes-triggers-federal-probe/; Amy Abdnor & Alexandra Spratt, *Part 2: Hotspots for COVID Deaths, Nursing Homes Have Long Been Targeted—and Gutted—by Private Equity*, ARNOLD VENTURES (Sept. 8, 2020), https://www.arnoldventures.org/stories/hotspots-for-covid-deaths-nursing-homes-have-long-been-targeted-and-gutted-by-private-equity.

71. *Id.*; Atul Gupta *et al.*, *Does Private Equity Investment in Healthcare Benefit Patients? Evidence from Nursing Homes* (National Bureau of Economic Research, Working Paper No. 28474, Feb. 2021), https://www.nber.org/papers/w28474.

72. Abdnor & Spratt, *supra* note 70.

73. Gupta *et al.*, *supra* note 71.

74. Appelbaum & Batt, *supra* note 67.

75. Adam Lewis, *PE Firms Keep Deploying Dividend Recaps Despite the Risks*, PITCHBOOK (Aug. 15, 2019), https://pitchbook.com/news/articles/pe-firms-keep-deploying-dividend-recaps-despite-the-risks.

76. Dan Primack, *Why Hertz Crashed*, AXIOS (May 26, 2020), https://www.axios.com/hertz-bankruptcy-6f16b3a4-141f-43cd-8f7b-e6a60a01d5dd.html.

77. Appelbaum & Batt, *supra* note 67, at 7.

78. Primack, *supra* note 76.

79. Tom Krisher, *Debt and Coronavirus Push Hertz into Bankruptcy Protection*, ASSOCIATED PRESS (May 23, 2020), https://apnews.com/article/3d73d765cb60bef45afc83fa0dd24775.

80. Lewis, *supra* note 75.

81. Eliza Ronalds-Hannon & Davide Scigliuzzo, *Sycamore Gets $1 Billion in Deal That Amazed Street*, BLOOMBERG (Apr. 11, 2019), https://www.bloomberg.com/news/articles /2019-04-11/sycamore-pockets-1-billion-from-deal-that-amazed-wall-street (Sycamore invested $1.6 billion in equity into the company, received $1 billion through a dividend recapitalization, and received another $300 million back through a separate deal).

82. Matthew Goldstein, *Private Equity Firms Are Piling on Debt to Pay Dividends*, N.Y. TIMES (Feb. 19, 2021), https://www.nytimes.com/2021/02/19/business/private-equity -dividend-loans.html; *Dividend Recapitalizations in Healthcare: How Private Equity Raids Critical Health Care Infrastructure for Short Term Profit*, PRIVATE EQUITY STAKEHOLDER PROJECT (Oct. 2020), https://pestakeholder.org/wp-content/uploads/2020/10/PESP-HC-dividends -10-2020.pdf.

83. Morgan Greene, *Hundreds More Lawsuits Filed over Ethylene Oxide Emissions at Sterigenics Plant in Willowbrook*, CHICAGO TRIB. (Aug. 21, 2020), https://www.chicagotribune .com/news/breaking/ct-sterigenics-lawsuits-20200821-mugtioojxvf2rfqoxnbfante2y -story.html. Sterigenics fought the lawsuits and argued that the quantities of chemicals it released were too small to be harmful. Nevertheless, in late 2022, a jury awarded $363 million to a plaintiff who lived near the facility and developed cancer. Sterigenics said that it would appeal the decision. Michelle Gallardo, *Sterigenics Trial Jury Reaches $363M Verdict in Favor of Woman Who Sued Willowbrook Company*, ABC7 CHICAGO (Sept. 19, 2022), https://abc7chicago.com/sterigenics-lawsuit-willowbrook-verdict-locations /12240473/.

84. *Sterigenics Funnels $1.3 Billion in Cash While Facing Increased Legal Pressure for Causing Cancers*, ROMANUCCI & BLANDIN (Feb. 3, 2020), https://jnswire.s3.amazonaws.com/jns -media/5f/59/11380855/Sterigenics_Amended_Complaint_2-3-20.pdf. The *Atlanta-Journal Constitution* exposed Sterigenics's use of dividend recapitalizations. In a statement to the paper, Sterigenics denied that the company "took actions with respect to capital structure at the expense of safety" but did not deny the recapitalizations themselves. Brian Eason, *Investor Payouts Put Sterigenics in Tenuous Financial Position as Pressure Mounts*, ATLANTA JOURNAL-CONSTITUTION (Feb. 3, 2022), https://www.ajc.com/news/atlanta-news /investor-payouts-put-sterigenics-in-tenuous-financial-position-as-pressure-mounts /EJC5VJYEH5CINFSN24TGN5C4RI/.

85. Goldstein, *supra* note 82.

86. Davide Scigliuzzo, *Private Equity's Dividend Spree Looks Like It's Just Starting*, BLOOMBERG (Sept. 15, 2021), https://www.bloomberg.com/news/articles/2021-09-15 /private-equity-s-dividend-spree-looks-like-it-s-just-starting.

87. *Id.*

88. Margalit Fox, *Alan Haberman, Who Ushered in the Bar Code, Dies at 81*, N.Y. TIMES (June 15, 2011), https://www.nytimes.com/2011/06/16/business/16haberman.html.

89. Peter Whoriskey, *As a Grocery Chain Is Dismantled, Investors Recover Their Money. Worker Pensions Are Short Millions*, WASH. POST (Dec. 28, 2018), https://wapo .st/32fIQFh.

90. *Id.*; Eileen Appelbaum & Rosemary Batt, *Private Equity Pillage: Grocery Stores and Workers at Risk*, CENTER FOR ECONOMIC AND POLICY RESEARCH (2018), https://cepr .shorthandstories.com/private-equity-pillage/index.html (estimating that Marsh's property was undervalued by $100 to $150 million).

91. Whoriskey, *supra* note 89.

92. *Id.*

93. *Id.*

94. *Id.*

95. *Id.*

96. *Id.*

97. Sun Capital allegedly received dividends on several of these investments. *See, e.g.,* Jonathan Shieber, *Sun Capital Sees Healthy Return on Fluid Routing Solutions,* WALL ST. J. (Mar. 9, 2012), https://www.wsj.com/articles/DJFLBO0020120308e838sjksd; Stephanie Gleason, *Indalex Sues Kirkland & Ellis, Alleges Investment Conflicts,* WALL ST. J. (May 15, 2021), https://www.wsj.com/articles/DJFDBS0020120515e85fjr2ah (In dalex alleged that Sun Capital received a substantial dividend from Indelex; the matter settled before the allegation could be resolved publicly).

98. *Sycamore Partners Completes Acquisition of Talbots,* CISION (Aug. 7, 2012), https://www.prnewswire.com/news-releases/sycamore-partners-completes-acquisition-of-talbots-165259216.html.

99. William Grimes, *Nancy Talbot, Who Helped Build a Retail Empire, Dies at 89,* N.Y. TIMES (Sept. 3, 2009), https://www.nytimes.com/2009/09/04/business/04talbot.html.

100. *Id.*

101. Khadeeja Safdar & Miriam Gottfried, *How One Investor Made a Fortune Picking Over the Retail Apocalypse,* WALL ST. J. (Mar. 21, 2018), https://www.wsj.com/articles/how-one-investor-made-a-fortune-picking-over-the-retail-apocalypse-1521643491.

102. Steve Gelsi, *Sycamore Pays Dividend Recap with $205 mln in Fresh Talbots Debt,* BUYOUTS (Apr. 27, 2015), https://www.buyoutsinsider.com/sycamore-pays-dividend-recap-with-205-mln-in-fresh-talbots-debt/.

103. Safdar & Gottfried, *supra* note 101.

104. Ben Unglesbee, *Talbots Downgraded by S&P as Pandemic Weighs on Sales, Cash Flow,* RETAIL DIVE (Jan. 22, 2021), https://www.retaildive.com/news/talbots-downgraded-by-sp-as-pandemic-weighs-on-sales-cash-flow/593821.

105. Debtors' Motion for an Order, *In re: Aeropostale Inc., et al.,* No. 16-bk-11275 (S.D.N.Y. July 22, 2016), ECF No. 496 at ¶ 5; Declaration of Julian R. Geiger, *In re: Aeropostale Inc., et al.,* No. 16-bk-11275 (S.D.N.Y. May 4, 2016), ECF No. 26.

106. Peg Brickley, *Aéropostale Loses Bid to Rein in Sycamore,* WALL ST. J. (Aug. 26, 2016), https://www.wsj.com/articles/aeropostale-loses-bid-to-rein-in-sycamore-1472243765; Memorandum of Decision, *In re: Aeropostale Inc., et al.,* No. 16-bk-11275 (S.D.N.Y. July 22, 2016), ECF No. 724 at 60-64; Jessica DiNapoli, *Aeropostale to Challenge Sycamore's Status as Creditor,* REUTERS (July 21, 2016), https://www.reuters.com/article/us-aeropostale-claims-bankruptcy/aeropostale-to-challenge-sycamores-status-as-creditor-idUSKCN10130P.

107. Jana Kasperkevic, *All the Stores You Shopped at as a Teen Are Going Bankrupt,* MARKETPLACE (Mar. 20, 2018), https://www.marketplace.org/2018/03/20/all-stores-you-shopped-teen-are-going-bankrupt/.

108. Nathan Bomey, *Will Your Aeropostale Close? Here's the List,* USA TODAY (May 4, 2016), https://www.usatoday.com/story/money/2016/05/04/aeropostale-chapter-11-bankruptcy-store-closure-list/83916028/.

109. Eileen Appelbaum & Rosemary Batt, *Private Equity Partners Get Rich at Taxpayer Expense,* CENTER FOR ECONOMIC AND POLICY RESEARCH (July 2017), https://cepr.net/images/stories/reports/private-equity-partners-2017-07.pdf.

110. Gregg D. Polsky, *Private Equity Management Fee Conversions* 12 (FSU College of Law, Public Law Research Paper No. 337, 2012), https://papers.ssrn.com/sol3/papers.cfm?abstract_id=1295443.

111. Jesse Drucker & Danny Hakim, *Private Inequity: How a Powerful Industry Conquered the Tax System*, N.Y. Times (Sept. 8, 2021), https://www.nytimes.com/2021/06/12/business/private-equity-taxes.html.

112. Appelbaum & Batt, *supra* note 67, at 79.

113. *Robert F. Smith*, Forbes, https://www.forbes.com/profile/robert-f-smith/?sh=45b9d7bb2236.

114. Ted Andersen, *Billionaire Private Equity Firm Founder, CEO Caught Up in Federal Tax Fraud*, San Francisco Bus. Times (Oct. 15, 2020), https://www.bizjournals.com/sanfrancisco/news/2020/10/16/sf-private-equity-firm-founder-federal-cuts-deal.html.

115. Laura Saunders, *The IRS Reels In a Whale of an Offshore Tax Cheat—and Goes for Another*, Wall St. J. (Oct. 23, 2020), https://www.wsj.com/articles/the-irs-reels-in-a-whale-of-an-offshore-tax-cheatand-goes-for-another-11603445399.

116. *Id.*

117. David Voreacos & Neil Weinberg, *Lawyer to Billionaire Who Died on Eve of Tax-Fraud Trial Took His Own Life*, Bloomberg (Nov. 29, 2022), bloomberg.com/news/articles/2022-11-29/lawyer-to-billionaire-died-by-suicide-on-eve-of-tax-fraud-trial.

118. Suhas Gondi & Zirui Song, *Potential Implications of Private Equity Investments in Health Care Delivery*, JAMA (Feb. 28, 2019), https://www.ncbi.nlm.nih.gov/pmc/articles/PMC6682417/.

119. Complaint, *Jones et al. v. Varsity Brands, LLC et al.*, 2:20-cv-02892 (W.D. Tenn. Dec. 10, 2020).

120. *Complaint to the FTC*, https://www.dropbox.com/s/f4o6w112dnzqv0x/Complaint%20to%20the%20FTC.pdf; Matt Stoller, *The Coming Collapse of a Cheerleading Monopolist*, BIG (May 27, 2020), https://mattstoller.substack.com/p/the-coming-collapse-of-a-cheerleading.

121. Varsity Defendants' Answer to the Class Action Complaint, *Jones et al. v. Varsity Brands, LLC et al.*, 2:20-cv-02892 (W.D. Tenn. Aug. 15, 2022), ECF No. 340; Bain Capital Private Equity's Answer to the Class Action Complaint, *Jones et al. v. Varsity Brands, LLC et al.*, 2:20-cv-02892 (W.D. Tenn. Aug. 15, 2022), ECF No. 338.

122. Leslie Helm, *Wellhaven's Pet Project*, Seattle Bus. (Apr. 2019), https://wellhaven.com/wp-content/uploads/2019/03/SBM-WellHavenArticle-3.29.19.pdf.

123. *Private Equity—What Veterinarians Should Know*, Veterinary Idealist (Feb. 12, 2020), https://vetidealist.com/private-equity-veterinarians/.

124. *Wall Street's Secret Pet Profiteering*, Americans for Financial Reform (Apr. 2020), https://ourfinancialsecurity.org/2020/04/blog-posts-wall-streets-secret-pet-profiteering/.

125. *Id.*

126. *Toys 'R' Us to Close 75 Stores and Cut 11% of Work Force*, N.Y. Times (Jan. 10, 2006), https://www.nytimes.com/2006/01/10/business/toys-r-us-to-close-75-stores-and-cut-11-of-work-force.html.

127. Ben Unglesbee, *Ex-Toys R Us Employees Win $2M Severance Agreement*, Retail Dive (June 28, 2019), https://www.retaildive.com/news/ex-toys-r-us-employees-win-2m-severance-agreement/557888/.

128. *Id.*

129. Mayra Rodriguez Valladares, *Private Equity Firms Have Caused Painful Job Losses and More Are Coming*, Forbes (Oct. 30, 2019), https://www.forbes.com/sites/mayrarodriguezvalladares/2019/10/30/private-equity-firms-have-caused-painful-job-losses-and-more-are-coming/?sh=35bbe1b37bff.

130. Jim Baker *et al.*, *Pirate Equity: How Wall Street Firms Are Pillaging American Retail*, Center for Popular Democracy *et al.* 40–44 (2019), https://united4respect.org

/wp-content/uploads/2019/07/Pirate-Equity-How-Wall-Street-Firms-are-Pillaging-American-Retail-July-2019.pdf.

131. Valladares, *supra* note 129.

132. Appelbaum & Batt, *supra* note 67, at 217; Julie Creswell, *Oh, No! What Happened to Archway?*, N.Y. TIMES (May 30, 2009), https://www.nytimes.com/2009/05/31/business/31archway.html.

133. *Id.*

134. *Id.* Catterton denied allegations of financial mismanagement made in a subsequent complaint by unsecured creditors. A spokeswoman for Catterton told the *Times* that "Archway notwithstanding, Catterton has helped to capitalize and grow nearly 75 successful consumer companies in its 20-year history."

135. *Warren, Pocan, and Ocasio-Cortez Investigate Private Equity Firms Profiteering Off Incarcerated People and Their Families*, OFFICE OF SENATOR ELIZABETH WARREN (Oct. 1, 2019), https://www.warren.senate.gov/oversight/letters/warren-pocan-and-ocasio-cortez-investigate-private-equity-firms-profiteering-off-incarcerated-people-and-their-families.

136. Letter from Senator Elizabeth Warren *et al.* to Andrew Feldstein *et al.* at 8 (Sept. 30, 2019), https://www.warren.senate.gov/imo/media/doc/2019-09-30%20Letters%20to%20PE%20Firms%20re%20Prison%20Services.pdf.

137. Steve Coll, *The Jail Health-Care Crisis*, NEW YORKER (Feb., 25, 2019), https://www.newyorker.com/magazine/2019/03/04/the-jail-health-care-crisis.

138. *Id.*

139. Neil Irwin, *How Private Equity Buried Payless*, N.Y. TIMES (Feb. 1, 2020), https://www.nytimes.com/2020/01/31/upshot/payless-private-equity-capitalism.html.

140. *Id.*

141. Alicia McElhaney, *LBOs Make (More) Companies Go Bankrupt, Research Shows*, INSTITUTIONAL INVESTOR (July 26, 2019), https://www.institutionalinvestor.com/article/b1gfygl4r8661f/LBOs-Make-More-Companies-Go-Bankrupt-Research-Shows.

142. *Capabilities*, BLUE WOLF CAPITAL, http://bluewolfcapita.wpengine.com/about/capabilities/.

143. Stephen Steed, *Arkansas Town Sees More Jobs with Sawmill Revival*, ARK. DEMOCRAT-GAZETTE (June 8, 2017), https://www.capitalpress.com/nation_world/profit/arkansas-town-sees-more-jobs-with-sawmill-revival/article_8332864c-0459-55a6-9bf4-a6fafe409f03.html.

144. *Capabilities, supra* note 142.

145. Steed, *supra* note 143.

146. Stephen Steed, *Sawmill's Revival Gives Arkansas Town a Lift*, ARK. DEMOCRAT-GAZETTE (June 1, 2017), https://www.arkansasonline.com/news/2017/jun/01/sawmill-s-revival-gives-town-a-lift-201/.

147. *Id.*

148. Steed, *supra* note 143.

149. *Investment Strategy*, BLUE WOLF CAPITAL, https://www.bluewolfcapital.com/strategy/investment-strategy.

150. Interview with Charlie Miller, partner and chief compliance officer, Blue Wolf Capital (Mar. 14, 2022).

151. *Conifex Buying U.S. Sawmills for $258 Million to Add 50 per Cent More Capacity*, FIN. POST (May 15, 2018), https://financialpost.com/pmn/business-pmn/conifex-buying-u-s-sawmills-for-258-million-to-add-50-per-cent-more-capacity.

152. Robert Dalheim, *Conifex Shuts Down Arkansas Lumber Mill Indefinitely, Lays Off 92*, WOODWORKING NETWORK (Aug. 15, 2019), https://www.woodworkingnetwork.com

/news/woodworking-industry-news/conifex-shuts-down-arkansas-lumber-mill
-indefinitely-lays-92.

153. *Resolute Forest Products Buying El Dorado, Glenwood Mills from Conifex, Will Reopen Union County Site in 2021*, MAGNOLIA REP. (Jan. 4, 2020), http://www.magnoliareporter
.com/news_and_business/union_county/article_b1febdaa-2927-11ea-a8eb-27ef7d9357e1
.html.

154. *Glenwood*, RESOLUTE FOREST PRODUCTS, https://www.resolutefp.com/installation
_site.aspx?siteid=173&langtype=4105.

CHAPTER 2: ENDING HOMEOWNERSHIP AS WE KNOW IT

1. Amanda L. Gordon, *Schwarzman Parties at 70 with Camels, Cake and Trump's Entourage*, BLOOMBERG (Feb. 13, 2017), https://bloom.bg/3mS8hWK.

2. Bess Levin, *Populist Hero Stephen Schwarzman's Birthday Blowout Included Fireworks, Acrobats, and Live Camels*, VANITY FAIR (Feb. 13, 2017), https://www.vanityfair.com/news
/2017/02/stephen-schwarzmans-birthday-blowout-included-fireworks-acrobats-and-live
-camels; Sam Dangremond, *Steve Schwarzman Hosted an Epic 70th Birthday Party in Palm Beach*, TOWN & COUNTRY (Feb. 13, 2017), https://www.townandcountrymag.com/the
-scene/parties/news/a9556/steve-schwarzman-birthday-party/; Emily Smith, *Blackstone CEO Throws Himself "the Party of the Century,"* N.Y. POST (Feb. 13, 2017), https://
pagesix.com/2017/02/13/blackstone-ceo-throws-himself-the-party-of-the-century/.

3. Sam Dangremond, *Steve Schwarzman Hosted an Epic 70th Birthday Party in Palm Beach*, TOWN & COUNTRY (Feb. 13, 2017), https://www.townandcountrymag.com/the
-scene/parties/news/a9556/steve-schwarzman-birthday-party/.

4. Levin, *supra* note 2.

5. Smith, *supra* note 2.

6. Gordon, *supra* note 1.

7. Smith, *supra* note 2.

8. Julia Gordon, *The Dark Side of Single-Family Rental*, SHELTERFORCE (July 30, 2018), https://shelterforce.org/2018/07/30/the-dark-side-of-single-family-rental/.

9. Brett Christophers, *How and Why U.S. Single-Family Housing Became an Investor Asset Class*, J. URBAN HIST. 1, 6–7 (2021), https://journals.sagepub.com/doi/pdf
/10.1177/00961442211029601.

10. Francesca Mari, *A $60 Billion Housing Grab by Wall Street*, N.Y. TIMES (Mar. 4, 2020), https://www.nytimes.com/2020/03/04/magazine/wall-street-landlords.html.

11. Elora Raymond et al., *Corporate Landlords, Institutional Investors, and Displacement: Eviction Rates in Single-Family Rentals*, 04-16 COMMUNITY & ECONOMIC DEVELOPMENT DISCUSSION PAPER 1, 2 (Dec. 2016), https://www.atlantafed.org/-/media/documents
/community-development/publications/discussion-papers/2016/04-corporate-landlords
-institutional-investors-and-displacement-2016-12-21.pdf.

12. Gordon, *supra* note 8.

13. Rachel Bogardus Drew, *Single-Family Rentals Have Risen to Nearly a Third of Rental Housing*, JOINT CENTER FOR HOUSING STUDIES OF HARVARD UNIVERSITY (Oct. 5, 2015), https://www.jchs.harvard.edu/blog/single-family-rentals-have-risen-to-nearly-a-third
-of-rental-housing.

14. Julianne Pepitone, *Foreclosures: Worst-hit Cities*, CNN (Oct. 28, 2009), https://
money.cnn.com/2009/10/28/real_estate/foreclosures_worst_cities/.

15. George Packer, THE UNWINDING 260 (2013).

16. Andrew Clark, *Mortgage Crisis: Welcome to Sub-prime Capital, USA*, GUARDIAN (July 27, 2008), https://www.theguardian.com/business/2008/jul/28/subprimecrisis .useconomy.

17. *Id.*

18. Christopher J. Goodman & Steven M. Mance, *Employment Loss and the 2007–09 Recession: An Overview*, MONTHLY LAB. REV. 1, 3 (April 2011), https://www.bls.gov/opub /mlr/2011/04/art1full.pdf.

19. Maya Abood *et al.*, *Wall Street Landlords Turn American Dream into a Nightmare*, ACCE INSTITUTE *ET AL.* 4, https://www.publicadvocates.org/wp-content/uploads/wallstreetland lordsfinalreport.pdf.

20. Charles Duhigg, *Loan-Agency Woes Swell from a Trickle to a Torrent*, N.Y. TIMES (July 11, 2008), https://www.nytimes.com/2008/07/11/business/11ripple.html?ex=1373515200.

21. *Reduce, Refinance, and Rent? The Economic Incentives, Risks, and Ramifications of Housing Market Policy Options*, CONGRESSIONAL RESEARCH SERVICE 13 (Aug. 28, 2012), https:// crsreports.congress.gov/product/pdf/R/R42480/12.

22. *Id.*

23. Ben Hallman, *Edward DeMarco's Lonely Stand Against Mortgage Debt Relief*, HUFFPOST (Aug. 2, 2012), https://www.huffpost.com/entry/edward-demarco-principal-reduction _n_1730806.

24. Letter from Edward J. DeMarco, acting director, Federal Housing Finance Authority to Tim Johnson, chairman of the House Committee on Banking, Housing and Urban Affairs *et al.* (July 31, 2012), https://www.fhfa.gov/Media/PublicAffairs/Documents /PF_LetterToCong_73112_N508.pdf.

25. Ben Hallman, *Ed DeMarco, Top Housing Official, Defies White House; Geithner Fires Back*, HUFFPOST (Sept. 30, 2012), https://www.huffpost.com/entry/ed-demarco-principal -reduction_n_1724880.

26. *President Obama, Fire Edward J. DeMarco*, CHANGE.ORG, https://www.change.org /p/president-obama-fire-edward-j-demarco?redirect=false.

27. *FHFA's DeMarco Opposes Mortgage Help*, UPI (July 31, 2012), https://www .upi.com/Business_News/2012/07/31/FHFAs-Demarco-opposes-mortgage -help/88651343773559/.

28. Ben Hallman, *Edward DeMarco Threatens Action Against Communities Weighing Principal Reduction Proposal*, HUFFPOST (Aug. 9, 2012), https://www.huffpost.com/entry /edward-demarco-principal-reduction_n_1759767?utm_hp_ref=business.

29. *Id.*; *Use of Eminent Domain to Restructure Performing Loans*, FEDERAL HOUSING FINANCE AGENCY (Aug. 9, 2012), https://www.fhfa.gov/SupervisionRegulation/Rules/Pages/Use -of-Eminent-Domain-to-Restructure-Performing-Loans.aspx.

30. *Welcome to HPC*, HOUSING POLICY COUNCIL, https://www.housingpolicycouncil .org/mission.

31. *FHFA Announces Pilot REO Property Sales in Hardest-Hit Areas*, FEDERAL HOUSING FINANCE AGENCY (Feb. 27, 2012), https://www.fhfa.gov/Media/PublicAffairs/Pages/FHFA -Announces-Pilot-REO-Property-Sales-in-HardestHit-Areas.aspx.

32. *Housing Markets in Transition*, FEDERAL RESERVE (Feb. 10, 2012), https://www.federal reserve.gov/newsevents/speech/bernanke20110210a.htm (Bernanke said that "[w]ith home prices falling and rents rising, it could make sense in some markets to turn some of the foreclosed homes into rental properties.").

33. *Id.* ("[A]ppropriately structured programs could help some involuntary renters become owners again by giving them options to purchase the homes they are renting.").

34. Lorraine Woellert, *FHFA Will Sell Foreclosed Homes to Investors for Rentals*, BLOOMBERG (Feb. 27, 2012), https://www.bloomberg.com/news/articles/2012-02-27/fhfa-to-begin-selling-foreclosed-homes-to-investors-for-rentals.

35. Meredith Abood, *Securitizing Suburbia: The Financialization of Single-Family Rental Housing and the Need to Redefine "Risk,"* MIT 13 (2017), https://dspace.mit.edu/handle/1721.1/111349.

36. *Id.*

37. *FHFA Statement on REO Pilot Transactions*, FEDERAL HOUSING FINANCE AGENCY (Nov. 1, 2012), https://www.fhfa.gov/Media/PublicAffairs/Pages/FHFA-Statement-on-REO-Pilot-Transactions.aspx.

38. Lisa Bartley, *Billion-Dollar Landlords: Rental-Home Giant Under Fire for Unsavory Conditions*, ABC7 (Nov. 18, 2017), https://abc7.com/starwood-waypoint-homes-tom-barrack-donald-trump-invitation/2663400/.

39. Christophers, *supra* note 9, at 1, 5.

40. Robbie Whelan, *Firms Flock to Foreclosure Auctions*, WALL ST. J. (Sept. 12, 2012), https://www.wsj.com/articles/SB10000872396390443696604577644700448760254.

41. *Id.*

42. Starwood Waypoint Homes, *Quarterly Report (Form 10-Q)* (Nov. 2017), https://www.sec.gov/Archives/edgar/data/1579471/000156459017023253/sfr-10q_20170930.htm.

43. Robbie Whelan, *Colony Capital to Acquire 10% Stake in Fannie Housing Pool*, WALL ST. J. (Oct. 25, 2012), https://www.wsj.com/articles/SB10001424052970204076204578079183382983270.

44. Allison Bisbey, *Invitation Homes Obtains Financing from Fannie Mae*, NAT'L MORTGAGE NEWS (Jan. 26, 2017), https://www.nationalmortgagenews.com/news/invitation-homes-obtains-financing-from-fannie-mae; Abood et al., *supra* note 19, at 37.

45. Stephanie Zimmerman, *Through Fannie Mae, US Taxpayers Provide Backing for Some Rental Home Giants*, ABC NEWS (Nov. 16, 2017), https://abcnews.go.com/US/fannie-mae-us-taxpayers-provide-backing-rental-home/story?id=51194097.

46. Elora Lee Raymond et al., *From Foreclosure to Eviction: Housing Insecurity in Corporate-Owned Single-Family Rentals*, 20 CITYSCAPE: J. POL'Y DEV. RES. 159, 160 (2018), https://bit.ly/3C7lEZu.

47. Abood, *supra* 35, at 12.

48. In 2015, Starwood Waypoint Residential Trust announced plans to buy Colony American. Barry Sternlicht and Tom Barrack were set to become nonexecutive cochairmen of the combined board of trustees. Chad Bray, *Starwood Waypoint Residential Trust to Acquire a Rival*, N.Y. TIMES (Sept. 21, 2015), https://www.nytimes.com/2015/09/22/business/dealbook/starwood-waypoint-residential-trust-to-acquire-a-rival.html. The deal was completed along these terms in 2016. *Colony Starwood Homes Announces Closing of $7.7 Billion Merger of Starwood Waypoint Residential Trust with Colony American Homes, Creating the Premier Single-Family REIT*, BUSINESS WIRE (Jan. 5, 2016), https://www.businesswire.com/news/home/20160105006880/en/Colony-Starwood-Homes-Announces-Closing-of-7.7-Billion-Merger-of-Starwood-Waypoint-Residential-Trust-with-Colony-American-Homes-Creating-the-Premier-Single-Family-REIT. The new venture was initially called Colony Starwood Homes but in 2017 rebranded as Starwood Waypoint Homes. Ben Lane, *Colony Starwood Homes Rebranding as Starwood Waypoint Homes*, HOUSING WIRE (July 9, 2017), https://www.housingwire.com/articles/40722-colony-starwood-homes-rebranding-as-starwood-waypoint-homes/. Then in July 2017, Blackstone's Invitation Homes bought Starwood

Waypoint. Ben Lane, *Invitation Homes, Starwood Waypoint Homes Merge to Create Largest Single-Family Landlord*, HOUSING WIRE (Nov. 16, 2017), https://www.housingwire.com /articles/41839-invitation-homes-starwood-waypoint-homes-merge-to-create-largest -single-family-landlord/. When they changed names, Barrack sold his stake in the firm. Ryan Dezember, *Blackstone, Starwood to Merge Rental-Home Businesses in Bet to Be America's Biggest Home Landlord*, WALL ST. J. (Aug. 10, 2017), https://www.wsj.com/articles /with-merger-deal-blackstone-starwood-bet-on-being-americas-biggest-home-landlord -1502361000. In the discussion that follows, "Colony" refers to any of the iterations of the company.

49. Abood, *supra* 35, at 73.

50. *Affordability Issues Aid Spike in Single-Family Rent Growth*, DS NEWS (July 20, 2021), https://dsnews.com/daily-dose/07-20-2021/affordability-aids-spike-in-single -family-rent-growth.

51. Abood *et al.*, *supra* note 19, at 17.

52. Mari, *supra* note 10.

53. *Rivera v. Invitation Homes, Inc.*, No. 4:18-cv-3158 (N.D. Cal. 2018); *McCumber et al. v. Invitation Homes Inc.*, 3:21-cv-2194 (N.D. Tex. 2021). As of November 2022, the parties in the Texas case have neared a settlement. Joint Status Report, *McCumber et al. v. Invitation Homes Inc.*, 3:21-cv-2194 (N.D. Tex. Nov. 22, 2022), ECF No. 86.

54. Order Denying Motion for Class Certification and Dismissing Action at 8, *Rivera v. Invitation Homes, Inc.*, No. 4:18-cv-3158 (N.D. Cal. Feb. 18, 2022), ECF No. 70.

55. Alexandra Stevenson & Matthew Goldstein, *Rent-to-Own Homes: A Win-Win for Landlords, a Risk for Struggling Tenants*, N.Y. TIMES (Aug. 21, 2016), https://www .nytimes.com/2016/08/22/business/dealbook/rent-to-own-homes-a-win-win-for -landlords-a-risk-for-struggling-tenants.html; *Invitation Homes Makes Dreams of Home Ownership a Reality for Residents*, INVITATION HOMES (Nov. 8, 2018), https://www .prnewswire.com/news-releases/invitation-homes-makes-dreams-of-home-ownership -a-reality-for-residents-300746216.html; Matthew Goldstein & Alexandra Stevenson, *Market for Fixer-Uppers Traps Low-Income Buyers*, N.Y. TIMES (Feb. 20, 2016), https:// www.nytimes.com/2016/02/21/business/dealbook/market-for-fixer-uppers-traps-low -income-buyers.html?_r=0 (Blackstone and its Invitation Homes offered such "opportunities," and KKR invested in a company that did the same).

56. Stevenson & Goldstein, *supra* note 55.

57. Abood, *supra* 35, at 77.

58. Capitol Forum, *Single Family Rental Industry: Companies Lean on Tenant Chargebacks to Effectively Cut Operating Expenses* (Feb. 21, 2018).

59. *Id.*

60. *Id.*

61. Mari, *supra* note 10; Abood *et al.*, *supra* note 19, at 21.

62. Raymond *et al.*, *supra* note 46, at 159–160.

63. Joshua Akers *et al.*, *Toxic Structures: Speculation and Lead Exposure in Detroit's Single-Family Rental Market* 3 (2019), https://npr-brightspot.s3.amazonaws.com/legacy/sites /michigan/files/toxic_structures_2019-final.pdf.

64. *A Brief Guide to Mold, Moisture and Your Home*, ENVIRONMENTAL PROTECTION AGENCY (Mar. 25, 2022), https://www.epa.gov/mold/brief-guide-mold-moisture-and-your-home.

65. Abood, *supra* 35, at 74.

66. Complaint, *Lisboa v. Colfin AI-FL 4, LLC et al.*, No. 5:16-cv-312 (M.D. Fla. May 3, 2016).

67. *Id.*

68. *Id.*

69. *Id.*

70. Abood *et al., supra* note 19, at 12.

71. Mari, *supra* note 10.

72. Maya Abood, *Wall Street Landlords Turn American Dream into a Nightmare,* ACCE INSTITUTE *ET AL.*, 33, https://www.publicadvocates.org/wp-content/uploads/wallstreetland lordsfinalreport.pdf ("Members of the Council include Invitation Homes, American Homes 4 Rent, Tricon American Homes, Altisource Rental Homes, FirstKey Homes, Roofstock, National Rental Homes, and over a dozen others."); *Renter's Rights,* NATIONAL RENTAL HOME COUNCIL, https://www.rentalhomecouncil.org/advocacy/ (promising to prevent "harmful rent control policies from being established that undermine rental choices for consumers").

73. *Homeowners vs Renters Statistics,* PROPERTY MANAGEMENT (July 12, 2022), https://ipropertymanagement.com/research/renters-vs-homeowners-statistics.

74. Mari, *supra* note 10 ("Blackstone contributed $5.6 million to the No campaign, and Invitation Homes contributed nearly $1.3 million.").

75. Eli Vitulli, *Hedge Papers No. 69: Billionaire Corporate Landlords,* 20 (2019), https://hedgeclippers.org/wp-content/uploads/2019/08/HP69_CorpLandlords-CA-Housing_V14.pdf.

76. Prop 10 Flaws, *Bad Future,* YOUTUBE, https://www.youtube.com/watch?v=Bde X1UTy5wo.

77. Eli Vitulli, HEDGE PAPERS NO. 69: BILLIONAIRE CORPORATE LANDLORDS 20 (2019), https://hedgeclippers.org/wp-content/uploads/2019/08/HP69_CorpLandlords-CA-Housing_V14.pdf.

78. Raymond *et al., supra* note 46, at 159, 162 n.2.

79. Ben Lane, *Blackstone Cashes Out on Invitation Homes,* HOUSING WIRE (Nov. 22, 2019), https://www.housingwire.com/articles/blackstone-cashes-out-on-invitation-homes/; Peter Grant, *Blackstone Bets $6 Billion on Buying and Renting Homes,* WALL ST. J. (June 22, 2021), https://www.wsj.com/articles/blackstone-bets-6-billion-on-buying-and-renting-homes-11624359600.

80. Ryan Dezember, *KKR Doubles Down on House Flippers,* WALL ST. J. (June 12, 2019), https://www.wsj.com/articles/kkr-doubles-down-on-house-flippers-11560331806.

81. *Blackstone Establishes Single-Family Buy-to-Rent Lending Platform,* BLACKSTONE (Nov. 15, 2013), https://www.blackstone.com/news/press/blackstone-establishes-single-family-buy-to-rent-lending-platform/.

82. Julia Gordon, *The Dark Side of Single-Family Rental,* SHELTERFORCE (July 30, 2018), https://shelterforce.org/2018/07/30/the-dark-side-of-single-family-rental/.

83. Diana Click, *Government's Fannie Mae Will Back PE Giant Blackstone's Rental Homes Debt,* CNBC (Jan. 25, 2017), https://www.cnbc.com/2017/01/25/governments-fannie-mae-will-back-pe-giant-blackstones-rental-business-debt.html.

84. Kevin Schaul & Jonathan O'Connell, *Investors Bought a Record Share of Homes in 2021. See Where,* WASH. POST (Feb. 16, 2022), https://www.washingtonpost.com/business/interactive/2022/housing-market-investors/.

85. *Investor Relations,* INVITATION HOMES, https://www.invh.com/home/default.aspx.

86. Daniel Immergluck, *Renting the Dream: The Rise of Single-Family Rentership in the Sunbelt Metropolis,* 2 (2018), https://scholarworks.gsu.edu/cgi/viewcontent.cgi?article=1010&context=urban_studies_institute.

87. Mari, *supra* note 10.

88. Alana Semuels, *When Wall Street Is Your Landlord*, ATLANTIC (Feb. 13, 2019), https://www.theatlantic.com/technology/archive/2019/02/single-family-landlords-wall-street/582394/.

89. Mari, *supra* note 10.

90. Hanna Ziady, *Wall Street Is Buying Up Family Homes. The Rent Checks Are Too Juicy to Ignore*, MERCURY NEWS (Aug. 2, 2021), https://www.mercurynews.com/2021/08/02/wall-street-is-buying-up-family-homes-the-rent-checks-are-too-juicy-to-ignore/.

91. *Id.*

92. Jacob Passy, *Black Homeownership Rate Hits Lowest Level Since the 1960s—That's Unlikely to Change in Pandemic Year 2*, MARKETWATCH (Mar. 23, 2021), https://www.marketwatch.com/story/most-black-americans-arent-homeowners-how-can-we-change-that-11615431459.

93. Amanda Lee et al., *U.S. Homeownership Rates Fall Among Young Adults, African Americans*, POPULATION REFERENCE BUREAU (Feb. 13,202), https://www.prb.org/resources/u-s-homeownership-rates-fall-among-young-adults-african-americans/.

94. *Id.*

95. Rani Molla, *The Home Sales Boom Means You Might End Up Renting*, VOX (May 4, 2021), https://www.vox.com/recode/22407667/home-sales-boom-rent-housing-single-family-rental.

96. Matthew Goldstein, *As Banks Retreat, Private Equity Rushes to Buy Troubled Home Mortgages*, N.Y. TIMES (Sept. 28, 2015), https://www.nytimes.com/2015/09/29/business/dealbook/as-banks-retreat-private-equity-rushes-to-buy-troubled-home-mortgages.html.

97. *Nationstar Mortgage LLC*, FORTRESS, https://www.fortress.com/businesses/private-equity/select-investments/nationstar.

98. *Nationstar Mortgage Announces Completion of Greenlight Financial Services Acquisition*, MR. COOPER GROUP (June 3, 2013), https://investors.mrcoopergroup.com/events-and-presentations/press-releases/press-release-details/2013/Nationstar-Mortgage-Announces-Completion-of-Greenlight-Financial-Services-Acquisition/default.aspx.

99. *TEXT-S&P Monitoring Nationstar on ResCap Acquisition Plans*, REUTERS (May 21, 2012), https://www.reuters.com/article/idUSWNA774420120521.

100. *Nationstar Mortgage Announces Agreement to Acquire Approximately $215 Billion in Mortgage Servicing Assets from Bank of America*, NATIONSTAR (Jan. 7, 2013), https://www.sec.gov/Archives/edgar/data/1520566/000119312513009512/d461579dex991.htm.

101. Complaint for a Permanent Injunction and Other Relief, *CFPB v. Nationstar Mortgage LLC*, No. 1:20-cv-3550 (D.D.C. Dec. 7, 2020), ECF No. 1.

102. Matthew Goldstein et al., *How Housing's New Players Spiraled into Banks' Old Mistakes*, N.Y. TIMES (June 26, 2016), https://www.nytimes.com/2016/06/27/business/dealbook/private-equity-housing-missteps.html.

103. *Id.*

104. *Quarterly Report to Congress*, OFFICE OF THE INSPECTOR GENERAL FOR THE TROUBLED ASSET RELIEF PROGRAM 72 (Apr. 26, 2017), https://www.sigtarp.gov/sites/sigtarp/files/Quarterly_Reports/April_26_2017_Report_to_Congress.pdf.

105. *Id.*

106. *Consumer Financial Protection Bureau and Multiple States Enter into Settlement with Nationstar Mortgage, LLC for Unlawful Servicing Practices*, CONSUMER FINANCIAL PROTECTION BUREAU (Dec. 7, 2020), https://www.consumerfinance.gov/about-us/newsroom/consumer-financial-protection-bureau-multiple-states-enter-settlement-nationstar

-mortgage-llc-unlawful-servicing-practices/; Complaint for a Permanent Injunction and Other Relief, *supra* note 101.

107. *Consumer Financial Protection Bureau and Multiple States Enter into Settlement with Nationstar Mortgage, LLC for Unlawful Servicing Practices, supra* note 106.

108. *National Creditor Settlements*, DEPARTMENT OF JUSTICE (Sept. 27, 2022), https://www.justice.gov/ust/national-creditor-settlements.

109. Goldstein *et al.*, *supra* note 102.

110. *Id.* Nationstar declined to comment on the Browns' case to the *New York Times*.

111. *Nationstar Mortgage LLC*, FORTRESS, https://www.fortress.com/businesses/private -equity/select-investments/nationstar; *Nationstar's Merger with WMIH*, CRAVATH, SWAINE & MOORE LLP, https://www.cravath.com/news/nationstar-s-merger-with-wmih.html; Ben Lane, *Invitation Homes, Starwood Waypoint Homes Merge to Create Largest Single-Family Landlord*, HOUSING WIRE (Nov. 16, 2017) (In 2012, Fortress organized an initial public offering for Nationstar, but continued to own a majority stake in the company into 2018).

112. Alexander Hermann, *New Paper Details the Dramatic Decline of Low-Cost Rentals*, JOINT CENTER FOR HOUSING STUDIES (Sept. 17, 2019), https://www.jchs.harvard.edu /blog/new-paper-details-the-dramatic-decline-of-low-cost-rentals.

113. Rana Foroohar, *Why Big Investors Are Buying Up American Trailer Parks*, FIN. TIMES (Feb. 7, 2020), https://www.ft.com/content/3c87eb24-47a8-11ea-aee2-9ddbdc86190d.

114. *Id.*; Dori Zinn, *How Much Does It Cost to Buy a Mobile Home?*, FORBES (Sept. 7, 2022), https://www.forbes.com/advisor/mortgages/mobile-home-cost/; Geoff Williams & Devon Thorsby, *How Much Does It Cost to Buy a Mobile Home?*, U.S. NEWS & WORLD REPORT (May 4, 2022), https://realestate.usnews.com/real-estate/articles/how-much-does -it-cost-to-buy-a-mobile-home.

115. Foroohar, *supra* note 113.

116. Andrew Keel, *Mobile Home Park Trends: Big Money and Improvements*, FORBES (Sept. 14, 2021), https://www.forbes.com/sites/forbesbusinesscouncil/2021/09/14/mobile-home -park-trends-big-money-and-improvements/?sh=4b9c851c5a89.

117. *Private Equity Giants Converge on Manufactured Homes*, PRIVATE EQUITY STAKE-HOLDER PROJECT, 1 (Feb. 2019), https://pestakeholder.org/wp-content/uploads/2019/02 /Private-Equity-GIants-Converge-on-Manufactured-Homes-PESP-MHAction-AFR -021419.pdf.

118. Sheelah Kolhatkar, *What Happens When Investment Firms Acquire Trailer Parks*, NEW YORKER (Mar. 8, 2021), https://www.newyorker.com/magazine/2021/03/15/what -happens-when-investment-firms-acquire-trailer-parks.

119. Peter Whoriskey, *A Billion-Dollar Empire Made of Mobile Homes*, WASH. POST (Feb. 14, 2019), https://www.washingtonpost.com/business/economy/a-billion-dollar-empire -made-of-mobile-homes/2019/02/14/ac687342-2b0b-11e9-b2fc-721718903bfc_story .html.

120. Peter Grant, *Singapore Fund GIC Is in Talks to Buy Owner of Manufactured-Home Com-munities*, WALL ST. J. (June 28, 2016), https://www.wsj.com/articles/singapores-sovereign -wealth-fund-is-in-talks-to-buy-manufactured-home-owner-1467106203.

121. Sam Tabachnik, *Raise Rent Repeatedly, Remove Amenities: The Core Tenets of Colorado's Mobile Home University and the People Who Suffer*, DENVER POST (Sept. 14, 2021), https://www .denverpost.com/2021/09/05/mobile-home-university-rv-horizons-impact-communities -frank-rolfe-dave-reynolds/.

122. Gillian Tan, *Blackstone to Boost Mobile-Home Bet with $550 Million Deal*, BLOOMBERG (Sept. 14, 2020), https://www.bloomberg.com/news/articles/2020-09-14/blackstone-said -to-boost-mobile-home-bet-with-550-million-deal.

123. Kolhatkar, *supra* note 118.

124. Jacob Channel, *Mobile Home Values Are Rising Faster Than Single-Family Home Values—Here's Where They're the Most, Least Expensive,* LENDINGTREE (Nov. 30, 2021), https://www.lendingtree.com/home/mortgage/mobile-home-values-study/.

125. *Private Equity Giants Converge on Manufactured Homes, supra* note 117, at 1–4.

126. *Id.* at 2 (Sunrise Capital Investors describes itself as a "real estate private equity investment firm."); Sunrise Capital Investors, *Sunrise Capital Investors Distributes Over $4.5 Million to Fund 2 Investors,* CISION (Oct. 21, 2021), https://www.prnewswire.com/news -releases/sunrise-capital-investors-distributes-over-4-5-million-to-fund-2-investors -301405867.html.

127. *Private Equity Giants Converge on Manufactured Homes, supra* note 117, at 2.

128. *Id.* at 6.

129. Whoriskey, *supra* note 119.

130. *Id.* Stockbridge said in a statement to the *Post* that "Stockbridge is proud of its association with YES Communities, which has met the affordable housing needs of its residents nationwide for the past 11 years."

131. Tracy Lien, *In Silicon Valley, Even Mobile Homes Are Getting Too Pricey for Longtime Residents,* L.A. TIMES (May 4, 2017), https://www.latimes.com/business/technology /la-fi-tn-silicon-valley-mobile-homes-20170504-htmlstory.html.

132. Whoriskey, *supra* note 119.

133. Foroohar, *supra* note 113.

134. Chris Arnold, *Why Are Investors Buying Up Mobile Home Parks and Evicting Residents?,* NPR (Sept. 3, 2021), https://www.npr.org/2021/09/03/1033910731/why-are-investors -buying-up-mobile-home-parks-and-evicting-residents.

135. *Duty to Serve Underserved Markets Plan: 2022–2024,* FANNIE MAE, 8 (2021), https:// www.novoco.com/sites/default/files/atoms/files/fannie-mae-duty-to-serve-2022-24 -proposed-052021.pdf.

136. *Id.*

137. *San Jose-Sunnyvale-Santa Clara Home Values,* ZILLOW, https://www.zillow.com /home-values/54626/sunnyvale-ca/. The Zillow Home Value Index is "[a] smoothed, seasonally adjusted measure of the typical home value and market changes across a given region and housing type. It reflects the typical value for homes in the 35th to 65th percentile range." *Housing Data,* ZILLOW, https://www.zillow.com/research/data/.

138. Lien, *supra* note 131.

139. *Id.* Carlyle declined to comment to the *Los Angeles Times* about its rent increases or plans after its lease ended.

140. *Id.*

141. Victoria Keira, *Sunnyvale: Council Will Select Top Issues to Study This Year,* MERCURY NEWS (Jan. 21, 2017), https://www.mercurynews.com/2017/01/21/sunnyvale-council -will-select-top-issues-to-study-this-year/.

142. Interview with Fred Kameda (Feb. 9, 2022).

143. *Id.*

144. *Id.*

145. Ben Silverfarb, *"Last Man Standing": Woman Will Not Accept Relocation Package After Being Evicted from Mobile Home Park,* DAILY J. (Jan. 11, 2016), https://www .smdailyjournal.com/news/local/last-man-standing-woman-will-not-accept-relocation -package-after-being-evicted-from-mobile-home/article_b6c227bc-f94b-5406-9508 -cdfccaaa6a9c.html.

146. Lien, *supra* note 131.

147. George Avalos, *Big Sunnyvale Mobile Home Park Is Bought by Chicago Investors*, MERCURY NEWS (Aug. 30, 2019). https://www.mercurynews.com/2019/08/30/big -sunnyvale-mobile-home-park-is-bought-by-chicago-investors/.

148. Leonardo Castañeda, *"It's Absolute Desperation": Mobile Park Residents Say Rent Increases Threaten One of Silicon Valley's Last Affordable Housing Options*, MERCURY NEWS (May 10, 2021), https://www.mercurynews.com/2021/05/08/were-like-hostages-mobile-park -residents-say-rent-increases-threaten-silicon-valleys-last-affordable-housing-option/.

149. Omar Pérez, *Sunnyvale Mobile Home Park Residents Express Frustrations over Rent Increases*, KRON4 (May 26, 2021), https://www.kron4.com/news/sunnyvale-mobile -home-park-residents-express-frustrations-over-rent-increases/.

150. *Id.*

151. *Sunnyvale Mobile Home Park Owners Agree on Deal to Keep Lots Affordable*, KRON4 (Oct. 22, 2021), https://www.kron4.com/news/bay-area/sunnyvale-mobile -home-park-owners-agree-on-deal-to-keep-lots-affordable/.

152. Kavish Harjai, *Sunnyvale's Mobile Homeowners Are Eligible for Key Financial Perks—if They Sign Up in Time*, PENINSULA PRESS (Nov. 4, 2021), https://peninsulapress .com/2021/11/04/sunnyvales-mobile-homeowners-are-eligible-for-key-financial-perks -if-they-sign-up-in-time/.

153. Resident interview (Feb. 10, 2022).

154. *GOP Candidate's Private Equity Resume Draws Scrutiny in Va.*, WTOP (July 1, 2021), https://wtop.com/virginia/2021/07/gop-candidates-private-equity-resume-draws -scrutiny-in-va/.

CHAPTER 3: PROFITING OFF BANKRUPTCY

1. *Charles Lazarus*, WIKIPEDIA, https://en.wikipedia.org/wiki/Charles_Lazarus.

2. *Toys "R" Us*, WIKIPEDIA, https://en.wikipedia.org/wiki/Toys_%22R%22_Us.

3. *Geoffrey Through the Years*, TOYS R US, https://www.toysrus.com/geoffrey.html.

4. Julia Horowitz, *How Toys 'R' Us Went from Big Kid on the Block to Bust*, CNN (Mar. 17, 2018), https://money.cnn.com/2018/03/17/news/companies/toys-r-us-history/index.html.

5. Jake Pearson, *Toys R Us Closes Flagship Store: Ferris Wheel, T-Rex and All*, SEATTLE TIMES (Dec. 30, 2015), https://www.seattletimes.com/business/toys-r-us-closes-flagship -store-ferris-wheel-t-rex-and-all/.

6. Mylene Mangalindan, *How Amazon's Dream Alliance with Toys 'R' Us Went So Sour*, WALL ST. J. (Jan. 23, 2006), https://www.wsj.com/articles/SB113798030922653260.

7. Toys "R" Us, *Form 10-K* (May 15, 2007), https://www.sec.gov/Archives/edgar /data/1005414/000119312507115768/d10k.htm.

8. Jeff Spross, *How Vulture Capitalists Ate Toys 'R' Us*, WEEK (Mar. 16, 2018), https:// theweek.com/articles/761124/how-vulture-capitalists-ate-toys-r.

9. *Id.* (Toys "R" Us's debt servicing ranged from $425 million to $527 million per year.)

10. *Id.*

11. Bryce Covert, *The Demise of Toys 'R' Us Is a Warning*, ATLANTIC (July 2018), https://www.theatlantic.com/magazine/archive/2018/07/toys-r-us-bankruptcy-private -equity/561758/ ("After its buyout, Toys "R" Us acquired a number of companies, including FAO Schwarz, eToys.com, and assets from KB Toys (itself a failed reclamation project of Bain's). Consolidating brick-and-mortar and online toy businesses may have been a good-faith strategy. What's certain is that the deals helped generate $128 million in transaction fees for the owners.").

12. *KKR, Bain Capital, Vornado Repeatedly Rewarded Themselves for Adding Debt to Toys "R" Us*, PRIV. EQUITY STAKEHOLDER PROJECT (May 29, 2018), https://pestakeholder.org /news/kkr-bain-capital-vornado-repeatedly-rewarded-themselves-for-adding-debt-to -toys-r-us/.

13. Spross, *supra* note 8.

14. Covert, *supra* note 11.

15. Ben Unglesbee, *Inside the 20-Year Decline of Toys R Us*, RETAIL DIVE (June 26, 2018), https://www.retaildive.com/news/inside-the-the-20-year-decline-of-toys-r-us/526364/.

16. *Toys "R" Us, supra* note 2.

17. Covert, *supra* note 11.

18. Alina Selyukh, *Game Over for Toys R Us: Chain Going out of Business*, NPR (Mar. 14, 2018), https://www.npr.org/sections/thetwo-way/2018/03/14/592882488/game -over-for-toys-r-us-chain-going-out-of-business.

19. Tara Lachapelle, *Lessons Learned from the Downfall of Toys 'R' Us*, BLOOMBERG (Mar. 29, 2018), https://www.bloomberg.com/news/articles/2018-03-09/toys-r-us-downfall -is-ominous-reminder-about-debt-laden-deals#xj4y7vzkg (Interest expenses tended to near or even exceed operating income. In 2017, had $460 million in operating income, $457 million in interest expenses.).

20. David A. Brandon, *Experience*, LINKEDIN, https://www.linkedin.com/in/david -a-brandon-5b826654/details/experience/ ("In March 1999, Brandon was named Chairman and CEO of Domino's Pizza by Bain Capital Partners, LLC after they acquired the world's largest pizza delivery company in December 1998.").

21. Complaint at ¶ 71, *TRU Creditor Litigation Trust v. David A. Brandon et al.*, No. 651637/2020 (N.Y. Sup. Ct. Mar. 12, 2020). The case was eventually transferred to the Eastern District of Virginia and settled without a final adjudication on the creditors' allegations, while broader bankruptcy litigation remains ongoing. Order Granting Joint Stipulation of Dismissal, *TRU Creditor Litigation Trust v. David A. Brandon et al.*, No. 3:20-cv-311 (E.D. Va. Nov. 15, 2022) ECF No. 92; *TRU Creditor Litigation Trust v. Raether et al.*, No. 3:20-ap-3038 (E.D. Va.).

22. *Central Park + The Plaza District*, ONE57, https://one57.com/location#location-hero.

23. JC Reindl, *Ex-U-M Athletic Director Dave Brandon Couldn't Save Toys R Us*, DETROIT FREE PRESS (Mar. 15, 2018), https://www.freep.com/story/money/2018/03/15/dave -brandon-toysrus-liquidates/423756002/.

24. Complaint, *TRU Creditor Litigation Trust v. David A. Brandon et al.*, No. 651637 /2020 (N.Y. Sup. Ct. Mar. 12, 2020).

25. *Id*. at ¶ 7.

26. *Id*. at ¶ 87, 170; Jeremy Hill & Eliza Ronalds-Hannon, *Former Toys 'R' Us Executives Face Trial over Botched Bankruptcy*, BLOOMBERG (June 28, 2022), https://www .bloomberg.com/news/articles/2022-06-28/former-toys-r-us-execs-to-stand-trial-over -botched-bankruptcy.

27. Complaint ¶ 88, *TRU Creditor Litigation Trust v. David A. Brandon et al.*, No. 651637/2020 (N.Y. Sup. Ct. Mar. 12, 2020).

28. *Id*. at ¶ 89.

29. *Id*. Brandon and the legal entity managing Toy's "R" Us's bankruptcy subsequently denied the allegation that Brandon misled the store employee. Answer at 44, *TRU Creditor Litigation Trust v. Raether et al.*, No. 3:20-ap-3038 (E.D. Va. Oct. 1, 2020), ECF No. 66. The case remains ongoing.

30. *See Kirkland & Ellis: Bankruptcy/Restructuring*, CHAMBERS AND PARTNERS, https:// chambers.com/department/kirkland-ellis-llp-bankruptcy-restructuring-usa-5:513:127

88:1:3636 (an interviewee comments, "I think they are the very best; they are aggressive and extremely commercially minded."); Roy Strom, *Kirkland's Bankruptcy Business Out-Billing Peers in Pandemic*, BLOOMBERG L. (June 9, 2020), https://news .bloomberglaw.com/business-and-practice/kirklands-bankruptcy-business-out-billing -peers-during-pandemic.

31. Kate Gibson, *Toys R Us' Bankruptcy Lawyers Get $56 Million While Laid-Off Workers Get $2 Million*, CBS NEWS (June 28, 2019), https://www.cbsnews.com/news/bankruptcy -court-gives-toys-r-us-workers-2-million-and-retailers-lawyers-56-million/.

32. Samantha Stokes, *Kirkland Secures $56M in Fees for Toys R Us Bankruptcy*, AM. LAWYER (June 10, 2019), https://www.law.com/americanlawyer/2019/06/10/kirkland -ellis-secures-56m-in-fees-for-toys-r-us-bankruptcy/.

33. *Average Hourly Rate for Toys 'R' Us Inc Employees*, PAYSCALE, https://www.payscale .com/research/US/Employer=Toys_%27R%27_Us_Inc/Hourly_Rate (Jan. 15, 2021).

34. Melanie Anzidei, *Toys R Us Workers Win $2 Million Severance Settlement*, N. JERSEY (June 27, 2019), https://www.northjersey.com/story/money/2019/06/27/toys-r-us-workers -win-2-million-severance-settlement/1587364001/.

35. Interview with Jack Raisner (Nov. 10, 2021).

36. Jeremy Hill & Eliza Ronalds-Hannon, *Former Toys 'R' Us Executives Face Trial over Botched Bankruptcy*, BLOOMBERG (June 28, 2022), https://www.bloomberg.com /news/articles/2022-06-28/former-toys-r-us-execs-to-stand-trial-over-botched -bankruptcy; Kate Gibson, *Toys R Us' Bankruptcy Lawyers Get $56 Million While Laid-Off Workers Get $2 Million*, CBS NEWS (June 28, 2019, 2:36 PM), https://www.cbsnews .com/news/bankruptcy-court-gives-toys-r-us-workers-2-million-and-retailers-lawyers -56-million/.

37. Gibson, *supra* note 36.

38. *Id.*

39. Gibson, *supra* note 31.

40. *Id.*

41. Gretchen Morgenson & Lillian Rizzo, *Who Killed Toys 'R' Us? Hint: It Wasn't Only Amazon*, WALL ST. J. (Aug. 23, 2018), https://www.wsj.com/articles/who-killed-toys-r-us -hint-it-wasnt-only-amazon-1535034401.

42. Chris Cumming, *Lawmakers Question KKR, Bain Capital over Toys 'R' Us Failure*, WALL ST. J. (July 6, 2018), https://www.wsj.com/articles/lawmakers-question-kkr-bain -capital-over-toys-r-us-failure-1530896043 ("Even accounting for fees received from Toys 'R' Us, we have lost many millions of dollars. To find anyone who profited, one would need to look at the institutions that pushed for Toys to liquidate its U.S. busi-ness,' the firm wrote.").

43. Dan Primack, *Toys "R" Us Not a Total Loss for Private Equity Fund Managers*, AXIOS (Oct. 5, 2017), https://www.axios.com/2017/12/15/toys-r-us-not-a-total-loss-for -private-equity-fund-managers-1513305992.

44. Complaint at ¶ 48, *TRU Creditor Litigation Trust v. David A. Brandon et al.*, No. 651637/2020 (N.Y. Sup. Ct. Mar. 12, 2020) (the private equity firms allegedly ex-tracted over $250 million in advisory fees).

45. Jim Baker *et al.*, *Pirate Equity: How Wall Street Firms Are Pillaging American Retail*, CENTER FOR POPULAR DEMOCRACY ET AL. 9 (2019), https://united4respect.org/wp-content /uploads/2019/07/Pirate-Equity-How-Wall-Street-Firms-are-Pillaging-American-Retail -July-2019.pdf.

46. *Id.*

47. *Id.* at 3.

48. *Id.* at 15, 21.

49. *Id.* at 3.

50. Steve LeVine, *Vulture Capitalists Are Killing Off Retail Jobs*, Axios (Jan. 10, 2018), https://www.axios.com/private-equity-1515603080-efd39541-a9fb-474b-8c24 -04623ee518fd.html.

51. Baker *et al., supra* note 45, at 13.

52. *Id. at* 40–44.

53. *Id.* at 5.

54. *Amazon and Walmart Are Nearly Tied in Full-Year Share of Retail Sales*, PYMNTS (Mar. 11, 2021), https://www.pymnts.com/news/retail/2021/amazon-walmart-nearly -tied-in-full-year-share-of-retail-sales/.

55. McKinsey & Company, FUTURE OF RETAIL OPERATIONS: WINNING IN A DIGITAL ERA 25 (2020), https://www.mckinsey.com/~/media/McKinsey/Industries/Retail/Our %20Insights/Future%20of%20retail%20operations%20Winning%20in%20a%20digital %20era/McK_Retail-Ops-2020_FullIssue-RGB-hyperlinks-011620.pdf (discussing Macy's, Nordstrom, and Walmart).

56. Sapna Maheshwari & Vanessa Friedman, *The Pandemic Helped Topple Two Retailers. So Did Private Equity.*, N.Y. TIMES (June 18, 2020), https://www.nytimes.com/2020/05 /14/business/coronavirus-retail-bankruptcies-private-equity.html.

57. *Id.*

58. *PetSmart-Chewy*, BC PARTNERS, https://www.bcpartners.com/private-equity -strategy/portfolio/petsmart-chewy.

59. Lauren Kaori Gurley, *Some Understaffed PetSmarts Are Dealing with Freezers Overflowing with Dead Pets*, VICE (Mar. 9, 2022), https://www.vice.com/en/article/3ab4ek /some-understaffed-petsmarts-are-dealing-with-freezers-overfilled-with-dead-pets.

60. *Id.*

61. *Id.*

62. *Id.*

63. *Id.*

64. *Id.*

65. Neil Irwin, *How Private Equity Buried Payless*, N.Y. TIMES (Feb. 1, 2020), https:// www.nytimes.com/2020/01/31/upshot/payless-private-equity-capitalism.html.

66. *Id.*

67. *Id.*

68. *Friendly's*, WIKIPEDIA, https://en.wikipedia.org/wiki/Friendly%27s.

69. Emily Langer, *S. Prestley Blake, a Founder of Friendly's Ice Cream Chain, Dies at 106*, WASH. POST (Feb. 12, 2021), https://www.washingtonpost.com/local/obituaries/s -prestley-blake-dead/2021/02/12/acbb76d0-6d4b-11eb-9f80-3d7646ce1bc0_story.html.

70. Emily Langer, *Curtis Blake, Co-founder of the Friendly's Ice Cream Chain, Dies at 102*, WASH. POST (May 31, 2019), https://www.washingtonpost.com/local/obituaries /curtis-blake-co-founder-of-the-friendlys-ice-cream-chain-dies-at-102/2019/05/31 /bc0a502c-83b2-11e9-95a9-e2c830afe24f_story.html.

71. Langer, *supra* note 69.

72. *Id.*

73. *Rhode Island's Awful Awful Love Affair: A History*, NEW ENG. HIST. SOC'Y, https://www .newenglandhistoricalsociety.com/rhode-islands-awful-awful-love-affair-history (Aug. 15, 2022).

74. Langer, *supra* note 69.

75. *Friendly's, supra* note 68.

76. Edwin Durgy, *Friendly's Files for Bankruptcy*, FORBES (Oct. 5, 2011), https:// www.forbes.com/sites/edwindurgy/2011/10/05/friendlys-files-for-bankruptcy /?sh=108c15144da3.

77. *Id.*

78. *Sun to Buy Friendly Ice Cream in $337 Million Deal*, REUTERS (June 17, 2007), https://www .reuters.com/article/friendlyicecream-suncapital/sun-to-buy-friendly-ice-cream -in-337-million-deal-idUSWEN881220070618; Mia Lamar & Jacqueline Palank, *Friendly's Files for Chapter 11 Bankruptcy*, WALL ST. J. (Oct. 6, 2011), https://www.wsj.com/articles /SB10001424052970203388804576612531340661442.

79. *See* Tom Hals, *UPDATE 3-Friendly's Chain Files for Bankruptcy*, REUTERS (Oct. 5, 2011), https://www.reuters.com/article/friendlys/update-3-friendlys-chain-files-for-bank ruptcy-idUSL3E7L51GD20111005 ("The company's debt load also prevented it from sprucing up its restaurants, which got their start in Springfield, Massachusetts, in 1935."). *See also* Motion for Joint Administration Filed by Friendly Ice Cream Corpo- ration at 4, *In re: Friendly Ice Cream Corp.*, No. 11-13167 (Bankr. D. Del., Oct. 5, 2011), ECF No. 2 ("As the Debtors' liquidity position deteriorated, the Debtors struggled to meet their debt service obligations and failed to satisfy financial covenants under their prepetition revolving credit agreement, resulting in a default.").

80. *Friendly Sells 160 Units in Sales-Leaseback Deal*, NATION'S REST. NEWS (Oct. 22, 2007), https://www.nrn.com/corporate/friendly-sells-160-units-sales-leaseback-deal.

81. Ch. 11 Voluntary Petition at 1925–26, *In re: Friendly Ice Cream Corp.*, No. 11-13167 (Bankr. D. Del., Oct. 5, 2011), ECF No. 1 (Friendly Ice Cream Corporation had its headquarters or principal place of business in Massachusetts. Its various sub- sidiaries were headquartered or had their principal places of business in Delaware); Motion for Joint Administration Filed by Friendly Ice Cream Corporation at 5, *In re: Friendly Ice Cream Corp.*, No. 11-13167 (Bankr. D. Del., Oct. 5, 2011), ECF No. 2.

82. Motion for Joint Administration Filed by Friendly Ice Cream Corporation at 9, *In re: Friendly Ice Cream Corp.*, No. 11-13167 (Bankr. D. Del., Oct. 5, 2011), ECF No. 2.

83. *In re: Humboldt Creamery, LLC*, No. 09-11078 (Bankr. N.D. Cal. 2009).

84. Mike Spector, *Two Hats a Fit for Friendly's Owner*, WALL ST. J. (July 26, 2012), https://www.wsj.com/articles/SB10000872396390443477104577551000555121714.

85. Omnibus Objection of the Official Committee of Unsecured Creditors ¶ 19, *In re: Friendly Ice Cream Corp.*, No. 11-13167 (Bankr. D. Del., Oct. 28, 2011), ECF No. 242. Technically, Friendly's owner—the Sun Capital affiliate Freeze LLC—had lent the money, then transferred ownership of the debt to the second affiliate, Sundae Group Holdings II; Omnibus Objection of Pension Benefit Guaranty Corporation at 7, *In re: Friendly Ice Cream Corp.*, No. 11-13167 (Bankr. D. Del., Oct. 28, 2011), ECF No. 241.

86. Lamar & Palank, *supra* note 78.

87. Spector, *supra* note 84.

88. Order Approving Bidding Procedures at 5, *In re: Friendly Ice Cream Corp.*, No. 11-13167 (Bankr. D. Del., Nov. 3, 2011), ECF No. 289.

89. Notice of Service/Notice of Cancellation of Auction and Successful Bidder Filed by Friendly Ice Cream Corporation, *In re: Friendly Ice Cream Corp.*, No. 11-13167 (Bankr. D. Del., Dec. 30, 2011), ECF No. 526.

90. Spector, *supra* note 84; Lamar & Palank, *supra* note 78.

91. Motion to Approve Debtor in Possession Financing at 2, *In re: Friendly Ice Cream Corp.*, No. 11-13167 (Bankr. D. Del., Oct. 5, 2011), ECF No. 16.

92. Israel Goldowitz *et al.*, *The PBGC Wins a Case Whenever the Debtor Keeps Its Pension Plan*, 16 MARQ. BEN. & SOC. WELFARE L. REV. 257, 297 (2015), https://

scholarship.law.marquette.edu/cgi/viewcontent.cgi?referer=&httpsredir=1&article
=1005&context=benefits.

93. Douglas J. Elliott, *A Guide to the Pension Benefit Guaranty Corporation*, BROOK-INGS INSTITUTION, 7 (May 20, 2009), https://www.brookings.edu/wp-content/uploads /2016/06/0520_pensions_elliott.pdf.

94. Omnibus Objection of Pension Benefit Guaranty Corporation at 1, *In re: Friendly Ice Cream Corp.*, No. 11-13167 (Bankr. D. Del., Oct. 28, 2011), ECF No. 241.

95. Order Approving Bidding Procedures at 5, *In re: Friendly Ice Cream Corp.*, No. 11-13167 (Bankr. D. Del., Nov. 3, 2011), ECF No. 289.

96. Motion to Authorize Debtors' Motion for Entry of an Order Approving Bidding Procedures and Notice Procedures at 28, *In re: Friendly Ice Cream Corp.*, No. 11 -13167 (Bankr. D. Del., Nov. 3, 2011), ECF No. 15.

97. *Statement of Hon. Joshua Gotbaum*, ABI COMMISSION TO STUDY REFORM OF CHAPTER 11 (Mar. 14, 2013), https://www.pbgc.gov/documents/Gotbaum-ABI-Statement.pdf.

98. *Friendly's Bankruptcy: Full List of Closed Friendly's Restaurants*, MASSLIVE (Oct. 5, 2011), https://www.masslive.com/business-news/2011/10/full_list_of_closed_friendlys _restaurants.html.

99. Eric Anderson, *Friendly Emerges from Bankruptcy*, TIMES UNION (Jan. 9, 2012), https://www.timesunion.com/business/article/Friendly-emerges-from-bankruptcy -2452103.php.

100. Aisha Al-Muslim, *Friendly's Restaurant Owner Files for Bankruptcy amid Pandemic*, WALL ST. J. (Nov. 2, 2020), https://www.wsj.com/articles/friendlys-restaurant-owner -files-for-bankruptcy-amid-pandemic-11604318761.

101. Jonathan Maze, *Friendly's Declares Bankruptcy and Will Be Sold to the Owner of Red Mango*, REST. BUS. (Nov. 2, 2020), https://www.restaurantbusinessonline.com /financing/friendlys-declares-bankruptcy-will-be-sold-owner-red-mango.

102. Al-Muslim, *supra* note 100.

103. Julie Creswell, *In a Romney Believer, Private Equity's Risks and Rewards*, N.Y. TIMES (Jan. 21, 2012), https://www.nytimes.com/2012/01/22/business/in-a-romney -believer-private-equitys-risks-and-rewards.html.

104. Baker *et al., supra* note 45, at 38 ("A National Bureau of Economic Research analysis of over 3,000 private equity acquisitions found that retail companies acquired by private equity experienced a 12 percent drop in employment over the subsequent five years.").

105. Elizabeth Lewis, *A Bad Man's Guide to Private Equity and Pensions* 7 (Edmond J. Safra Working Papers No. 68, 2015), https://papers.ssrn.com/sol3/papers.cfm ?abstract_id=2620320.

106. Lynn M. LoPucki, COURTING FAILURE: HOW COMPETITION FOR BIG CASES IS CORRUPTING THE BANKRUPTCY COURTS 16 (2006) (Forum shopping provisions became part of bankruptcy code in 1978, went into effect 1979).

107. Lynn M. LoPucki, *Chapter 11's Descent into Lawlessness* 4 (UCLA Sch. of L. L.-Econ., Working Paper No. 21–12, 2022), https://ssrn.com/abstract=3946577.

108. *Id.*

109. LoPucki, *supra* note 106, at 18.

110. *Id.*

111. *Id.* at 20.

112. Tom Hals, *Ever-Shorter U.S. Bankruptcies Have Creditors Scrambling*, REUTERS (Feb. 1, 2017), https://www.reuters.com/article/us-usa-bankruptcy/ever-shorter-u-s-bank ruptcies-have-creditors-scrambling-idUSKBN15G5FO.

113. LoPucki, *supra* note 106, at 2, 8.

114. *Id.* at 16.

115. *Id.* at 3.

116. Stephen Kurczy, *Annmarie Reinhart Smith, Who Battled for Retail Workers, Dies at 61*, N.Y. TIMES (Mar. 15, 2021), https://www.nytimes.com/2021/03/06/obituaries/annmarie -reinhart-smith-dead-coronavirus.html; Sarah Jaffe, *Service with a Smile: A Retail Worker Learns to Fight for Her Rights*, PROGRESSIVE MAG. (Jan. 26, 2021), https://progressive.org /magazine/service-with-a-smile-jaffe/.

117. Jaffe, *supra* note 116.

118. Rachel Siegel, *$20 Million Fund Set Aside for Laid-Off Toys R Us Workers*, WASH. POST (Nov. 20, 2018), https://www.washingtonpost.com/business/2018/11/20/million-fund-set -aside-laid-off-toys-r-us-workers/.

119. Jaffe, *supra* note 116.

120. *Id.*

121. Kurczy, *supra* note 116.

122. Letter from Rep. Mark Pocan *et al.*, to Joshua Bekenstein, cofounder of Bain Capital, L.P., *et al.* (July 5, 2018), http://online.wsj.com/public/resources/document s/toysrusletter_0706.pdf.

123. *Menendez, Booker, Pascrell Demand Fairness for Toys 'R' Us Workers Following Bankruptcy*, OFFICE OF SENATOR BOB MENENDEZ (June 1, 2018), https://www.menendez .senate.gov/newsroom/press/menendez-booker-pascrell-demand-fairness-for-toys-r-us -workers-following-bankruptcy.

124. Kurczy, *supra* note 116.

125. Chris Isidore, *Toys 'R' Us Employees Protest Lack of Severance Pay*, CNN (June 4, 2018), https://money.cnn.com/2018/06/04/news/companies/toys-r-us-employees-severance -protests/index.html.

126. Michael Corkery, *Laid-off Toys R Us Workers Find Powerful Ally in Public Pensions*, ALBUQUERQUE BUS. J. (Oct. 8, 2018), https://www.bizjournals.com/albuquerque/news /2018/10/08/laid-off-toys-r-us-workers-find-powerful-ally-in.html.

127. Mark Vandevelde, *KKR Faces Pension Fund Ire over Toys R Us Collapse*, FIN. TIMES (June 24, 2018), https://www.ft.com/content/7370b1fc-763a-11e8-a8c4-408cfba4327c.

128. Siegel, *supra* note 118.

129. Memorandum Opinion, *TRU Creditor Litig. Tr. v. Brandon* (In re: Toys "R" U.S., Inc.), No. 17-34665-KLP (Bankr. E.D. Va. June 27, 2022).

130. Corinne Ruff, *Former Toys R Us Employees Receive Hardship Fund Checks*, RETAIL DIVE (Jan. 4, 2019), https://www.retaildive.com/news/former-toys-r-us-employees-receive -hardship-fund-checks/545295/.

131. Siegel, *supra* note 118 (The employees would get payments from $20 million fund. Rise Up Retail said that they were owed $75 million, however.)

132. *Id.*

133. *United for Respect Mourns the Loss of Ann Marie Reinhart Smith, Leader in Toys 'R' Us, Private Equity Campaigns*, UNITED FOR RESPECT (Feb. 18, 2021), https://united4respect.org /statement/ann-marie-reinhart-smith/ (Employees will get between $200 and $12,000).

134. Kurczy, *supra* note 116.

135. Anne D'Innocenzio, *Former Toys R Us Workers to Get $20 Million in Hardship Fund*, TELEGRAPH (Nov. 25, 2018), https://www.telegraphherald.com/news/business /article_9bcaa561-2f95-5e3e-9308-81d36e5e4d87.html/.

136. Jaffe, *supra* note 116.

137. Kurczy, *supra* note 116.

138. *United for Respect Mourns the Loss of Ann Marie Reinhart Smith, supra* note 133.

139. Jaffe, *supra* note 116.

140. Kurczy, *supra* note 116.

141. *United for Respect Mourns the Loss of Ann Marie Reinhart Smith, supra* note 133.

CHAPTER 4: DEADLY CARE

1. David Gelles, *Billionaire Confessional: David Rubenstein on Wealth and Privilege*, N.Y. TIMES (Mar. 12, 2020), https://www.nytimes.com/2020/03/12/business/david-rubenstein -carlyle-corner-office.html.

2. Greg Schneider, *Connections and Then Some*, WASH. POST (Mar. 16, 2003), https:// www.washingtonpost.com/archive/lifestyle/2003/03/16/connections-and-then-some /faaece9e-0225-4310-a8f9-8137d2329d52/.

3. David Montgomery, *David Rubenstein, Co-founder of Carlyle Group and Washington Philanthropist*, WASH. POST (May 14, 2012), https://www.washingtonpost.com/lifestyle /style/david-rubenstein-co-founder-of-carlyle-group-and-washington-philanthropist /2012/05/14/gIQA7XcvPU_story.html.

4. *Id.*; *Interview with David Rubenstein, Deputy Director Domestic Policy Staff*, JIMMY CARTER PRESIDENTIAL LIBRARY (Dec. 3, 1980), https://www.jimmycarterlibrary.gov /assets/documents/oral_histories/exit_interviews/Rubenstein.pdf.

5. Schneider, *supra* note 2.

6. *Id.* (President Carter said, "He devoted probably more hours to his work in the White House than anyone on my staff, so far as I ever knew.... He was a reticent person as far as putting himself forward. He was very modest, and never claimed credit for successes when they did materialize.").

7. Thomas DeFrank & Eleanor Clift, *Inside the Carter White House*, Wash. Post (Jan. 18, 1981), https://www.washingtonpost.com/archive/opinions/1981/01/18/inside-the -carter-white-house/31f3eb8e-038e-48c0-ae29-a805adb92a7a/; *Collection: Office of Staff Secretary; Series: Presidential Files; Folder: 8/27/80; Container 173*, JIMMY CARTER PRESIDENTIAL LIBRARY (Aug. 27, 1980), https://www.jimmycarterlibrary.gov/digital_library/sso /148878/173/SSO_148878_173_05.pdf; *Folder Citation: Collection: Office of Staff Secretary; Series: Presidential Files; Folder: 9/13/77; Container 40*, JIMMY CARTER PRESIDENTIAL LIBRARY (Sept. 13, 1977), https://www.jimmycarterlibrary.gov/digital_library/sso/148878/40/SSO _148878_040_08.pdf; *Folder Citation: Collection: Office of Staff Secretary; Series: Presidential Files; Folder: 7/2/80; Container 168*, JIMMY CARTER PRESIDENTIAL LIBRARY (July 2, 1980), https://www.jimmycarterlibrary.gov/digital_library/sso/148878/168/SSO_148878 _168_03.pdf; *Folder Citation: Collection: Office of Staff Secretary; Series: Presidential Files; Folder: 12/13/77; Container 54*, JIMMY CARTER PRESIDENTIAL LIBRARY (Dec. 13, 1977), https://www.jimmycarterlibrary.gov/digital_library/sso/148878/54/SSO_148878_054 _12.pdf.

8. *Jimmy Carter entering presidential helicopter, fr 1-5; David Rubenstein, fr 8-28*, NATIONAL ARCHIVES CATALOG (Apr. 13, 1979), https://catalog.archives.gov/id/184343.

9. Schneider, *supra* note 2.

10. David A. Vise, *Area Merchant Banking Firm Formed*, WASH. POST (Oct. 5, 1987), https://www.washingtonpost.com/archive/business/1987/10/05/area-merchant-banking -firm-formed/c567202c-e8ed-409a-8c08-d552e1857844/.

11. *Hotel Fact Sheet*, CARLYLE, A ROSEWOOD HOTEL, https://www.rosewoodhotels .com/en/the-carlyle-new-york/media/press-kit/hotel-fact-sheet.

12. Schneider, *supra* note 2.

13. *Carlucci Takes Job at Carlyle Group*, N.Y. TIMES (Jan. 30, 1989), https://www.nytimes .com/1989/01/30/business/carlucci-takes-job-at-carlyle-group.html.

14. Kenneth N. Gilpin, *Little-Known Carlyle Scores Big*, N.Y. TIMES (Mar. 26, 1991), https://www.nytimes.com/1991/03/26/business/little-known-carlyle-scores-big .html.

15. *Id.*

16. Schneider, *supra* note 2.

17. David Ignatius, *The President as Businessman: The Fancy Financial Footwork of George W. Bush*, N.Y. TIMES (Aug. 7, 2002), https://www.nytimes.com/2002/08/07/opinion/IHT -the-president-as-businessman-the-fancy-financial-footwork-of.html.

18. Schneider, *supra* note 2; *Biography: William E. Kennard*, DEPARTMENT OF STATE, https://2009-2017.state.gov/s/p/fapb/185588.htm; *Julius Genachowski*, CARLYLE, https:// www.carlyle.com/about-carlyle/team/julius-genachowski.

19. Schneider, *supra* note 2.

20. *Id.*

21. *Bain Capital Partners, the Carlyle Group and Thomas H. Lee Partners Agree to Acquire Dunkin' Brands, Inc. from Pernod Ricard S.A. for $2.425 Billion*, CARLYLE GROUP (Dec. 11, 2005), https://www.carlyle.com/media-room/news-release-archive/bain-capital -partners-carlyle-group-and-thomas-h-lee-partners-agree; *The Carlyle Group and Getty Images Management to Acquire Getty Images from Hellman and Friedman for $3.3 Billion*, CARLYLE GROUP (Aug. 14, 2012), https://www.carlyle.com/media-room/news-release-archive /carlyle-group-and-getty-images-management-acquire-getty-images; Austen Hufford, *Carlyle to Sell Remaining Stake in Booz Allen Hamilton*, PRIVATE EQUITY NEWS (Dec. 2, 2016), https://www.penews.com/articles/carlyle-remaining-stake-in-booz-allen-hamilton -20161202; Dan Primack, *Why Hertz Crashed*, AXIOS (May 26, 2020), https://www .axios.com/2020/05/26/hertz-bankruptcy.

22. *The Carlyle Group*, WIKIPEDIA, https://en.wikipedia.org/wiki/The_Carlyle_Group.

23. Schneider, *supra* note 2; Tina Sfondeles & Alex Thompson, *Why "Scranton Joe" Loves Nantucket*, POLITICO (Nov. 24), https://www.politico.com/newsletters/west-wing -playbook/2021/11/24/why-scranton-joe-loves-nantucket-495223.

24. *David Rubenstein*, FORBES, https://www.forbes.com/profile/david-rubenstein/?sh =2c0fcd8792fd (Oct. 2, 2022).

25. Mikaela Lefrak, *Why This Billionaire Is Spending a Fortune on Washington's Monuments*, WAMU 88.5 (Feb. 12, 2020), https://wamu.org/story/20/02/12/why-this-billionaire-is -spending-a-fortune-on-washingtons-monuments/.

26. Gelles, *supra* note 1.

27. Schneider, *supra* note 2.

28. *The David Rubenstein Show*, BLOOMBERG, https://www.bloomberg.com/peer-to -peer (Sept. 29, 2022).

29. *David Rubenstein*, WIKIPEDIA, https://en.wikipedia.org/wiki/David_Rubenstein; Daniel Trotta, *Carlyle CEO Buys 1776 Printing of Declaration of Independence*, REUTERS (June 25, 2013), https://www.reuters.com/article/us-usa-declaration-carlyle/carlyle-ceo-buys -1776-printing-of-declaration-of-independence-idUSBRE95O1HK20130626; Newseum, *First Newspaper Printing of the Declaration of Independence Goes on Display at the Newseum*, CISION (June 29, 2016), https://www.prnewswire.com/news-releases/first -newspaper-printing-of-the-declaration-of-independence-goes-on-display-at-the -newseum-300292229.html; *Smithsonian Announces $10 Million Gift from David Rubenstein to the National Museum of African American History and Culture*, NATIONAL MUSEUM OF

AFRICAN AMERICAN HISTORY AND CULTURE (Jan. 20, 2016), https://www.si.edu/newsdesk/releases/smithsonian-announces-10-million-gift-david-rubenstein-national-museum-african-american-his.

30. *David Rubenstein, supra* note 29.

31. Benjamin Wofford, *How Did David Rubenstein—Yes, That David Rubenstein—Become a TV Star?*, WASHINGTONIAN (Oct. 26, 2017), https://www.washingtonian.com/2017/10/26/david-rubenstein-become-tv-star/.

32. Martin Pengelly, *"America Is Not a Perfect Country": David Rubenstein on Trump, Biden and a Nation's Troubled History*, GUARDIAN (Sept. 6, 2021), https://www.theguardian.com/books/2021/sep/06/david-rubenstein-interview-trump-biden-america.

33. David Matthews, *"Sesame Street" Stars Feted at the Kennedy Center Honors, on Day Big Bird Puppeteer Caroll Spinney Died*, N.Y. DAILY NEWS (Dec. 8, 2019), https://www.nydailynews.com/news/national/ny-sesame-street-kennedy-center-honors-big-bird-elmo-20191209-ezraqh3o6rhgfpll74rltyrexm-story.html.

34. Schneider, *supra* note 2.

35. *Overview*, CARLYLE GROUP (Dec. 2017), https://www.carlyle.com/sites/default/files/inline-files/CarlyleFactSheet_Dec2017.pdf; Dan Primack, *David Rubenstein Steps Down as Carlyle Group Co-CEO*, AXIOS (Oct. 25, 2017), https://www.axios.com/2017/12/15/david-rubenstein-steps-down-as-carlyle-group-co-ceo-1513306434.

36. Grace Birnstengel, *How'd We Get Here? The History of Nursing Homes*, NEXT AVE. (Mar. 5, 2021), https://www.nextavenue.org/history-of-nursing-homes/.

37. Charlene Harrington *et al.*, *Marketization in Long-Term Care: A Cross-Country Comparison of Large For-Profit Nursing Home Chains*, 10 HEALTH SERVS. INSIGHTS (2017) ("Major growth occurred in the 1990s with many acquisitions and mergers by chains.").

38. *Nursing Home Care*, CENTERS FOR DISEASE CONTROL AND PREVENTION (Sept. 6, 2022), https://www.cdc.gov/nchs/fastats/nursing-home-care.htm.

39. Peter Whoriskey & Dan Keating, *Overdoses, Bedsores, Broken Bones: What Happened When a Private-Equity Firm Sought to Care for Society's Most Vulnerable*, WASH. POST (Nov. 25, 2018), https://www.washingtonpost.com/business/economy/opioid-overdoses-bedsores-and-broken-bones-what-happened-when-a-private-equity-firm-sought-profits-in-caring-for-societys-most-vulnerable/2018/11/25/09089a4a-ed14-11e8-baac-2a674e91502b_story.html.

40. Charlene Harrington *et al.*, *Improving the Financial Accountability of Nursing Facilities*, KAISER COMMISSION ON MEDICAID AND THE UNINSURED, 6 (June 2013), https://www.kff.org/wp-content/uploads/2013/06/8455-improving-the-financial-accountability-of-nursing-facilities.pdf.

41. Mike Shepard, *Carlyle to Buy Nursing Home Operator Manor Care*, WASH. POST (July 2, 2007), http://voices.washingtonpost.com/washbizblog/2007/07/carlyle_to_buy_nursing_home_op_1.html.

42. David A. Vise, *Manor Care Keeps Growing*, WASH. POST (Aug. 8, 1982), https://www.washingtonpost.com/archive/business/1982/08/08/manor-care-keeps-growing/3a77db32-e28f-40a9-b567-b1358d088ddc/. *See also Despite Recent Troubles, HCR ManorCare Has a Rich History*, INS. NEWSNET (Apr. 29, 2018), https://insurancenewsnet.com/oarticle/despite-recent-troubles-hcr-manorcare-has-a-rich-history (The former head of HCR, prior to its merger with ManorCare, said that today "the elderly are more wealthy... [and] increasingly able to pay for their own care.").

43. Vise, *supra* note 42.

44. *Carlyle to Buy Manor Care for $4.9 Billion*, REUTERS (July 2, 2007), https://www.reuters.com/article/us-manorcare-carlyle/carlyle-to-buy-manor-care-for-4-9-billion-idUSWNAS513520070702.

45. *HCP to Acquire the Real Estate Assets of HCR ManorCare, Inc. for $6.1 Billion*, CARLYLE (Dec. 12, 2010), https://www.carlyle.com/media-room/news-release-archive/hcp-acquire-real-estate-assets-hcr-manorcare-inc-61-billion.

46. Whoriskey & Keating, *supra* note 39.

47. *Id.*

48. *Id.*

49. Matthew Goldstein *et al.*, *Push for Profits Left Nursing Homes Struggling to Provide Care*, N.Y. TIMES (May 7, 2020), https://www.nytimes.com/2020/05/07/business/coronavirus-nursing-homes.html.

50. Whoriskey & Keating, *supra* note 39.

51. Harrington *et al.*, *supra* note 40.

52. Eileen O'Grady, *Pulling Back the Veil on Today's Private Equity Ownership of Nursing Homes*, PRIVATE EQUITY STAKEHOLDER PROJECT (2021), https://pestakeholder.org/wp-content/uploads/2021/07/PESP_Report_NursingHomes_July2021.pdf (discussing issues with Genesis (owned by Formation) and Golden Living (owned by Fillmore)); *Sava Senior Care*, NURSING HOME ABUSE GUIDE, https://www.nursinghomeabuseguide.org/resources/sava-senior-care (discussing Sava).

53. Harrington *et al.*, *supra* note 40.

54. *Genesis Healthcare Inc. Agrees to Pay Federal Government $53.6 Million to Resolve False Claims Act Allegations Relating to the Provision of Medically Unnecessary Rehabilitation Therapy and Hospice Services*, DEPARTMENT OF JUSTICE (June 16, 2017), https://www.justice.gov/opa/pr/genesis-healthcare-inc-agrees-pay-federal-government-536-million-resolve-false-claims-act (Genesis settled for $53.6 million); Alex Spanko, *DOJ Drops False Claims Act Case Against HCR ManorCare*, SKILLED NURSING NEWS (Nov. 9, 2017), https://skillednursingnews.com/2017/11/doj-drops-false-claims-act-case-hcr-manorcare/; *Golden Living Nursing Homes Settle Allegations of Substandard Wound Care*, DEPARTMENT OF JUSTICE (Jan. 2, 2013), https://www.justice.gov/usao-ndga/pr/golden-living-nursing-homes-settle-allegations-substandard-wound-care; *SavaSeniorCare LLC Agrees to Pay $11.2 Million to Resolve False Claims Act Allegations*, DEPARTMENT OF JUSTICE (May 21, 2021), https://www.justice.gov/opa/pr/savaseniorcare-llc-agrees-pay-112-million-resolve-false-claims-act-allegations.

55. R. Tamara Konetzka *et al.*, *The Staffing—Outcomes Relationship in Nursing Homes*, 42 HEALTH SERVICES RESEARCH (2008), https://www.ncbi.nlm.nih.gov/pmc/articles/PMC2442239/.

56. Atul Gupta *et al.*, *Does Private Equity Investment in Healthcare Benefit Patients? Evidence from Nursing Homes* 4 (Nat'l Bureau of Econ. Rsch., Working Paper No. 28474, 2021).

57. Nalea Ko, *Licensed Practical Nurses (LPN) vs. Registered Nurses (RN)*, NURSE J. (Aug. 29, 2022), https://nursejournal.org/resources/lpn-vs-rn-roles/; Rohit Pradhan *et al.*, *Private Equity Ownership of Nursing Homes: Implications for Quality*, 42 J. HEALTHCARE FIN. 1, 9 (2014), https://healthfinancejournal.com/index.php/johcf/article/view/12 ("In terms of structural (staffing) variables, results suggest that private equity nursing homes have 29% lower RN hours PPD compared to the control group (p<.001). On the other hand, private equity owned facilities have 7% higher LPN hours PPD (p<.05).").

58. Gupta *et al.*, *supra* note 56, at 2–4.

59. *Id.* at 2–3.

60. *The Deadly Combination of Private Equity and Nursing Homes During a Pandemic*, AMERICANS FOR FINANCIAL REFORM 1 (Aug. 2020), https://ourfinancialsecurity.org /wp-content/uploads/2020/08/AFREF-NJ-Private-Equity-Nursing-Homes-Covid.pdf.

61. O'Grady, *supra* note 52, at 7 ("Regency's West Oaks Nursing and Rehabilitation Center experienced the deadliest coronavirus outbreak at a nursing home in Austin, TX, where at least 18 patients died and 72 of its 98 current patients were infected."); Anita Chabria & Melissa Gomez, *How Nursing Homes Became California Coronavirus Hot Zones*, L.A. TIMES (May 2, 2020), https://www.latimes.com/california /story/2020-05-02/how-nursing-homes-became-coronavirus-hot-zones-in-california (Plum Healthcare Group had the nursing home with the biggest outbreak in California).

62. *6 Most Common Nursing Injuries*, UNITEKCOLLEGE (Dec. 15, 2020), https://www .unitekcollege.edu/blog/most-common-nursing-injuries/.

63. *Occupational Injuries and Illnesses Resulting in Musculoskeletal Disorders (MSDs)*, BUREAU OF LABOR STATISTICS (May 2020), https://www.bls.gov/iif/oshwc/case/msds.htm; Daniel Zwerdling, *Hospitals Fail to Protect Nursing Staff from Becoming Patients*, NPR (Feb. 4, 2015), https://www.npr.org/2015/02/04/382639199/hospitals-fail-to-protect -nursing-staff-from-becoming-patients.

64. Testimony of Milly Silva, executive vice president, 1199SEIU United Healthcare Workers East before the House Ways and Means Oversight Subcommittee (Mar. 25, 2021), https://waysandmeans.house.gov/sites/democrats.waysandmeans.house.gov/files /documents/M.%20Silva%20Testimony.pdf.

65. *Id.*

66. *Id.*

67. Gupta *et al.*, *supra* note 56, at 34.

68. *Id.* at 20 ("In our data, more than 90% of the billed amount is paid by taxpayers through Medicare and patients pay the balance.").

69. *Investor-Owned Nursing Homes Draw Scrutiny as Deals Flourish*, BLOOMBERG LAW (April 6, 2021), https://news.bloomberglaw.com/health-law-and-business/investor-owned -nursing-homes-draw-scrutiny-as-deals-flourish.

70. *Nursing Home Law Basics*, FINDLAW (May 17, 2021), https://www.findlaw.com /elder/elder-care-law/nursing-home-law-basics.html; MaryBeth Musumeci & Priya Chidambaram, *Key Questions About Nursing Home Regulation and Oversight in the Wake of COVID-19*, KAISER FAMILY FOUNDATION (Aug. 3, 2020), https://www.kff.org /coronavirus-covid-19/issue-brief/key-questions-about-nursing-home-regulation-and -oversight-in-the-wake-of-covid-19/ ("Certification of nursing home compliance with federal Medicare and/or Medicaid requirements generally is performed by states through regular inspections known as surveys.").

71. *LTCCC Report: Identification of Resident Harm in Nursing Home Citations*, LONG TERM CARE COMMUNITY COALITION 3 (Feb. 2017), https://nursinghome411.org /identification-of-resident-harm-in-nursing-home-citations/ ("[I]t is highly unlikely that a facility will face a penalty for deficient care unless a violation is identified as having caused harm or immediate jeopardy to a resident.").

72. *Id.* at 5.

73. *House Ways & Means Committee Issues Testimony from Long Term Care Community Coalition*, INSURANCE NEWSNET (Nov. 16, 2019), https://insurancenewsnet.com/oarticle/house -ways-means-committee-issues-testimony-from-long-term-care-community-coalition; *EJ-Issue-Guide-Fall-2019*, LONG TERM CARE COMMUNITY COALITION (2019), https:// nursinghome411.org/wp-content/uploads/2019/12/EJ-Issue-Guide-Fall-2019.xlsx.

74. *EJ-Issue-Guide-Fall-2019*, *supra* note 73.

75. *Id.*

76. Interview with Lori Smetanka, executive director, National Consumer Voice (Oct. 12, 2021).

77. Robert Gebeloff *et al.*, *How Nursing Homes' Worst Offenses Are Hidden from the Public*, N.Y. TIMES (Dec. 10, 2021), https://www.nytimes.com/2021/12/09/business /nursing-home-abuse-inspection.html.

78. Interview with Lori Smetanka, *supra* note 76.

79. *American Health Care Assn*, OPEN SECRETS, https://www.opensecrets.org/orgs /american-health-care-assn/summary?toprecipcycle=2022&contribcycle=2022&lobcycle =2022&outspendcycle=2022&id=D000000192&topnumcycle=A.

80. *Genesis Healthcare*, OPEN SECRETS, https://www.opensecrets.org/orgs/genesis -healthcare/summary?toprecipcycle=2022&contribcycle=2022&lobcycle=2022& outspendcycle=2022&id=D000022002&topnumcycle=A; *ManorCare Inc.*, OPEN SECRETS, https://www.opensecrets.org/orgs/manor-care-inc/summary?toprecipcycle=2022& contribcycle=2022&lobcycle=2022&outspendcycle=2022&id=D000022097&topnumcycle =A; *Golden Living*, OPEN SECRETS, https://www.opensecrets.org/orgs/golden-living /summary?toprecipcycle=2022&contribcycle=2022&lobcycle=2022&outspendcycle=2022 &id=D000066613&topnumcycle=A.

81. Matthew Cunningham-Cook, *Nursing Home Industry Avoids Scrutiny for Covid-19 Deaths as Powerful Lobby Goes to Work*, INTERCEPT (Feb. 20, 2021), https://theintercept .com/2021/02/20/covid-nursing-home-cuomo-clyburn/.

82. Robert Gebeloff *et al.*, *How Nursing Homes' Worst Offenses Are Hidden from the Public*, N.Y. TIMES (Dec. 10, 2021), https://www.nytimes.com/2021/12/09/business/nursing -home-abuse-inspection.html.

83. *Id.*

84. Ryan Mills & Melanie Payne, *Neglected: Florida's Largest Nursing Home Chain Survives Despite Legacy of Poor Patient Care*, NAPLES DAILY NEWS (Jan. 24, 2019), https:// www.naplesnews.com/story/news/special-reports/2018/05/31/neglected-fraud-and -abuse-nursing-homes-florida/542609002/.

85. *Id.*

86. Interview with Nicole Snapp-Holloway, attorney (Oct. 15, 2021).

87. *Id.*

88. Interview with Ernest C. Tosh, attorney (Oct. 8, 2021).

89. *Id.*

90. David G. Stevenson *et al.*, *Nursing Home Ownership Trends and Their Impact on Quality of Care: A Study Using Detailed Ownership Data from Texas*, 25 J. AGING & SOC. POL'Y 30 (2013).

91. Jordan Rau, *Care Suffers as More Nursing Homes Feed Money into Corporate Webs*, N.Y. TIMES (Jan. 2, 2018), https://www.nytimes.com/2018/01/02/business/nursing-homes -care-corporate.html. *See, e.g.*, Mills & Payne, *supra* note 84 ("Despite the big money generated from Medicare and Medicaid programs serving the poor and elderly, Consulate's nursing homes are designed to appear cash-strapped. While individual nursing home LLCs are essentially empty shells, they pay rent, management and rehabilitation service fees to Consulate or Formation Capital–affiliated companies.").

92. Stevenson, *supra* note 90, at 30.

93. Rau, *supra* note 91.

94. *Id.*

95. *Id.*

96. *Id.*

97. Mills & Payne, *supra* note 84.

98. Margaret Cronin Fisk, *Nursing Home Neglect Trial Fights Shell Company Transfers*, BLOOMBERG (Sept. 22, 2014), https://www.bloomberg.com/news/articles/2014-09-22 /nursing-home-neglect-trial-fights-shell-company-transfers#xj4y7vzkg.

99. *In re: Fundamental Long Term Care Inc.*, No. 11-bk-22258 (M.D. Fla. Bankr. 2011).

100. Ed Williams, *"An Anything-Goes Situation": Assessing Arbitration Agreements at Nursing Homes*, LAS CRUCES SUN NEWS (July 12, 2020), https://www.lcsun-news.com /story/news/2020/07/11/an-anything-goes-situation/5421301002/.

101. *The Truth About Forced Arbitration*, AMERICAN ASSOCIATION FOR JUSTICE 27 (Sept. 2019), https://www.justice.org/resources/research/the-truth-about-forced-arbitration.

102. *About Us*, AMERICAN HEALTH CARE ASSOCIATION, https://members.ahcancal.org /About-Us/NCAL-Board (Michael Wylie of Genesis was the immediate past chair of the AHCA); *AHCA/NCAL Elects Board of Governors, Directors*, AMERICAN HEALTH CARE ASSOCIATION (Oct. 7, 2020), https://www.ahcancal.org/News-and-Communications /Press-Releases/Pages/AHCANCAL-Elects-Board-of-Governors,-Directors.aspx (Phil Fogg of Marquis served as AHCA vice chair).

103. Alex Spanko, *CMS Finalizes Reversal of Arbitration Ban in Nursing Homes, Proposes Partial Phase 3 RoP Delay*, SKILLED NURSING NEWS (July 16, 2019), https://skillednursingnews .com/2019/07/cms-finalizes-reversal-of-arbitration-ban-in-nursing-homes-proposes -partial-phase-3-rop-delay/.

104. Scott Loftin & Ragini A. Acharya, *Federal District Court Upholds CMS Pre-Dispute Arbitration Rule*, HUSCH BLACKWELL (April 13, 2020), https://www.healthcarelawinsights .com/2020/04/federal-district-court-upholds-cms-pre-dispute-arbitration-rule/.

105. Christopher Rowland, *Long-Term-Care Facilities Are Using the Pandemic as a Shield, Even in Lawsuits Unrelated to Covid-19*, WASH. POST (Aug. 20, 2021), https://www .washingtonpost.com/business/2021/08/20/nursing-home-immunity-covid-lawsuits/.

106. Debbie Cenziper *et al.*, *As Nursing Home Residents Died, New Covid-19 Protections Shielded Companies from Lawsuits. Families Say That Hides the Truth*, WASH. POST (June 8, 2020), https://www.washingtonpost.com/business/2020/06/08/nursing-home-immunity-laws/.

107. *Id.*

108. *Id.*

109. Interview with Ernie Tosh (Oct. 5, 2021).

110. O'Grady, *supra* note 52, at 15.

111. Jessica Silver-Greenberg & Robert Gebeloff, *Maggots, Rape and Yet Five Stars: How U.S. Ratings of Nursing Homes Mislead the Public*, N.Y. TIMES (Aug. 4, 2021), https:// www.nytimes.com/2021/03/13/business/nursing-homes-ratings-medicare-covid .html.

112. Amended Complaint ¶ 27, *US ex rel. Ruckh v. La Vie Health Care Centers, Inc.* No. 8:11-cv-1303 (M.D. Fla. Aug. 2, 2012), ECF No. 16; Mills & Payne, *supra* note 84.

113. Amended Complaint ¶ 36, *US ex rel. Ruckh v. La Vie Health Care Centers, Inc.* No. 8:11-cv-1303 (M.D. Fla. Aug. 2, 2012), ECF No. 16.

114. Second Amended Complaint ¶ 164–184, *US ex rel. Ruckh v. La Vie Health Care Centers, Inc.* No. 8:11-cv-1303 (M.D. Fla. June 3, 2013), ECF No. 75.

115. Mills & Payne, *supra* note 84.

116. *Id.*

117. *Id.* The company was also organized so that, in practice, it was difficult to immediately understand who actually is the owner of a nursing homes' owners. For instance, Ruckh's initial suit was not against Consulate, but "La Vie Health Care Centers, Inc.," only later identified to be the nursing home chain. *Compare* Amended Complaint,

US ex rel. Ruckh v. La Vie Health Care Centers, Inc. No. 8:11-cv-1303 (M.D. Fla. Aug. 2, 2012), ECF No. 16 *with* Second Amended Complaint ¶ 164–184, *supra* note 114.

118. Mills & Payne, *supra* note 84.

119. Docket, *US ex rel. Ruckh v. La Vie Health Care Centers, Inc.* No. 8:11-cv-1303 (M.D. Fla. June 10, 2011).

120. Jury Verdict, *US ex rel. Ruckh v. La Vie Health Care Centers, Inc.* No. 8:11-cv-1303 (M.D. Fla. Feb. 15, 2017), ECF No. 430; Order Granting Judgment as a Matter of Law, *US ex rel. Ruckh v. La Vie Health Care Centers, Inc.*, No. 8:11-cv-1303 (M.D. Fla. Jan. 11, 2018), ECF No. 468.

121. *Angela Ruckh v. Salus Rehabilitation, LLC, et al.*, No. 18-10500 (11th Cir. June 25, 2020).

122. Order on Damages, *US ex rel. Ruckh v. La Vie Health Care Centers, Inc.* No. 8:11-cv-1303 (M.D. Fla. Feb. 8, 2021), ECF No. 562.

123. The complaint was filed on June 10, 2011, and judgment was issued on Feb. 8, 2021.

124. Order Staying Proceedings, *US ex rel. Ruckh v. La Vie Health Care Centers, Inc.* No. 8:11-cv-1303 (M.D. Fla. Feb. 8, 2021), ECF No. 570.

125. Danielle Brown, *Approved: Consulate Health Care to Pay Just $4.5 Million of $258 Million Judgment in Inherited Upcoding Case*, McKnights Long-Term Care News (Sept. 30, 2021), https://www.mcknights.com/news/approved-consulate-health-care-to -pay-just-4-5-million-of-258-million-judgment-in-inherited-upcoding-case/; Christopher Rowland, *How One of the Largest Nursing Home Chains in Florida Could Avoid Nearly All of $256 Million Fraud Judgment*, Wash. Post (Sept. 14, 2021), https://www .washingtonpost.com/business/2021/09/14/nursing-home-bankruptcy-fraud/.

126. Verdict, *US ex rel. Ruckh v. La Vie Health Care Centers, Inc.* No. 8:11-cv-1303 (M.D. Fla. Feb. 15, 2017), ECF No. 430 (Finding over $80 million in Medicare fraud, the Medicaid verdict was vacated).

127. *About*, Formation Capital, https://formationcapital.com/about/ (May 19, 2022).

128. Interview with Lori Smetanka, *supra* note 76.

129. *Id.*

130. *Id.*

CHAPTER 5: MAKING IT ALL WORSE

1. Alex Montero *et al.*, *Americans' Challenges with Health Care Costs*, KFF (July 14, 2022), https://www.kff.org/health-costs/issue-brief/americans-challenges-with-health-care-costs/.

2. *Id.*

3. Charlotte Morabito, *Why Health-Care Costs Are Rising in the U.S. More Than Anywhere Else*, CNBC (Feb. 28 2022), https://www.cnbc.com/2022/02/28/why-health -care-costs-are-rising-in-the-us-more-than-anywhere-else-.html.

4. Nirad Jain *et al.*, *Healthcare Private Equity Market 2021: The Year in Review*, Bain (Mar. 16, 2022), https://www.bain.com/insights/year-in-review-global-healthcare-private -equity-and-ma-report-2022/.

5. *See* Erin C. Fuse *et al.*, *Private Equity Investment as a Divining Rod for Market Failure: Policy Responses to Harmful Physician Practice Acquisitions*, Brookings Institution (Oct. 5, 2021), https://www.brookings.edu/essay/private-equity-investment-as-a-divining-rod-for -market-failure-policy-responses-to-harmful-physician-practice-acquisitions/.

6. Sally Tan *et al.*, *Trends in Private Equity Acquisition of Dermatology Practices in the United States*, 155 JAMA Dermatol 1013 (2019).

7. Heather Perlberg, *How Private Equity Is Ruining American Health Care*, BLOOMBERG (May 20, 2020), https://www.bloomberg.com/news/features/2020-05-20/private-equity -is-ruining-health-care-covid-is-making-it-worse#xj4y7vzkg.

8. *Id.*

9. *Id.*

10. Fuse *et al.*, *supra* note 5.

11. Kara Grant, *Is Private Equity a Dangerous Employer?*, MEDPAGE TODAY (Oct. 14, 2021), https://www.medpagetoday.com/special-reports/exclusives/95022.

12. *See, e.g., Dermatologist, Not Private Equity, Group*, CHEGG INTERNSHIPS, https://www .internships.com/posting/bug_39194282087 ("Dermatologist, Not Private Equity, Group"); *Dermatologist, NOT Private Equity, Permanent Group Position (Physician)*, WBOY12 (Aug. 4, 2022), https://jobs.wboy.com/jobs/dermatologist-not-private-equity-permanent -group-position-physician-naperville-illinois/677322663-2/; *Dermatologist—Private Group, NOT Private Equity—Sunset Beach (Physician)*, KRQE (Aug. 4, 2022), https://jobs.krqe .com/jobs/dermatologist-private-group-not-private-equity-sunset-beach-physician -california/677295888-2/; *Houston, TX Dermatology—NOT Private Equity (Physician)*, WANE (Aug. 18, 2022), https://jobs.wane.com/jobs/houston-tx-dermatology-not-private -equity-physician-texas/688815409-2/.

13. *See* Alexander Borsa, *When Private Equity Firms Invest in Women's Health Clinics, Who Benefits?*, STAT NEWS (Sept. 14, 2020), https://www.statnews.com/2020/09/14/private -equity-firms-invest-womens-health-clinics-who-benefits/ ("The industry has set its sights on women's health in part because of its high profitability and the limited regulation of fertility services"); EILEEN APPELBAUM & ROSEMARY BATT, PRIVATE EQUITY BUYOUTS IN HEALTHCARE: WHO WINS, WHO LOSES? 52–53 (Mar. 15, 2020), https://www.ineteconomics .org/uploads/papers/WP_118-Appelbaum-and-Batt-2-rb-Clean.pdf; Alpesh Patel, *Private Equity and Its Emergence in Orthopaedics*, 29 J. AM. ORTHO. SURG. (2021), https://journals .lww.com/jaaos/Abstract/2021/10150/Private_Equity_and_Its_Emergence_in _Orthopaedics.4.aspx#JCL-P-4; Fuse *et al.*, *supra* note 5; Jane M. Zhu *et al.*, *Private Equity Acquisitions of Physician Medical Groups Across Specialties, 2013-2016*, JAMA (Feb. 18, 2020), https://jamanetwork.com/journals/jama/fullarticle/2761076?guestAccessKey =4eb6959c-7cec-43f1-95b3-93a8c6ea6f6b; Justin Doshi *et al.*, *Healthcare Providers: New Roll-Up Candidates and a New Look for Risk-Bearing Providers*, BAIN (Mar. 16, 2021), https://www.bain.com/insights/providers-global-healthcare-private-equity-and-ma -report-2021/; *Private Equity Investing in Dental Companies*, PRIVATE EQUITY INFO (Sept. 9, 2021), https://blog.privateequityinfo.com/index.php/2021/09/09/private-equity-investing -in-dental-companies/; Jane M. Zhu, *Private Equity Investment in Physician Practices*, PENN LDI (Feb. 15, 2020), https://ldi.upenn.edu/our-work/research-updates/private-equity -investment-in-physician-practices/.

14. Appelbaum & Batt, *supra* note 13. (Eileen Appelbaum and Rosemary Batt estimate that private equity firms have bought 2,500 health care clinics and service. Together, private equity firms bought 2,500 clinics and small health care services over twenty years and spent over $150 billion to do so.); Fuse *et al.*, *supra* note 5 (estimating private equity purchase of 1,283 clinics over eleven years).

15. BAIN & CO., GLOBAL HEALTHCARE PRIVATE EQUITY AND M&A REPORT 2022 (2022), https://www.bain.com/insights/topics/global-healthcare-private-equity-ma-report/.

16. *The Blackstone Group Completes Major Investment in Vanguard Health Systems, Inc.*, BLACKSTONE (Sept. 23, 2004), https://www.blackstone.com/news/press/the-blackstone -group-completes-major-investment-in-vanguard-health-systems-inc/.

17. *Blackstone Buying Majority of Vanguard Health Systems*, PHOENIX BUS. J. (July 26, 2004), https://www.bizjournals.com/phoenix/stories/2004/07/26/daily14.html.

18. Kevin Dowd, *This Day in Buyout History: KKR, Bain Capital Complete the Biggest LBO Ever*, PITCHBOOK (Nov. 17, 2027), https://pitchbook.com/news/articles/this-day-in-buyout-history-kkr-bain-capital-complete-the-biggest-lbo-ever.

19. Appelbaum & Batt, *supra* note 13.

20. Jack O'Brien, *Steward Health Care Buys Back Control from Cerberus*, HEALTHLEADERS (June 2, 2020), https://www.healthleadersmedia.com/finance/steward-health-care-buys-back-control-cerberus.

21. John Hechinger & Sabrina Willmer, *Life and Debt at a Private Equity Hospital*, BLOOMBERG (August 6, 2020), https://www.bloomberg.com/news/features/2020-08-06/cerberus-backed-hospitals-face-life-and-debt-as-virus-rages#xj4y7vzkg.

22. Appelbaum & Batt, *supra* note 13.

23. *Regionals: Vanguard Health Systems Acquires Two Hospitals and More News*, MOD. HEALTHC. (Aug. 9, 2010), https://www.modernhealthcare.com/article/20100809/MAGAZINE/308099981/regionals-vanguard-health-systems-acquires-two-hospitals-and-more-news (Vanguard bought two hospitals in 2010); *HCA Healthcare*, WIKIPEDIA, https://en.wikipedia.org/wiki/HCA_Healthcare#United_States. In 2017, HCA made a number of acquisitions. The company had gone public a number of years earlier, but KKR continued to hold a small stake in it. *KKR Rep Leaves HCA Board*, NASHV. POST (May 17, 2016), https://www.nashvillepost.com/kkr-rep-leaves-hca-board/article_1bd2e76f-584e-5cd5-87ea-9ff7418b4847.html; *Steward Health Care Completes Acquisition of Five South Florida Hospitals Bringing Physician-Led Care to More Communities in the Region*, ST. ELIZABETH'S MEDICAL CENTER (Aug. 2, 2021), https://www.semc.org/domain-specific/720191/newsroom/2021-08-02/steward-health-care-completes-acquisition-five-south-florida-hospitals-bringing (Steward bought five additional hospitals).

24. Appelbaum & Batt, *supra* note 13, at 22–23.

25. Josh Kosman, *Bain's Huge HCA IPO Gain*, N.Y. POST (Mar. 11, 2011), https://nypost.com/2011/03/11/bains-huge-hca-ipo-gain/.

26. Hechinger & Willmer, *supra* note 21.

27. *Id.*

28. *Id.*

29. *Id.*

30. *Id.*

31. *Id.*

32. Envision estimates that about 65 percent of hospitals outsource their emergency staffing to a third-party company. Envision Healthcare Holdings, Inc., *Form 10-K* (Mar. 2, 2015), https://www.sec.gov/Archives/edgar/data/1578318/000104746915001498/a2223319z10-k.htm. TeamHealth estimates that it controls about 20 percent of the emergency department and hospital medicine market. It says that the fragmented market "represents an attractive opportunity for further consolidation." TeamHealth, *Ex.-99.1*, https://www.sec.gov/Archives/edgar/data/1082754/000119312517003669/d267388dex991.htm.

33. Ellie Kincaid, *Envision Healthcare Infiltrated America's ERs. Now It's Facing a Backlash*, FORBES (May 15, 2018), https://www.forbes.com/sites/elliekincaid/2018/05/15/envision-healthcare-infiltrated-americas-ers-now-its-facing-a-backlash/?sh=6853c2c4284f.

34. *IPO of Onex's Emergency Medical Services Priced*, CBC NEWS (Dec. 6, 2005), https://www.cbc.ca/news/business/ipo-of-onex-s-emergency-medical-services-priced

-1.539892; *Onex Sells U.S. Medical Investment*, CBC NEWS (Feb. 14, 2011), https://www
.cbc.ca/news/business/onex-sells-u-s-medical-investment-1.1102276.

35. *Clayton, Dubilier & Rice Completes $3.2 Billion Acquisition of Emergency Medical
Services Corporation*, CLAYTON, DUBILIER & RICE (May 25, 2011), https://www.cdr-inc.com
/news/press-release/clayton-dubilier-rice-completes-3.2-billion-acquisition-emergency
-medical.

36. Gretchen Morgenson, *Doctor Fired from ER Warns About Effect of For-Profit Firms on
U.S. Health Care*, NBC NEWS (Mar. 28, 2022), https://www.nbcnews.com/health/health
-care/doctor-fired-er-warns-effect-profit-firms-us-health-care-rcna19975.

37. Aisha Al-Muslim, *KKR to Acquire Envision Healthcare for $5.5 Billion*, WALL ST. J.
(June 11, 2018), https://www.wsj.com/articles/kkr-to-acquire-envision-healthcare-for
-5-5-billion-1528718957.

38. *Brovont vs. KS-I Medical Services, P.A. et al.*, 622 S.W.3d 671 (Mo. Ct. App. Oct.
13, 2020).

39. *Id.*

40. *Id.*

41. *Id.*

42. *Id.*

43. *Id.*

44. *Id.*

45. *Id.*

46. William Sullivan, *$26M Judgment Against EmCare in Wrongful Termination Lawsuit*,
EMERGENCY PHYSICIANS MONTHLY (Aug. 2, 2021), https://epmonthly.com/article/26m
-judgment-against-emcare-in-wrongful-termination-lawsuit/.

47. Dan Margolies, *Appeals Court Restores Most of $29M Verdict to ER Doctor Who Com-
plained of Staffing Shortages*, KCUR 89.3 (Oct. 13, 2020), https://www.kcur.org/health
/2020-10-13/appeals-court-restores-most-of-29m-verdict-to-er-doctor-who-complained
-of-staffing-shortages.

48. Ming Lin, *I just sent this letter to our cmo*, FACEBOOK (Mar. 15, 2020),https://
m.facebook.com/story.php?story_fbid=10216583796603708&id=1122938346.

49. *Id.*

50. Complaint ¶ 3.37, *Lin v. Peacehealth et al.*, No. 20-2-00700 (Wash. Sup. Ct. May
28, 2020).

51. Gretchen Morgenson & Emmanuelle Saliba, *Private Equity Firms Now Control Many
Hospitals, ERs and Nursing Homes. Is It Good for Health Care?*, NBC NEWS (May 13, 2020),
https://www.nbcnews.com/health/health-care/private-equity-firms-now-control-many
-hospitals-ers-nursing-homes-n1203161; Docket, *Lin v. Peacehealth et al.*, No. 20-2-00700
(Wash. Sup. Ct. May 28, 2020).

52. Isaac Arnsdorf, *Overwhelmed Hospitals Face a New Crisis: Staffing Firms Are Cutting
Their Doctors' Hours and Pay*, PROPUBLICA (Apr. 3, 2020), https://www.propublica.org
/article/overwhelmed-hospitals-face-a-new-crisis-staffing-firms-are-cutting-their-
doctors-hours-and-pay.

53. *Id.*

54. *Edited Transcript, Q4 2018 KKR & Co Inc Earnings Call*, KKR 10 (Feb. 1, 2019)
(KKR's head of investor relations, Craig Larson, said that "Envision is an investment where we're going to be focused together with management on a series of operational improvement initiatives."); Kiran Stacey, *US Doctors Fear Patients at Risk as
Cost Cuts Follow Private Equity Deals*, FIN. TIMES (Nov. 11, 2021), https://www.ft.com

/content/9eac6649-2df5-4663-aecf-632885462288 (Envision subsequently put doctors on new salary plans, which it estimated would lower pay by 15% and link pay to doctors' ability to bill patients. Also increasingly relied on the use of nurses.); TeamHealth, *Ex.-99.1*, https://www.sec.gov/Archives/edgar/data/1082754/000119312517003669/d267388dex991.htm. (According to SEC filings, Blackstone decided to reinvest in TeamHealth in 2016 (it previously owned the company in 2005) because of "near-term cost reduction opportunities.")

55. Isaac Arnsdorf, *How Rich Investors, Not Doctors, Profit from Marking Up ER Bills*, ProPublica (June 12, 2020), https://www.propublica.org/article/how-rich-investors-not-doctors-profit-from-marking-up-er-bills.

56. Interview with Robert McNamara, chief medical officer, Temple University Physicians (Jan. 7, 2022).

57. *Id.*

58. *Two Physician Groups Pay Over $33 Million to Resolve Claims Involving HMA Hospitals*, Department of Justice (Dec. 19, 2017), https://www.justice.gov/opa/pr/two-physician-groups-pay-over-33-million-resolve-claims-involving-hma-hospitals (The offending conduct occurred between 2008 and 2012. The private equity firm Onex bought EmCare in 2004); *EmCare*, Wikipedia, https://en.wikipedia.org/wiki/EmCare; *IPO of Onex's Emergency Medical Services priced*, CBC News (Dec. 6, 2005), https://www.cbc.ca/news/business/ipo-of-onex-s-emergency-medical-services-priced-1.539892; *Onex Sells U.S. Medical Investment*, CBC News (Feb. 14, 2011), https://www.cbc.ca/news/business/onex-sells-u-s-medical-investment-1.1102276.

59. *Two Physician Groups Pay Over $33 Million to Resolve Claims Involving HMA Hospitals*, Department of Justice (Dec. 19, 2017), https://www.justice.gov/opa/pr/two-physician-groups-pay-over-33-million-resolve-claims-involving-hma-hospitals.

60. *See* Robert W. Derlet et al., *Corporate and Hospital Profiteering in Emergency Medicine: Problems of the Past, Present, and Future*, 50 J. Emerg. Med. 902, 905 (2016) ("Hospital stays of any length of time increase the risk of infection and medical mishaps.").

61. *Two Physician Groups Pay Over $33 Million to Resolve Claims Involving HMA Hospitals*, Department of Justice (Dec. 19, 2017), https://www.justice.gov/opa/pr/two-physician-groups-pay-over-33-million-resolve-claims-involving-hma-hospitals.

62. Julie Creswell & Reed Abelson, *Hospital Chain Said to Scheme to Inflate Bills*, N.Y. Times (Jan. 23, 2014), https://www.nytimes.com/2014/01/24/business/hospital-chain-said-to-scheme-to-inflate-bills.html

63. Jeff Lagasse, *TeamHealth Wins Lawsuit Against UnitedHealth*, Healthcare Fin. (Nov. 30, 2021), https://www.healthcarefinancenews.com/news/teamhealth-wins-lawsuit-against-unitedhealth.

64. Complaint ¶ 9, *United Healthcare Services, Inc. et al., v. Team Health Holdings, Inc. et al.*, No. 3:21-cv-00364 (E.D. Tenn. Dec. 27, 2021) ECF No. 1. TeamHealth largely denied United's allegations. Answer, *United Healthcare Services, Inc. et al., v. Team Health Holdings, Inc. et al.*, No. 3:21-cv-00364 (E.D. Tenn. June 9, 2022) ECF No. 49.

65. Paige Minemyer, *UnitedHealth Lawsuit Claims TeamHealth Upcoded Claims for $100M in Fraud*, Fierce Healthcare (Oct. 28, 2021), https://www.fiercehealthcare.com/payer/unitedhealth-lawsuit-claims-teamhealth-upcoded-claims-for-100m-fraud.

66. Scheduling Order, *United Healthcare Services, Inc. et al., v. Team Health Holdings, Inc. et al.*, No. 3:21-cv-00364 (E.D. Tenn. Feb. 16, 2022) ECF No. 43.

67. Yeganeh Torbati, *How Private Equity Extracted Hundreds of Millions of Dollars from a Firm Accused of Medicare Fraud*, Wash. Post (Mar. 1, 2021), https://www.washingtonpost.com/business/2021/03/01/blackstone-healthcare-private-equity-dividend-apria/.

68. *Acting Manhattan U.S. Attorney Announces $40.5 Million Settlement with Durable Medical Equipment Provider Apria Healthcare for Fraudulent Billing Practices*, DEPARTMENT OF JUSTICE (Dec. 21, 2020), https://www.justice.gov/usao-sdny/pr/acting-manhattan-us-attorney-announces-405-million-settlement-durable-medical-equipment. In a statement to the *Washington Post*, Apria said that "[w]e fully cooperated throughout the review and are pleased to have resolved this civil matter.... As always, our patients are our top priority and we remain committed to providing outstanding care and exceptional service." Torbati, *supra* note 67.

69. Matthew Goldstein, *Private Equity Firms Are Piling on Debt to Pay Dividends*, N.Y. TIMES (Feb. 19, 2021), https://www.nytimes.com/2021/02/19/business/private-equity-dividend-loans.html.

70. Torbati, *supra* note 67.

71. *Id.* (Nominally the Trump administration did this in response to the pandemic, but Apria Healthcare had been lobbying on the issue for years.)

72. Torbati, *supra* note 67.

73. Jacob T. Elberg, *Health Care Fraud Means Never Having to Say You're Sorry*, PROGRAM ON CORPORATE COMPLIANCE AND ENFORCEMENT (Apr. 28, 2021), https://wp.nyu.edu/compliance_enforcement/2021/04/28/health-care-fraud-means-never-having-to-say-youre-sorry/.

74. *Issue Brief: Corporate Practice of Medicine*, AMERICAN MEDICAL ASSOCIATION (2015), https://www.ama-assn.org/media/7661/download.

75. Janice Davis & Banee Pachuca, *Private Equity and Physician Practice Acquisitions: Key Legal Considerations*, MORGAN LEWIS 9 (Apr. 13, 2021), https://www.morganlewis.com/-/media/files/publication/presentation/webinar/2021/private-equity-and-physician-practice-acquisitions-key-legal-considerations.pdf; Rosemary Batt & Eileen Appelbaum, *Private Equity Tries to Protect Another Profit Center*, AM. PROSPECT (Sept. 9, 2019), https://prospect.org/power/private-equity-tries-protect-another-profit-center/.

76. AHealthcareZ, *Private Equity Owning Doctor Practices ... Corporate Practice of Medicine Laws Explained*, YOUTUBE, https://www.youtube.com/watch?v=2epmk4_-kUI.

77. Redacted First Amended Complaint at 8, *American Academy of Emergency Medicine Physician Group, Inc. v. Envision Healthcare Corporation et al.*, No. 3:22-cv-421 (N.D. Cal. Feb. 18, 2022), ECF No. 18-2.

78. Complaint at ¶ 26, *American Academy of Emergency Medicine Physician Group, Inc. v. Envision Healthcare Corporation et al.*, No. 3:22-cv-421 (Jan. 21, 2022), ECF No. 1; Redacted First Amended Complaint at 32, *American Academy of Emergency Medicine Physician Group, Inc. v. Envision Healthcare Corporation et al.*, No. 3:22cv421 (N.D. Cal. Feb. 18, 2022), ECF No. 18-2; Gretchen Morgenson, *Doctor Fired from ER Warns About Effect of For-Profit Firms on U.S. Health Care*, NBC NEWS (Mar. 28, 2022), https://www.nbcnews.com/health/health-care/doctor-fired-er-warns-effect-profit-firms-us-health-care-rcna19975 (describing a figurehead doctor at EmCare facilities in Missouri).

79. Complaint at ¶ 26, *American Academy of Emergency Medicine Physician Group, Inc. v. Envision Healthcare Corporation et al.*, No. 3:22-cv-421 (Jan. 21, 2022), ECF No. 1.

80. *Id.* at ¶ 38.

81. Redacted First Amended Complaint at ¶ 45, *American Academy of Emergency Medicine Physician Group, Inc. v. Envision Healthcare Corporation et al.*, No. 3:22-cv-421 (N.D. Cal. Feb. 18, 2022), ECF No. 18-2.

82. *Id.* at ¶ 38.

83. *AAEM-PG Files Suit Against Envision Healthcare Alleging the Illegal Corporate Practice of Medicine*, AMERICAN ACADEMY OF EMERGENCY MEDICINE (Dec. 21, 2021), https://

www.aaemphysiciangroup.com/news-and-updates/aaem-pg-files-suit-envision
-healthcare-alleging-the-illegal-corporate-practice-of-medicine.

84. Docket, *American Academy of Emergency Medicine Physician Group, Inc. v. Envision Healthcare Corporation et al.*, No. 3:22-cv-421 (N.D. Cal. Jan. 1, 2022) (as of Oct. 6, 2022, the parties were litigating over a motion to dismiss).

85. Cory Capps, *Physician Practice Consolidation Driven by Small Acquisitions, so Antitrust Agencies Have Few Tools to Intervene*, 36 HEALTH AFFAIRS (Sept. 2017), https://www.healthaffairs.org/doi/full/10.1377/hlthaff.2017.0054.

86. *Id.*

87. *FTC Requires Community Health Systems, Inc. to Divest Two Hospitals as a Condition of Acquiring Rival Hospital Operator*, FTC (Jan. 22, 2014), https://www.ftc.gov/news-events/news/press-releases/2014/01/ftc-requires-community-health-systems-inc-divest-two-hospitals-condition-acquiring-rival-hospital.

88. Melanie Evans, *Steward Health Care to Buy Iasis Healthcare for $1.9 Billion*, WALL ST. J. (May 19, 2017), https://www.wsj.com/articles/steward-health-care-to-buy-iasis-healthcare-for-1-9-billion-1495199135.

89. Vince Gallaro, *FTC Won't Block Vanguard-DMC Deal*, MODERN HEALTHCARE (Sept. 8, 2010), https://www.modernhealthcare.com/article/20100908/NEWS/309089983/ftc-won-t-block-vanguard-dmc-deal; Melanie Evans, *Steward Health Care to Buy Iasis Healthcare for $1.9 Billion*, WALL ST. J. (May 19, 2017), https://www.wsj.com/articles/steward-health-care-to-buy-iasis-healthcare-for-1-9-billion-1495199135.

90. Eileen Applebaum, *How Private Equity Makes You Sicker*, AM. PROSPECT (Oct. 7, 2019), https://prospect.org/health/how-private-equity-makes-you-sicker/; *The Courage to Learn*, AMERICAN ECONOMIC LIBERTIES PROJECT 9 (2021), https://www.economicliberties.us/wp-content/uploads/2021/01/Courage-to-Learn-Final.pdf.

91. *Northern Pacific Railroad Co. v. U.S.*, 356 U.S. 1, 4 (1958).

92. *William Howard Taft*, WIKIPEDIA, https://en.wikipedia.org/wiki/William_Howard_Taft; Peri Arnold, *William Taft: Domestic Affairs*, https://millercenter.org/president/taft/domestic-affairs.

93. Einer Elhauge, *Horizontal Shareholding*, 129 HARV. L. REV. 1267, 1286 (2016).

94. *Id.* at 1287 (citing Joseph Alsop & Robert Kintner, *Trust Buster: The Folklore of Thurman Arnold*, SATURDAY EVENING POST, Aug. 12, 1939, at 5, 7).

95. Tim Wu, THE CURSE OF BIGNESS 107 (2018).

96. Christopher R. Leslie, *Antitrust Made (Too) Simple*, 79 ANTITRUST L. J. 917 (2014), https://papers.ssrn.com/sol3/papers.cfm?abstract_id=2589598.

97. *Modern Antitrust Enforcement*, THURMAN ARNOLD PROJECT, https://som.yale.edu/centers/thurman-arnold-project-at-yale/modern-antitrust-enforcement.

98. Fred Barbash, *Big Corporations Bankroll Seminars for U.S. Judges*, WASH. POST (Jan. 20, 1980), https://www.washingtonpost.com/archive/politics/1980/01/20/big-corporations-bankroll-seminars-for-us-judges/8385bf9f-1eb7-451a-8f3d-bdabb4648452/.

99. William E. Kovacic, *The Antitrust Paradox Revisited: Robert Bork and the Transformation of Modern Antitrust Policy*, 36 WAYNE L. REV. 1413, 1434 n.97 (1990).

100. Henry N. Butler, *The Manne Programs in Economics for Federal Judges*, 50 CASE WESTERN L. REV. 351, 352 (1999).

101. Barbash, *supra* note 98.

102. *Mason Judicial Education Program*, ANTONIN SCALIA LAW SCHOOL LAW & ECONOMICS CENTER, https://masonlec.org/divisions/mason-judicial-education-program/.

103. Kovacic, *supra* note 99.

104. *Reiter v. Sonotone Corp.*, 442 U.S. 330 (1979).

105. *Matsushita v. Zenith Radio Corp.*, 475 U.S. 574 (1986).

106. *Brooke Group Ltd. v. Brown & Williamson Tobacco Corp.*, 509 U.S. 209 (1993).

107. *Verizon Commc'ns Inc. v. L. Offs. of Curtis V. Trinko, LLP*, 540 U.S. 398, 407 (2004).

108. In 2001, the Antitrust Division of the Justice Department had a budget of approximately $121 million; in 2021, $185 million. *Appropriation Figures for the Antitrust Division*, DEPARTMENT OF JUSTICE (Feb. 2020), https://www.justice.gov/atr/appropriation-figures-antitrust-division. Accounting for inflation, funding for the office actually shrank at a time when merger and acquisition activity exploded. Similarly, in 2020, the FTC actually had fewer than 1,200 people working for it, 600 fewer than it had in 1979. *Appropriation and Full-Time Equivalent (FTE) History*, FTC, https://www.ftc.gov/about-ftc/bureaus-offices/office-executive-director/financial-management-office/ftc-appropriation (last visited Oct. 7, 2022).

109. *1968 Merger Guidelines*, DEPARTMENT OF JUSTICE (Aug. 4, 2015), https://www.justice.gov/archives/atr/1968-merger-guidelines.

110. *Id.*

111. *Id.*

112. *Modern Antitrust Enforcement*, THURMAN ARNOLD PROJECT, https://som.yale.edu/centers/thurman-arnold-project-at-yale/modern-antitrust-enforcement.

113. *Horizontal Merger Guidelines*, DEPARTMENT OF JUSTICE AND FTC (Aug. 19, 2010), https://www.justice.gov/atr/horizontal-merger-guidelines-08192010.

114. Robert H. Lande & Sandeep Vaheesan, *Preventing the Curse of Bigness Through Conglomerate Merger Legislation*, 52 ARIZONA STATE L. J. 75 (2020).

115. *Summary of Antitrust Division Health Care Cases (Since August 25, 1983)*, DEPARTMENT OF JUSTICE, https://www.justice.gov/atr/page/file/1077686/download.

116. *Domestic market share of leading U.S. airlines from January to December 2021*, STATISTA (Mar. 2022), https://www.statista.com/statistics/250577/domestic-market-share-of-leading-us-airlines/.

117. *Wireless subscriptions market share by carrier in the U.S. from 1st quarter 2011 to 2nd quarter 2022*, STATISTA (July 2022), https://www.statista.com/statistics/199359/market-share-of-wireless-carriers-in-the-us-by-subscriptions/.

118. Corey Stern, *CVS and Walgreens Are Completely Dominating the US Drugstore Industry*, BUSINESS INSIDER (July 29, 2015), https://www.businessinsider.com/cvs-and-walgreens-us-drugstore-market-share-2015-7.

119. Harris Meyer, *Biden's FTC Has Blocked 4 Hospital Mergers and Is Poised to Thwart More Consolidation Attempts*, KAISER HEALTH NEWS (July 17, 2022), https://khn.org/news/article/biden-ftc-block-hospital-mergers-antitrust/.

120. David McCabe, *Justice Dept. Sues to Block $13 Billion Deal by UnitedHealth Group*, N.Y. TIMES (Feb. 24, 2022), https://www.nytimes.com/2022/02/24/business/doj-antitrust-lawsuit-unitedhealth.html.

CHAPTER 6: THIS TIME WILL BE DIFFERENT

1. Andrew F. Tuch, *The Remaking of Wall Street*, 7 HARV. BUS. L. REV. 315, 316–317, 333–334 (2017).

2. *Id.* at 319–320.

3. *Id*. at 366–367 ("For example, they [private equity] recruited proprietary trading teams from BHCs that downsized in anticipation of the Volcker Rule's ban on engaging in proprietary trading.").

4. Paul J. Davies, *Private-Debt Funds Withstand Covid-19, but Bigger Test Comes Next Year*, WALL ST. J. (Dec. 23, 2020), https://www.wsj.com/articles/private-debt-funds -withstand-covid-19-but-bigger-test-comes-next-year-11608732001.

5. *Report to Congress on Regulation A/Regulation D Performance*, SEC 3 (Aug. 2020), https://www.sec.gov/files/report-congress-regulation-a-d.pdf.

6. Michael Wursthorn & Gregory Zuckerman, *Fewer Listed Companies: Is That Good or Bad for Stock Markets?*, WALL ST. J. (Jan. 4, 2018), https://www.wsj.com/articles/fewer -listed-companies-is-that-good-or-bad-for-stock-markets-1515100040?mod=article _inline.

7. Miriam Gottfried, *Sixth Street Partners Amasses One of the Largest Private-Capital Funds*, WALL ST. J. (Aug. 16, 2020), https://www.wsj.com/articles/sixth-street-partners -amasses-one-of-the-largest-private-capital-funds-11597575600.

8. Debora Vrana, *Ares Management to Take New Fund Public*, L.A. TIMES (Apr. 22, 2004), https://www.latimes.com/archives/la-xpm-2004-apr-22-fi-ares22-story.html.

9. *Investor Day*, ARES 17 (Aug. 12, 2021), https://s1.q4cdn.com/524527723/files /doc_downloads/2021/08/Ares-Investor-Day-8.12.21-vF.pdf.

10. Arleen Jacobins, *Blackstone AUM Skyrockets 42% in Year to $880.9 Billion*, PEN-SION & INVESTMENTS (Jan. 27, 2022), https://www.pionline.com/alternatives/blackstone -aum-skyrockets-42-year-8809-billion.

11. *Growth of Private Credit Has Systemic Implications*, MOODY'S (Nov. 3, 2021), https:// www.moodys.com/web/en/us/about/insights/podcasts/moodys-talks-focus-on-finance /growth-of-private-credit-has-systemic-implications.html.

12. *Id.*

13. Daniel Rasmussen & Greg Obenshain, *High-Yield Was Oxy. Private Credit Is Fentanyl*, INSTITUTIONAL INVESTOR (Jan. 28, 2020), https://www.institutionalinvestor .com/article/b1k369v2lg69qt/High-Yield-Was-Oxy-Private-Credit-Is-Fentanyl.

14. Interview with Dan Rasmussen, founder, Verdad (Dec. 8, 2021).

15. *Private Credit's Rapid Growth: A Secular Trend*, BLACKSTONE (Apr. 2022), https:// www.bcred.com/wp-content/uploads/sites/11/2020/10/Private-Credits-Rapid-Growth _A-Secular-Trend.pdf?v=1649296149.

16. Elisabeth de Fontenay, *The Deregulation of Private Capital and the Decline of the Public Company*, 68 HASTINGS L. J. 445, 467–468 (2017).

17. *Id.* at 467–468.

18. *Id.* at 468.

19. National Securities Markets Improvement Act of 1996, H.R. 3005, 104th Cong. (1996).

20. de Fontenay, *supra* note 16, at 445, 468–469.

21. Jumpstart Our Business Startups, H.R. 3606, 112th Cong. (2011).

22. Critics argue that it was actually the overregulation of the stock market, rather than the deregulation of the private credit market, that led to the fall in public companies. But this tells, at best, only part of the story, given that the number of public companies started falling years before then. *Why Are There So Few Public Companies in the U.S.?*, NBER (Sept. 2015), https://www.nber.org/digest/sep15/why-are -there-so-few-public-companies-us. And even if overregulation burdened public companies, borrowers would have had no place to go without the deregulation around syndication and solicitation in the private credit markets.

23. *2018 Blackstone Investor Day*, BLACKSTONE 5 (Sept. 21, 2018), https://www.blackstone.com/wp-content/uploads/sites/2/2018/10/2018-blackstone-investor-day-conference_pdfdownload_2.pdf.

24. *Blackstone Life Sciences (BXLS)*, BLACKSTONE, https://www.blackstone.com/our-businesses/life-sciences/.

25. Tuch, *supra* note 1, at 315, 343; Shawn Tully, *How Blackstone Became the World's Biggest Corporate Landlord*, FORBES (Feb. 17, 2020), https://fortune.com/2020/02/17/blackstone-commercial-real-estate-business-brep-breit/.

26. *See, e.g., Investor Day*, KKR & CO. INC. 16 (Apr. 13, 2021), https://ir.kkr.com/app/uploads/2021/05/April-2021-Investor-Day.pdf (KKR lists private equity as just one of its businesses, which include real estate, infrastructure, credit, and hedge funds); *Deutsche Bank Global Financial Services Conference*, CARLYLE 3 (June 2022), https://ir.carlyle.com/static-files/84a996cd-9328-4772-9914-70af12a4b0df (Carlyle's business is organized around private equity, credit, and "investment solutions"); *Investor Presentation*, APOLLO GLOBAL MANAGEMENT 3 (2020) (Apollo describes four groups of assets under management: institutional, retail, capital markets, and retirement services).

27. *Apollo Closes Second Dedicated Infrastructure Fund with More Than $2.5 Billion in Capital Commitments*, APOLLO GLOBAL MANAGEMENT (Jan. 6, 2022), https://www.apollo.com/media/press-releases/2022/01-06-2022-130444186.

28. *Health Care Growth*, KKR, https://www.kkr.com/businesses/health-care-growth.

29. *Id.*

30. Davies, *supra* note 4. See, *e.g.,* Jeanine Prezioso, *Blackstone Eyes More Funding for Prop Trading*, REUTERS (Sept. 28, 2010), https://www.reuters.com/article/us-blackstone-creditsuisse/blackstone-eyes-more-funding-for-prop-trading-idUSTRE68R3YH20100928; Steve Eder & Megan Davies, *Goldman Proprietary Traders Jump to KKR*, REUTERS (Oct. 21, 2010), https://www.reuters.com/article/us-kkr-goldman/goldman-proprietary-traders-jump-to-kkr-idUSTRE69K3A020101021.

31. Tuch, *supra* note 1, at 315, 344.

32. *See, e.g., The Carlyle Group Completes Acquisition of Diversified Global Asset Management*, CARLYLE GROUP (Feb. 4, 2014), https://www.carlyle.com/media-room/news-release-archive/carlyle-group-completes-acquisition-diversified-global-asset (Carlyle describes itself as an "alternative asset manager"); *Ares Management Corporation*, ARES, https://www.aresmgmt.com/ (Ares describes itself as an "alternative asset manager").

33. Tuch, *supra* note 1, at 315, 337–349.

34. *Id.* at 341.

35. *Id.* at 349.

36. William Alden, *A Mad Scramble for Young Bankers*, N.Y. TIMES (July 5, 2014), https://www.nytimes.com/2014/07/06/business/wall-street-banks-and-private-equity-firms-compete-for-young-talent.html (Private equity firms pay "around $300,000 a year, including salary and bonus, roughly double what a second-year banker might earn at Goldman.").

37. Tomi Kilgore, *Goldman Sachs CEO David Solomon Total Compensation Slipped 3% to Below $24 Million in 2020*, MKT. WATCH (Mar. 19, 2021), https://www.marketwatch.com/story/goldman-sachs-ceo-david-solomon-total-compensation-slipped-3-to-below-24-million-in-2020-2021-03-19.

38. *Blackstone (BX) CEO Receives 20% Hike in 2020 Compensation*, YAHOO!, https://www.yahoo.com/now/blackstone-bx-ceo-receives-20-165704021.html ("Blackstone's president, Jonathan Gray received a total pay package of $216.1 million. This consisted of $123.2 million in compensation and $92.8 million in dividends.").

39. Mark Vandevelde, *How Private Equity Came to Resemble the Sprawling Empires It Once Broke Up*, FIN. TIMES (Oct. 15, 2021), https://www.ft.com/content/2c56a7da-6435-469c-90d8-28e966f20379.9.

40. The CEOs of the largest full-service investment banks are Jamie Dimon (JP Morgan Chase), David Solomon (Goldman Sachs), Brian Moynihan (BofA Securities), Jamie Gorman (Morgan Stanley), and Jane Fraser (Citigroup). Jamie Dimon is worth an estimated $1.9 billion. *Jamie Dimon*, FORBES, https://www.forbes.com/profile/jamie-dimon/?sh=6c4e32135063. None of the rest appear on *Forbes*'s list of billionaires.

41. Davies, *supra* note 4.

42. KKR & Co. Inc., *Form 425* (June 1, 2009), https://ir.kkr.com/sec-filings-annual-letters/sec-filings/?attchment=1&secFilingId=38ea3895-0b6e-47dd-8a6c-f88e8b9c40b6&format=convpdf.

43. Davies, *supra* note 4.

44. *FACTBOX-Blackstone IPO Reveals Firm's Financials*, REUTERS (Mar. 22, 2007), https://www.reuters.com/article/blackstone-ipo-stats/factbox-blackstone-ipo-reveals-firms-financials-idUSN2239653520070322.

45. BLACKSTONE 2020 LETTER 1 (on file); APOLLO INVESTOR DAY PRESENTATION 23 (2020) (on file); *Apollo Aims to Double Its Asset Under Management to $1 Trillion by 2026*, REUTERS (Oct. 19, 2021), https://www.reuters.com/business/finance/apollo-aims-double-its-asset-under-management-1-trillion-by-2026-2021-10-19/.

46. Unless stated otherwise, I refer to life insurance and annuity companies interchangeably.

47. Miriam Gottfried, *Carlyle Signs New Advisory Deal with Fortitude Re*, WALL ST. J. (Mar. 31, 2022), https://www.wsj.com/articles/carlyle-signs-new-advisory-deal-with-fortitude-re-11648720800.

48. Katherine Chiglinsky & Heather Perlberg, *Blackstone to Buy an Allstate Life Insurance Business for $2.8 Billion*, BLOOMBERG (Jan. 27, 2021), https://www.bloomberg.com/news/articles/2021-01-26/blackstone-to-buy-an-allstate-life-business-for-2-8-billion#xj4y7vzkg.

49. *KKR Closes Acquisition of Global Atlantic Financial Group Limited*, GLOBAL ATLANTIC FINANCIAL GROUP (Feb. 1, 2021), https://www.globalatlantic.com/news/KKR-closes-acquisition-of-Global-Atlantic-Financial-Group-Limited.

50. *Apollo Completes Merger with Athene and Finalizes Key Governance Enhancements*, APOLLO (Jan. 3, 2022), https://www.apollo.com/media/press-releases/2022/01-03-2022-120051006.

51. Alwyn Scott, *Analysis: Chasing Yield, U.S. Private Equity Firms Nudge Up Risk on Insurers*, REUTERS (June 1, 2021), https://www.reuters.com/business/finance/chasing-yield-us-private-equity-firms-nudge-up-risk-insurers-2021-06-01/.

52. Alexander R. Cochran *et al.*, *Insurance Investments: Key Considerations for Investors in the United States, Europe and Asia*, DEBEVOISE & PLIMPTON (May 2021), https://www.debevoise.com/insights/publications/2021/05/insurance-investments-key-considerations-for.

53. Michael J. Mishak, *Drinks, Junkets and Jobs: How the Insurance Industry Courts State Commissioners*, WASH. POST (Oct. 2, 2016), https://www.washingtonpost.com/investigations/drinks-junkets-and-jobs-how-the-insurance-industry-courts-state-commissioners/2016/10/02/1069e7a0-6add-11e6-99bf-f0cf3a6449a6_story.html.

54. *Id.*

55. *See, e.g.*, Alwyn Scott & David French, *U.S. Insurance Asset Sales Attract New Private Equity Players, Strategies*, REUTERS (Feb. 8, 2021), https://www.reuters.com/article

/us-insurance-m-a/u-s-insurance-asset-sales-attract-new-private-equity-players-strategies
-idUSKBN2A811G (Apollo charges Athene for identifying higher yielding assets).

56. Greg Iacurci, *Private Equity Is Buying Up Annuity and Life Insurance Policies. That May Be Bad for Consumers*, CNBC (Apr. 24 2021), https://www.cnbc.com/2021/04/24 /private-equity-is-buying-up-annuity-and-life-insurance-policies.html.

57. Kerry Pechter, *Bermuda's Role in a Changing Annuity Industry*, RETIREMENT INCOME J. (Sept. 10, 2021), https://retirementincomejournal.com/article/bermudas-role-in-a -changing-annuity-industry/.

58. *Id.*; Leslie Scism, *Private-Equity Firms Put Retirees' Annuities in Higher Risks but Also More Cash*, WALL ST. J. (July 1, 2021), https://www.wsj.com/articles/private-equity -firms-put-retirees-annuities-in-higher-risks-but-also-more-cash-11625130001.

59. Zachary R. Mider, *Apollo-to-Goldman Embracing Insurers Spurs State Concerns*, BLOOMBERG (Apr. 22, 2013), https://www.bloomberg.com/news/articles/2013-04-22 /apollo-to-goldman-embracing-insurers-spurs-state-concerns#xj4y7vzkg.

60. *Id.*

61. Miriam Gottfried, *A $433 Billion Wall Street Giant Has a Reputation Problem. It's Josh Harris's Job to Fix It.*, WALL ST. J. (Oct. 31, 2020), https://www.wsj.com/articles/a-433-billion -wall-street-giant-has-a-reputation-problem-its-josh-harriss-job-to-fix-it-11604116827; Sabrina Willmer *et al.*, *A Brawl Between Billionaire Founders at Apollo Sidelines One of Its Own*, BLOOMBERG (April 30, 2021), https://www.bloomberg.com/news/articles/2021-04-30 /apollo-apo-billionaire-founders-brawl-shunting-aside-josh-harris; Matthew Goldstein, *Leon Black Leaves Apollo Sooner Than Expected*, N.Y. TIMES (Mar. 26, 2021), https://www .nytimes.com/2021/03/22/business/leon-black-apollo.html.

62. Miriam Gottfried, *A $433 Billion Wall Street Giant Has a Reputation Problem. It's Josh Harris's Job to Fix It.*, WALL ST. J. (Oct. 31, 2020), https://www.wsj.com /articles/a-433-billion-wall-street-giant-has-a-reputation-problem-its-josh-harriss-job -to-fix-it-11604116827.

63. Daniel Davies, *Morning Coffee: 28 Year-Olds Working 20 Hour Days for $450k Salaries Decide to Quit. The Biggest Egomaniacs in Banking*, EFINANCIALCAREERS (Mar. 18, 2021), https://www.efinancialcareers.com/news/2021/03/working-hours-private-equity.

64. Willmer *et al.*, *supra* note 61.

65. Matthew Goldstein & Steve Eder, *What Jeffrey Epstein Did to Earn $158 Million from Leon Black*, NEW YORK TIMES (Jan. 26, 2021), https://www.nytimes.com/2021/01/26 /business/jeffrey-epstein-leon-black-apollo.html; Sabrina Willmer & Miles Weiss, *Apollo Co-Founder Harris Steps Back After Missing Out on CEO*, BLOOMBERG (May 20, 2021), https://www.bloomberg.com/news/articles/2021-05-20/apollo-co-founder-harris -stepping-back-after-missing-out-on-ceo#xj4y7vzkg.

66. Matthew Goldstein *et al.*, *The Billionaire Who Stood by Jeffrey Epstein*, N.Y. TIMES (Oct. 13, 2020), https://www.nytimes.com/2020/10/12/business/leon-black-jeffrey -epstein.html; Memorandum from Dechert LLP to Apollo Conflicts Committee (Jan. 22, 2021), https://www.sec.gov/Archives/edgar/data/1411494/000119312521016405 /d118102dex991.htm.

67. @GuzelGanieva3, TWITTER, https://twitter.com/guzelganieva3?lang=en; Reuters, *Woman's Lawsuit Accuses Leon Black of Defamation, Violent Behavior*, CNBC (June 2, 2021), https://www.cnbc.com/2021/06/02/womans-lawsuit-accuses-leon-black-of-defamation -violent-behavior.html.

68. Miriam Gottfried & Leslie Scism, *Apollo Reabsorbs Athene in All-Stock Deal That Values Firm at $11 Billion*, WALL ST. J. (Mar. 8, 2021), https://www.wsj.com/articles /apollo-strikes-11-billion-all-stock-merger-with-athene-11615211824.

69. Athene Holding Ltd., *Athene Announces $4.9 Billion Pension Risk Transfer Transaction with Lockheed Martin*, CISION (Aug. 3, 2021), https://www.prnewswire.com/news-releases/athene-announces-4-9-billion-pension-risk-transfer-transaction-with-lockheed-martin-301347561.html.

70. Athene Holding Ltd., *Athene Completes Significant Pension Risk Transfer Transaction with JCPenney*, CISION (Apr. 1, 2021), https://www.prnewswire.com/news-releases/athene-completes-significant-pension-risk-transfer-transaction-with-jcpenney-301261013.html.

71. Gottfried & Scism, *supra* note 68.

72. *Id.*; Paul J. Davies, *Apollo Wants to Be a Bit Like Buffett, But It's Complicated*, WASH. POST (Nov. 1, 2021), https://www.washingtonpost.com/business/apollo-wants-to-be-a-bit-like-buffett-but-its-complicated/2021/10/29/42677550-387e-11ec-9662-399cfa75efee_story.html.

73. *Tom Gober*, http://tomgober.com/.

74. Email with Tom Gober, forensic accountant (Mar. 8, 2022).

75. Interview with Tom Gober, forensic accountant (Feb. 17, 2022).

76. Email with Tom Gober, *supra* note 74.

77. *Guaranty Funds Safeguard Consumers When Insurance Companies Fail*, NATIONAL CONFERENCE OF INSURANCE GUARANTY FUNDS (Oct. 10, 2018), https://www.ncigf.org/about-us/guaranty-funds-safeguard-consumers-when-insurance-companies-fail/.

78. John Pitlosh, *Are You Protected if Your Insurance Company Goes Belly-Up?*, INVESTOPEDIA (Aug. 31, 2021), https://www.investopedia.com/articles/insurance/09/insurance-company-guarantee-fund.asp.

79. *See* Miriam Gottfried, *Blackstone, Other Large Private-Equity Firms Turn Attention to Vast Retail Market*, WALL ST. J. (June 7, 2022), https://www.wsj.com/articles/blackstone-other-large-private-equity-firms-turn-attention-to-vast-retail-market-11654603201.

80. Andrew Ackerman, *Labor Nominee Scalia Earned More Than $6 Million as Corporate Law Partner*, WALL ST. J. (Aug. 30, 2019), https://www.wsj.com/articles/labor-nominee-scalia-earned-more-than-6-million-as-corporate-law-partner-11567179475.

81. Noam Scheiber, *Trump's Labor Pick Has Defended Corporations, and One Killer Whale*, N.Y. TIMES (July 19, 2019), https://www.nytimes.com/2019/07/19/business/economy/eugene-scalia-labor-lawsuits.html.

82. Ackerman, *supra* note 80.

83. Eyal Press, *Trump's Labor Secretary Is a Wrecking Ball Aimed at Workers*, NEW YORKER (Oct. 19, 2020), https://www.newyorker.com/magazine/2020/10/26/trumps-labor-secretary-is-a-wrecking-ball-aimed-at-workers ("This fall, however, OSHA informed employers that they no longer have to report COVID-19 hospitalizations unless an employee was admitted within twenty-four hours of a workplace exposure—a highly unlikely scenario, given that symptoms are usually delayed.").

84. Sarah Chaney, *Labor Secretary Eugene Scalia Opposes Extension of Extra $600 in Unemployment Benefits*, WALL ST. J. (June 9, 2020), https://www.wsj.com/articles/labor-secretary-eugene-scalia-opposes-extension-of-extra-600-in-unemployment-benefits-11591728182.

85. Ben Protess & Matthew Goldstein, *Trump's S.E.C. Nominee Disclosure Offers Rare Glimpse of Clients and Conflicts*, N.Y. TIMES (Mar. 8, 2017), https://www.nytimes.com/2017/03/08/business/dealbook/sec-nominee-jay-clayton-client-list-conflicts-interest.html.

86. Dave Michael & Liz Hoffman, *SEC Pick Jay Clayton Is a 180 from Chairman Mary Jo White*, WALL ST. J. (Jan. 4, 2017), https://www.wsj.com/articles/president-elect

-trump-to-nominate-jay-clayton-securities-and-exchange-commission-chairman -1483545999; *About Us*, PHILADELPHIA CRICKET CLUB, https://www.philacricket.com /about-us (Oct. 7, 2022).

87. Joseph Walter Clayton, *Executive Branch Personnel Public Financial Disclosure Report (OGE Form 278e)* 2 (Mar. 10, 2017), https://s3.documentcloud.org/documents/4388156/Jay -Clayton-Financial-Disclosure.pdf (Jay Clayton was directly invested in funds from Apollo, Warburg Pincus, TPG, Bain, Centerbridge Hellman & Friedman, and Thoma Bravo).

88. Dave Michaels, *SEC Chair Nominee Clayton's Ethics Report Reveals Range of Possible Conflicts*, WALL ST. J. (Mar. 8, 2017), https://www.wsj.com/articles/sec-chair-nominee -claytons-ethics-report-reveals-range-of-possible-conflicts-1488988744.

89. Tom Dreisbach, *Under Trump, SEC Enforcement of Insider Trading Dropped to Lowest Point in Decades*, NPR (August 14, 2020), https://www.npr.org/2020/08/14/901862355 /under-trump-sec-enforcement-of-insider-trading-dropped-to-lowest-point-in-decade.

90. *Id.*

91. Mark Schoeff Jr., *Clayton Wants Retirement Investors to Have More Access to Private Funds*, INV. NEWS (Apr.9, 2019), https://www.investmentnews.com/clayton-wants-retirement -investors-to-have-more-access-to-private-funds-79000.

92. *Id.*

93. Chris Cumming, *U.S. Labor Department Allows Private Equity in 401(k) Plans*, WALL ST. J. (June 3, 2020), https://www.wsj.com/articles/u-s-labor-department-allows -private-equity-in-401-k-plans-11591229396; Warren Rojas, *Private Equity Cracks 401(k)s with Teamwork, Help from D.C. Firm*, BLOOMBERG TAX (June 19, 2020), https://news .bloombergtax.com/crypto/private-equity-cracks-401ks-with-teamwork-help-from -d-c-firm?context=article-related (Bloomberg reports that Clayton "len[t] his support" to advocate for the information letter).

94. Chris Cumming, *U.S. Labor Department Allows Private Equity in 401(k) Plans*, WALL ST. J. (June 3, 2020), https://www.wsj.com/articles/u-s-labor-department-allows -private-equity-in-401-k-plans-11591229396.

95. *Private Equity Trend Report 2020*, PRICEWATERHOUSECOOPERS (2020), https://www .mergermarket.com/assets/42033_PETR_2020_200225_SCREEN.pdf.

96. Chris Cumming, *U.S. Labor Department Allows Private Equity in 401(k) Plans*, WALL ST. J. (June 3, 2020), https://www.wsj.com/articles/u-s-labor-department-allows -private-equity-in-401-k-plans-11591229396.

97. Melissa Mittelman, *Schwarzman's "Dream" Tested as Private Equity Eyes Your Nest Egg*, BLOOMBERG (Apr. 20, 2017), https://www.bloomberg.com/news/articles/2017-04-20 /schwarzman-s-dream-tested-as-private-equity-eyes-your-nest-egg.

98. *What They Are Saying: Expanding Access to Private Equity Will Strengthen Retirement Security for Millions of Americans*, AM. INV. COUNCIL (June 10, 2020), https://www .investmentcouncil.org/what-they-are-saying-expanding-access-to-private-equity-will -strengthen-retirement-security-for-millions-of-americans/.

99. *Id.*

100. David Bradley Isenberg, *Wall Street Is Looting the American Retirement System. The Trump Administration Is Helping*, ROLLING STONE (Aug. 23, 2020), https://www.rollingstone .com/politics/politics-features/retirement-private-equity-trump-administration-wall -street-1047576/.

101. *Id.*

102. *Jay Clayton (Attorney)*, WIKIPEDIA, https://en.wikipedia.org/wiki/Jay_Clayton _(attorney).

103. Noor Zainab Hussain & Chibuike Oguh, *Leon Black Leaves Apollo Executive Roles After Epstein Investigation*, REUTERS (Mar. 22, 2021), https://www.reuters.com/business /apollo-names-ex-sec-chief-clayton-non-executive-chairman-2021-03-22/.

104. *Former U.S. Secretary of Labor Eugene Scalia Returns to Gibson Dunn*, GIBSON DUNN (Mar. 30, 2021), https://www.gibsondunn.com/former-u-s-secretary-of-labor -eugene-scalia-returns-to-gibson-dunn/.

105. Eugene Scalia, *Biden's Policies Will Hurt America's Laborers in the Long Run*, WALL ST. J. (Sept. 2, 2021), https://www.wsj.com/articles/american-laborers-unemployment -trump-biden-jobs-11630597010.

106. Daniel Rasmussen & Greg Obenshain, *High-Yield Was Oxy. Private Credit Is Fentanyl.*, INSTITUTIONAL INV. (Jan. 28, 2020), https://www.institutionalinvestor.com /article/b1k369v2lg69qt/High-Yield-Was-Oxy-Private-Credit-Is-Fentanyl.

107. Tuch, *supra* note 1 at 357. ("Accordingly, if a firm's funds suffered significant losses or failed, the firm's management fees would dry up, cutting off its primary reve- nue source. It would lose its (typically modest) investments in those funds, but the bulk of the funds' losses would be borne by outside investors and creditors, rather than by the firm.").

108. William J. Marx & Julie K. Stapel, *Department of Labor Waves Caution Flag for 401(k) Private Equity Investing*, MORGAN LEWIS (Jan. 4, 2022), https://www.morganlewis .com/blogs/mlbenebits/2022/01/department-of-labor-waves-caution-flag-for-401k -private-equity-investing.

109. Austin R. Ramsey, *Private Equity Firms Are Winning the Fight for Your 401(k)*, BLOOMBERG L. (Jan. 31, 2022), https://news.bloomberglaw.com/daily-labor-report /private-equity-firms-are-winning-the-fight-for-your-401k.

CHAPTER 7: CAPTIVE AUDIENCE

1. Marcus Henderson, *US Prison Commissary Giants Are Set to Merge*, SAN QUENTIN NEWS (Jan. 31, 2017), https://sanquentinnews.com/us-prison-commissary-giants-merge/; *H.I.G. Capital Acquires Trinity Services Group*, MERGR, https://mergr.com/h.i.g.-capital -acquires-trinity-services-group.

2. *Aventiv*, PLATINUM EQUITY, https://www.platinumequity.com/our-portfolio /portfolio/2017/aventiv.

3. David Shepardson, *Inmate Calling Services Companies Drop Merger Bid After U.S. Regulatory Opposition*, REUTERS (Apr. 2, 2019), https://www.reuters.com/article/us -fcc-inmate-merger/inmate-calling-services-companies-drop-merger-bid-after-u-s -regulatory-opposition-idUSKCN1RE2L7.

4. *Global Tel Link Acquired by American Securities*, CRUNCHBASE, https://www .crunchbase.com/acquisition/american-securit-acquires-global-tel-link--ddf38327.

5. *Wellpath*, H.I.G. CAPITAL, https://higcapital.com/portfolio/company/403.

6. Matt Blois, *Investment Firm Acquires Corizon*, NASHV. POST (June 30, 202), https:// www.nashvillepost.com/investment-firm-acquires-corizon/article_eeba5a0a-486c -5779-886c-2d50b1befc5a.html.

7. *3M Sells Israeli Subsidiary to Apax for $200M*, GLOBES (Oct. 10, 2017), https://en .globes.co.il/en/article-3m-sells-israeli-subsidiary-to-apax-for-200m-1001207560.

8. *Release Cards*, PRISON POLICY INITIATIVE, https://www.prisonpolicy.org/release cards/.

9. *Aventiv*, *supra* note 2.

10. *Pay-per-Minute E-Readers in West Virginia Prisons Jeopardize Access to Literature*, PEN AMERICA (Nov. 22, 2019), https://pen.org/press-release/pay-per-minute-e-readers-in-west-virginia-prisons-jeopardize-access-to-literature/.

11. Eli Hager, *Debtors' Prisons, Then and Now: FAQ*, THE MARSHALL PROJECT (Feb. 24, 2015), https://www.themarshallproject.org/2015/02/24/debtors-prisons-then-and-now-faq.

12. *Convict Leasing*, WIKIPEDIA, https://en.wikipedia.org/wiki/Convict_leasing.

13. *Recovering Correctional Costs Through Offender Fees*, NATIONAL INSTITUTE OF JUSTICE 1 (June 1990), https://www.ojp.gov/pdffiles1/Digitization/125084NCJRS.pdf.

14. Steven J. Jackson, *Ex-Communication: Competition and Collusion in the U.S. Prison Telephone Industry*, CRITICAL STUD. IN MEDIA COMMC'NS 263, 267 (2005).

15. *Id.* at 268; Stephen Raher, *The Company Store and the Literally Captive Market: Consumer Law in Prisons and Jails*, 17 HASTINGS RACE & POVERTY L. J. 3, 24 (2020) ("The Commission's involvement with the industry dates back to 1993, when ICS carriers asked the FCC to deregulate payphone rates in correctional facilities. The FCC ultimately granted the request mere days before the entire telecommunications industry changed with the enactment of the Telecommunications Act of 1996.").

16. Jackson, *supra* note 14, at 268.

17. *Id.*

18. *H.I.G. Capital Acquires Evercom Holdings, Inc.—Forms Securus Technologies, Inc.*, H.I.G. CAPITAL (Sept. 10, 2004), https://higcapital.com/news/release/h.i.g.-capital-acquires-evercom-holdings-inc.-forms-securus-technologies-inc.

19. *Castle Harlan Acquires Securus Technologies*, CASTLE HARLAN (Nov. 10, 2011), http://castleharlan.com/news/item/194-castle-harlan-acquires-securus-technologies.

20. Greg Roumeliotis, *Platinum Equity Nears Deal to Buy Prison Phone Company Securus: Sources*, REUTERS (May 16, 2017), https://www.reuters.com/article/us-securus-tech-m-a-abrypartners/platinum-equity-nears-deal-to-buy-prison-phone-company-securus-sources-idUSKCN18C2FU.

21. *Aventiv, supra* note 2.

22. *Global Tel Link Acquired by American Securities, supra* note 4.

23. Davide Scigliuzzo, *HIG Plans Spinoff of Prison Phone Operator After Failed Merger*, BLOOMBERG (Jan. 24, 2020), https://www.bloomberg.com/news/articles/2020-01-24/hig-plans-spinoff-of-prison-phone-operator-after-failed-merger?leadSource=uverify%20wall.

24. See Tom McLaughlin, *"Families Die by a Thousand Cuts." Companies Like JPay Make Big Bucks Billing Florida Inmates for Essentials*, NW. FLA. NEWS (May 5, 2022), https://www.nwfdailynews.com/story/news/2021/12/22/companies-like-jpay-make-big-bucks-billing-florida-inmates-essentials/5469115001/.

25. Peter Wagner & Alexi Jones, *The Biggest Priorities for Prison and Jail Phone Justice in 40 States*, PRISON POLICY INITIATIVE (Sept. 11, 2019), https://www.prisonpolicy.org/blog/2019/09/11/worststatesphones/.

26. Tim Requarth, *How Private Equity Is Turning Public Prisons into Big Profits*, NATION (Apr. 30, 2019), https://www.thenation.com/article/archive/prison-privatization-private-equity-hig/.

27. Timothy Williams, *The High Cost of Calling the Imprisoned*, N.Y. TIMES (Mar. 30, 2015), https://www.nytimes.com/2015/03/31/us/steep-costs-of-inmate-phone-calls-are-under-scrutiny.html.

28. Omari Sankofa II & Angie Jackson, *Detroit Pistons Owner Tom Gores Speaks About Controversy over Securus*, DETROIT FREE PRESS (Feb. 6, 2021), https://www.freep .com/story/sports/nba/pistons/2021/02/04/tom-gores-detroit-pistons-securus-prison -phone-calls/4139871001/.

29. *Id.*

30. Colin Lecher, *Criminal Charges*, VERGE, https://www.theverge.com/a/prison -phone-call-cost-martha-wright-v-corrections-corporation-america (May 11, 2016).

31. *Id.*

32. Saneta deVuono-powell *et al.*, *Who Pays? The True Cost of Incarceration on Families*, ELLA BAKER CENTER, FORWARD TOGETHER, RESEARCH ACTION DESIGN 30 (2015), http://whopaysreport.org/wp-content/uploads/2015/09/Who-Pays-FINAL.pdf.

33. Requarth, *supra* note 26.

34. *Tom Gores*, WIKIPEDIA, https://en.wikipedia.org/wiki/Tom_Gores; *Buyout Buccaneer*, FORBES (July 9, 2001), https://www.forbes.com/forbes/2001/0723/065.html?sh =1716ef9562f9.

35. *Tom Gores*, *supra* note 34; Steven Bertoni, *Meet Tom Gores: The Detroit Piston's New Billionaire Boss*, FORBES (June 3, 2011), https://www.forbes.com/sites/stevenbertoni /2011/06/03/meet-tom-gores-the-detroit-pistons-new-billionaire-boss/?sh=4a380 e52069c.

36. Steven Bertoni, *Ready to Play*, FORBES (Oct. 2, 2009), https://www.forbes.com /forbes/2009/1019/forbes-400-rich-list-09-buyout-firms-gores-ready-to-play.html?sh =6357fc611464.

37. *McGraw-Hill*, PLATINUM EQUITY, https://www.platinumequity.com/mcgraw-hill.

38. *Jostens*, PLATINUM EQUITY, https://www.platinumequity.com/jostens.

39. Lisa Bannon, *Gores Brothers Jockey for Same Deals in Grown-Up Game of Sibling Rivalry*, WALL ST. J. (Apr. 9, 2002), https://www.wsj.com/articles/SB1018299410443735120; Jason Dean, *Tom Gores: Balancing Family, Business, and the Detroit Pistons*, CSQ (July 9, 2011), https://csq.com/2011/07/tom-gores-balancing-family-business-detroit-pistons/#.YW ShzRDMIUQ.

40. Bianca Barragan, *Ridiculous Holmby Hills Spec House Now Belongs to Detroit Pistons Owner Tom Gores*, CURBED L.A. (Oct. 24, 2016), https://la.curbed.com/2016/10/24 /13388372/detroit-pistons-tom-gores-la-spec-house.

41. *Id.*

42. *Id.*; Neal J. Leitereg, *Tom Gores Buys Holmby Hills Spec House in $100-Million Deal Involving Multiple Properties*, L.A. TIMES (Oct. 21, 2016), https://www.latimes.com/business /realestate/hot-property/la-fi-hotprop-100-million-home-sale-los-angeles-20161021 -snap-story.html.

43. Roumeliotis, *supra* note 20.

44. *See* Jabari Young, *Detroit Pistons Owner Tom Gores Has a New Perspective as Team Tries to Restore Its Brand and Culture*, CNBC (Oct. 8, 2021), https://www.cnbc.com /2021/10/08/pistons-owner-tom-gores-has-a-new-perspective-as-team-enters-restoration -process.html.

45. Vince Ellis, *Pistons Owner Gores to Taise $10M for Flint Crisis*, DETROIT FREE PRESS (Jan. 28, 2016), https://www.freep.com/story/sports/nba/pistons/2016/01/28/flint -water-crisis-tom-gores/79452146/.

46. Young, *supra* note 44.

47. *Statement from Tom Gores and the Detroit Pistons*, NBA (June 2, 2020), https:// www.nba.com/pistons/news/statement-tom-gores-and-detroit-pistons.

48. Interview with Bianca Tylek, executive director, Worth Rises (Oct. 26, 2021).

49. Letter from Bianca Tylek, director, Corrections Accountability Project, to commissioner's secretary, FCC (July 16, 2018), https://ecfsapi.fcc.gov/file/10717225630127/2018.07.16%20-%20Corrections%20Accountability%20Project%2018-193%20Comment%20.pdf.

50. *Chairman Pai Statement on Withdrawal of Inmate Calling Merger*, FCC (Apr. 2, 2019), https://www.fcc.gov/document/chairman-pai-statement-withdrawal-inmate-calling-merger.

51. Stephen Caruso, *State Employee Retirement Board Balks at Investing in Prison-Linked Private Equity Firm*, PA. CAPITAL-STAR (Sept. 27, 2019), https://www.penncapital-star.com/blog/state-employee-retirement-board-balks-at-investing-in-prison-linked-private-equity-firm/.

52. *Id.*

53. *Id.*

54. Shiri, *Tom Gores Resigns from Board of the LACMA*, CANYON NEWS (Oct. 11, 2020), https://www.canyon-news.com/tom-gores-resigns-from-the-board-of-the-lacma/134727.

55. @scavendish, TWITTER (Dec. 20, 2020), https://twitter.com/scavendish/status/1340699398242709504.

56. Eric Woodyard, *As Nonprofit Group Pushes for Him to Sell Team, Detroit Pistons Owner Tom Gores Says He's Committed to Changing System, but Needs Time*, ESPN (Dec. 26, 2020), https://www.espn.com/nba/story/_/id/30602718/as-nonprofit-group-pushes-sell-team-detroit-pistons-owner-tom-gores-says-committed-changing-system-needs.

57. Sankofa II & Jackson, *supra* note 28.

58. *Victory: San Francisco Makes Jail Phone Calls Free and Eliminates Jail Commissary Markups*, WORTH RISES (June 21, 2019), https://worthrises.org/pressreleases/2019/6/12/victory-san-francisco-makes-jail-phone-calls-free-and-eliminates-jail-commissary-markups.

59. *Campaigns*, WORTH RISES, https://worthrises.org/ourcampaigns.

60. *Connecticut Makes History as First State to Make Prison Calls Free*, WORTH RISES (June 16, 2021), https://worthrises.org/pressreleases/connecticut-makes-history-as-first-state-to-make-prison-calls-free.

61. *Families of Prisoners Sue Nation's Largest Providers of Inmate Calling Services for Fixing and Lying About Services*, JUSTICE CATALYST LAW (July 20, 2021), https://catalystlaw.org/2020/06/30/prison-telecom-press-release/.

62. Keaton Ross, *"Sued Every Way and Sunday." New Prison Phone Provider Has Troubled History*, OKLAHOMA WATCH (Aug. 27, 2020), https://oklahomawatch.org/2020/08/27/sued-every-way-and-sunday-new-prison-phone-provider-has-troubled-history/.

63. *Id.*; Brigette Honaker, *Securus Prison Call Recording Class Action Settlement Gets OK*, TOP CLASS ACTIONS (June 22, 2020), https://topclassactions.com/lawsuit-settlements/jail-prison/securus-prison-call-recording-class-action-settlement-gets-ok/ (The defendants admitted no wrongdoing as part of the lawsuit); Final Approval Order and Judgment, *Crane v. Corrections Corporation of America et al.*, No. 4:16-cv-00947 (W.D. Mo. Dec. 23, 2020), ECF No. 275; *Largest Detention Communications Companies*, NATIONAL ASSOCIATION OF CRIMINAL DEFENSE LAWYERS, https://www.nacdl.org/getattachment/da45649f-b63c-4fbd-a155-c5243592fecb/detention-facilities-communication-companies.pdf; Karl Bode, *Securus Quietly Settles Lawsuit over Illegally Spying on Inmate Attorney Conversations*, TECHDIRT (June 1, 2020), https://www.techdirt.com/2020/06/01/securus-quietly-settles-lawsuit-over-illegally-spying-inmate-attorney-conversations/.

64. *Dave Abel Named Chief Executive Officer of Aventiv Technologies and Its Corrections Subsidiary Securus Technologies*, CISION (Jan. 13, 2020), https://www.prnewswire.com

/news-releases/dave-abel-named-chief-executive-officer-of-aventiv-technologies
-and-its-corrections-subsidiary-securus-technologies-300985675.html.

65. Sankofa II & Jackson, *supra* note 28.

66. Eric Woodyard, *As Nonprofit Group Pushes for Him to Sell Team, Detroit Pistons Owner Tom Gores Says He's Committed to Changing System, but Needs Time*, ESPN (Dec. 26, 2020), https://www.espn.com/nba/story/_/id/30602718/as-nonprofit-group-pushes-sell
-team-detroit-pistons-owner-tom-gores-says-committed-changing-system-needs.

67. Tyler J. Davis, *Why Detroit Pistons' Tom Gores Says It's a "Blessing" to Own Prison Telecom Firm*, DETROIT FREE PRESS (Dec. 28, 2020), https://www.freep.com/story/sports/nba/pistons/2020/12/28/tom-gores-detroit-pistons-securus-worth-rises/4050901001/.

68. Woodyard, *supra* note 66.

69. *Id.*

70. *Aventiv, supra* note 2.

71. *Wright, et al. v. Corrections Corp et al.*, No. 1:00-cv-293 (D.D.C. Feb. 16, 2000).

72. Lecher, *supra* note 30.

73. Interview with Mignon Clyburn, former FCC commissioner (Oct. 29, 2021).

74. *Id.*

75. *Id.*

76. *Id.*

77. Requarth, *supra* note 26.

78. Letter from Larry D. Amerson, president of the National Sheriff's Association to Marlene H. Dortch, secretary, FCC (Mar. 25, 2013), https://www.sheriffs.org/sites/default/files/1.%202013.03.25%20NSA%20Comments.pdf.

79. Barbara Koeppel, *The Prison Phone Rip-Off*, WASH. SPECTATOR (July 5, 2021), https://washingtonspectator.org/the-prison-phone-rip-off/; *Corporate Partnership Information*, NATIONAL SHERIFF'S ASSOCIATION, https://www.sheriffs.org/partners/corporate
-partnership-information.

80. Lecher, *supra* note 30.

81. Ann E. Marimow, *FCC Made a Case for Limiting Cost of Prison Phone Calls. Not Anymore.*, WASH. POST (Feb. 5, 2017), https://www.washingtonpost.com/local/public-safety/fcc-made-a-case-for-limiting-cost-of-prison-phone-calls-not-anymore/2017/02/04/9306fbf8-e97c-11e6-b82f-687d6e6a3e7c_story.html.

82. Kate Rose Quandt, *Lawsuit Reveals How Tech Companies Profit off the Prison -Industrial Complex*, THINKPROGRESS (Feb. 9, 2018), https://archive.thinkprogress.org/prison
-technology-companies-inmates-9d4242805363/.

83. Shepardson, *supra* note 3; Memorandum Opinion and Order, *In the Matter of Joint Application of Securus Investment Holdings, LLC*, No. 17-126 (FCC Oct. 30, 2017).

84. *Ajit Pai*, LINKEDIN, https://www.linkedin.com/in/ajit-pai-bb014816a/.

85. Interview with Mignon Clyburn, *supra* note 73.

86. Marie Feyche, *FCC Approves Plan to Lower Interstate and International Jail and Prison Phone Call Rates*, JURIST (May 23, 2021), https://www.jurist.org/news/2021/05/fcc-approves-plan-to-lower-interstate-and-international-jail-and-prison-phone-call
-rates/.

87. Harper Neidig, *Court Strikes Down FCC Caps on In-State Prison Phone Rates*, THE HILL (June 13, 2017), https://thehill.com/policy/technology/337593-court-strikes-down-in
-state-prison-call-rates/.

88. Marie Feyche, *FCC Approves Plan to Lower Interstate and International Jail and Prison Phone Call Rates*, JURIST (May 23, 2021), https://www.jurist.org/news/2021/05/fcc
-approves-plan-to-lower-interstate-and-international-jail-and-prison-phone-call-rates/.

89. *Id.*

90. *Duckworth, Portman, Booker, Schatz Introduce Bipartisan Bill to Ensure Just and Reasonable Phone Rates in Criminal Justice System*, OFFICE OF SENATOR TAMMY DUCKWORTH (May 10, 2021), https://www.duckworth.senate.gov/news/press-releases/duckworth-portman-booker-schatz-introduce-bipartisan-bill-to-ensure-just-and-reasonable-phone-rates-in-criminal-justice-system.

91. Interview with Mignon Clyburn, *supra* note 73.

92. *Id.*

93. Léon Digard *et al.*, VERA INST. OF JUST., CLOSING THE DISTANCE: THE IMPACT OF VIDEO VISITS IN WASHINGTON STATE PRISONS (2017), https://www.vera.org/downloads/publications/The-Impact-of-Video-Visits-on-Washington-State-Prisons.pdf.

94. Wendy Sawyer, *How Much Do Incarcerated People Earn in Each State?*, PRISON POLICY INITIATIVE (Apr. 10, 2017), https://www.prisonpolicy.org/blog/2017/04/10/wages/.

95. *Securus Ends Its Ban on In-Person Visits, Shifts Responsibility to Sheriffs*, PRISON POLICY INITIATIVE (May 6, 2015), https://www.prisonpolicy.org/blog/2015/05/06/securus-ends-ban/ (70% of the contracts the Prison Policy Initiative reviewed had terms saying that "[f]or non-professional visitors, Customer will eliminate all face to face visitation through glass or otherwise at the Facility.").

96. Natasha Haverty, *Video Calls Replace In-Person Visits in Some Jails*, NPR (Dec. 5, 2016), https://www.npr.org/2016/12/05/504458311/video-calls-replace-in-person-visits-in-some-jails.

97. *Id.*

98. *Securus Ends Its Ban on In-Person Visits, Shifts Responsibility to Sheriffs*, PRISON POLICY INITIATIVE (May 6, 2015), https://www.prisonpolicy.org/blog/2015/05/06/securus-ends-ban/.

99. *See, e.g.*, Teresa Mathew, *How Jails Are Replacing Visits with Video*, THE APPEAL (Apr. 22, 2019), https://theappeal.org/how-jails-are-replacing-visits-with-video/ (discussing two Missouri counties that ended in-person visits).

100. Nate Raymond, *Private Equity Firm HIG Capital Settles Fraud Case for $20 Million*, REUTERS (Oct. 14, 2021), https://www.reuters.com/legal/government/private-equity-firm-hig-capital-settles-fraud-case-20-million-2021-10-14/.

101. David M. Reutter, *Michigan's New Prison Food Service Provider Failing to Meet Contract Terms*, PRISON LEGAL NEWS (Jan. 8, 2018), https://www.prisonlegalnews.org/news/2018/jan/8/michigans-new-prison-food-service-provider-failing-meet-contract-terms/.

102. Paul Egan, *More Problems for State's Prison Food Contractor: Maggots Found in Chow Served to Inmates*, DETROIT FREE PRESS (Nov. 6, 2017), https://www.freep.com/story/news/local/michigan/2017/11/06/maggots-food-cotton-prison-jackson-michigan-trinity-services/825834001/ (Trinity declined to comment); *Michigan Prison Food Worker Says He Was Fired for Refusing to Serve Rotten Potatoes*, CBS NEWS DETROIT (Aug. 25, 2017), https://www.cbsnews.com/detroit/news/rotten-prison-potatoes/.

103. Paul Egan, *Prison Food Worker: "I Was Fired for Refusing to Serve Rotten Potatoes,"* DETROIT FREE PRESS (Aug. 25, 2017), https://www.freep.com/story/news/local/michigan/2017/08/25/prison-trinity-kinross-fired-rotten-potatoes/596849001/ (Trinity did not respond to a request for comment).

104. Tom Perkins, *Michigan's Failed Effort to Privatize Prison Kitchens and the Future of Institutional Food*, SALON (Aug. 29, 2018), https://www.salon.com/2018/08/29/michigans-failed-effort-to-privatize-prison-kitchens-and-the-future-of-institutional-food_partner/ (Trinity did not respond to a request for comment).

105. Tom Perkins, *Something Still Stinks in Michigan and Ohio's Prison Kitchens*, Cleve Scene (Feb. 17, 2016), https://www.clevescene.com/news/empty-promises-something -still-stinks-in-michigan-and-ohios-prison-kitchens-4705549.

106. Reutter, *supra* note 101.

107. Tom Perkins, *We Spoke with Michigan Inmates About Rotten Food, Maggots, and More Prison Kitchen Problems*, Metro Times (Jan. 18, 2018), https://www.metrotimes.com/food -drink/we-spoke-with-michigan-inmates-about-rotten-food-maggots-and-more-prison -kitchen-problems-8686387.

108. *Id.*

109. Paul Egan, *Riot or Reined-In? Prison Officials Disagree on U.P. Skirmish*, Detroit Free Press (Sept. 20, 2016), https://www.freep.com/story/news/local/michigan/2016 /09/20/disturbance-kinross-prison-riot/90742082/ (according to the *Detroit Free Press*, two issues that motivated the riot were poor food and low wages).

110. Tom Perkins, *Michigan's Failed Effort to Privatize Prison Kitchens and the Future of Institutional Food*, Salon (Aug. 29, 2018), https://www.salon.com/2018/08/29/michigans -failed-effort-to-privatize-prison-kitchens-and-the-future-of-institutional-food_partner/.

111. Paul Egan, *Prison Worker Fired After Kitchen Sex with Inmate*, WUSA9 (May 11, 2017), https://www.wusa9.com/article/news/local/michigan/prison-worker-fired-after -kitchen-sex-with-inmate/69-438865568.

112. April Stevens, *MDOC Ends Contract with Private Food Service, Going Back to State-Run Resources*, WZZM13 (Feb. 7, 2018), https://www.wzzm13.com/article/news/local /michigan/mdoc-ends-contract-with-private-food-service-going-back-to-state-run -resources/69-51566592.

113. Perkins, *supra* note 110.

114. Elizabeth Whitman, *Arizona Prison Food Was Labeled "Not for Human Consumption,"* *Ex-Inmates Say*, Phoenix New Times (Sept. 25, 2019), https://www.phoenixnewtimes .com/news/ex-inmates-arizona-prison-food-was-not-for-human-consumption -11362468.

115. *Id.* Trinity said in a statement to the *Phoenix New Times* that "[w]e have never intentionally bought expired food. Just as in any food service operation or high end restaurant, on occasion, a vendor may deliver a product that does not meet our quality standard and in such an instance, that product is either discarded or returned."

116. Complaint at 9, *Young v. Trinity Services Group, Inc. et al.*, No. 3:19-cv-2465 (N.D. Oh. Oct. 22, 2019), ECF No. 1 (Trinity largely denied the allegations, and the litigation remains ongoing); Answer, *Young v. Trinity Services Group, Inc. et al.*, No. 3:19-cv-2465 (N.D. Oh. Nov. 5, 2019), ECF No. 5.

117. Mark Shenefelt, *Maggots, Mold and Dirt Reported in Weber Jail Food*, Standard Exam'r (Jan. 14, 2018), https://www.standard.net/police-fire/2018/jan/14/maggots -mold-and-dirt-reported-in-weber-jail-food/ (Trinity did not comment).

118. Alan Judd, *Jail Food Complaints Highlight Debate over Outsourcing Public Services*, Atlanta J.-Const. (Jan. 1, 2015), https://www.ajc.com/news/public-affairs/jail -food-complaints-highlight-debate-over-outsourcing-public-services/PpVFFB46k OLExOmv6UX7SJ/ (Trinity said that the company's dieticians ensure prisoners "the right product in the right amount and served correctly."); letter from Sarah Geraghty, Southern Center for Human Rights, to Sheriff Mitch Ralston, Gordon County sheriff's office (Oct. 28, 2014), https://www.schr.org/files/post/files/SCHR%20to%20Sheriff %20Ralston%2010%2028%2014.pdf.

119. Judd, *supra* note 118.

120. *See, e.g.*, *Lyons v. Trinity Servs. Grp., Inc.*, 401 F. Supp. 2d 1290 (S.D. Fla. 2005).

121. *See, e.g., Spurling v. Trinity Servs. Grp., Inc.*, No. 4:19-cv-2872, 2020 WL 1862674, at *2 (N.D. Ohio Apr. 14, 2020).

122. *Cradle v. Trinity Food Servs.*, No. 2:10-cv-1962, 2010 WL 4340336, at *2 (D.S.C. Aug. 9, 2010), *Report and Recommendation Adopted*, No. 2:10-cv-01962, 2010 WL 4281790 (D.S.C. Oct. 21, 2010).

123. *Wilson v. White*, No. 3:19-cv-441HTW, 2020 WL 5163528, at *2 (S.D. Miss. Aug. 2, 2020), *Report and Recommendation Adopted*, No. 3:19-cv-441, 2020 WL 5121348 (S.D. Miss. Aug. 31, 2020).

124. *Est. of Ricardez v. Cty. of Ventura*, No. 20-cv-79, 2020 WL 3891460, at *4 (C.D. Cal. June 24, 2020), *cert. denied sub nom. Ricardez v. Cty. of Ventura*, No. 20-cv-79, 2020 WL 7862129 (C.D. Cal. Aug. 6, 2020).

125. Steve Coll, *The Jail Health-Care Crisis*, NEW YORKER (Feb. 25, 2019), https://www.newyorker.com/magazine/2019/03/04/the-jail-health-care-crisis.

126. Jason Szep, *Special Report: U.S. Jails Are Outsourcing Medical Care—and the Death Toll Is Rising*, REUTERS (Oct. 26, 2020), https://www.reuters.com/article/us-usa-jails-privatization-special-repor/special-report-u-s-jails-are-outsourcing-medical-care-and-the-death-toll-is-rising-idUSKBN27B1DH.

127. Coll, *supra* note 125.

128. Beth Schwartzapfel, *How Bad Is Prison Health Care? Depends on Who's Watching*, MARSHALL PROJECT (Feb. 26, 2018), https://www.themarshallproject.org/2018/02/25/how-bad-is-prison-health-care-depends-on-who-s-watching. The litigation in which this was alleged remains ongoing. Docket, *Jensen et al. v. Shinn et al.*, No. 2:12-cv-601 (D. Ariz. 2022).

129. *Inmate Correctional Healthcare Contract Awarded*, ARIZONA DEPARTMENT OF CORRECTIONS (Jan. 18, 2019), https://corrections.az.gov/article/inmate-correctional-healthcare-contract-awarded.

130. Schwartzapfel, *supra* note 128.

131. Notice of Impending Death, *Parsons v. Ryan*, No. 2:12-cv-601 (D. Ariz. Aug. 29, 2017), ECF No. 2262.

132. Schwartzapfel, *supra* note 128.

133. AFT, *Private Prisons and Investment Risks: How Private Prison Companies Fuel Mass Incarceration—and How Public Pension Funds Are at Risk*, AMERICAN FEDERATION OF TEACHERS 6 (2020), https://www.aft.org/sites/default/files/media/2020/private-prisons-invest-2019-part2.pdf.

134. Kristine Phillips, *"Something Is Eating My Brain," an Inmate Said. A Lawsuit Claims He Was Left to Die*, WASH. POST (Oct. 30, 2017), https://www.washingtonpost.com/news/post-nation/wp/2017/10/27/something-is-eating-my-brain-an-inmate-said-a-lawsuit-says-he-was-left-to-die/.

135. Order Granting Motion for Summary Judgment, *Walker et al. v. Corizon Health, Inc. et al.*, No. 2:17-cv-2601 (D. Kans. June 3, 2022), ECF No. 311 (The matter is now on appeal).

136. Marsha McLeod, *The Private Option*, ATLANTIC (Sept. 12, 2019), https://www.theatlantic.com/politics/archive/2019/09/private-equitys-grip-on-jail-health-care/597871/; Mark Lungariello, *Controversies Swirl as Westchester County Jail Considers New Health Care Provider*, LOHUD (Apr. 12, 2019), https://www.lohud.com/story/news/local/westchester/2019/04/12/westchester-county-jail-health-care-correct-care-correct-care-solutions-wellpath-tennessee-mcnulty/3237201002/.

137. Blake Ellis & Melanie Hicken, *Dangerous Jail Births, Miscarriages, and Stillborn Babies Blamed on the Same Billion Dollar Company*, CNN (May 7, 2019), https://www.cnn.com/2019/05/07/health/jail-births-wellpath-ccs-invs/index.html; David M. Reutter, *Medical, Mental Health Care Lacking at Florida Jail Despite 43 Years of Court Oversight*, PRISON

LEGAL NEWS (Dec. 10, 2019), https://www.prisonlegalnews.org/news/2019/dec/10
/medical-mental-health-care-lacking-florida-jail-despite-43-years-court-oversight/.

138. Coll, *supra* note 125.

139. Susan Sharon, *Maine State Prison Inmate Files Suit, Says Hundreds of Inmates Were Denied Hepatitis C Treatment*, MAINE PUBLIC (June 26, 2019), https://www.mainepublic.org/courts-and-crime/2019-06-26/maine-state-prison-inmate-files-suit-says-hundreds-of-inmates-were-denied-hepatitis-c-treatment; Susan Sharon, *Maine Expands Chronic Hepatitis C Treatment for Prisoners After Lawsuit Settlement*, MAINE PUBLIC (Oct. 1, 2020), https://www.mainepublic.org/health/2020-10-01/maine-expands-chronic-hepatitis-c-treatment-for-prisoners-after-lawsuit-settlement.

140. Letter from Grace Kingman, Office of the Pierce County Prosecuting Attorney, to Keith Kubik, Kubik Mediation 2 (Mar. 26, 2016), https://www.documentcloud.org/documents/5978547-Pierce-County-March-2016-memo-to-CCS.html.

141. *Id.* at 3.

142. *Id.*

143. *Jury Sides with Pierce County in Jail Health Care Lawsuit*, ASSOCIATED PRESS (Mar. 9, 2019), https://apnews.com/article/f8f7558ae11c49429515ad7f386aed3a; Blake Ellis & Melanie Hicken, *Jail Heath Care CSS Investigation*, CNN (June 25, 2019), https://www.cnn.com/interactive/2019/06/us/jail-health-care-ccs-invs/ (Correct Care Solutions appealed the decision).

144. *See e.g.*, *Sanchez v. Oliver*, 995 F.3d 461, 472 (5th Cir. 2021) (Predecessor to Wellpath had an indemnification clause); *Crawford v. Corizon Health, Inc.*, No. 17-cv-113, 2019 WL 3208001, at *1 (W.D. Pa. July 15, 2019) (Corizon had an indemnification clause).

145. For instance, Corizon repeatedly relies on the law firm O'Connor Kimball, LLP to handle its defense, *see, e.g.*, *Rosado v. Aramark et al.*, No. 2:14cv3033 (E.D. Pa. May 29, 2014); *Rodriguez v. Corizon Health, Inc. et al.*, No. 2:12cv7250 (E.D. Pa. Dec. 31, 2012), while Wellpath repeatedly relied on Cassiday Schade LLP; see, e.g., *Hall-Adejola v. Will County et al.*, No. 1:20-cv-2699 (N.D. Ill. May 4, 2020); *Hirsch v. Will County et al.*, No. 1:19-cv-7398 (N.D. Ill. Nov. 7, 2019).

146. *HIG Capital's and Wellpath's Correctional Healthcare Investment Risks*, PRIVATE EQUITY STAKEHOLDER PROJECT (July 2019), https://pestakeholder.org/wp-content/uploads/2019/07/HIG-Capitals-Correctional-Healthcare-Investment-Risks-PESP-070819.pdf (CMFG was bought by H.I.G. Capital and eventually merged into Wellpath).

147. Rupert Neate, *Welcome to Jail Inc: How Private Companies Make Money off US Prisons*, GUARDIAN (June 16, 2016), https://www.theguardian.com/us-news/2016/jun/16/us-prisons-jail-private-healthcare-companies-profit.

148. Order Granting Motion to Dismiss at 2, *Bible-Marshall et al. V. Montgomery County et al.*, No. 4:20-cv-28 (S.D. Tex. June 1, 2021), ECF No. 47.

149. *Id.* at 7.

150. *Id.*

151. Complaint, *Reichert et al., v. Keefe Commissary Network, LLC et al.*, No. 3:17-cv-5848 (W.D. Wash. Oct. 20, 2017), ECF No. 1. Keefe largely initially denied the accusations, though as noted below, it ultimately settled a portion of the case and agreed to repay a percentage of the fees it took from prisoners. *See* Answer by Defendant Keefe Commissary Network, LLC, *Reichert et al., v. Keefe Commissary Network, LLC et al.*, No. 3:17-cv-5848 (W.D. Wash. May 15, 2018), ECF No. 55.

152. Complaint at ¶ 74–75, *Reichert et al., v. Keefe Commissary Network, LLC et al.*, No. 3:17-cv-5848 (W.D. Wash. Oct. 20, 2017), ECF No. 1.

153. *Id.* at ¶ 82–83.

154. Quandt, *supra* note 82.

155. Unopposed Motion for Approval of Settlement Agreement at 1–2, *Reichert et al. v. Keefe Commissary Network, LLC et al.*, No. 3:17-cv-5848 (W.D. Wash. June 9, 2022), ECF No. 166.

156. Aaron Gregg, *CFPB Orders Prison Banker to Pay $6 Million for Charging Inmates 'Unfair' Fees*, WASH. POST (Oct. 19, 2021), https://www.washingtonpost.com/business/2021/10/19/cfpb-jpay-fine/.

157. *Id.*

158. *An Introduction to Platinum Equity*, PLATINUM EQUITY 4 (July 2022), https://www.platinumequity.com/wp-content/uploads/2022/08/Platinum-Equity-Introduction-July-2022.pdf.

CHAPTER 8: SUING THEIR OWN CUSTOMERS

1. Complaint, *Castellanos v. Mariner Finance, LLC*, No. 1:17-cv-3168 (D. Md. Oct. 27, 2017) ECF No. 2.

2. *Id.*

3. *Id.*

4. *Id.*

5. *Id.*

6. *Santoni, Vocci, & Ortega*, https://www.svolaw.com/.

7. Motion to Compel Arbitration at 4, *Castellanos v. Mariner Fin., LLC*, No. 17-cv-3168 (D. Md. Nov. 3, 2017), ECF No. 7-2.

8. Motion to Compel Arbitration at 15, *Castellanos v. Mariner Fin., LLC*, No. 17-cv-3168 (D. Md. Nov. 3, 2017), ECF No. 7.

9. Opposition to Motion to Compel Arbitration at 5–7, *Castellanos v. Mariner Fin., LLC*, No. 17-cv-3168 (D. Md. Nov. 15, 2017), ECF No. 12.

10. *Castellanos v. Mariner Fin., LLC*, No. 17-cv-3168, 2018 WL 488725, at *1 (D. Md. Jan. 19, 2018).

11. Marginal Order Granting Stipulation of Dismissal with Prejudice, Opposition to Motion to Compel Arbitration, *Castellanos v. Mariner Fin., LLC*, No. 17-cv-3168 (D. Md. May 8, 2018), ECF No. 19.

12. *Mariner Finance*, WARBURG PINCUS, https://warburgpincus.com/investments/mariner-finance/.

13. *Curo Financial Technologies*, FFL PARTNERS, https://www.fflpartners.com/investments/curo-financial-technologies.

14. PRIV. EQUITY STAKEHOLDER PROJECT, PRIVATE EQUITY PILES INTO PAYDAY LENDING AND OTHER SUBPRIME CONSUMER LENDING (2017), https://pestakeholder.org/wp-content/uploads/2017/12/PE-Investment-in-Payday-Installment-Lending-AFR-PESP-121117-with-links.pdf.

15. David French, *Blackstone to Sell Lendmark Financial to Lightyear Capital: Sources*, REUTERS (June 24, 2019), https://www.reuters.com/article/us-lendmarkfinancial-m-a-lightyearcapita/blackstone-to-sell-lendmark-financial-to-lightyear-capital-sources-idUSKCN1TP2C7.

16. *Lone Star Funds Completes Acquisition of DFC Global Corp.*, BUSINESS WIRE (June 13, 2014), https://www.businesswire.com/news/home/20140613005800/en/Lone-Star-Funds-Completes-Acquisition-of-DFC-Global-Corp.

17. *Consumer Financial Protection Bureau*, CFPB DATA POINT: PAYDAY LENDING 4 (2014), https://files.consumerfinance.gov/f/201403_cfpb_report_payday-lending.pdf.

18. *JLL Partners Completes Acquisition of ACE Cash Express, Inc.*, TMCNET (Oct. 5, 2006), https://www.tmcnet.com/usubmit/2006/10/05/1961548.htm; *Populous Financial Group*, JLL PARTNERS, https://www.jllpartners.com/our-companies/populus-financial -group/ (JLL continues to own the company through Populus Financial Group).

19. *Advance America*, ZOOMINFO, https://www.zoominfo.com/c/advance-america-cash -advance-centers-inc/1985111 (estimating $2 billion in annual revenue for Advance America); *ACE Cash Express*, ZOOMINFO, https://www.zoominfo.com/c/ace-cash-express -inc/427413.

20. *Consumer Complaint Database—Advance America*, CONSUMER FINANCIAL PROTECTION BUREAU (Oct. 7, 2022), https://www.consumerfinance.gov/data-research/consumer -complaints/search/?chartType=line&dateInterval=Month&date_received_max=2022 -01-01&date_received_min=2012-01-01&lens=Overview&searchField=all&searchText =%22advance%20america%22&tab=Trends.

21. *Complaint Database—ACE Cash Express*, CONSUMER FINANCIAL PROTECTION BUREAU (Oct. 7, 2022), https://www.consumerfinance.gov/data-research/consumer -complaints/search/?chartType=line&dateInterval=Month&date_received_max=2022 -01-01&date_received_min=2012-01-01&lens=Overview&searchField=all&searchText =%22ace%20cash%22&tab=Trends.

22. *Complaint 5287308*, CONSUMER FINANCIAL PROTECTION BUREAU (Mar. 4, 2022), https://www.consumerfinance.gov/data-research/consumer-complaints/search/detail /5287308; *Complaint 5199725*, CONSUMER FINANCIAL PROTECTION BUREAU (Feb. 8, 2022), https://www.consumerfinance.gov/data-research/consumer-complaints/search/detail /5199725.

23. *Complaint 5195180*, CONSUMER FINANCIAL PROTECTION BUREAU (Feb. 7, 2022), https://www.consumerfinance.gov/data-research/consumer-complaints/search/detail /5195180.

24. *Complaint 5249656*, CONSUMER FINANCIAL PROTECTION BUREAU (Feb. 22, 2022), https://www.consumerfinance.gov/data-research/consumer-complaints/search/detail /5249656.

25. Danielle Douglas, *Payday Lender Ace Cash Express to Pay $10 Million over Debt-Collection Practices*, WASH. POST (July 10, 2014), https://www.washingtonpost.com/business /economy/payday-lender-ace-cash-express-fined-over-abusive-debt-collection-practices /2014/07/10/04e9fa08-0858-11e4-8a6a-19355c7e870a_story.html.

26. *Consumer Complaint Database—Lendmark*, CONSUMER FINANCIAL PROTECTION BUREAU (Oct. 7, 2022), https://www.consumerfinance.gov/data-research/consumer -complaints/search/?chartType=line&dateInterval=Month&dateRange=All&date _received_max=2022-10-07&date_received_min=2011-12-01&lens=Overview&search Field=all&searchText=lendmark&tab=Trends.

27. Search for "Plaintiff-Litigant (Mariner Ginance)," LEXIS COURTLINK, https:// advance.lexis.com/search/?pdmfid=1519217&crid=a4e6f7ec-90ff-438d-9d28-390925e3 cf61&pdsearchterms=plaintiff-litigant(mariner+finance)&pdstartin=hlct%3A1%3A1& pdcaseshlctselectedbyuser=false&pdtypeofsearch=searchboxclick&pdsearchtype=SearchBox &pdqttype=and&pdpsf=hlct%3A1%3A1&pdquerytemplateid=&ecomp=pbrwk&earg =pdpsf&prid=69facea1-c07b-43dc-b9fd-a272a9ad5557.

28. Bailey McCann, *Fortress Backed Springleaf to Acquire OneMain*, PRIVATE EQUITY INTERNATIONAL (Mar. 3, 2015), https://www.privateequityinternational.com/fortress -backed-springleaf-to-acquire-onemain/.

29. Search for "Plaintiff-Litigant (OneMain)," LEXIS COURTLINK, https://advance.lexis
.com/search/?pdmfid=1519217&crid=9bea117a-6d62-4da5-b4f9-dfc6ae9e75e0&
pdsearchterms=plaintiff-litigant(onemain)&pdstartin=hlct%3A1%3A1&pdcaseshlctse
lectedbyuser=false&pdtypeofsearch=searchboxclick&pdsearchtype=SearchBox&pdqttype
=and&pdpsf=hlct%3A1%3A1&pdquerytemplateid=&ecomp=pbrwk&earg=pdpsf
&prid=a4e6f7ec-90ff-438d-9d28-390925e3cf61.

30. *See, e.g.*, *Writ of Attachment on a Judgment*, SUPERIOR COURT OF THE DISTRICT OF
COLUMBIA, https://www.dccourts.gov/sites/default/files/pdf-forms/writ_wages.pdf.

31. *Arbitration Schedule of Fees and Costs*, JAMS, https://www.jamsadr.com/arbitration
-fees.

32. *See, e.g.*, Mark D. Gough, *The High Costs of an Inexpensive Forum: An Empirical Analysis
of Employment Discrimination Claims Heard in Arbitration and Civil Litigation*, 35 BERKELEY
J. EMP. & LAB. L. 91, 91 (2014); *Arbitration Study*, CONSUMER FINANCIAL PROTECTION BU-
REAU (Mar. 2015), https://files.consumerfinance.gov/f/201503_cfpb_arbitration-study
-report-to-congress-2015.pdf.

33. Scott Horsley, *Payday Loans—and Endless Cycles of Debt—Targeted by Federal Watchdog*,
NPR (Mar. 26, 2015), https://www.npr.org/2015/03/26/395421117/payday-loans-and
-endless-cycles-of-debt-targeted-by-federal-watchdog.

34. Katherine Kirkpatrick *et al.*, *CFPB Focus on Payday Lending: A Look Around the
Corner*, JD SUPRA (Jan. 15, 2021), https://www.jdsupra.com/legalnews/cfpb-focus-on
-payday-lending-a-look-7629208/.

35. Aliyyah Camp, *What Is the Community Financial Services Association of America?*,
FINDER (Oct. 16, 2021), https://www.finder.com/community-financial-services-association
-of-america. Private equity-backed lenders included Community Choice Financial and
Speedy Cash.

36. Katherine Kirkpatrick *et al.*, *CFPB Focus on Payday Lending: A Look Around the
Corner*, JD SUPRA (Jan. 15, 2021), https://www.jdsupra.com/legalnews/cfpb-focus-on
-payday-lending-a-look-7629208/; PRIV. EQUITY STAKEHOLDER PROJECT, PRIVATE EQ-
UITY PILES INTO PAYDAY LENDING AND OTHER SUBPRIME CONSUMER LENDING 7 (2017),
https://pestakeholder.org/wp-content/uploads/2017/12/PE-Investment-in-Payday
-Installment-Lending-AFR-PESP-121117-with-links.pdf.

37. Katherine Kirkpatrick *et al.*, *CFPB Focus on Payday Lending: A Look Around the
Corner*, JD SUPRA (Jan. 15, 2021), https://www.jdsupra.com/legalnews/cfpb-focus-on
-payday-lending-a-look-7629208/; PRIVATE EQUITY STAKEHOLDER PROJECT, PRIVATE
EQUITY PILES INTO PAYDAY LENDING AND OTHER SUBPRIME CONSUMER LENDING 7 (2017),
https://pestakeholder.org/wp-content/uploads/2017/12/PE-Investment-in-Payday
-Installment-Lending-AFR-PESP-121117-with-links.pdf.

38. Jackie Wattles, *Cordray Resignation Sets Off Scramble over Consumer Financial Protection Bureau*, CNN MONEY (Nov. 25, 2017), https://money.cnn.com/2017/11/24/news
/cfpb-richard-cordray-resignation/index.html.

39. Emily Stewart, *Mick Mulvaney Once Called the CFPB a "Sick, Sad" Joke. Now
He Might Be in Charge of It*, VOX (Nov. 16, 2017), https://www.vox.com/policy-and
-politics/2017/11/16/16667266/mick-mulvaney-cfpb-cordray-omb-joke.

40. *Client Profile: JLL Partners*, OPEN SECRETS, https://www.opensecrets.org/federal
-lobbying/clients/summary?cycle=2018&id=D000052577.

41. *Client Profile: Lendmark Financial Services*, OPEN SECRETS, https://www.opensecrets
.org/federal-lobbying/clients/summary?cycle=2018&id=D000071049.

42. *Client Profile: Mariner Finance*, OPEN SECRETS, https://www.opensecrets.org/federal
-lobbying/clients/summary?cycle=2018&id=D000084066.

43. *Client Profile: OneMain Financial*, OPEN SECRETS, https://www.opensecrets.org /federal-lobbying/clients/summary?cycle=2018&id=D000020937.

44. Katherine Kirkpatrick *et al.*, *CFPB Focus on Payday Lending: A Look Around the Corner*, JD SUPRA (Jan. 15, 2021), https://www.jdsupra.com/legalnews/cfpb-focus-on -payday-lending-a-look-7629208/.

45. *Congress Overturns CFPB Arbitration Rule*, BAKER & HOSTETLER (Nov. 1, 2017), https://www.bakerlaw.com/alerts/congress-overturns-cfpb-arbitration-rule.

46. *Cotton Statement on the CFPB's New Arbitration Rule*, OFFICE OF SENATOR TOM COTTON (July 11, 2017), https://www.cotton.senate.gov/news/press-releases/2017/07/11 /cotton-statement-on-the-cfpb-and-146s-new-arbitration-rule.

47. *AFR Report: Payday Lobbying and Campaign Spending Top $15 Million for 2014 Election Cycle*, AMERICANS FOR FINANCIAL REFORM (July 7, 2015), https://ourfinancialsecurity .org/2015/07/payday-lender-lobbying-and-campaign-spending-top-15-million-for-2014 -election-cycle-afr-report-finds/.

48. Search for "Cotton for Senate, Inc," "Cotton Victory," and "Blackstone," FEDERAL ELECTION COMMISSION, https://www.fec.gov/data/receipts/individual-contributions /?committee_id=C00499988&committee_id=C00571018&contributor_employer =blackstone.

49. Jessica Silver-Greenberg, *Consumer Bureau Loses Fight to Allow More Class-Action Suits*, N.Y. TIMES (Oct. 24, 2017), https://www.nytimes.com/2017/10/24/business/senate -vote-wall-street-regulation.html.

50. Letter from Keith A. Noreika, acting comptroller of the currency, to Richard Cordray, director, Consumer Financial Protection Bureau (July 10, 2017), https://finservblog .bakerhostetlerblogs.com/wp-content/uploads/sites/20/2017/11/07-10-2017.pdf.

51. Jeffrey L. Hare & Adam Dubin, *Congress Overturns CFPB's Arbitration Rule*, DLA PIPER (Nov. 1, 2017), https://www.dlapiper.com/en/us/insights/publications/2017/11 /congress-overturns-cfpb-arbitration-rule/.

52. *Cotton Statement on Senate Vote to Repeal the CFPB's Arbitration Rule*, OFFICE OF SENATOR TOM COTTON (Oct. 24, 2017), https://www.cotton.senate.gov/news/press-releases /cotton-statement-on-senate-vote-to-repeal-the-cfpb-and-146s-arbitration-rule.

53. *Tom Cotton*, OPEN SECRETS https://www.opensecrets.org/members-of-congress /tom-cotton/summary?cid=N00033363&cycle=2018&type=I.

54. Peter Whoriskey, *"A Way of Monetizing Poor People": How Private Equity Firms Make Money Offering Loans to Cash-Strapped Americans*, WASH. POST (July 1, 2018, https:// www.washingtonpost.com/business/economy/a-way-of-monetizing-poor-people -how-private-equity-firms-make-money-offering-loans-to-cash-strapped-americans /2018/07/01/5f7e2670-5dee-11e8-9ee3-49d6d4814c4c_story.html.

55. Wendi C. Thomas *et al.*, *A Private Equity–Owned Doctors' Group Sued Poor Patients Until It Came Under Scrutiny*, NPR (Nov. 27, 2019), https://www.npr.org/sections/health -shots/2019/11/27/783449133/a-private-equity-owned-doctors-group-sued-poor-patients -until-it-came-under-scru.

56. *Id.*

57. Jordan Rau, *Patients Eligible for Charity Care Instead Get Big Bills*, KAISER HEALTH NEWS (Oct. 11, 2019), https://khn.org/news/patients-eligible-for-charity-care-instead -get-big-bills/.

58. Thomas *et al.*, *supra* note 55.

59. *Id.*

60. Consent Order ¶ 15, *In the Matter of: Transworld Systems, Inc.*, No. 2017-CFPB-0018, (US Consumer Financial Protection Bureau, Sept. 18, 2017) (Transworld

provided documentation in support of the National Collegiate Student Loan Trusts' lawsuits).

61. Priv. Equity Stakeholder Project, Platinum Equity-Owned Transworld Systems Fined $2.5 Million for Illegal Student Debt Collection Lawsuits, Draws Thousands of Consumer Complaints 1 (2019), https://pestakeholder.org/wp-content/uploads/2019/07/Platinum-Equity-Owned-Transworld-Systems-Fined-2.5-Million-PESP-071619.pdf.

62. *Id.*

63. Ori Lev, *CFPB Suffers Embarrassing Court Loss*, Mayer Brown (June 4, 2020), https://www.mayerbrown.com/en/perspectives-events/blogs/2020/06/cfpb-suffers-embarrassing-court-loss; Transworld System's Motion to Intervene, *CFPB v. National Collegiate Master Student Loan Trust, et al.*, 1:17-cv-1323 (D. Del. Sept. 22, 2017), ECF No. 9.

64. *Platinum Equity-Owned Transworld Systems Fined $2.5 Million for Illegal Student Debt Collection Lawsuits, Draws Thousands of Consumer Complaints*, Private Equity Stakeholder Project 4 (July 2019), https://pestakeholder.org/wp-content/uploads/2019/07/Platinum-Equity-Owned-Transworld-Systems-Fined-2.5-Million-PESP-071619.pdf (Transworld bought Nationwide Credit, Inc. and NCC Business Services). It also bought debt collection management company Altisource. *PE-backed Transworld Systems to acquire Altisource's financial services business*, S&P Global (Mar. 29, 2019), https://www.spglobal.com/marketintelligence/en/news-insights/trending/3QTPWjMZlN9q1P7Hs21fjg2.

65. Pilar Sorensen, *Pandemic Evictor: Don Mullen's Pretium Partners Files to Evict Black Renters, Collects Billions from Investors*, Private Equity Stakeholder Project (Apr. 2021), https://pestakeholder.org/wp-content/uploads/2021/04/Pandemic-Evictor-Pretium-Partners-PESP-041421.pdf.

66. *See, e.g.*, *Vero Beach v. Harvey Smith Jr.*, No. 05-2018-CC-027948 (Fla. Cir. Ct., Brevard Cty., May 11, 2018) (suit by consulate to collect unpaid debts of resident and demanding attorney's fees).

67. *See, e.g.*, *Dowell Properties v. Ellen Balentine and Justin Balentine*, No. SC-2012-2915 (Okla. Dist. Ct. July 13, 2012) (suit alleging indebtedness of resident).

68. James Fontanella-Khan, Sujeet Indap & Barney Thompson, How a Private Equity Boom Fuelled the World's Biggest Law Firm, Fin. Times (June 6, 2019), https://www.ft.com/content/13696928-86d5-11e9-a028-86cea8523dc2.

69. *Id.*

70. *Id.*

71. *Id.*

72. *See, e.g.*, *Private Equity*, Latham & Watkins, https://www.lw.com/practices/privateequity; *Private Equity*, HoganLovells, https://www.hoganlovells.com/en/service/private-equity; *Private Equity Fund Litigation*, Quinn Emanuel Urquhart & Sullivan, LLP, https://www.quinnemanuel.com/practice-areas/investment-fund-litigation/private-equity-fund-litigation/; *Private Equity*, Gibson Dunn, https://www.gibsondunn.com/practice/private-equity/; *Private Equity*, Greenberg Traurig, https://www.gtlaw.com/en/capabilities/corporate/private-equity.

73. *Private Equity Fund Litigation*, Quinn Emanuel Urquhart & Sullivan, LLP, https://www.quinnemanuel.com/practice-areas/investment-fund-litigation/private-equity-fund-litigation/.

74. *Private Equity Litigation*, Sidley Austin, https://www.sidley.com/en/services/commercial-litigation-and-disputes/private-equity-litigation.

75. Complaint, *Salley v. Heartland-Charleston of Hanahan, SC, LLC et al.*, No. 2:10-cv-791 (D.S.C. Mar. 29, 2010), ECF No. 1.

76. *Id.*

77. *Id.*

78. Motion to Dismiss at 4, *Salley v. Heartland-Charleston of Hanahan, SC, LLC et al.*, No. 2:10-cv-791 (D.S.C. June 25, 2010), ECF No. 15.

79. Order on Motion to Dismiss at 9, *Salley v. Heartland-Charleston of Hanahan, SC, LLC et al.*, No. 2:10-cv-791 (D.S.C. Dec. 10, 2010), ECF No. 45.

80. *Id.*

81. David G. Stevenson, *Nursing Home Ownership Trends and Their Impact on Quality of Care: A Study Using Detailed Ownership Data from Texas*, 25 J. AGING SOC. POL'Y (2013), https://www.ncbi.nlm.nih.gov/pmc/articles/PMC4825679/.

82. *Scott Brass Overview*, PITCHBOOK, https://pitchbook.com/profiles/company/10474-03#overview.

83. *Sun Capital Acquires Scott Brass*, MERGERS & ACQUISITIONS (Feb. 19, 2007), https://www.themiddlemarket.com/news/sun-capital-acquires-scott-brass.

84. Complaint, *Sun Capital Partners III, LP, et al. v. New England Teamsters & Trucking Industry Pension Fund*, (D. Mass. June 4, 2010), ECF No. 1.

85. *Federal Court Finds Investment Funds Not Liable for Portfolio Company-Employer's Withdrawal Liability*, AKIN GUMP (Nov. 9, 2012), https://www.akingump.com/en/news-insights/federal-court-finds-investment-funds-not-liable-for-portfolio.html.

86. *First Circuit Sun Capital Decision Increases ERISA Exposure for Private Equity Funds*, DAVIS POLK (Aug. 6, 2013), https://www.davispolk.com/sites/default/files/08.06.13.Sun_.Capital.pdf.

87. *First Circuit Overturns Sun Capital Decision*, SULLIVAN & CROMWELL LLP (Dec. 2, 2019), https://www.sullcrom.com/files/upload/SC-Publication-First-Circuit-Overturns-Sun-Capital-Decision.pdf.

88. Martina Barash, *Sun Capital Advisors Wins Battle over Teamsters Pension Fund*, BLOOMBERG LAW (Nov. 22, 2019), https://news.bloomberglaw.com/employee-benefits/teamsters-pension-fund-cant-recover-from-private-equity-funds.

89. Maria Glover, *Mass Arbitration*, 74 STAN. L. REV. 1283 (2022); Myriam Giles, *The Day Doctrine Died: Private Arbitration and the End of Law*, U. ILL. L. REV. 371, 278–290 (2016).

90. Robert H. Klonoff, *The Decline of Class Actions*, 90 WASH. U. L. REV. 729 (2013).

91. *AT&T Mobility LLC v. Concepcion*, 563 U.S. 333, 339 (2011); *Moses H. Cone Mem'l Hosp. v. Mercury Constr. Corp.*, 460 U.S. 1, 24 (1983) ("Section 2 is a congressional declaration of a liberal federal policy favoring arbitration agreements.").

92. *AT&T Mobility LLC v. Concepcion*, 563 U.S. 333 (2011).

93. *American Express Co. v. Italian Colors Restaurant*, 133 S. Ct. 2304 (2013).

94. *Epic Systems v. Lewis*, 138 S. Ct. 1612, 1626 (2018).

95. Glover, *supra* note 89.

96. *Id.*; Scott Medintz, *Forced Arbitration: A Clause for Concern*, CONSUMER REPORTS (Jan. 30, 2020), https://www.consumerreports.org/mandatory-binding-arbitration/forced-arbitration-clause-for-concern.

97. Glover, *supra* note 89.

98. *See, e.g.*, Ed Williams, *"An Anything-Goes Situation": Assessing Arbitration Agreements at Nursing Homes*, LAS CRUCES SUN NEWS (July 11, 2020), https://www.lcsun-news.com/story/news/2020/07/11/an-anything-goes-situation/5421301002/ (Discussing arbitration agreements at the private equity–owned Genesis nursing home chain).

99. *Preston Darron v. Invitation Homes*, No. 2020-M6-001029 (Ill. Cir. Jan. 23, 2020) (compelling case to arbitration).

100. Complaint at ¶ 206, *Mayberry et al., v. KKR & Co., LP, et al.*, No. CI-17-1348 (Ky. Cir. Ct. Feb. 26, 2018).

101. *Overstreet v. Mayberry*, 603 S.W.3d 244, 256 (Ky. 2020).

102. *Id.*

103. *Kentucky Supreme Court Dismisses $50 Billion Derivative Action Against Hedge Fund Managers for Lack of Standing*, PAUL WEISS, https://www.paulweiss.com/practices /transactional/investment-management/publications/kentucky-supreme-court-dismisses -50-billion-derivative-action-against-hedge-fund-managers-for-lack-of-standing?id =37533.

104. *E.g.*, Michael Corkery, *Amazon Ends Use of Arbitration for Customer Disputes*, N.Y. TIMES (Sept. 28, 2021), https://www.nytimes.com/2021/07/22/business/amazon -arbitration-customer-disputes.html (Noting that "Amazon faces potentially tens of millions of dollars in fees that it will have to pay the private arbitrators to have those cases heard."); Alison Frankel, *Forced into Arbitration, 12,500 Drivers Claim Uber Won't Pay Fees to Launch Cases*, REUTERS (Dec. 6, 2018), https://www.reuters.com/article /legal-us-otc-uber/forced-into-arbitration-12500-drivers-claim-uber-wont-pay -fees-to-launch-cases-idUSKBN1O52C6. ("Under Uber's arbitration provisions, it's up to the company to pay initial arbitration fees."); Nicholas Iovino, *DoorDash Ordered to Pay $9.5M to Arbitrate 5,000 Labor Disputes*, COURTHOUSE NEWS (Feb. 10, 2020), https:// www.courthousenews.com/doordash-ordered-to-pay-12m-to-arbitrate-5000-labor -disputes/ ("DoorDash refused to pay its share of fees").

105. Glover, *supra* note 89; *FanDuel Announces Series E Financing of $275 Million from KKR, Google Capital and Time Warner*, BUSINESS WIRE (July 14, 2015), https:// www.businesswire.com/news/home/20150714005506/en/FanDuel-Announces -Series-E-Financing-of-275-Million-from-KKR-Google-Capital-and-Time-Warner9 /26/2022; Ben Penn, *Buffalo Wild Wings Case Tests Future of Class Action Waivers*, BLOOMBERG L. (July 12, 2018), https://news.bloomberglaw.com/daily-labor-report /buffalo-wild-wings-case-tests-future-of-class-action-waivers.

106. Alison Frankel, *"This Hypocrisy Will Not Be Blessed": Judge Orders DoorDash to Arbitrate 5,000 Couriers' Claims*, REUTERS (Feb. 11, 2020), https://www.reuters.com/article /us-otc-doordash/this-hypocrisy-will-not-be-blessed-judge-orders-doordash-to-arbitrate -5000-couriers-claims-idUSKBN2052S1.

107. *Id.*

108. Glover, *supra* note 89; Michael Holecek, *As Mass Arbitrations Proliferate, Companies Have Deployed Strategies for Deterring and Defending Against Them*, GIBSON DUNN (May 24, 2021), https://www.gibsondunn.com/as-mass-arbitrations-proliferate-companies -have-deployed-strategies-for-deterring-and-defending-against-them/.

109. Order on Motion to Dismiss at 2, *In re: Nine West LBO Securities Litigation*, No. 1:20-md-2941 (S.D.N.Y. Dec. 4, 2020), ECF No. 423.

110. *Id.* at 6.

111. *Id.* at 29.

112. William D. Cohan, *The Private Equity Party Might Be Ending. It's About Time.*, N.Y. TIMES (Feb. 28, 2021), https://www.nytimes.com/2021/02/28/opinion/private -equity-reckoning.html.

113. Stipulation of Voluntary Dismissal, *In re: Nine West LBO Securities Litigation*, No. 1:20-md-2941 (S.D.N.Y. Dec. 4, 2020), ECF No. 429.

114. Cohan, *supra* note 112.

115. Interview with Cathy Hershcopf, partner, Cooley (Jan. 12, 2022).

116. Gillian Tan, *Debt Rises in Leveraged Buyouts Despite Warnings*, WALL ST. J. (May 20, 2014), https://www.wsj.com/articles/SB10001424052702304422704579574184101045614; Chibuike Oguh, *Analysis: Private Equity Investors Fret over Record U.S. Buyout Prices*, REUTERS (Mar. 16, 2021), https://www.reuters.com/business/private-equity-investors -fret-over-record-us-buyout-prices-2021-03-16.

CHAPTER 9: PRIVATIZING THE PUBLIC SECTOR

1. Julianne Mattera, *Middletown Approves 50-Year Water, Sewer Lease with United Water*, PENN-LIVE (Sept. 30, 2014), https://www.pennlive.com/midstate/2014/09/middletown _approves_50-year_wa.html.

2. *Comprehensive Annual Financial Report for the Fiscal Year Ended December 31, 2014*, TOWNSHIP OF MIDDLETOWN 19 (2015), https://www.middletownbucks.org/Departments /Finance/Financial-Reports/Reports/CAFR_2014.

3. *Middletown, Dauphin County, Pennsylvania*, WIKIPEDIA, https://en.wikipedia.org /wiki/Middletown,_Dauphin_County,_Pennsylvania.

4. *Middletown Borough, Pennsylvania*, CENSUS BUREAU, https://www.census.gov/quick facts/fact/table/middletownboroughpennsylvania,US/SEX255221 (the Middletown per capita income is $29,575; the US per capita income is $37,638).

5. Complaint at ¶ 59, *Middletown Borough v. Middletown Water Joint Venture LLC*, No. 1:18-cv-861 (M.D. Pa. Apr. 20, 2018), ECF No. 1.

6. Mattera, *supra* note 1.

7. *Id.*

8. Complaint at ¶ 12, *Middletown Borough v. Middletown Water Joint Venture LLC*, No. 1:18-cv-861 (M.D. Pa. Apr. 20, 2018).

9. Memorandum on Order on Motion to Dismiss at 4, *Middletown Borough v. Middletown Water Joint Venture LLC*, No. 1:18-cv-861 (M.D. Pa. Mar. 27, 2019), ECF No. 66 (Middletown Water ultimately made a final offer of a $43 million payment, with annual payments of $750,000).

10. *United Water and KKR Sign Utility Partnership with Borough of Middletown*, BUSINESS WIRE (Dec. 11, 2014), https://www.businesswire.com/news/home/20141211006533/en /United-Water-and-KKR-Sign-Utility-Partnership-with-Borough-of-Middletown-PA.

11. Memorandum on Order on Motion to Dismiss at 2, *Middletown Borough v. Middletown Water Joint Venture LLC*, No. 1:18-cv-861 (M.D. Pa. Mar. 27, 2019), ECF No. 66.

12. Complaint at ¶ 56, *Middletown Borough v. Middletown Water Joint Venture LLC*, No. 1:18cv861 (M.D. Pa. Apr. 20, 2018).

13. Jackie Foster, FACEBOOK (Mar. 8, 2018). https://www.facebook.com/middletown .borough/posts/1263031863827564.

14. Sheila Hinkson, FACEBOOK (Mar. 9, 2018), https://www.facebook.com/middletown .borough/posts/1263031863827564.

15. Tom Buck, FACEBOOK (Mar. 9, 2018), https://www.facebook.com/middletown .borough/posts/1263031863827564.

16. Julianne Mattera, *Middletown Approves 50-Year Water, Sewer Lease with United Water*, PENNLIVE 9 (Sept. 30, 2014) https://www.pennlive.com/midstate/2014/09/middletown _approves_50-year_wa.html; *Benjamin Kapenstein*, LINKEDIN, https://www.linkedin.com /in/benjamin-kapenstein-798a3756/.

17. Complaint at ¶ 24-27, *Middletown Borough v. Middletown Water Joint Venture LLC*, No. 1:18-cv-861 (M.D. Pa. Apr. 20, 2018).

18. Docket, *Middletown Borough v. Middletown Water Joint Venture LLC*, No. 1:18-cv-861 (M.D. Pa. Apr. 20, 2018).

19. Memorandum on Order on Motion to Dismiss at 13, *Middletown Borough v. Middletown Water Joint Venture LLC*, No. 1:18-cv-861 (M.D. Pa. Mar. 27, 2019), ECF No. 66 (Middletown Water ultimately made a final offer of a $43 million payment, with annual payments of $750,000).

20. *Public Notice*, Suez (2018), https://middletownborough.com/wp-content/uploads/2018/07/Middletown-Boil-Water-Advisory-FAQs.pdf.

21. Andrew Vitelli, *KKR Makes Splash with US Water PPP Exits*, Infrastructure Investor (Jan. 26, 2018), https://www.infrastructureinvestor.com/66833-2/.

22. *A Tale of Two Public-Private Partnership Cities*, Knowledge at Wharton (June 10, 2015), https://knowledge.wharton.upenn.edu/article/a-tale-of-two-public-private-partnership-cities/.

23. *United Water and KKR Sign Unique Utility Partnership with City of Bayonne, NJ*, KKR (Dec. 20, 2012), https://media.kkr.com/news-details/?news_id=a371ff23-5bc6-48ab-8ca8-c4b8769837d0&type=1&download=1.

24. United Water, *United Water Announces Commitment to Action at 2012 Clinton Global Initiative Annual Meeting*, Cision (Sept. 25, 2012), https://www.prnewswire.com/news-releases/united-water-announces-commitment-to-action-at-2012-clinton-global-initiative-annual-meeting-171193121.html; *United Water and KKR Sign Unique Utility Partnership with City of Bayonne, NJ*, Business Wire (Dec. 20, 2012), https://www.businesswire.com/news/home/20121220005674/en/United-Water-and-KKR-Sign-Unique-Utility-Partnership-with-City-of-Bayonne-NJ.

25. Peter D'Auria, *Frustration over Bayonne's Water Contract Has Reached a Boiling Point. Can the City Find a Way Out?*, Jersey J. (June 8, 2021), https://www.nj.com/hudson/2021/06/frustration-over-bayonnes-water-contract-has-reached-a-boiling-point-can-the-city-find-a-way-out.html.

26. Dan Israel, *Come Hell or High Water*, Hudson Rptr. (May 19, 2021), https://hudsonreporter.com/2021/05/19/come-hell-or-high-water/.

27. Corey W. McDonald, *Bayonne Hit with 9 Percent Water Rate Hike—Second Highest Increase Since 2012 Contract*, Jersey J. (Feb. 13, 2019), https://www.nj.com/hudson/2019/02/bayonne-hit-with-9-percent-water-rate-hike-second-highest-increase-since-2012-contract.html.

28. Andrew Vitelli, *KKR Makes Splash with US Water PPP Exits*, Infrastructure Inv. (Jan. 26, 2018), https://www.infrastructureinvestor.com/66833-2/.

29. Israel, *supra* note 26.

30. D'Auria, *supra* note 25.

31. Danielle Ivory et al., *In American Towns, Private Profits from Public Works*, N.Y. Times (Dec. 24, 2016), https://www.nytimes.com/2016/12/24/business/dealbook/private-equity-water.html.

32. Ray C. Fair, *U.S. Infrastructure: 1929–2019* (Cowles Foundation Discussion Paper No. 2187, July 2019), https://papers.ssrn.com/sol3/papers.cfm?abstract_id=3432670.

33. Michael A. Pagano & Christopher W. Hoene, *City Budgets in an Era of Increased Uncertainty*, Brookings Institution 4–5 (July 2018), https://www.brookings.edu/wp-content/uploads/2018/07/20180718_Brookings-Metro_City-fiscal-policy-Pagano-Hoene-final.pdf.

34. *Carlyle Commits Over $100 Million in Battery Storage and Electric Vehicle Infrastructure Technologies to Accelerate the Energy Transition*, Carlyle (Jan. 14, 2022), https://www

.carlyle.com/media-room/news-release-archive/carlyle-commits-over-100-million
-battery-storage-electric-vehicle-infrastructure-energy-transition.

35. *KKR Portfolio*, KKR, https://www.kkr.com/businesses/private-equity/kkr
-portfolio (KKR invested in Genesis Energy, LP and Rocky Mountain Midstream).

36. *As Climate Change Requires Cuts to Coal, Private Equity Buys More*, PRIVATE EQUITY
STAKEHOLDER PROJECT (June 2020), https://pestakeholder.org/wp-content/uploads/2020
/07/PESP-As-Coal-Declines-PE-Buys-More.pdf.

37. *Blackstone Infrastructure Partners Acquires Stake in Phoenix Tower International*, BLACK-
STONE (Jan. 18, 2022), https://www.blackstone.com/news/press/blackstone-infrastructure
-partners-acquires-stake-in-phoenix-tower-international/.

38. Macky Tall & Pooja Goyal, *Addressing the Global Infrastructure Funding Gap*,
CARLYLE (Oct. 15, 2021), https://www.carlyle.com/global-insights/addressing-global
-infrastructure-funding-gap-macky-tall-pooja-goyal.

39. Greg Roumeliotis, *KKR Joins Private Equity Charge in U.S. Water*, REUTERS
(Dec. 20, 2012), https://www.reuters.com/article/us-kkr-water/kkr-joins-private-equity
-charge-in-u-s-water-idUSBRE8BJ0GL20121220.

40. *Investor Group Buys West Corp.*, N.Y. TIMES (June 1, 2006), https://www.nytimes
.com/2006/06/01/business/01west.html. Despite several changes, the company stayed
in the hands of private equity. Lee and Quadrangle took the company public again
in 2013, though along with the companies' founders, continued to hold a near
majority of shares in the business. *West Corporation Enters into Definitive Agreement to Be Acquired by Certain Funds Affiliated with Apollo Global Management for
$23.50 per Share in Cash*, THOMAS H. LEE PARTNERS (May 10, 2017), https://thl
.com/news-post/west-corporation-enters-into-definitive-agreement-to-be-acquired
-by-certain-funds-affiliated-with-apollo-global-management-for-23-50-per-share
-in-cash/. In 2017, Apollo Global Management bought the business outright, taking
it private once again. *Apollo Global to Buy West Corp for About $2 billion*, REUTERS (May
8, 2017), https://www.reuters.com/article/us-west-m-a-apollo-global/apollo-global-to
-buy-west-corp-for-about-2-billion-idUSKBN1852RN.

41. *April 2014 Multistate 911 Outage Report*, FCC 4 (Oct. 17, 2014), https://www.fcc
.gov/document/april-2014-multistate-911-outage-report.

42. Order, *In the Matter of Intrado Communications Inc.*, No. EB-SED-14-00017191
(FCC Apr. 6, 2015), https://apps.fcc.gov/edocs_public/attachmatch/DA-15-421A1.pdf.

43. Colin Wood, *911 Vendor Intrado Takes Responsibility for Widespread Outage*, STATE-
SCOOP (Oct. 2, 2020), https://statescoop.com/911-outage-intrado/.

44. Phil Harvey, *CenturyLink, West Safety Agree to Pay Up for 911 Outage*, LIGHT
READING (Nov. 5, 2019), https://www.lightreading.com/automation/centurylink-west
-safety-agree-to-pay-up-for-911-outage/d/d-id/755381; *WSC Settles for $175K over
Multi-State 911 Outage in Aug 2018*, FCC (Nov. 4, 2019), https://www.fcc.gov/document
/wsc-settles-175k-over-multi-state-911-outage-aug-2018.

45. *FCC Report on CenturyLink Network Outage*, FCC 3 (Aug. 19, 2019), https://
www.fcc.gov/document/fcc-report-centurylink-network-outage.

46. Colin Wood, *911 Vendor Intrado Takes Responsibility for Widespread Outage*, STATE
SCOOP (Oct. 2, 2020), https://statescoop.com/911-outage-intrado/.

47. *FCC Reaches Settlement of Intrado 911 Outage Investigation*, FCC (Dec. 17, 2021), https://
www.fcc.gov/document/fcc-reaches-settlement-intrado-911-outage-investigation.

48. *West Corporation Reports Fourth Quarter and Full Year 2006 Results*, WEST COR-
PORATION (Jan. 31, 2007), https://ir.intrado.com/static-files/240d47fc-e3e4-48b2-839a
-8669d88924f3.

49. *West Corporation Annual Report 2016*, WEST CORPORATION 31 (2017), https://www.annualreports.com/HostedData/AnnualReports/PDF/NASDAQ_WSTC_2016_0efc2cea0e5740f881650788b08ebab2.pdf.

50. *Apollo Global to Buy West Corp for About $2 Billion*, REUTERS (May 9, 2017), https://www.reuters.com/article/us-west-m-a-apollo-global/apollo-global-to-buy-west-corp-for-about-2-billion-idUSKBN1852RN.

51. *Fitch Downgrades Intrado's IDR to "B-," Outlook Stable*, FITCHRATINGS (Aug. 25, 2021), https://www.fitchratings.com/research/corporate-finance/fitch-downgrades-intrado-idr-to-b-outlook-stable-25-08-2021.

52. Robin A. Johnson, *The Future of Local Emergency Medical Service: Ambulance Wars or Public-Private Truce?*, REASON PUBLIC POLICY INSTITUTE (2001), https://reason.org/wp-content/uploads/2001/08/02987706670b6394141064d6c60f0d80.pdf.

53. *Id.*

54. Steven Potter, *Sounding the Alarm*, PROGRESSIVE MAGAZINE (Feb. 1, 2019), https://progressive.org/magazine/sounding-the-alarm/.

55. Tom Corrigan, *Ambulance Operator Controlled by Lynn Tilton Files for Bankruptcy*, WALL ST. J. (Feb. 25, 2016), https://www.wsj.com/articles/ambulance-operator-controlled-by-lynn-tilton-files-for-bankruptcy-1456438453; Olivia Webb, *Private Equity Chases Ambulances*, AM. PROSPECT (Oct. 3, 2019), https://prospect.org/health/private-equity-chases-ambulances-emergency-medical-transport/; Chris Anderson, *Private Equity Firm Buys Emergency Medical Services for $3.2 Billion*, HEALTHCARE FINANCE (Feb. 15, 2011), https://www.healthcarefinancenews.com/news/private-equity-firm-buys-emergency-medical-services-32-billion; *KKR Buys AMR for $2.4bn*, FINANCIER WORLDWIDE (Oct. 2017), https://www.financierworldwide.com/kkr-buys-amr-for-24bn.

56. John Tozzi, *Air Ambulances Are Flying More Patients Than Ever, and Leaving Massive Bills Behind*, BLOOMBERG (June 11, 2018), https://www.bloomberg.com/news/features/2018-06-11/private-equity-backed-air-ambulances-leave-behind-massive-bills.

57. Danielle Ivory *et al.*, *When You Dial 911 and Wall Street Answers*, N.Y. TIMES (June 25, 2016), https://www.nytimes.com/2016/06/26/business/dealbook/when-you-dial-911-and-wall-street-answers.html. (Envision Healthcare, which bought Rural/Metro, told the *New York Times* that "[w]e are continuing to hire paramedics and E.M.T.s," while Warburg Pincus said that "[d]espite several initiatives undertaken by the company's board and management team… [the] challenges Rural/Metro faced were too difficult to overcome.").

58. *Id.*

59. *See, e.g.*, *PatientCare EMS Solutions Acquires MedFleet Ambulance Service*, A&M CAPITAL PARTNERS (Feb. 12, 2020), https://www.a-mcapital.com/patientcare-ems-solutions-acquires-medfleet-ambulance-service; *Harbour Point Capital Completes Investment in Midwest Medical Transport*, PRIVATE EQUITY WIRE (Jan. 27, 2022), https://www.privateequitywire.co.uk/2022/01/27/311601/harbour-point-capital-completes-investment-midwest-medical-transport.

60. Rebecca Pifer, *Ground Ambulance Costs Continue to Soar, Study Finds*, HEALTH CARE DIVE (Feb. 22, 2022), https://www.healthcaredive.com/news/ground-ambulance-costs-continue-to-soar-study-finds/619195/.

61. *Analysis: Half of Emergency Ambulance Rides Lead to Out-of-Network Bills for Privately Insured Patients*, KAISER FAMILY FOUNDATION (June 24, 2021), https://www.kff.org/health-costs/press-release/analysis-half-of-emergency-ambulance-rides-lead-to-out-of-network-bills-for-privately-insured-patients/.

62. Loren Adler, *High Air Ambulance Charges Concentrated in Private Equity–Owned Carriers*, BROOKINGS INSTITUTION (Oct. 13, 2020), https://www.brookings.edu/blog

/usc-brookings-schaeffer-on-health-policy/2020/10/13/high-air-ambulance-charges
-concentrated-in-private-equity-owned-carriers/.

63. David Lohr, *Arizona Firefighters Charge Family Nearly $20,000 After Home Burns Down*, HuffPost (Nov. 11, 2013), https://www.huffpost.com/entry/justin-purcell-fire _n_4242734.

64. *Id.*

65. Ivory *et al.*, *supra* note 57.

66. *Henry Kravis*, Bloomberg, https://www.bloomberg.com/billionaires/profiles /henry-r-kravis/.

67. *Two Decades of Change in Federal and State Higher Education Funding*, Pew Charitable Trust (2019), https://www.pewtrusts.org/en/research-and-analysis/issue-briefs/2019/10 /two-decades-of-change-in-federal-and-state-higher-education-funding.

68. *Id.* (In 1990, state per student funding was almost 140 percent more than federal government. As of 2018, state per student funding was 18 percent more than the federal government.)

69. *Tuition Costs of Colleges and Universities*, National Center for Education Statistics, https://nces.ed.gov/fastfacts/display.asp?id=76.

70. Richard D. Kahlenberg *et al.*, *Policy Strategies for Pursuing Adequate Funding of Community Colleges*, Century Foundation (Oct. 25, 2018), https://tcf.org/content /report/policy-strategies-pursuing-adequate-funding-community-colleges/; Melanie Hanson, *Average Cost of Community College*, Education Data Initiative (Dec. 27, 2021), https://educationdata.org/average-cost-of-community-college.

71. Alex Goldstein & Jim Baker, *Private Equity's Failing Grade: Private Equity Investment in For-Profit Colleges*, Private Equity Stakeholder Project 10 (Mar. 2018), https:// pestakeholder.org/wp-content/uploads/2018/03/Private-Equitys-Failing-Grade-PESP -AFR-032218-2.pdf.

72. Stephanie Hall, *The Students Funneled into For-Profit Colleges*, Century Found. (May 11, 2021), https://tcf.org/content/report/students-funneled-profit-colleges/.

73. *10 Key Facts About Student Debt in the United States*, Peter G. Peterson Foundation (May 5, 2021), https://www.pgpf.org/blog/2021/05/10-key-facts-about-student -debt-in-the-united-states.

74. Hall, *supra* note 72.

75. Stephanie Riegg Cellini, *The Alarming Rise in For-Profit College Enrollment*, Brookings Institution (Nov. 2, 2020), https://www.brookings.edu/blog/brown-center -chalkboard/2020/11/02/the-alarming-rise-in-for-profit-college-enrollment/.

76. Charlie Eaton *et al.*, *When Investor Incentives and Consumer Interests Diverge: Private Equity in Higher Education* 2 (Nat'l Bureau of Econ. Rsch., Working Paper No. 24976, 2019) https://www.nber.org/papers/w24976.

77. Complaint ¶ 26, *California v. Ashford University, LLC et al.*, No. 37-2018-00046134 (Cal. Super. Ct., Alameda Cty. Nov. 29, 2017).

78. Bridgepoint Education, Inc.: A Case Study in For-Profit Education and Oversight, S. Hrg. 112-774 (Mar. 10, 2011), https://www.govinfo.gov/content/pkg/CHRG -112shrg81200/html/CHRG-112shrg81200.htm.

79. *Id.*

80. Complaint, *California v. Ashford University, LLC et al.*, No. 37-2018-00046134 (Cal. Super. Ct., Alameda Cty. Nov. 29, 2017).

81. *Id.* at ¶ 29.

82. *Id.* at ¶ 116.

83. *Veterans Education Success,* VETERAN AND SERVICEMEMBER COMPLAINTS ABOUT MISCONDUCT AND ILLEGAL PRACTICES AT ASHFORD UNIVERSITY 12 (2017), https:// vetsedsuccess.org/wp-content/uploads/2018/09/VES-Ashford-Report-2017-Fall.pdf.

84. *Id.*

85. Complaint at ¶ 37, *California v. Ashford University, LLC et al.*, No. 37-2018-00046134 (Cal. Super. Ct., Alameda Cty. Nov. 29, 2017). Ashford was eventually found guilty. Statement of Decision, *California v. Ashford University, LLC et al.*, (Cal. Super. Ct., San Diego Cty Nov. 8, 2021).

86. Complaint ¶ 107, *California v. Ashford University, LLC et al.*, No. 37-2018-00046134 (Cal. Super. Ct., Alameda Cty. Nov. 29, 2017).

87. *Id.*

88. *Id.* at ¶ 34.

89. *Trends in College Pricing and Student Aid 2021,* COLLEGE BOARD 3 (2021), https:// research.collegeboard.org/media/pdf/trends-college-pricing-student-aid-2021.pdf.

90. Complaint, *California v. Ashford University, LLC et al.*, No. 37-2018-00046134 (Cal. Super. Ct., Alameda Cty. Nov. 29, 2017).

91. *Veteran and Servicemember Complaints About Misconduct and Illegal Practices at Ashford University,* VETERANS EDUCATION SUCCESS 8 (2017), https://vetsedsuccess.org/wp -content/uploads/2018/09/VES-Ashford-Report-2017-Fall.pdf.

92. *Id.* at 12.

93. Complaint ¶ 48, *California v. Ashford University, LLC et al.*, No. 37-2018-00046134 (Cal. Super. Ct., Alameda Cty. Nov. 29, 2017).

94. *Id.* at ¶ 8.

95. *Id.* at ¶ 3.

96. *Id.* at ¶ 43.

97. *Attorney General Bonta: Ashford University Must Pay $22 Million in Penalties for Defrauding California Students,* CALIFORNIA DEPARTMENT OF JUSTICE (Mar. 7, 2022), https://oag.ca.gov/news/press-releases/attorney-general-bonta-ashford-university-must -pay-22-million-penalties.

98. *See, e.g.,* Bridgepoint Education, Inc., *supra* note 78 (In their materials to *U.S. News & World Report,* the college said that "[f]ounded in 1918, Ashford University is committed to providing accessible, affordable, innovative, high-quality degree programs to its campus, online, and accelerated students.").

99. Shellie Nelson, *Ashford University to Close Campus in Clinton, Iowa,* WQAD NEWS 8 (July 9, 2015), https://www.wqad.com/article/news/education/ashford-university-to -close-campus-in-clinton-iowa/526-f5b9cde9-b200-496b-84a9-07890263f254.

100. Tamar Lewin, *Hearing Sees Financial Success and Education Failures of For-Profit College,* N.Y. TIMES (Mar. 10, 2011), https://www.nytimes.com/2011/03/11/education /11college.html.

101. Bridgepoint Education, Inc., *supra* note 78.

102. *Id.*

103. *Consumer Financial Protection Bureau Takes Action Against Bridgepoint Education, Inc. for Illegal Student Lending Practices,* CONSUMER FINANCIAL PROTECTION BUREAU (Sept. 12, 2016), https://www.consumerfinance.gov/about-us/newsroom/consumer-financial-protection -bureau-takes-action-against-bridgepoint-education-inc-illegal-student-lending- practices/.

104. *Ashford University and Parent Company Bridgepoint Education Agree to $7.25 Million Payment and Major Changes After Miller Alleges Consumer Fraud,* OFFICE OF THE IOWA

ATTORNEY GENERAL (May 16, 2014), https://www.iowaattorneygeneral.gov/newsroom
/ashford-university-and-parent-company-bridgepoint-education-agree-to-7-25-million
-payment-and-majo.

105. *Law Enforcement Actions Against Predatory Colleges*, DEPARTMENT OF EDUCATION
(2018), https://sites.ed.gov/naciqi/files/2018/05/NACIQI-Enclosure-1-law-enforcement
.pdf.

106. Jake Steinberg, *UA Acquires For-Profit Ashford University, Launches New Online
"Campus."* ARIZ. PUB. MEDIA (Dec. 1, 2020), https://news.azpm.org/p/news-splash
/2020/12/1/184791-ua-acquires-for-profit-ashford-university-launches-new-online
-campus/ (Ashford was sold for a symbolic one dollar, but Zovio, Ashford's parent, was
entitled to over 19 percent of the tuition revenue coming from the school).

107. *Bridgepoint Education, Inc.*, PROSPECTUS (Aug. 3, 2011), https://www.sec.gov
/Archives/edgar/data/1305323/000119312511208297/d424b3.htm ("In January 2004,
our principal investor, Warburg Pincus Private Equity VIII, L.P. ('Warburg Pincus'),
and our CEO and president, Andrew Clark, as well as several other members of our
current executive management team, launched Bridgepoint Education, Inc. to establish a differentiated postsecondary education provider."). Andrew Clark, *How I Did
It: Andrew Clark, Bridgepoint Education*, INC.COM (Sept. 1, 2008), https://www.inc.com
/magazine/20080901/how-i-did-it-andrew-clark-bridgepoint-education.html (Andrew
Clark, cofounder of Bridgepoint's parent company, said that "I started knocking on the
doors of investors and soon forged a relationship with Warburg Pincus.").

108. Melissa Korn, *Bridgepoint Investor Files for Stake Sale*, WALL ST. J. (July 25, 2011),
https://www.wsj.com/articles/SB10001424053111903591104576468193396752056;
Megha Mandavia, *Investors Seen as Too Tough on Bridgepoint*, REUTERS (July 23, 2012),
https://www.reuters.com/article/us-bridgepoint-accreditation/investors-seen-as-too
-tough-on-bridgepoint-idUSBRE86M12I20120723.

109. *Bridgepoint Education, Inc.*, U.S. SENATE COMMITTEE ON HEALTH, EDUCATION, LA-
BOR AND PENSIONS 2, https://www.help.senate.gov/imo/media/for_profit_report/PartII
/Bridgepoint.pdf.

110. Senator Harkin's hearing was in March 2011. Warburg Pincus filed papers
to divest in July of that year. Tamar Lewin, *Hearing Sees Financial Success and Education Failures of For-Profit College*, N.Y. TIMES (Mar. 10, 2011), https://www.nytimes
.com/2011/03/11/education/11college.html; Melissa Korn, *Bridgepoint Investor Files for
Stake Sale*, WALL ST. J. (July 25, 2011), https://www.wsj.com/articles/SB1000142405311
1903591104576468193396752056.

111. Bridgepoint Education, Inc., *supra* note 78.

112. *Bridgepoint Education (BPI) Prices 7.56M Share Secondary Offering by Warburg Pincus LLC; Announces 2.1M Share Buyback*, STREET INSIDER (Nov. 17, 2017), https://www
.streetinsider.com/Corporate+News/Bridgepoint+Education+(BPI)+Prices+7.56M+Share
+Secondary+Offering+by+Warburg+Pincus+LLC;+Announces+2.1M+Share+Buyback
/13521346.html.

113. *Zovio*, WIKIPEDIA, https://en.wikipedia.org/wiki/Zovio ("On November 15,
2017, Bridgepoint suspended enrolling GI Bill students for Ashford University after
a controversial exposé on the school appeared in the *Chronicle of Higher Education*. On
November 17, 2017, Warburg Pincus, Bridgeport Education's major underwriter, announced its complete divestment from Bridgepoint.").

114. Bridgepoint Education, Inc., *supra* note 78.

115. Goldstein and Baker, *supra* note 71, at 2.

116. Ben Unglesbee, *Private Equity's Role in the Rise—and Fall—of For-Profit Colleges*, HIGHER ED DEEP DIVE (May 6, 2019), https://www.highereddive.com/news/private -equitys-role-in-the-rise-and-fall-of-for-profit-colleges/554077/.

117. *For-Profit College Company to Pay $95.5 Million to Settle Claims of Illegal Recruiting, Consumer Fraud and Other Violations*, DEPARTMENT OF JUSTICE (Nov. 16, 2015), https:// www.justice.gov/opa/pr/profit-college-company-pay-955-million-settle-claims-illegal -recruiting-consumer-fraud-and (As part of the settlement, Education Management did not admit to any liability).

118. *For-Profit Education Company to Pay $13 Million to Resolve Several Cases Alleging Submission of False Claims for Federal Student Aid*, DEPARTMENT OF JUSTICE (June 24, 2015), https://www.justice.gov/opa/pr/profit-education-company-pay-13-million-resolve -several-cases-alleging-submission-false (As part of the settlement, Education Affiliates did not admit to any liability).

119. Hayley Brown, *Private Equity in Higher Education: A Full Ride at Student and Taxpayer Expense?*, CENTER FOR ECONOMIC AND POLICY RESEARCH, https://cepr.net/private -equity-in-higher-education-a-full-ride-at-student-and-taxpayer-expense/; *Vatterott College System Closes All 15 Campuses*, ASSOCIATED PRESS (Dec. 18, 2018), https://apnews .com/article/us-news-education-st-louis-us-department-of-education-71a07fb863bf4e459 a7f1c2417cb1ecd; *Major For-Profit College Chain Abruptly Announces Closure of Dozens of Schools*, NBC NEWS (Dec. 6, 2018), https://www.nbcnews.com/news/education/major -profit-college-chain-abruptly-announces-closure-dozens-schools-n944696.

120. Complaint ¶ 30, *California v. Ashford University, LLC et al.*, No. 37-2018- 00046134 (Cal. Super. Ct., Alameda Cty. Nov. 29, 2017) (specifically, Ashford got between 80.9 and 86.8 percent of its revenue from the federal government).

121. Goldstein & Baker, *supra* note 71, at 2.

122. Allie Bidwell, *Education Department's Gainful Employment Rules Rebuffed*, U.S. NEWS & WORLD REPORT (Oct. 30, 2014), https://www.usnews.com/news/articles/2014/10/30 /obama-administrations-gainful-employment-rules-upset-student-groups-for-profits.

123. Danielle Douglas-Gabriel, *Biden Administration Clashes with Consumer Groups over the Reinstatement of Obama-Era Career Training Regulation*, WASH. POST (Nov. 18, 2021), https://www.washingtonpost.com/education/2021/11/17/gainful-employment -rule-biden-administration/.

124. Goldstein & Baker, *supra* note 71, at 5; Paul Fain, *Some U of Phoenix Programs Fail Gainful Employment Standard*, INSIDE HIGHER ED (Nov. 28, 2016), https:// www.insidehighered.com/quicktakes/2016/11/28/some-u-phoenix-programs-fail -gainful-employment-standard.

125. Goldstein & Baker, *supra* note 71, at 6.

126. Fain, *supra* note 124.

127. Jackie Roberts, *Erie's Fortis Institute to Close Its Doors*, YOUR ERIE (July 18, 2018), https://www.yourerie.com/news/local-news/eries-fortis-institute-to-close-its -doors/; *Fortis Institute-Baltimore*, COLLEGE TUITION COMPARE, https://www.collegetuition compare.com/edu/450076/fortis-institute-baltimore/.

128. Karen Campbell & Tim Tooten, *Brightwood College Suddenly Closes Leaving Students Frustrated*, WBAL-TV (Dec. 6, 2018), https://www.wbaltv.com/article/brightwood-college -suddenly-closes-leaving-students-frustrated/25425539.

129. Institute for College Access & Success, *Fact Sheet: What to Know About the Gainful Employment Rule,* HIGHER ED NOT DEBT (August 12, 2019), https://higherednotdebt .org/blog/fact-sheet-what-to-know-about-the-gainful-employment-rule.

130. Eric Lichtblau, *With Lobbying Blitz, For-Profit Colleges Diluted New Rules*, N.Y. TIMES (Dec. 9, 2011), https://www.nytimes.com/2011/12/10/us/politics/for-profit-college -rules-scaled-back-after-lobbying.html.

131. Russ Choma, *Rep. Kline Turns Chairmanship into Profitable For-Profit Haul*, OPEN SE- CRETS (July 15, 2013), https://www.opensecrets.org/news/2013/07/for-profit-education/; *The Gainful Employment Regulation: Limiting Job Growth and Student Choice*, House SUB- COMMITTEE ON REGULATORY AFFAIRS OF THE COMMITTEE ON OVERSIGHT AND GOVERN- MENT REFORM *ET AL.*, 11th Cong. (2012), https://www.govinfo.gov/content/pkg/CHRG -112hhrg71822/html/CHRG-112hhrg71822.htm; *Education Regulations: Roadblocks to Student Choice in Higher Education*, HOUSE COMMITTEE ON EDUCATION AND THE WORKFORCE, 112th Cong. (2011), https://www.govinfo.gov/content/pkg/CHRG-112hhrg65011/html /CHRG-112hhrg65011.htm.

132. Joseph Ax, *Judge Upholds U.S. "Gainful Employment" Rules for For-Profit Colleges*, REUTERS (May 25, 2015), https://www.reuters.com/article/us-usa-education-lawsuit /judge-upholds-u-s-gainful-employment-rules-for-for-profit-colleges-idUSKBN0 OC2J520150527.

133. *Id.*; Andy Thomason, *Federal Court Upholds Gainful-Employment Rule, Dealing For- Profit Group Another Loss*, CHRONICLE OF HIGHER EDUCATION (Mar. 8, 2016), https://www .chronicle.com/blogs/ticker/federal-court-upholds-gainful-employment-rule-dealing -for-profit-group-another-loss.

134. Danielle Douglas-Gabriel, *Biden Administration Clashes with Consumer Groups over the Reinstatement of Obama-Era Career Training Regulation*, WASH. POST (Nov. 18, 2021), https://www.washingtonpost.com/education/2021/11/17/gainful-employment -rule-biden-administration/.

135. Erica L. Green, *DeVos Repeals Obama-Era Rule Cracking Down on For-Profit Colleges*, N.Y. TIMES (June 28, 2019), https://www.nytimes.com/2019/06/28/us/politics /betsy-devos-for-profit-colleges.html.

136. Douglas-Gabriel, *supra* note 134.

137. Ben Miller & Laura Jimenez, *Inside the Financial Holdings of Billionaire Betsy De- Vos*, CENTER FOR AMERICAN PROGRESS (Jan. 27, 2017), https://www.americanprogress .org/article/inside-the-financial-holdings-of-billionaire-betsy-devos/.

138. Hayley Brown, *Private Equity in Higher Education: A Full Ride at Student and Taxpayer Expense?*, CENTER FOR ECONOMIC AND POLICY RESEARCH, https://cepr.net /private-equity-in-higher-education-a-full-ride-at-student-and-taxpayer-expense/.

139. Patricia Cohen, *Betsy DeVos's Hiring of For-Profit College Official Raises Impartial- ity Issues*, N.Y. TIMES (Mar. 17, 2017), https://www.nytimes.com/2017/03/17/business /education-for-profit-robert-eitel.html; Erin Dooley, *Exclusive: Former For-Profit Col- lege Executive Shaped Education Department Policy That Could Benefit Former Employers: Documents*, ABC NEWS (May 15, 2018), https://abcnews.go.com/US/exclusive-profit -college-executive-shaped-education-department-policy/story?id=55108981. Eitel began working for the Department of Education without leaving his old job, simply taking an unpaid leave of absence. He finally gave up his private employment in April 2018, after being hired to work full-time as a senior adviser to Secretary DeVos.

140. Stacy Cowley, *Delayed Obama-Era Rule on Student Debt Relief Is to Take Effect*, N.Y. TIMES (Oct. 16, 2018), https://www.nytimes.com/2018/10/16/business/student-loan -debt-relief.html.

141. Danielle Douglas-Gabriel, *House Falls Short of Overriding Trump's Veto of Measure to Overturn Student Loan Forgiveness Rule*, WASH. POST (June 26, 2020), https://www

.washingtonpost.com/education/2020/06/26/house-falls-short-overriding-trumps-veto
-measure-overturn-student-loan-forgiveness-rule/.

142. *Id.*

CHAPTER 10: THE INDUSTRY'S STRONGEST ADVOCATES

1. *Totals*, OPEN SECRETS, https://www.opensecrets.org/industries/totals.php?cycle
=2022&ind=F2600.

2. *Id.*

3. *Client Profile: KKR & Co*, OPEN SECRETS, https://www.opensecrets.org/federal
-lobbying/clients/lobbyists?cycle=2022&id=D000000358 (former reps. Dennis Car-
doza and Scott Klug lobbied for KKR); *Client Profile: Apollo Global Management*, OPEN
SECRETS, https://www.opensecrets.org/federal-lobbying/clients/lobbyists?cycle=2021
&id=D000021845&t0-Former+Members+of+Congress=Former+Members+of+Congress
(former senators Mark Pryor and Steven Symms lobbied for Apollo); *Client Profile: Blackstone
Group*, OPEN SECRETS, https://www.opensecrets.org/federal-lobbying/clients/lobbyists?cy
cle=2021&id=D000021873&t0-Former+Members+of+Congress=Former+Members+of
+Congress (former representative Luke Messer lobbied for Blackstone); *Client Profile: Carlyle
Group*, OPEN SECRETS, https://www.opensecrets.org/federal-lobbying/clients/lobbyists?
cycle=2020&id=D000000810&t0-Former+Members+of+Congress=Former+Members
+of+Congress (former representative Ileana Ros-Lehtinen lobbied for Carlyle).

4. *Employment History: Bayh, Evan*, OPEN SECRETS, https://www.opensecrets.org
/revolving/rev_summary.php?id=76382 (former senator Birch Bayh serves as a senior adviser to Apollo); *Corporate Governance*, BLACKSTONE, https://ir.blackstone.com/corporate
-governance/default.aspx (former Senator Kelly Ayotte serves on the board of Blackstone).

5. People who lobbied for Carlyle included Stacey A. Dion, former counsel to the
House Republican leader, Jeff Forbes, former chief of staff to Senator Max Baucus; Libby
Greer, former chief of staff to Congressman Allen Boyd, Dan Tate, former special assis-
tant to the president; Ryan Welch, former legislative director to Richard Shelby; *Client
Profile: Carlyle Group, supra* note 3; *Lobbyist Profile: Stacey A Dion*, OPEN SECRETS, https://
www.opensecrets.org/federal-lobbying/lobbyists/official_positions?cycle=2022&id
=Y0000037370L; *Stacey Dion*, LINKEDIN, https://www.linkedin.com/in/staceydion/;
Lobbyist Profile: Jeff Forbes, OPEN SECRETS, https://www.opensecrets.org/federal-lobbying
/lobbyists/official_positions?cycle=2022&id=Y0000032896L; *Lobbyist Profile: Libby Greer*,
OPEN SECRETS, https://www.opensecrets.org/federal-lobbying/lobbyists/official_positions
?cycle=2022&id=Y0000038065L; *Lobbyist Profile: Dan C Jr Tate*, OPEN SECRETS,
https://www.opensecrets.org/federal-lobbying/lobbyists/official_positions?cycle=2022
&id=Y0000040940L; *Lobbyist Profile: Ryan Welch*, OPEN SECRETS, https://www.open
secrets.org/federal-lobbying/lobbyists/official_positions?cycle=2022&id=Y0000042198L.

6. Chad Terhune, *Life-Threatening Heart Attack Leaves Teacher with $108,951 Bill*, NPR
(Aug. 27, 2018), https://www.npr.org/sections/health-shots/2018/08/27/640891882
/life-threatening-heart-attack-leaves-teacher-with-108-951-bill.

7. *Id.*

8. *Id.*

9. *Id.*

10. *Private Equity Is the Driving Force Behind Surprise Medical Billing*, AMERICANS
FOR FINANCIAL REFORM (Oct. 2021), https://ourfinancialsecurity.org/2021/10/fact
-sheet-private-equity-is-the-driving-force-behind-surprise-medical-billing/.

11. Rachel Bluth & Emmarie Huetterman, *Investors' Deep-Pocket Push to Defend Surprise Medical Bills*, KAISER HEALTH NEWS (Sept. 11, 2019), https://khn.org/news/investors-deep-pocket-push-to-defend-surprise-medical-bills/.

12. Eileen Appelbaum & Rosemary Batt, *Private Equity and Surprise Medical Billing*, INST. FOR NEW ECON. THINKING (Sept. 4, 2019), https://www.ineteconomics.org/perspectives/blog/private-equity-and-surprise-medical-billing.

13. Karen Pollitz *et al.*, *An Examination of Surprise Medical Bills and Proposals to Protect Consumers from Them*, PETERSON-KFF HEALTH SYSTEM TRACKER (Feb. 10, 2020), https://www.healthsystemtracker.org/brief/an-examination-of-surprise-medical-bills-and-proposals-to-protect-consumers-from-them-3/.

14. *Air Ambulance: Available Data Show Privately-Insured Patients Are at Financial Risk*, GOVERNMENT ACCOUNTABILITY OFFICE 2 (Mar. 2019), https://www.gao.gov/assets/gao-19-292.pdf.

15. Bluth & Huetterman, *supra* note 11.

16. Julie Creswell *et al.*, *Mystery Solved: Private-Equity-Backed Firms Are Behind Ad Blitz on "Surprise Billing,"* N.Y. TIMES (Sept. 13, 2019), https://www.nytimes.com/2019/09/13/upshot/surprise-billing-laws-ad-spending-doctor-patient-unity.html.

17. *TeamHealth Named to Fortune Magazine's List of "World's Most Admired Companies" for Third Consecutive Year*, TEAMHEALTH, https://www.teamhealth.com/news-and-resources/press-release/teamhealth-named-to-fortune-magazines-list-of-worlds-most-admired-companies-for-third-consecutive-year/?r=1.

18. Joel Stinnett, *Completion of $9.9B Deal Leaves Nashville with One Fewer Public Health Care Company*, NASHV. BUS. J. (Oct. 11, 2018), https://www.bizjournals.com/nashville/news/2018/10/11/completion-of-9-9b-deal-leaves-nashville-with-one.html.

19. Envision Healthcare Corporation, *Form 10-K* (Feb. 23, 2018), https://www.sec.gov/Archives/edgar/data/1678531/000167853118000033/evhc10k20171231.htm.

20. Miriam Gottfried, *Ill-Timed Health-Care Buyouts Bruise KKR and Blackstone*, WALL ST. J. (May 28, 2020), https://www.wsj.com/articles/ill-timed-health-care-buyouts-bruise-kkr-and-blackstone-11590658201; Gretchen Morgenson & Emmanuelle Saliba, *Private Equity Firms Now Control Many Hospitals, ERs and Nursing Homes. Is It Good for Health Care?*, NBC NEWS (May 13, 2020), https://www.nbcnews.com/health/health-care/private-equity-firms-now-control-many-hospitals-ers-nursing-homes-n1203161.

21. Loren Adler *et al.*, *High Air Ambulance Charges Concentrated in Private Equity–Owned Carriers*, BROOKINGS INSTITUTION (Oct. 13, 2020), https://www.brookings.edu/blog/usc-brookings-schaeffer-on-health-policy/2020/10/13/high-air-ambulance-charges-concentrated-in-private-equity-owned-carriers/.

22. Olivia Webb, *Private Equity Chases Ambulances*, AM. PROSPECT (Oct. 3, 2019), https://prospect.org/health/private-equity-chases-ambulances-emergency-medical-transport/.

23. Adler *et al.*, *supra* note 21.

24. Danielle Ivory *et al.*, *When You Dial 911 and Wall Street Answers*, N.Y. TIMES (June 25, 2016), https://www.nytimes.com/2016/06/26/business/dealbook/when-you-dial-911-and-wall-street-answers.html.

25. Julie Creswell *et al.*, *The Company Behind Many Surprise Emergency Room Bills*, N.Y. TIMES (July 24, 2017), https://www.nytimes.com/2017/07/24/upshot/the-company-behind-many-surprise-emergency-room-bills.html.

26. *Id.*

27. *Id.*

28. Richard M. Scheffler, *Soaring Private Equity Investment in the Healthcare Sector: Consolidation Accelerated, Competition Undermined, and Patients at Risk*, AMERICAN ANTITRUST

INSTITUTE 13 (May 2021), https://publichealth.berkeley.edu/wp-content/uploads/2021/05/Private-Equity-I-Healthcare-Report-FINAL.pdf.

29. Creswell *et al.*, *supra* note 25.

30. *Id.*

31. Appelbaum & Batt, *supra* note 12.

32. Paul McLeod, *A Deal to End Surprise Medical Billing Was Tanked at the Last Minute*, BUZZFEED NEWS (Dec. 19, 2019), https://www.buzzfeednews.com/article/paulmcleod/surprise-billing-deal-richard-neal.

33. *Id.*

34. Zack Cooper *et al.*, *Surprise! Out-of-Network Billing for Emergency Care in the United States*, 128 J. OF POLITICAL ECONOMY 3626–3677 (2020), https://isps.yale.edu/research/publications/isps17-22.

35. TeamHealth owes $2.7 billion by 2024, Envision owes $5.4 billion by 2021. Eileen Appelbaum & Rosemary Batt, *Why It's So Hard to End Surprise Medical Bills*, CENTER FOR ECONOMIC POLICY RESEARCH (Feb. 19, 2020), https://cepr.net/report/why-its-so-hard-to-end-surprise-medical-bills/.

36. Eileen Applebaum, *A Surprise Ending for Surprise Billing?*, AM. PROSPECT (Dec. 16, 2020), https://prospect.org/health/surprise-ending-for-surprise-billing/.

37. Creswell *et al.*, *supra* note 25.

38. *Id.*

39. Applebaum & Batt, *supra* note 35.

40. Jessie Hellman, *Private Equity–Funded Doctors Coalition Spends $4 Million Lobbying on "Surprise" Medical Billing*, THE HILL (Oct. 21, 2019), https://thehill.com/policy/healthcare/466756-doctors-coalition-funded-by-private-equity-spends-4-million-lobbying-on/.

41. *Physicians for Fair Coverage*, POLITIFACT (Aug. 7, 2019), https://www.politifact.com/factchecks/2019/aug/07/physicians-fair-coverage/doctors-argue-plans-remedy-surprise-medical-bills-/.

42. Bob Herman, *Doctors Flood Congress with Lobbyists on Surprise Medical Bills*, AXIOS (Aug. 20, 2019), https://www.axios.com/2019/08/20/surprise-medical-billing-lobbying-congress; *Client: US Physician Partners (Informal Coalition), Lobbying Firm: Akin, Gump, Strauss, Hauer & Feld*, PROPUBLICA (July 1, 2019–June 30, 2022), https://projects.propublica.org/represent/lobbying/r/301022149.

43. Herman, *supra* note at 42.

44. Adam Lewis, *PE Digs in as Battle to End Surprise Medical Bills Rages On*, PITCHBOOK (Mar. 6, 2020), https://pitchbook.com/news/articles/pe-digs-in-as-battle-to-end-surprise-medical-bills-wages-on.

45. *Ways and Means Committee Surprise Medical Billing Plan*, HOUSE COMMITTEE ON WAYS AND MEANS, https://waysandmeans.house.gov/sites/democrats.waysandmeans.house.gov/files/documents/WM%20Surprise%20Billing%20Summary.pdf.

46. McLeod, *supra* note 32.

47. Paul McLeod, *Surprise Medical Billing Is Finally Coming to an End After Congress Reached a Last-Minute Deal*, BUZZFEED NEWS (Dec. 22, 2020), https://www.buzzfeednews.com/article/paulmcleod/suprise-medical-billing-banned-congress-coronavirus; Akela Lacy, *Effort to Take on Surprise Medical Billing in Coronavirus Stimulus Collapses*, THE INTERCEPT (Dec. 8 2020), https://theintercept.com/2020/12/08/surprise-medical-billing-neal-covid/ (One member of Congress said, "The one stumbling block has been of course, Richie trying to scuttle it." Neal himself said he wanted to wait another year to address the issue).

48. McLeod, *supra* note 47.

49. Susannah Luthi & Rachel Roubein, *How Powerful Health Providers Tamed a "Surprise" Billing Threat*, POLITICO (Dec. 21, 2020), https://www.politico.com/news/2020/12/21/surprise-billing-health-providers-congress-449759.

50. Andrew Hurst, *Ambulance Rides Have Cost $1,189 on Average Since 2010—Totaling More Than $46 Billion*, VALUEPENGUIN (Sept. 13, 2021), https://www.valuepenguin.com/cost-ambulance-services.

51. Hailey Mensik, *Ground Ambulances, Excluded from Surprise Billing Ban, to Get Scrutiny from Federal Committee*, HEALTHCARE DIVE (Nov. 22, 2021), https://www.healthcaredive.com/news/federal-committee-ground-ambulances-no-surprises-act/610451/.

52. Luthi & Roubein, *supra* note 49.

53. Marty Stempniak, *150 Members of Congress Pressure Administration to Fix Surprise Billing Rule They Say Favors Insurers*, RADIOLOGY BUS. (Nov. 10, 2021), https://radiologybusiness.com/topics/healthcare-policy/congress-administration-surprise-billing-insurers.

54. Thomas Suozzi (D-N.Y.) received $7,500 from US Anesthesia Partners; Brad Wenstrup (R-Ohio) received $11,200 from Blackstone; Raul Ruiz (D-Calif.) received $31,605 from KKR (his largest contribution that cycle); Larry Bucshon (R-Ind.) received $12,500 from US Anesthesia Partners. US Anesthesia Partners was in turned owned by Welsh, Carson, Anderson & Stowe. *Tom Suozzi*, OPEN SECRETS, https://www.opensecrets.org/members-of-congress/tom-suozzi/contributors?cid=N00038742&cycle=2020&recs=100&type=I; *Brad Wenstrup*, OPEN SECRETS, https://www.opensecrets.org/members-of-congress/brad-wenstrup/contributors?cid=N00033310&cycle=2020&recs=100&type=I; *Raul Ruiz*, OPEN SECRETS, https://www.opensecrets.org/members-of-congress/raul-ruiz/contributors?cid=N00033510&cycle=2020&type=I; *Larry Bucshon*, OPEN SECRETS, https://www.opensecrets.org/members-of-congress/larry-bucshon/contributors?cid=N00031227&cycle=2020&recs=100&type=I; *Welsh, Carson, Anderson & Stowe and Healthcare Industry Veteran Announce Formation of U.S. Anesthesia Partners, Inc.*, US ANESTHESIA PARTNERS, https://www.usap.com/news-and-events/news/welsh-carson-anderson-stowe-and-healthcare-industry-veteran-announce-formation.

55. *Bill Cassidy*, OPEN SECRETS, https://www.opensecrets.org/members-of-congress/bill-cassidy/contributors?cid=N00030245&cycle=2020&recs=100&type=I.

56. *Maggie Hassan*, OPEN SECRETS, https://www.opensecrets.org/members-of-congress/maggie-hassan/contributors?cid=N00038397&cycle=2020&recs=100&type=I; https://www.opensecrets.org/members-of-congress/maggie-hassan/contributors?cid=N00038397&cycle=2020&recs=100&type=I. US Acute Care Solutions was then owned by Welsh Carson Anderson & Stowe.

57. Austin Ahlman, *Congressional Democrats Join Republicans to Undermine Biden Administration's Surprise Medical Billing Rule*, THE INTERCEPT (Jan. 17 2022), https://theintercept.com/2022/01/17/surprise-medical-billing-lawsuit/.

58. *Kevin Brady*, OPEN SECRETS, https://www.opensecrets.org/members-of-congress/kevin-brady/contributors?cid=N00005883&cycle=2020&recs=100&type=I; Austin Ahlman, *Congressional Democrats Join Republicans to Undermine Biden Administration's Surprise Medical Billing Rule*, THE INTERCEPT (Jan. 17, 2022), https://theintercept.com/2022/01/17/surprise-medical-billing-lawsuit/.

59. *Richard E Neal*, OPEN SECRETS, https://www.opensecrets.org/members-of-congress/richard-e-neal/contributors?cid=N00000153&cycle=2020&recs=100&type=I.

60. *AHA, AMA and Others File Lawsuit over No Surprises Act Rule That Jeopardizes Access to Care*, American Hospital Association (Dec. 9, 2021), https://www.aha.org /news/news/2021-12-09-aha-ama-and-others-file-lawsuit-over-no-surprises-act-rule -jeopardizes-access.

61. Victor Fleischer, *Two and Twenty: Taxing Partnership Profits in Private Equity Funds*, 83 NYU L. Rev. 1 (2008) (While published in 2008, the draft article reached congressional staffers in 2006); Andrew Ross Sorkin, *A Professor's Word on a Buyout Tax Battle*, N.Y. Times (Oct. 3, 2007), https://www.nytimes.com/2007/10/03/business/03tax.html.

62. H.R. 3970, Tax Reduction and Reform Act of 2007, 110th Cong. (2007); *Levin— Legislation Fixes Carried Interest Loophole*, House Ways & Means Committee (Jan. 18, 2012), https://waysandmeans.house.gov/media-center/press-releases/levin-legislation -fixes-carried-interest-loophole; Louis Jacobson & Molly Moorhead, *Tax Carried Interest as Ordinary Encome*, PolitiFact (Jan. 2, 2013), https://www.politifact.com/truth-o-meter /promises/obameter/promise/42/tax-carried-interest-as-ordinary-income/.

63. *Client Profile: Blackstone Group, supra* note 3.

64. *Apollo Global Management*, Open Secrets, https://www.opensecrets.org/orgs/apollo -global-management/lobbying?id=D000021845; *KKR & Co*, Open Secrets, https:// www.opensecrets.org/orgs/kkr-co/lobbying?id=D000000358; *Carlyle Group*, Open Secrets, https://www.opensecrets.org/orgs/carlyle-group/lobbying?id=D000000810.

65. Peter Lattman, *Carried Interest Tax Break Comes Under Fire Again*, N.Y. Times (Sept. 12, 2011), https://archive.nytimes.com/dealbook.nytimes.com/2011/09/12/carried -interest-tax-break-comes-under-fire-again/.

66. Richard Rubin, *Obama Attacks Carried Interest Again to Shrugs in Congress*, Bloomberg (May 12, 2015), https://www.bloomberg.com/news/articles/2015-05-12 /obama-attacks-carried-interest-again-to-shrugs-in-u-s-congress.

67. *Id.*

68. Alan Rappeport, *Trump Promised to Kill Carried Interest. Lobbyists Kept It Alive.*, N.Y. Times (Dec. 22, 2017), https://www.nytimes.com/2017/12/22/business/trump -carried-interest-lobbyists.html.

69. Justin Elliott & Theodoric Meyer, *Susan Collins Backed Down from a Fight with Private Equity. Now They're Underwriting Her Reelection.*, ProPublica (Oct. 29, 2020), https://www.propublica.org/article/susan-collins-backed-down-from-a-fight-with -private-equity-now-theyre-underwriting-her-reelection.

70. *Susan Collins*, Open Secrets, https://www.opensecrets.org/members-of-congress /susan-collins/contributors?cid=N00000491&cycle=2020&type=I.

71. Elliott & Meyer, *supra* note 69.

72. Alan Rappeport, *Mnuchin's Private Equity Fund Raises $2.5 Billion*, N.Y. Times (Oct. 28, 2021), https://www.nytimes.com/2021/09/20/us/politics/mnuchin-saudi-private -equity.html.

73. Jesse Drucker & Danny Hakim, *Private Inequity: How a Powerful Industry Conquered the Tax System*, N.Y. Times (Sept. 8, 2021), https://www.nytimes.com/2021/06/12/business /private-equity-taxes.html.

74. *Id.*

75. Nancy Cook & Bernie Beckert, *Top Treasury Aide to Leave Administration for Private Equity Trade Group*, Politico (June 7, 2018), https://www.politico.com/story/2018/06 /07/drew-maloney-treasury-leaving-white-house-631547.

76. Allyson Versprille, *Carried-Interest Tax Break Shrinks, Survives in Democrats' Plan*, Bloomberg (Sept. 13, 2021), https://www.bloomberg.com/news/articles/2021-09-13

/house-democrats-maintain-a-scaled-back-private-equity-tax-break; Michael A. Bloom et al., *Summer Update: Where Do We Stand on President Biden's Proposal to Eliminate the Carried Interest Loophole?*, VENABLE (July 2021), https://www.venable.com/insights/publications /2021/07/summer-update-where-do-we-stand-on-pres.

77. Versprille, *supra* note 76.

78. Christina Wilkie, *Lobbyists Shielded Carried Interest from Biden's Tax Hikes, Top White House Economist Says*, CNBC (Sept. 30, 2021), https://www.cnbc.com/2021/09 /30/lobbying-kept-carried-interest-out-of-bidens-tax-plan-bernstein-says.html.

79. *Id.*

80. *Id.*

81. *Carlyle Group, supra* note 64; *Blackstone Group*, OPEN SECRETS, https://www.open secrets.org/orgs/blackstone-group/lobbying?id=D000021873; *KKR & Co, supra* note 64.

82. *Apollo Global Management, supra* note 64.

83. *Lobbyist Profile: Marc Lampkin*, OPEN SECRETS, https://www.opensecrets.org/federal -lobbying/lobbyists/official_positions?cycle=2021&id=Y0000015980L5.

84. *Lobbyist Profile: Brian Wild*, OPEN SECRETS, https://www.opensecrets.org/federal -lobbying/lobbyists/official_positions?cycle=2021&id=Y0000009894L.

85. *Lobbyist Profile: Nadeam Elshami*, OPEN SECRETS, https://www.opensecrets.org/federal -lobbying/lobbyists/official_positions?cycle=2021&id=Y0000054026L.

86. *Client Profile: Apollo Global Management, supra* note 3.

87. *Kyrsten Sinema*, OPEN SECRETS, https://www.opensecrets.org/members-of-congress /kyrsten-sinema/contributors?cid=N00033983&cycle=2022.

88. *Reckless Tax and Spend Spree Amendment Tracker*, SENATE REPUBLICAN POLICY COMMITTEE, https://www.rpc.senate.gov/policy-papers/reckless-tax-and-spend-spree -amendment-tracker; Christopher Hickey, *Not the Year for Women and Parents*, CNN (Aug. 12, 2022), https://www.cnn.com/2022/08/12/politics/inflation-reduction-children -families/index.html.

89. Jennifer L. Bragg, *Senate Passes Landmark Bill with Climate, Tax, Energy and Health Care Implications*, SKADDEN (Aug. 7, 2022), https://www.skadden.com/insights /publications/2022/08/senate-passes-landmark-bill.

90. Oscar Valdes-Viera et al., *Public Money for Private Equity: Pandemic Relief Went to Companies Backed by Private Equity Titans*, Anti-Corruption Data Collective ET AL. 2 (2021), https://ourfinancialsecurity.org/wp-content/uploads/2021/09/public-money-for-private -equity-9-13-21.pdf.

91. *Id.* at 8.

92. David Kocieniewski & Caleb Melby, *Private Equity Lands Billion-Dollar Backdoor Hospital Bailout*, BLOOMBERG (June 2, 2020), https://www.bloomberg.com/news /features/2020-06-02/private-equity-lands-billion-dollar-backdoor-hospital-bailout.

93. *Id.*

94. *Id.*; *CMS Announces New Repayment Terms for Medicare Loans Made to Providers During COVID-19*, CENTER FOR MEDICARE AND MEDICAID SERVICES (Oct. 8, 2020), https://www .cms.gov/newsroom/press-releases/cms-announces-new-repayment-terms-medicare -loans-made-providers-during-covid-19.

95. Kocieniewski & Melby, *supra* note 92.

96. Valdes-Viera et al., *supra* note 90, at 7.

97. *Id.* at 21.

98. Ryan Gallagher, *SolarWinds Adviser Warned of Lax Security Years Before Hack*, BLOOMBERG (Dec. 21, 2020), https://www.bloomberg.com/news/articles/2020-12-21 /solarwinds-adviser-warned-of-lax-security-years-before-hack.

99. Drew Harris & Doug MacMillan, *Investors in Breached Software Firm SolarWinds Traded $280 Million in Stock Days Before Hack Was Revealed*, WASH. POST (Dec. 15, 2020), https://www.washingtonpost.com/technology/2020/12/15/solarwinds-russia-breach-stock-trades/.

100. Ezequiel Minaya, *SolarWinds to Be Bought by Silver Lake, Thoma Bravo*, WALL ST. J. (Oct. 21, 2015), https://www.wsj.com/articles/solarwinds-to-be-bought-by-silver-lake-and-thoma-bravo-1445438835.

101. Miriam Gottfried, *Orlando Bravo Rides Software Deals to Heights of Private-Equity Industry*, WALL ST. J. (Sept. 22, 2020), https://www.wsj.com/articles/orlando-bravo-rides-software-deals-to-heights-of-private-equity-industry-11600767001.

102. Antoine Gara, *Buyout Firm Thoma Bravo Goes from Niche to Big League*, FIN. TIMES (Dec. 6 2021), https://www.ft.com/content/456f2fd7-f868-4ea6-abd7-fce34e783333.

103. *E.g.*, *SolarWinds Worldwide, SolarWinds MSP Acquires SpamExperts to Enhance Its Growing Product Portfolio*, GLOBENEWSWIRE (Aug. 29, 2017), https://www.globenewswire.com/news-release/2017/08/29/1101687/0/en/SolarWinds-MSP-Acquires-SpamExperts-to-Enhance-its-Growing-Product-Portfolio.html; *SolarWinds Adds Access Rights Management to Its IT Management Portfolio, Following the Acquisition of 8MAN*, SOLARWINDS (Nov. 15, 2018), https://investors.solarwinds.com/news/news-details/2018/SolarWinds-Adds-Access-Rights-Management-to-Its-IT-Management-Portfolio-following-the-Acquisition-of-8MAN/default.aspx; Frederic Lardinois, *SolarWinds Acquires Real-time Threat-Monitoring Service Trusted Metrics*, TECHCRUNCH (July 10, 2018), https://techcrunch.com/2018/07/10/solarwinds-acquires-real-time-threat-monitoring-service-trusted-metrics/; Frederic Lardinois, *SolarWinds Acquires Log-Monitoring Service Loggly*, TECHCRUNCH (Jan. 8, 2018), https://techcrunch.com/2018/01/08/solarwinds-acquires-log-monitoring-service-loggly/.

104. The *New York Times* reported that the company shifted software engineering resources to Poland, the Czech Republic, and Belarus. The last of these appears to have occurred under Silver Lake and Thoma Bravo's oversight. In the company's 2015 quarterly statement, its last year before its acquisition, it makes no reference to operations in Belarus, while its 2021 financial statement after acquisition does. *Compare* SolarWinds Corporation, *Form 10-Q* (Nov. 3, 2015), https://www.sec.gov/Archives/edgar/data/1428669/000142866915000067/swi-2015930x10q.htm *with* SolarWinds Corporation, *Form 10-K* (Feb. 24, 2021), https://d18rn0p25nwr6d.cloudfront.net/CIK-0001739942/48bd02f7-3c52-4abc-a5e9-60401f9a4e8b.pdf.

105. David E. Sanger *et al.*, *As Understanding of Russian Hacking Grows, So Does Alarm*, N.Y. TIMES (May 28, 2021), https://www.nytimes.com/2021/01/02/us/politics/russian-hacking-government.html. This appears to have occurred during the private equity firms' ownership of the company: between 2020 and 2021, for instance, the company managed to reduce the overall cost of revenue. *2021 Analyst & Investor Day*, SOLARWINDS 75 (2021), https://s22.q4cdn.com/673701899/files/doc_downloads/2021/11/Analyst-Day-PDF-Version-(2).pdf.

106. Ryan Gallagher, *SolarWinds Adviser Warned of Lax Security Years Before Hack*, BLOOMBERG (Dec. 21, 2020), https://www.bloomberg.com/news/articles/2020-12-21/solarwinds-adviser-warned-of-lax-security-years-before-hack.

107. Consolidated Complaint ¶ 8, *In re: SolarWinds Corporation Securities Litigation*, No. 1:21-cv-138 (W.D. Tex. (June 1, 2021), ECF No. 26.

108. Raphael Satte *et al.*, *Hackers Used SolarWinds' Dominance Against It in Sprawling Spy Campaign*, REUTERS (Dec. 15, 2020), https://www.reuters.com/article/global-cyber-solarwinds/hackers-at-center-of-sprawling-spy-campaign-turned-solarwinds-dominance-against-it-idUSKBN28P2N8.

109. *Id.*

110. Consolidated Complaint ¶ 111, *In re: SolarWinds Corporation Securities Litigation,* No. 1:21-cv-138 (W.D. Tex. June 1, 2021), ECF No. 26.

111. David E. Sanger *et al., As Understanding of Russian Hacking Grows, So Does Alarm,* N.Y. TIMES (May 28, 2021), https://www.nytimes.com/2021/01/02/us/politics/russian -hacking-government.html.

112. Consolidated Complaint ¶ 6, *In re: SolarWinds Corporation Securities Litigation,* No. 1:21-cv-138 (W.D. Tex. June 1, 2021), ECF No. 26.

113. *Id.*; Ryan Gallagher, *SolarWinds Adviser Warned of Lax Security Years Before Hack,* BLOOMBERG (Dec. 21, 2020), https://www.bloomberg.com/news/articles/2020-12-21 /solarwinds-adviser-warned-of-lax-security-years-before-hack.

114. Dave Sebastian, *SolarWinds Discloses Earlier Evidence of Hack,* WALL ST. J. (Jan. 12, 2021), https://www.wsj.com/articles/solarwinds-discloses-earlier-evidence-of-hack -11610473937.

115. Dina Temple-Raston, *A "Worst Nightmare" Cyberattack: The Untold Story of the SolarWinds Hack,* NPR (Apr. 16, 2021), https://www.npr.org/2021/04/16/985439655 /a-worst-nightmare-cyberattack-the-untold-story-of-the-solarwinds-hack.

116. Consolidated Complaint ¶ 151, *In re: SolarWinds Corporation Securities Litigation,* No. 1:21-cv-138 (W.D. Tex. June 1, 2021), ECF No. 26.

117. Julia Kisielius, *Breaking Down the SolarWinds Supply Chain Attack,* SPYCLOUD (Mar. 11, 2021), https://spycloud.com/solarwinds-attack-breakdown/.

118. The federal agencies were the Treasury, State, Justice, Commerce, Defense, and Energy Departments. Sanger et al., *supra* note 105; Catalin Cimpanu, *DOJ Says SolarWinds Hack Impacted 27 US Attorneys' Offices,* RECORD (July 30, 2021), https://therecord .media/doj-says-solarwinds-hack-impacted-27-state-attorneys-offices/.

119. David E. Sanger & Alan Rappeport, *Treasury Department's Senior Leaders Were Targeted by Hacking,* N.Y. TIMES (Jan. 6, 2021), https://www.nytimes.com/2020/12/21 /us/politics/russia-hack-treasury.html.

120. Alan Suderman & Eric Tucker, *Justice Department Says Russians Hacked Federal Prosecutors,* ASSOCIATED PRESS (July 30, 2021), https://apnews.com/article/technology -europe-russia-election-2020-5486323e455277b39cd3283d70a7fd64.

121. Consolidated Complaint ¶ 150, *In re: SolarWinds Corporation Securities Litigation,* No. 1:21-cv-138 (W.D. Tex. June 1, 2021), ECF No. 26.

122. David E. Sanger *et al., As Understanding of Russian Hacking Grows, So Does Alarm,* N.Y. TIMES (May 28, 2021), https://www.nytimes.com/2021/01/02/us/politics /russian-hacking-government.html.

123. *Hearings on the SolarWinds Hack and Possible Policy Responses,* NAT'L L. REV. (Oct. 9, 2022), https://www.natlawreview.com/article/hearings-solarwinds-hack-and -possible-policy-responses; *Prevention, Response, and Recovery: Improving Federal Cybersecurity Post-SolarWinds,* SENATE COMMITTEE ON HOMELAND SECURITY AND GOVERNMENTAL AFFAIRS (May 11, 2021), https://www.hsgac.senate.gov/hearings/prevention-response -and-recovery-improving-federal-cybersecurity-post-solarwinds; *SolarWinds and Beyond: Improving the Cybersecurity of Software Supply Chains,* HOUSE COMMITTEE ON SCIENCE, SPACE, AND TECHNOLOGY, SUBCOMMITTEE ON INVESTIGATIONS AND OVERSIGHT & SUBCOMMITTEE RESEARCH AND TECHNOLOGY (May 25, 2021), https://science.house.gov/hearings /solarwinds-and-beyond-improving-the-cybersecurity-of-software-supply-chains.

124. Michael Novinson, *$286M of SolarWinds Stock Sold Before CEO, Hack Disclosures,* CRN (Dec. 16, 2020), https://www.crn.com/news/security/-286m-of-solarwinds

-stock-sold-before-ceo-hack-disclosures?itc=refresh (Silver Lake and Thoma Bravo together owned three-fourths of the company's stock and controlled a majority of its board).

125. Search for "SolarWinds," 116th and 117th Cong., CONGRESS.GOV; search for "Silver Lake," 116th and 117th Cong., CONGRESS.GOV (all references to Silver Lake are to geographies, not the private equity firm); search for "Thoma Bravo," CONGRESS.GOV.

126. Drew Harris & Doug MacMillan, *Investors in Breached Software Firm Solar-Winds Traded $280 Million in Stock Days Before Hack Was Revealed*, WASH. POST (Dec. 15, 2020), https://www.washingtonpost.com/technology/2020/12/15/solarwinds-russia -breach-stock-trades/.

127. Douglas MacMillan & Aaron Schaffer, *Breached Software Firm SolarWinds Faces SEC Inquiry After Insider Stock Sales*, WASH. POST (Mar. 1, 2021), https://www .washingtonpost.com/business/2021/03/01/solarwinds-sec-inquiry/ (Thoma Bravo and Silver Lake declined to comment to the *Washington Post* on the inquiry).

128. Miriam Gottfried, *China's Sovereign Fund Sells Out of Pre-Crisis Blackstone Investment*, WALL ST. J. (Mar. 13, 2018), https://www.wsj.com/articles/chinas-sovereign -fund-sells-out-of-pre-crisis-blackstone-investment-1520981281.

129. *China's Forex Investment Company to Invest US$3 BLN in Blackstone*, XINHUA (May 21, 2007), http://en.people.cn/200705/21/print20070521_376576.html.

130. Alexandra Stevenson, *China Sells Stake in Blackstone as Deal Scene Turns Sour*, N.Y. TIMES (Mar. 14, 2018), nytimes.com/2018/03/14/business/blackstone-cic-china.html.

131. Michael Kranish, *Trump's China Whisperer: How Billionaire Stephen Schwarzman Has Sought to Keep the President Close to Beijing*, WASH. POST (Mar. 12, 2018), https:// www.washingtonpost.com/politics/trumps-china-whisperer-how-billionaire-stephen -schwarzman-has-sought-to-keep-the-president-close-to-beijing/2018/03/11 /67e369a8-0c2f-11e8-95a5-c396801049ef_story.html.

132. *E.g.*, *Blackstone Completes Acquisition of Majority Stake in the Largest Logistics Park in China's Greater Bay Area*, BLACKSTONE (Jan. 20, 2021), https://www.blackstone.com /news/press/blackstone-completes-acquisition-of-majority-stake-in-the-largest-logistics -park-in-chinas-greater-bay-area/; Carol Zhong & Kane Wu, *Blackstone Buys China -based Packager ShyaHsin in $800–900 Million Deal—Sources*, YAHOO NEWS (Nov. 10, 2017), https://www.yahoo.com/news/blackstone-buys-china-based-packager-072804958.html.

133. Miriam Gottfried, *China's Sovereign Fund Sells Out of Pre-Crisis Blackstone Investment*, WALL ST. J. (Mar. 13, 2018), https://www.wsj.com/articles/chinas -sovereign-fund-sells-out-of-pre-crisis-blackstone-investment-1520981281.

134. Kranish, *supra* note 131.

135. Simon Clark, *American Billionaires Vanish from Russian Fund's Website*, WALL ST. J. (Sept. 3, 2014), https://www.wsj.com/articles/names-of-u-s-billionaires-vanish-from -russian-funds-website-1409747234.

136. *Id.*

137. Dylan Tokar & Kristin Broughton, *Russian Fund Behind Coronavirus Aid Shipment Is on U.S. Lending Blacklist*, WALL ST. J. (Apr. 2, 2020), https://www.wsj.com/articles/russian -fund-behind-coronavirus-aid-shipment-is-on-u-s-lending-blacklist-11585873617.

138. Jessica Silver-Greenberg *et al.*, *The Benefits of Standing by the President*, N.Y. TIMES (Aug. 19, 2017), https://www.nytimes.com/2017/08/19/business/the-benefits -of-standing-by-the-president.html.

139. Kate Kelly & Andrew Ross Sorkin, *Massive United States–Saudi Infrastructure Fund Struggles to Get Going*, N.Y. TIMES (Apr. 4, 2018), https://www.nytimes .com/2018/04/04/business/blackstone-infrastructure-fund-saudi.html.

140. Natasha Turak, *What's Happening in Saudi Arabia Is "Extraordinary," Says Blackstone CEO*, CNBC (Jan. 25, 2018), https://www.cnbc.com/2018/01/25/blackstone-ceo-schwarzman-saudi-arabia-reforms-are-extraordinary.html.

141. *Id.*

142. Ben Hubbard, *Saudis Say Arrests Target Foreign-Funded Dissidents*, N.Y. TIMES (Sept. 15, 2017), https://www.nytimes.com/2017/09/15/world/middleeast/saudi-arabia-arrests.html?mcubz=3&_r=0.

143. Kevin Sullivan & Kareem Fahim, *A Year After the Ritz-Carlton Roundup, Saudi Elites Remain Jailed by the Crown Prince*, WASH. POST (Nov. 5, 2018), https://www.washingtonpost.com/world/a-year-after-the-ritz-carlton-roundup-saudi-elites-remain-jailed-by-the-crown-prince/2018/11/05/32077a5c-e066-11e8-b759-3d88a5ce9e19_story.html.

144. Jeanne Whalen, *Finance CEOs Pull Out of Saudi "Davos in the Desert" over Khashoggi, Risking Lucrative Role in Kingdom's Economic Reforms*, WASH. POST (Oct. 15, 2018), https://www.washingtonpost.com/business/economy/finance-ceos-pull-out-of-saudi-davos-in-the-desert-over-khashoggi-risking-lucrative-role-in-kingdoms-economic-reforms/2018/10/15/b10afea4-d0b8-11e8-b2d2-f397227b43f0_story.html.

145. *Third Quarter 2018 Earnings Investor Call*, BLACKSTONE (Oct. 18, 2018), https://s23.q4cdn.com/714267708/files/doc_events/BLACKSTONE-Third-Quarter-2018-Investor-Call.pdf (On an earnings call, Blackstone's president said that its investment with Saudi was set to grow, regardless of "some near-term challenges," that is, Khashoggi's murder).

146. Nicholas Comfort, *Women Were Scared of Working at Blackstone, Schwarzman Says*, BLOOMBERG (Oct. 26, 2021), https://www.bloomberg.com/news/articles/2021-10-26/women-were-scared-of-working-at-blackstone-schwarzman-says.

147. Cristina Alesci, *Stephen Schwarzman Writes in New Book About His Role as Trump Interlocutor with China*, CNN BUSINESS (Sept. 17, 2019), https://www.cnn.com/2019/09/17/economy/stephen-schwarzman-trump-china-trade/index.html.

148. Kate Kelly, *In Trump, Stephen Schwarzman Found a Chance to Burnish His Legacy*, N.Y. TIMES (Jan. 19, 2021), https://www.nytimes.com/2021/01/19/business/schwarzman-blackstone-trump.html.

149. Kranish, *supra* note 131.

150. *Id.*; Cristina Alesci, *Stephen Schwarzman Writes in New Book About His Role as Trump Interlocutor with China*, CNN (Sept. 19, 2019), https://www.cnn.com/2019/09/17/economy/stephen-schwarzman-trump-china-trade/index.html; Kelly, *supra* note 148.

151. Phleim Kine, *From "Momentous" to "Meh"—Trump's China Trade Deal Letdown*, POLITICO (Jan. 13, 2022), https://www.politico.com/newsletters/politico-china-watcher/2022/01/13/from-momentous-to-meh-the-phase-one-trade-deal-letdown-495705.

152. Silver-Greenberg *et al., supra* note 138.

CHAPTER 11: WHAT WE MUST DO

1. Lawrence Mishel & Jori Kandra, *Wages for the Top 1% Skyrocketed 160% Since 1979 While the Share of Wages for the Bottom 90% Shrunk*, ECONOMIC POLICY INSTITUTE (Dec. 1, 2020), https://www.epi.org/blog/wages-for-the-top-1-skyrocketed-160-since-1979-while-the-share-of-wages-for-the-bottom-90-shrunk-time-to-remake-wage-pattern-with-economic-policies-that-generate-robust-wage-growth-for-vast-majority/.

2. *How Does COVID Relief Compare to Great Recession Stimulus?*, COMMITTEE FOR A RESPONSIBLE FEDERAL BUDGET (July 1, 2020), https://www.crfb.org/blogs

/how-does-covid-relief-compare-great-recession-stimulus; Juliana Menasce Horowitz *et al.*, *Trends in Income and Wealth Inequality*, PEW RESEARCH CENTER (Jan. 9, 2020), https:// www.pewresearch.org/social-trends/2020/01/09/trends-in-income-and-wealth -inequality/.

3. *Value Added by Industry: Manufacturing as a Percentage of GDP*, ST. LOUIS FEDERAL RESERVE, https://fred.stlouisfed.org/series/VAPGDPMA; *Value Added by Industry: Finance, Insurance, Real Estate, Rental, and Leasing: Finance and Insurance as a Percentage of GDP*, ST. LOUIS FEDERAL RESERVE, https://fred.stlouisfed.org/series/VAPGDPFI.

4. Elizabeth Warren, *End Wall Street's Stranglehold on Our Economy*, MEDIUM.COM (July 18, 2019), https://medium.com/@teamwarren/end-wall-streets-stranglehold-on-our -economy-70cf038bac76.

5. William M. Tsutsui & Stefano Mazzotta, *The Bubble Economy and the Lost Decade: Learning from the Japanese Economic Experience*, 9 J. GLOBAL INITIATIVES: POLICY, PEDAGOGY, PERSPECTIVE 57, 65 (2015), https://digitalcommons.kennesaw.edu/cgi/viewcontent.cgi ?article=1164&context=jgi.

6. *Id.* at 71; Matt Jancer, *How Eight Conglomerates Dominate Japanese Industry*, SMITHSONIAN MAG. (Sept. 7, 2016), https://www.smithsonianmag.com/innovation/how-eight -conglomerates-dominate-japanese-industry-180960356/.

7. *Lost Decades*, WIKIPEDIA, https://en.wikipedia.org/wiki/Lost_Decades.

8. Tsutsui & Mazzotta, *supra* note 5.

9. Bruce Stokes, *Japanese More Satisfied with Economy, but Doubts About Future Persist*, PEW RESEARCH CENTER (Oct. 17, 2017), https://www.pewresearch.org/global/2017/10/17 /japanese-more-satisfied-with-economy-but-doubts-about-future-persist/.

10. Kim Parker *et al.*, *America in 2050*, PEW RESEARCH CENTER (Mar. 21, 2019), https://www.pewresearch.org/social-trends/2019/03/21/america-in-2050/ (An almost identical number—20 percent—of Americans believe that the standard of living for the average American family will improve over the next thirty years).

11. Daniel A. Crane, *Antitrust and Democracy: A Case Study from German Fascism* 1, 16 (U. of Michigan Law & Econ. Research Paper No. 18-009, U. of Michigan Public Law Research Paper No. 595, Apr. 17, 2018), https://papers.ssrn.com/sol3/papers.cfm ?abstract_id=3164467.

12. Jack Beatty, AGE OF BETRAYAL: THE TRIUMPH OF MONEY IN AMERICA, 1865–1900, 12, 40–41, 33–34, 109 (2008).

13. *Id.* at 42, 157, 187, 218.

14. *Id.* at 219.

15. *Id.* at 476.

16. *Adamson Act*, WIKIPEDIA, https://en.wikipedia.org/wiki/Adamson_Act.

17. *Hepburn Act*, WIKIPEDIA, https://en.wikipedia.org/wiki/Hepburn_Act.

18. *Federal Farm Loan Act*, WIKIPEDIA, https://en.wikipedia.org/wiki/Federal_Farm _Loan_Act.

19. *United States Postal Savings System*, WIKIPEDIA, https://en.wikipedia.org/wiki /United_States_Postal_Savings_System.

20. *Inspection, Enforcement, Compliance*, DEPARTMENT OF LABOR, https://www.dol.gov /general/aboutdol/history/mono-regsafepart03.

21. *Progressive Ideas*, DEPARTMENT OF LABOR, https://www.dol.gov/general/aboutdol /history/mono-regsafepart03.

22. Bill Kovarik, *Air Pollution*, ENVIRONMENTAL HISTORY, https://environmentalhistory .org/about/airpollution/ (Pittsburgh established smoke abatement ordinances); Scott Klinger, *Breathing Easier Because of the Clean Air Act*, CENTER FOR EFFECTIVE GOVERNMENT

(Dec. 31, 2014), https://www.foreffectivegov.org/blog/breathing-easier-because-clean-air -act (1910, Massachusetts passes clean air laws regulating smoke output).

23. *The Agrarian and Populist Movements*, COURSE HERO, https://www.coursehero .com/study-guides/boundless-ushistory/the-agrarian-and-populist-movements/.

24. *Our Labor History Timeline*, AFL-CIO, https://aflcio.org/about-us/history.

25. Henny Sender & Monica Langley, *How Blackstone's Chief Became $7 Billion Man*, WALL ST. J. (June 13, 2007), https://www.wsj.com/articles/SB118169817142333414.

26. Beatty, *supra* note 12, at 278; *see generally* Sven Beckert, THE MONIED METROP-OLIS: NEW YORK CITY AND THE CONSOLIDATION OF THE AMERICAN BOURGEOISIE, 1850–1896 293–295 (2001).

27. James B. Stewart, *The Birthday Party*, NEW YORKER (Feb. 18, 2008).

28. Alec Tyson & Brian Kennedy, *Two-Thirds of Americans Think Government Should Do More on Climate*, PEW RESEARCH CENTER (June 23, 2020), https://www.pewresearch .org/science/2020/06/23/two-thirds-of-americans-think-government-should-do -more-on-climate/ (showing widespread support for climate action, including among Republicans); Katherine Schaeffer, *Key Facts About Americans and Guns*, PEW RESEARCH CEN-TER (Sept. 12, 2021), https://www.pewresearch.org/fact-tank/2021/09/13/key-facts -about-americans-and-guns/ (showing support for some gun control policies, includ-ing among Republicans); Gaby Galvin, *About 7 in 10 Voters Favor a Public Health Insurance Option. Medicare for All Remains Polarizing*, MORNING CONSULT (Mar. 24, 2021), https:// morningconsult.com/2021/03/24/medicare-for-all-public-option-polling/ (showing large support for a public option, including among Republicans).

29. *Summary*, OPEN SECRETS, https://www.opensecrets.org/industries/indus.php?ind =F2600.

CHAPTER 12: AN AGENDA FOR REFORM

1. Brendan Ballou, *The "No Collusion" Rule*, 32 STAN. L. & POL'Y REV. 213 (2021).

2. Beth Schwartzapfel, *How Bad Is Prison Health Care? Depends on Who's Watching*, MARSHALL PROJECT (Feb. 26, 2018), https://www.themarshallproject.org/2018/02/25 /how-bad-is-prison-health-care-depends-on-who-s-watching.

3. Elizabeth Whitman, *Arizona Prison Food Was Labeled "Not for Human Consumption," Ex-Inmates Say*, PHOENIX NEW TIMES (Sept. 25, 2019), https://www.phoenixnewtimes .com/news/ex-inmates-arizona-prison-food-was-not-for-human-consumption-11362468.

4. Alan Judd, *Jail Food Complaints Highlight Debate over Outsourcing Public Services*, AT-LANTA J. CONST. (Jan. 1, 2015), https://bit.ly/31wc8Tn.

5. Peter Whoriskey, *As a Grocery Chain Is Dismantled, Investors Recover Their Money. Worker Pensions Are Short Millions.*, WASH. POST (Dec. 28, 2018), https://www .washingtonpost.com/business/economy/as-a-grocery-chain-is-dismantled-investors -recover-their-money-worker-pensions-are-short-millions/2018/12/28/ea22e398-0a0e -11e9-85b6-41c0fe0c5b8f_story.html.

6. Stephen Miller, *DOL Pulls Back on Private Equity in 401(k)s*, SHRM (Jan. 11, 2022), https://www.shrm.org/resourcesandtools/hr-topics/benefits/pages/dol-pulls-back-on -private-equity-in-401k-plans.aspx.

7. *Consumer Financial Protection Bureau Proposes Rule to End Payday Debt Traps*, CON-SUMER FINANCIAL PROTECTION BUREAU (June 2, 2016), https://bit.ly/31DQFrc.

8. Kate Berry, *CFPB Poised to Reinstate Tough Stance on Payday Lenders*, AMERICAN BANKER (Mar. 29, 2021), https://www.americanbanker.com/news/cfpb-poised-to-reinstate-tough -stance-on-payday-lenders. *But see* Alan S. Kaplinsky, *CFPB Issues Report on State*

Payday Loan Extended Payment Plans, BALLARD SPAHR (Apr. 7, 2022), https://www
.consumerfinancemonitor.com/2022/04/07/cfpb-issues-report-on-state-payday
-loan-extended-payment-plans/ ("Perhaps more significant than what the report says
is what it does not say—namely, that the CFPB intends to launch a new rulemaking in
the payday lending space that would purport to reinstate the "ability-to-repay" provisions in former Director Cordray's original payday lending rule.").

9. *Questions for the Record, Committee on Banking, Housing, and Urban Affairs Nomina-
tions of the Honorable Gary Gensler and the Honorable Rohit Chopra*, SENATE BANKING COMMITTEE
8 (Mar. 2, 2021), https://www.banking.senate.gov/imo/media/doc/Chopra%20Resp
%20to%20QFRs%203-2-211.pdf.

10. *CFPB Penalizes JPay for Siphoning Taxpayer-Funded Benefits Intended to Help People Re-enter Society After Incarceration*, CONSUMER FINANCIAL PROTECTION BUREAU (Oct. 19,
2021), https://www.consumerfinance.gov/about-us/newsroom/cfpb-penalizes-jpay-for
-siphoning-taxpayer-funded-benefits-intended-to-help-people-re-enter-society-after
-incarceration/.

11. *Nursing Homes Need More Staff*, NATIONAL CONSUMER VOICE, https://theconsumer
voice.org/uploads/files/issues/Consumer-Fact-Sheet-Nursing-Home-Staffing.pdf

12. *Fact Sheet: Protecting Seniors by Improving Safety and Quality of Care in the Nation's
Nursing Homes*, WHITE HOUSE (Feb. 28, 2022), https://www.whitehouse.gov/briefing
-room/statements-releases/2022/02/28/fact-sheet-protecting-seniors-and-people-with
-disabilities-by-improving-safety-and-quality-of-care-in-the-nations-nursing-homes/.

13. Charlene Harrington *et al.*, *These Administrative Actions Would Improve Nursing
Home Ownership and Financial Transparency in the Post COVID-19 Period*, HEALTH AF-
FAIRS (Feb. 11, 2021), https://www.healthaffairs.org/do/10.1377/hblog20210208.597573
/full/.

14. Ariel Gelrud Shiro & Richard V. Reeves, *The For-Profit College System Is Broken and
the Biden Administration Needs to Fix It*, BROOKINGS INSTITUTION (Jan. 12, 2021), https://
www.brookings.edu/blog/how-we-rise/2021/01/12/the-for-profit-college-system-is
-broken-and-the-biden-administration-needs-to-fix-it/.

15. *Id.*

16. *Id.*

17. Stephanie Hall *et al.*, *What States Can Do to Protect Students from Predatory For-Profit
Colleges*, CENTURY FOUND (May 26, 2020), https://tcf.org/content/report/states-can
-protect-students-predatory-profit-colleges/.

18. *Id.*

19. Ben Miller, *College Executives Need to Pay Up When Their Schools Close Abruptly*,
CENTER FOR AMERICAN PROGRESS (Mar. 19, 2019), https://www.americanprogress.org
/article/college-executives-need-pay-schools-close-abruptly/.

20. Shiro & Reeves, *supra* note 14.

21. *Form PF Presentation*, SEC (Sept. 13, 2013), https://www.sec.gov/info/cco/cco
-2013-09-13-presentation-form-pf.pdf.

22. Chris Witowsky, *LPs Fear an "Erosion" of Fiduciary Duty in Fund Contracts: ILPA
Survey*, BUYOUTS (July 13, 2020), https://www.buyoutsinsider.com/lps-fear-an-erosion
-of-fiduciary-duty-in-fund-contracts-ilpa-survey/ (Limited partners are concerned
about agreements with general partners where the GPs eliminate their fiduciary duties
to the fund. Based on a survey by Institutional Limited Partners Association, 71% of
LPs have seen fiduciary duties modified or eliminated in the past year.).

23. *SEC Proposes to Enhance Private Fund Investor Protection*, SEC (Feb. 9, 2022),
https://www.sec.gov/news/press-release/2022-19.

24. *Id.*; Chris Cumming, *SEC Considering New Rules on Private-Fund Fees, Conflicts, Gensler Says*, WALL ST. J. (Nov. 10, 2021), https://www.wsj.com/articles/sec-considering -new-rules-on-private-fund-fees-conflicts-gensler-says-11636580410.

25. *Dodd-Frank Wall Street Reform and Consumer Protection Act*, Pub. L. 111-203, § 956, 124 Stat. 1905 (2010).

26. Victor Fleischer, *Two and Twenty Revisited: Taxing Carried Interest as Ordinary Income Through Executive Action Instead of Legislation* (Working Paper Sept. 16, 2015), https://papers.ssrn.com/sol3/papers.cfm?abstract_id=2661623.

27. Jesse Drucker & Danny Hakim, *How Accounting Giants Craft Favorable Tax Rules from Inside Government*, N.Y. TIMES (Sept. 19, 2021), https://www.nytimes.com /2021/09/19/business/accounting-firms-tax-loopholes-government.html (For instance, Craig Gerson, who was a tax specialist at PwC who specialized in advising PE firms, led the development of fee waiver rulemaking, which was watered down and allowed some forms. Two months after issuing the regulation, Gerson rejoined PwC).

28. Jesse Drucker & Danny Hakim, *Private Inequity: How a Powerful Industry Conquered the Tax System*, N.Y. TIMES (Sept. 8, 2021), https://www.nytimes.com/2021/06 /12/business/private-equity-taxes.html.

29. Ryan Tracy, *Feds Win Fight over Risky-Looking Loans*, WALL ST. J. (Dec. 2, 2015), https://www.wsj.com/articles/feds-win-fight-over-risky-looking-loans-1449110383.

30. Joe Rennison, *US Borrowers Breach Loan Limit Guidance at Record Pace*, FIN. TIMES (Dec. 16, 2021), https://www.ft.com/content/67b625e7-87ab-478e-aca1-995f15 0e6b9c.

31. Maya Abood *et al.*, *Wall Street Landlords Turn American Dream into a Nightmare*, ACCE INSTITUTE ET AL. 41–43, https://www.publicadvocates.org/wp-content/uploads /wallstreetlandlordsfinalreport.pdf.

32. *Id.*

33. *See, e.g., Duty to Serve Underserved Markets Plan: 2022–2024*, FANNIE MAE 8 (2021), https://www.novoco.com/sites/default/files/atoms/files/fannie-mae-duty-to-serve -2022-24-proposed-052021.pdf (proposing to "[i]ncrease loan purchases of MHCs [Mobile Home Communities] owned by government entities, nonprofit organizations, or residents"); *Duty to Serve Underserved Markets Plan: For 2018–2021*, FREDDIE MAC 40 https://www.freddiemac.com/sites/g/files/ynjofi111/files/about/duty-to-serve/docs /Freddie-Mac-Underserved-Markets-Plan.pdf (proposing to "Develop a New Offering for Resident-Owned Communities").

34. Alan Rappeport, *Former Top Financial Regulators Warn Against Move to Ease Oversight of Firms*, N.Y. TIMES (May 13, 2019), https://www.nytimes.com/2019/05/13/us /politics/financial-regulation-trump-administration.html.

35. Richard M. Scheffler, *Soaring Private Equity Investment in the Healthcare Sector: Consolidation Accelerated, Competition Undermined, and Patients at Risk*, AMERICAN ANTITRUST INSTITUTE 50 (May 2021), https://publichealth.berkeley.edu/wp-content/uploads/2021/05 /Private-Equity-I-Healthcare-Report-FINAL.pdf.

36. Jack Hoadley *et al.*, *Surprise Billing Protections: Help Finally Arrives for Millions of Americans*, COMMONWEALTH FUND (Dec. 17, 2020), https://www.commonwealthfund .org/blog/2020/surprise-billing-protections-cusp-becoming-law.

37. Christopher J. Archibald, *Ninth Circuit Upholds California's Ban on Mandatory Arbitration of Employment Disputes*, BCLP (Sept. 24, 2021), https://www.bclplaw.com /en-US/insights/blogs/bclp-at-work/ninth-circuit-upholds-californias-ban-on-mandatory -arbitration-of-employment-disputes.html.

38. David Seligman, *Three June State Law Actions Helping Consumers Fight Arbitration Requirements*, NATIONAL CONSUMER LAW CENTER (July 31, 2019), https://library.nclc .org/three-june-state-law-actions-helping-consumers-fight-arbitration-requirements.

39. Sam Cleveland, *A Blueprint for States to Solve the Mandatory Arbitration Problem While Avoiding FAA Preemption*, 104 MINN. L. REV. 3266 (2020).

40. Seligman, *supra* note 38.

41. April Kuehnhoff, *What States Can Do to Help Consumer Debt Collection*, NATIONAL CONSUMER LAW CENTER, https://www.nclc.org/images/pdf/debt_collection/fact-sheets /fact-sheet-debt-collection-state-reform.pdf.

42. Robert J. Hobbs, *Model Family Financial Protection Act*, NATIONAL CONSUMER LAW CENTER 4 (2020), https://www.nclc.org/wp-content/uploads/2022/08/model_family _financial_protection_act.pdf.

43. *Common Defenses to Raise*, NATIONAL CONSUMER LAW CENTER, https://library.nclc .org/sd/0404 ("Ask that the debt buyer prove that your debt has been properly transferred to it. Amazingly, debt buyers often do not have that proof.").

44. Joe Bousquin, *How Rent Control Policies Could Impact the Single-Family Market*, BUILDER (Feb. 14, 2020), https://www.builderonline.com/money/how-rent-control -policies-could-impact-the-single-family-market_o.

45. Yonah Freemark *et al.*, *What Does the Rise in Single-Family Rentals Mean for the Twin Cities?*, URBAN INSTITUTE (June 11, 2021), https://www.urban.org/research/publication /what-does-rise-single-family-rentals-mean-twin-cities.

46. *Id.*

47. Will Parker, *House Rents Pop Up as New Investors Pile In*, WALL ST. J. (Aug. 31, 2021), https://www.wsj.com/articles/house-rents-pop-up-as-new-investors-pile-in -11630402201.

48. *Policy Agenda 2019–2020*, EQUITY IN PLACE (Jan. 2020), http://thealliancetc.org /wp-content/uploads/2020/01/EIP-Policy-Agenda-final-Jan-2020.pdf.

49. *Id.*

50. Hall *et al.*, *supra* note 17.

51. *Id.*

52. *Id.*

53. *Id.*

54. *Id.*

55. *Id.*

56. *Id.*; Anthony Walsh, *Obama-Era Rule Banning Mandatory Arbitration in College Contracts Carries the Day*, CENTURY FOUNDATION (Dec. 1, 2020), https://tcf.org/content /commentary/obama-era-rule-banning-mandatory-arbitration-college-contracts-carries -day/?session=1.

57. Hall *et al.*, *supra* note 17.

58. *See, e.g.*, Memorandum Opinion, *Frederick Hsu Living Trust v. ODN Holding Corp.*, No. C.A. No. 12108-VCL (Del. Ch. Jan. 31, 2017) (Plaintiff alleged that the board tried to maximize the VC firm's redemption rights, rather than the long-term value of the corporation. In its ruling, the court said that the board had to promote the interests of the shareholders in the aggregate, without regard to special rights). Julia Beskin & Samantha Yantko, *Fiduciary Duties of Directors Appointed by Private Equity Firms: Pitfalls and Best Practices*, FINANCIER WORLDWIDE (Oct. 2019), https://www.financierworldwide .com/fiduciary-duties-of-directors-appointed-by-private-equity-firms-pitfalls-and -best-practices#.Y0MTpOzMJKN.

59. *Warren, Baldwin, Brown, Pocan, Jayapal, Colleagues Unveil Bold Legislation to Fundamentally Reform the Private Equity Industry*, OFFICE OF SENATOR ELIZABETH WARREN (July 18, 2019), https://www.warren.senate.gov/newsroom/press-releases/warren-baldwin -brown-pocan-jayapal-colleagues-unveil-bold-legislation-to-fundamentally-reform -the-private-equity-industry.

60. *Public Money for Private Equity*, OUR FINANCIAL SECURITY 39 (Sept. 13, 2021), https://ourfinancialsecurity.org/wp-content/uploads/2021/09/public-money-for -private-equity-9-13-21.pdf.

61. Danielle Ivory *et al.*, *When You Dial 911 and Wall Street Answers*, N.Y. TIMES (June 25, 2016), https://www.nytimes.com/2016/06/26/business/dealbook/when-you-dial -911-and-wall-street-answers.html.

INDEX

Brendan Ballou is a federal prosecutor and served as Special Counsel for Private Equity at the U.S. Department of Justice. He began his legal career in the Department's National Security Division, where he advised the White House on counter-terrorism policy. He graduated from Columbia University and Stanford Law School.

The views expressed in this book do not necessarily represent those of the U.S. Department of Justice.

PublicAffairs is a publishing house founded in 1997. It is a tribute to the standards, values, and flair of three persons who have served as mentors to countless reporters, writers, editors, and book people of all kinds, including me.

I. F. Stone, proprietor of *I. F. Stone's Weekly*, combined a commitment to the First Amendment with entrepreneurial zeal and reporting skill and became one of the great independent journalists in American history. At the age of eighty, Izzy published *The Trial of Socrates*, which was a national bestseller. He wrote the book after he taught himself ancient Greek.

Benjamin C. Bradlee was for nearly thirty years the charismatic editorial leader of *The Washington Post*. It was Ben who gave the *Post* the range and courage to pursue such historic issues as Watergate. He supported his reporters with a tenacity that made them fearless and it is no accident that so many became authors of influential, best-selling books.

Robert L. Bernstein, the chief executive of Random House for more than a quarter century, guided one of the nation's premier publishing houses. Bob was personally responsible for many books of political dissent and argument that challenged tyranny around the globe. He is also the founder and longtime chair of Human Rights Watch, one of the most respected human rights organizations in the world.

·   ·   ·

For fifty years, the banner of Public Affairs Press was carried by its owner Morris B. Schnapper, who published Gandhi, Nasser, Toynbee, Truman, and about 1,500 other authors. In 1983, Schnapper was described by *The Washington Post* as "a redoubtable gadfly." His legacy will endure in the books to come.

Peter Osnos, *Founder*